The Haunting of America

William J. Birnes
and Joel Martin

Foreword by George Noory

The
Haunting
of
America

*From the Salem
Witch Trials to
Harry Houdini*

A Tom Doherty
Associates Book
New York

A Forge Book
Published by Tom Doherty Associates, LLC
175 Fifth Avenue
New York, NY 10010

www.tor-forge.com

Forge® is a registered trademark of Tom Doherty Associates, LLC.

Library of Congress Cataloging-in-Publication Data

Birnes, William J.
    The haunting of America : from the Salem witch trials to Harry Houdini / William
J. Birnes and Joel Martin ; foreword by George Noory.—1st ed.
        p. cm.
    "A Tom Doherty Associates Book."
    ISBN 978-0-7653-1381-2 (hardcover)—ISBN 978-0-7653-2618-8 (trade pbk.)
    1. United   States—History—Anecdotes.   2. Spiritualism—United   States—
Anecdotes.   3. Ghosts—United States—Anecdotes.   4. Parapsychology—United
States—Anecdotes.   I. Martin, Joel, 1945–   II. Title.
    E178.B56 2009
    973—dc22

                                                                      2009019362

First Edition: September 2009

Printed in the United States of America

0 9 8 7 6 5 4 3 2 1

To our parents and our children's grandparents, who are now in heaven, Abraham Kaplan and Viola Katz, Laura Bruni, Dave Duthie, Mom Mom and Pop Pop, Chuck Jordan and Kay Tice; to our children Geoff and Carly, Holly and David, and to Casey, Reese, and Marcus, the grandchildren upon whom our parents are smiling and under their grandparents' watchful eyes they will always remain.

To the memory of Marika Morgan, whose watchful eyes watched over UFO Magazine.

And to my wife, Nancy Birnes, the editor-in-chief of UFO Maga-zine *and the creator of* UFO Hunters, *for her support, strength, and commitment to finding the truth.*

—WILLIAM J. BIRNES

To the beloved memory of my wife, Chris—my inspiration, my guiding spirit, who passed from this life all too soon. I will miss you more than I ever realized I would.

—JOEL MARTIN

The authors also dedicate this book to the many generations of men and women whose courage and persistence, often in the face of unrelenting criticism and opposition, tell the true story of America's paranormal past. These pioneers never lost faith in their frequently misunderstood and controversial struggle to enlighten—and often mystify us.

In the "brave new world" of the twenty-first century, may their spirit be our guide.

Contents

We have made every effort to present historical facts as accurately as possible. However, in the course of researching and writing, we sometimes discovered variations in details such as dates, locations, events, dialogue, and even spellings of names and places. To the best of our ability, we have consulted several authoritative references to provide the greatest historical accuracy possible. However, some variations proved unavoidable and are a reflection of incomplete, inadequate, or contradictory historical recordkeeping.

In some instances, some names have been changed to protect privacy. However, while certain identifying characteristics have been altered, the incidents and experiences described are genuine. Where a name has been changed, we have indicated it with quotation marks.

Too many people take history for granted. What we read in our school textbooks is true, we are sure of that. But how many textbooks describe Washington's vision of an angel at Valley Forge, or Lincoln's premonition of his own death, or Woodrow Wilson's reliance on the psychic Edgar Cayce? Not many, I'll bet.

American history over the years has become almost formulaic. How many times do we hear people calling Abraham Lincoln our most psychic president, calling spiritual medium Nettie Colburn into the White House to try to communicate with Willie Lincoln, who died during Lincoln's first term. In a puritanical America, communicating with the dead is taboo, witchcraft, something the Pilgrims burned people at the stake for practicing. Yet, America has had a psychic history—filled with ghosts, prophets, spiritualists, and mediums—that is as exciting and challenging as any war story.

As authors Bill Birnes and Joel Martin recount it, America's psychic history informs many aspects of today's news. For example, during the Reagan administration, when stories leaked out about Nancy Reagan's reliance on astrologer Joan Quigley, many people, including Vice President George H. W. Bush, were shocked. But how many people realized that Franklin Pierce, Barbara Bush's great-great-grandfather's fourth cousin, also sought the advice of two famous mediums of the day, the Fox sisters? American history is replete with such stories, some old, some modern.

Perhaps the new First Family, having just taken up residence in the White House, will see President Lincoln's ghost walking the hallways or haunting his old bedroom. President Harry Truman wrote about that ghost in his famous diary. Maybe, because President Obama has spoken so much about Lincoln's importance, he will see President Lincoln himself and maybe even get some advice about how to deal with a cabinet, who are not simply, in Doris Kearns Goodwin's words, an "echo chamber." Will President Obama ever reveal any ghostly visitations to the American people? Will he ever disclose the truth about UFOs to the American people? If he ever does, maybe he will be the first president to talk openly about a hidden America, America's hidden psychic history.

Reading Bill's and Joel's book, the first volume in their two-book series, I had to wonder whether most of what I learned in school was simply another form of cover-up. Whether you think so or not, the stories in *The Haunting of America* will certainly challenge your belief system and make you rethink what you believe is real.

Acknowledgments

To my children, Geoff and Carly and Holly and David, who keep me honest and grounded in reality. And to the producers, cast, and crew of *UFO Hunters*: Pat Uskert and Kevin Cook and Ted Acworth from season 2; execs Jon Alon Walz, Dave Pavoni, Aaron Kass, and Steve Nigg; line producer Daniel Zarenkiewcz; field coordinator Kyle Crosby; and to our network execs at the History Channel, Mike Stiller and Dolores Gavin; thanks for giving me this wonderful opportunity to talk about my favorite subject, UFOs. And thanks as well to my talent agent, Mark Turner, at Abrams Artists, who urges me to step back when I, as usual, have gone too far.

And to my wife, Nancy, who defines reality, not just on television, and keeps everything going.

WILLIAM J. BIRNES

We are deeply grateful to many people who generously shared their knowledge, skills, and experiences with us, and thank each of them for his or her invaluable contributions, especially:

Bill Birnes—many, many thanks to a rare coauthor whose quick intelligence, support, and patience made this complex and all-consuming project much easier than it would otherwise have been; and who also represented this book.

Christina Martin—without whose help and encouragement this book would not have come to fruition. Thank you for your loyalty, patience, and belief in me. You're a giant.

Elise LeVaillant—for her enduring love, spirituality, strength, knowledge, and support in everything I do.

Kristina Rus—reference librarian, East Meadow (New York) Public Library, whose remarkable reference and research skills, and persistence in locating a vast amount of historical sources (many of them unique and out-of-print) were truly outstanding and tireless.

Catherine Erdelyi—for brilliantly organizing an immense number of books and articles, cataloging our enormous bibliography, and performing a myriad of other tasks.

Margaret Wendt—who opened doors to this and other worlds for me to explore; an incredible journey of wonder that has contributed vastly. She has my undying gratitude for sharing her singular knowledge of spiritual and psychic realms, and for our special friendship.

Gaylon Emerzian—everlasting thanks for bringing Bill Birnes and me together to collaborate as authors.

Max Toth—my eternal gratitude for generously sharing his vast knowledge about parapsychology, pyramids, photography, hypnotism, magic, Freemasonry, and more.

Roxanne Salch Kaplan—Director, Parapsychology Institute of America, with deep appreciation for years of friendship and joining forces through light and darkness.

My special thanks to: Carole Chin, R.N., N.P.; Donna DiBiase; Jayne Dietl; Warren Greene; Brian Hurst; Patricia Ippolito; Nancy Kaiser; Nick Lentzeres; Guy LeVaillant, Ed.D; Jacques LeVaillant; Robert Marcus, M.D.; Larry Naukam, Division Head, Local History and Genealogy, Rochester (New York) Public Library; Dean Radin, Ph.D., Institute for Noetic Sciences; John Ray, Esq.; Richard Romano; Dick Ruhl; Vladimir Rus, Ph.D.; Linda Russek, Ph.D., Human Energy Systems Laboratory, University of Arizona; Dale Saglimbene, D.O.; Thomas Santorelli, cinema historian; Jerry Shevick, Hearst Entertainment; John Smith; Al Ubert; Neil Vineberg; Patrice Ann Vohs; Edgar Cayce Foundation (A.R.E.); The David Library of the American Revolution; and the Vermont Historical Society. On a personal note, all my love to Cambria and Caleb Weintraub—two beautiful children, with my prayers for a bright and healthy future.

And, in loving memory: Evelyn Moleta, you are deeply missed. My dear friend and parapsychologist, Stephen Kaplan; Bill Marshall, accomplished astrologer and friend; D. C. "Ben" Webster, a true visionary; Muriel Horenstein; Douglas Johnson; Howard Metz; Joseph Matyas; Charles and Sadie Cohen; Shirleyann Martin; and Mary Moleta. Father John Papallo, always with me, and in the hearts of so many he touched; and John G. Fuller, my inspiration for writing about the paranormal.

JOEL MARTIN

The Haunting of America

Introduction: What Is New Age?

The past is but the beginning of a beginning.
—H. G. WELLS

How did it all occur, this business of human origins? What part did the paranormal play, and what influence have ancient psychic beliefs had through the centuries, to this very day? You may be surprised to discover that much of what we believe to be "New Age" actually dates back long before the birth of Jesus. Some parapsychologists have even wondered if primitive humans were more telepathic before the development of language by prehistoric tribes.

"How modern types of men originated is one of the unsolved puzzles of archaeology and physical anthropology," wrote William H. McNeill in *The Rise of the West: A History of the Human Community*.[1] "Cultural evolution must have begun among the pre-human ancestors of modern man."

Therein is the unresolved controversy: Humankind's "ancestor apes" may have been present on Earth as long ago as twenty-five million years. The evolution to hominids or manlike apes occurred perhaps fourteen million years ago. Eleven million more years passed until the first being described as homo or "manlike" appeared in Africa approximately two million years ago. Another million years would go by before *Homo erectus* arrived. Some 900,000 years later marked the advent of the first "primitive man," named Neanderthal, for the location where his remains were found. Remember, two million years went by between the "manlike creature" and Neanderthal; yet both types of beings looked alike and used similar stone tools.

But then, inexplicably, about 35,000 years ago, *Homo sapiens*, men with the ability to think, made their appearance in Europe. These "modern men" were dubbed Cro-Magnons, and bore a remarkable resemblance to people today. But what happened to Neanderthals? There is one theory that they somehow vanished and *Homo sapiens* replaced Neanderthals until the latter were extinct, and with no anthropological evidence to indicate the two interbred. Recent archaeological evidence, however, suggests that Neanderthals and Cro-Magnons coinhabited the planet for a while, during which time, the two species might have mated. In America, *Homo sapiens* first surfaced around 10,000 B.C., but McNeill noted that "even the skeletal characteristics of the first American immigrants remain unclear."

The author of *The 12th Planet*, biblical and ancient languages expert Zecharia Sitchin, wrote, "It is clear that *Homo sapiens* represent such an extreme departure from the slow evolutionary process that many of our features, such as the ability to speak, are totally unrelated to the earlier primates."[2] How did our ancestors appear long before they should have? Shouldn't their "evolutionary development" have taken more time? Sitchin, a leading proponent of the controversial theory that "Earth was visited in its past by astronauts from another planet," asked, "Was life imported to Earth from elsewhere?"

One puzzle about *Homo sapiens*, or Cro-Magnons, in Europe is how quickly they became the most adaptable of all species. Whether they were a product of creationism, evolution, or the result of "ancient astronauts" has been—and could be—debated endlessly. "All details of human evolution are uncertain," wrote McNeill.[3] Did outer space visitors many millennia ago play a role here on Earth? Are they the "gods" the ancients referred to in their writings?

For the first primitive beings that walked on planet Earth, the experience of life and death had to be both awe-inspiring and intimidating. There was a multitude of unknowns: the infinite sky above that grew dark at the end of each day, and might fill one with terror even as the moon, stars, and planets shined above; and what were those mysterious, faraway objects? Most important, what effect did they have? Who knew what lurked in the shadows and blackness of night, and when daylight returned, was some supernatural or magical force responsible?

By observing the cycles of light and dark, the phases of the moon, and the changing seasons, early man had unwittingly begun the notion, albeit crude, of the first calendar, a system of telling time, of when to plant, and even of navigation. Some early civilizations may have built megaliths or large stone monuments for this purpose, such as Stonehenge. Some parapsychologists have speculated that primitive peoples either spent inordinate amounts of time watching the sky to learn its patterns and vagaries, or they initially had help from some intelligent beings from outer space.

Nothing was more terrifying than death. How and why did people simply leave this physical existence? However and whenever human consciousness developed marked the start of man's first psychic experiences, possibly in dreams of the deceased.

If there were supernatural explanations of life and death, might all living things be endowed with a spirit or essence that survived death? Thus, nature understandably became an object of worship. The primitive belief known as animism considered that a spirit or soul was present even in nonhuman life, such as animals, trees, and plants. If a spirit survived, it suggested immortality.

Weather was a constant concern, and the battle to adapt to climate may have spurred beliefs, inventiveness, and ingenuity. What did winds, rain, and storms that poured from the heavens mean? Who above was angry when the sky flashed with lightning bolts accompanied by the inexplicable and frightening rumble of thunder? Had man done something to disturb powerful celestial beings?

Did illness and death mean humans had somehow displeased the immense forces? Could they ever master or harness these forces? Homage had to be paid to the invisible beings of nature people eventually called "gods." If deities could be pleased—or appeased—might both life and the afterlife be improved? The obvious answer was to satisfy the gods, but how? Rituals had to be developed.

Early "cave art" that has survived many millennia in parts of Africa, Asia, and Europe offers clues to the way man lived, worshipped, hunted, and dressed, and to his concern with the mystery of death. We surmise from these depictions that one of the first human psychic experiences by which man attempted to make some sense of life and death were his interpretations of dreams.

Not unlike our dream experiences, if the dead appeared during sleep, sometimes vividly, was that reason to believe they hadn't ceased to exist; that possibly they'd moved on to some other place, or never left Earth?

Sleep seemed to be a separate life. Might a dream vision offer a message or a glimpse of a future event? If it did, as it surely must have, wasn't that proof the spirit of the dead had survived—for better or worse? There was the persistent fear that spirits might return to exact revenge on the living; might ancient peoples, just like later ones, have seen—or been frightened by—apparitions or ghosts, a further confirmation of life after death?

If the deceased moved on to another—hopefully better—place, then the dead must be prepared for their journey. So began funereal practices. Primitive peoples often placed the deceased in a fetal position, for if that was how we were born then shouldn't we be sent to the next world in that posture, perhaps to be reborn? Shouldn't foods and tools accompany the departed? When the time came for interment, rituals became a part of the burial ceremony, and special words were spoken or chanted as a plea to the gods to care for the dead. Soon, man had invented what was later called "prayer" to communicate with the gods above and the spirits beyond.

Some people seemed to have a gift, they said, for communicating with the gods and the dead, similar to the mediums of our own time. Prehistoric tribes regarded these extraordinary and powerful individuals with special respect: they were the shamans, and could be found in every tribe. Their task was to act as mediators between the living and the spirits, providing the connection between this and the "next world."

The analogy of an ancient shaman to a modern medium is no exaggeration. The shamans of prehistoric times, like mediums today, offered advice from the spirit world, and might also help heal the sick and infirm. Shamans, often in trance states, typically worked in darkened caves or tents, similar to mediums many centuries later in America and Europe who held séances in dimly lit rooms. Often they dressed in animal skins and performed ritual dances to appease the spirits and plead for fertility; some ceremonies were a tribute to "Mother Earth," for the ancients believed in both gods and goddesses. Primitive people also developed magical practices, such as carrying the foot, tooth, or horn of an animal in the belief it would bring hunters greater success.

Homo sapiens, who'd primarily hunted, eventually became adept at farming, and built more permanent communities. Development of agriculture in the Near East led to the "first civilized societies" by around 6500 B.C., for farmers tending crops and flocks of domesticated animals could now settle in one place and have time to develop more complex cultures.

But what about our earlier question, the perplexing mystery of how the leap was made from Neanderthals to *Homo sapiens?* Put aside the long and contentious debate between creationists and evolutionists about which theory best explains the origins and advancement of humankind. Consider, for a moment, the provocative possibility of extraterrestrial intervention and influence on Earth.

Chaldea and Alien Intervention

Let's go back some six thousand years to what most historians, archaeologists, and anthropologists agree was "the world's first great civilization," Sumer in Mesopotamia. Called Chaldea in biblical times, this area between the Tigris and Euphrates rivers is known today as Iraq. Who were the Sumerians and where did they come from? For the two thousand years it existed, the Sumerian civilization had huge impact, and although it disappeared as inexplicably as it emerged, its contributions to life and culture were immense.

It wasn't until the 1840s that archaeologists discovered the buried remains of Sumerian cities and artifacts, as well as thousands of clay tablets written in the original Sumerian wedge-shaped cuneiform language, which had to be laboriously deciphered and translated. Before those remarkable discoveries, skeptics questioned whether Sumer had ever existed. Surprisingly, when skeletal remains were found, the Sumerians bore no physical resemblance to other civilizations or tribes in that part of the world, nor did their language resemble anything ever seen previously.

Before we question the mystery of Sumerian origins, let's look at their remarkable list of accomplishments. They're credited with creating the first system of cuneiform writing, schools, medical science, systematic recording of history, wheeled devices, laws, social reforms, taxation, the two-chambered legislature, coined money, cosmogony (theories about the origin of the universe), and cosmology, the science of the universe. They'd also learned shipbuilding and mapmaking, and Sumerian queens were familiar with cosmetics. Remember this was two thousand years before Rome.

The Sumerian civilization had remarkable celestial knowledge, far beyond anything one would expect in an ancient culture. British author Alan Alford wrote that the Sumerians inexplicably understood "spherical astronomy, including the 360-degree circle; the zenith (that part of the sky directly above observers); the horizon; heavenly bodies; the poles; the ecliptic (the sun's apparent path among the stars during the year); and the equinoxes."[4]

To the Sumerians we owe the first calendars and the way we still tell time, based on their mathematical principles of the number sixty. Because the Sumerians believed in twelve gods, each of which ruled an important city-state, they created the zodiac, the basis of astrology, with its twelve houses or parts, each thirty degrees, for a total of 360 degrees.

How was it possible for the Sumerians to have had such advanced knowledge and insight? Alford asked, "Is this a clue that [Sumerian] astronomy was a lesson from the gods?"

Alan and Sally Landsburg, coauthors of *In Search of Ancient Mysteries* (1974), wrote that the Sumerians "pop up like some devilish jack-in-the-box, around 3000 B.C., fully equipped," and suggested the Sumerians were "extraterrestrial colonists possessed of technology advanced well beyond our own today [who] settled on Earth."[5]

Author Jim Marrs, in his 2000 book *Rule by Secrecy*, reasoned that an explanation might come from the Sumerians themselves. In other words, to whom did the Sumerians attribute their knowledge? The Sumerians wrote, "Everything they achieved came from their gods."[6]

Most scholars explain away such a statement as mythology, noting that all primitive societies had a belief system that included gods who'd come down to Earth from somewhere above and rose again skyward. But who were these "gods," and when and how did they arrive here? Where did they come from, and what was their purpose once on Earth? Might there be more to the extraterrestrial theory than mere legend?

One of the recent scholars who seriously considered this possibility was Zecharia Sitchin, who is among only a handful able to read and translate ancient Sumerian writing. In his book, *The 12th Planet*, he wrote that

"Earth was indeed visited in its past by astronauts from another planet."[7] He asked, "Was life imported to Earth from elsewhere?"[8] He identified a twelfth planet as "the home planet of the ancient visitors to Earth."[9] It is an extraordinary paranormal theory for the origin of man's development, one seldom discussed.

The Sumerians rapidly built cities, including substantial temples for devotion to the gods, known as "temple communities."[10] But curiously, they never applied the term *gods* to whoever brought them advanced knowledge. The Sumerians credited those they called Anunnaki.[11] It was not until later that the ancient Greeks and Romans employed the term *gods*. Anunnaki, translated from the original Sumerian language, meant "those who came to Earth from Heaven."

Has an important paranormal theory for the origins of humankind and the Sumerian enigma been ignored by traditional historians and scientists?

Sitchin became convinced that beings from another planet visited Earth, mated with those they found here, and thus created a more advanced human species than would otherwise have been possible. And this theory actually comports with the Bible, where, in Genesis, the text refers to the "Giants in the Earth," later the Nefilim, whose daughters married the children of Adam and Eve.

This is not the conjecture of Erich von Däniken, whose book, *Chariots of the Gods?*, became a controversial best seller in the 1960s and '70s despite vociferous critics. Obdurate skeptics and debunkers dismiss the possibility of so-called "ancient astronauts" as myth.

But Sitchin and other scholars point out that in the Old Testament there are references to the Nefilim,[12] traditionally translated to mean "giants." When Sitchin dug further into the Sumerian origins of the word, it meant not giants, but translated into "Those Who Were Cast Down." Biblical and earlier Sumerian explanations are strangely similar.

The Old Testament Book of Genesis 6:4 states, "The Nefilim were on earth in those days and also afterward when the sons of God went to the daughters of men and had children by them. They were the heroes of old, men of renown."[13]

The *Holman Bible Dictionary* defines the Nefilim as "ancient heroes who according to most interpretations, are the products of sexual union of heavenly beings and human women." Were the Sumerian writings that date back thousands of years simply a traditional narrative or legend with a supernatural theme or were they the records of Sumerian history as it actually occurred?

Sitchin concluded that at several points during ancient times extraterrestrials brought to Earth both their seed and advanced intelligence, which would explain the mystery of the ancient Sumerian civilization's beginnings and vast accomplishments. The Sumerians said the visitors' origin was a large planet they called Nibru, the "twelfth planet in our solar system." Since the 1980s, scientists have been seeking a tenth planet, for which there was speculation as recently as 2004.[14]

The ancient Sumerians—without benefit of the telescope—were able to correctly identify the planets Uranus, Neptune, and even Pluto, dubbed the "outermost planet," which scientists discovered only in 1930. Why isn't it possible that the Sumerians were telling the truth?

Some 450,000 years ago the evolved beings from the planet Nibru, also called Marduk,[15] first traveled to Earth when the two planets were close to each other, and Sumerian records say they landed in ancient Mesopotamia. The outer-space visitors were believed to have made separate journeys or explorations to Earth at various intervals, the last around 3800 B.C. when they helped create Sumer.

The great Sumerian civilization lasted barely two millennia.[16] What happened to it? That's another mystery.

The possibility of extraterrestrial visitors deserves at least consideration along with other suppositions, especially when there are so many blank spaces and "missing links" that historians, archaeologists, and anthropologists have been unable to answer about human origins. Might it be that ancient peoples were accurately relating their contact with life from places other than Earth? Perhaps *our* modern version is the mythical one.

Babylonia

Following the demise of the Sumerians, next Babylonia arose in the same region of the Near East and became the third advanced civilization in Mesopotamia, after the Sumerians and Assyrians. Of course, the Babylonians had the advantage of building upon the ingenious contributions of the Sumerians. In fact, the famed biblical Tower of Babel was originally one of the Sumerians' ziggurats, or towers.

Babylonians were terrified of ghosts or "wandering spirits" they feared returned to Earth seeking vengeance, and were often tormented by dreams and nightmares they believed were cast upon them by spirits or demons.

As recourse they employed priests with magical abilities both to exorcise evil spirits and to clean or "purify" their homes. To protect dwellings from demonic attacks and disease, Babylonians positioned specific plants above windows and thresholds. To this day, observant Jews attach a *mezuzah*, a small case with religious writing in it to the doorposts of their houses, while many Catholics place a small crucifix inside the entryway. Whether you believe these are acts of faith or superstition, they owe their origins to ancient practice.

Often overlooked is the Babylonian dependence on astrology. In Mesopotamia, "the cradle of civilization," Western and Hindu astrology were born, while the Chinese astrological system developed separately. Many historians ignore the significance astrology played in shaping Mesopotamian life and religion.

Originally, astrology in Mesopotamia was a type of divination:[17] the foretelling of future events, such as eclipses—a menacing omen—as well as epidemics and famines. Like the Sumerians, the Babylonians did not consider astrology for one's own use as we do today; that came about later in Greece and Rome. Early astrologers were priests retained by kings to divine or interpret the celestial bodies as a way of predicting the intent of the gods.

Ancient Egypt is, to this day, a civilization that still rings with an aura of mystery and wonder.[18] Its origin dates back to about 4000 B.C.

For several millennia, debate has raged about Egypt's construction of the pyramids, with some people suggesting that the supernatural or extraterrestrials helped play a part, since these monumental structures seemed beyond human capacity to build. "Who taught the Egyptians?" Alan Landsburg asked in his book, *In Search of Ancient Mysteries*.[19]

In our modern world, where we tend to place occupations and disciplines in neat little boxes, it is sometimes difficult to comprehend the ancient world. An Egyptian physician or priest could draw upon any number of magical or supernatural practices and remedies. Unlike our culture, Egyptian caregivers wore many hats, so medicine, magic, and religion were not separate and apart from each other as they are now.

Egypt became widely admired throughout the ancient world for its intricate "magical system"[20] and for its priority and attention to death, the care of the corpse, and its preparation for passage to the next world.

All civilizations, ancient and modern, share a fear mingled with morbid fascination about death and what awaits us when we leave this mortal plane. But in ancient Egypt interest in death was elevated to near obsession:[21] it was the heart of the Egyptian religion with its strong emphasis on immortality. By 1580 B.C., the Egyptian Book of the Dead, a compilation of various funerary writings, contained many "words of power" meant to help the departed.[22] The book's title, *pert em hru,* translates into "coming forth by day" or "manifested in the light." Was what we call the "near-death experience" already known to the ancient Egyptians? Letters to the Dead[23] were messages written in clay containers that held food placed for the deceased. At the beginning of Egypt's long history, only pharaohs and royalty could attain immortality; later, the opportunity was available to nearly all.

Another ancient reference to near-death experiences appeared in the Bardo Thodol, also known as the Tibetan Book of the Dead.[24] Although not written until the eighth century A.D., its oral tradition dated back many generations earlier, and detailed continued existence following physical death.

Meanwhile in India, the Hindu Bhagavad Gita—"The Lord's Song"—was already long in use.[25] It comprised one of the most significant dialogues in world history about the soul's immortality, and the relationship between eternal life and our behavior in this physical world.

Thanatologists, researchers who study death and dying, have discovered in age-old writings definite comparisons between the stages of death and dying and what we've rediscovered in recent decades through medical and paranormal research.

Ancient Egyptians engaged in magical practices, of which some remain controversial to this day: necromancy, that is, communication with the dead; and black magic, the invocation of evil spirits. Magic was thought to afford protection from a myriad of terrors including disease, the wrath of storms, and, of course, phantoms of the dead.

One of the strongest means to ward off adversity was to utilize magical amulets or charms; written or carved words on them were believed to contain magical powers. One of the best-known symbols was the scarab, a gem or stone cut in the form of a scarabacus, or sacred dung beetle, a symbol of rising from the dead.

The ancient Egyptians also practiced "image magic" in which wax figures represented the bewitched, and if the figures were harmed, the power directed against them was meant to cause injury to the persons they portrayed.

Of all the "ceremonial magic" rituals the Egyptians used, the meticulous mummification process remains the most fascinating.[26] It was highly precise with bandages wrapped in specific configurations, accompanied by "words of power" to aid the preservation process. Once the body was disemboweled, cleaned, and treated or embalmed, the attending priest offered magical words to the deceased, then applied oil to the entire body, especially the head. Preserving the body involved the use of a special salt or chemical, aided by Egypt's hot, dry climate. Then the mummy was decorated with "precious stones" for magical purposes. As just one example, crystal was supposed to cast light on the face of the deceased. When the complex mummification process was finished, the deceased was interred, ready for its soul's journey to the afterlife, and the priest conducted ceremonies.

Dream interpretation was widely engaged in by ancient Egyptians.[27] Magicians, assumed to be among the wisest of men, foretold the future based on what people reported they'd envisioned while asleep; and Egyptians were convinced dreams originated from the gods.

There is still debate today about how much of the dream state can be attributed to communications from outside our being; that is, paranormal in nature, such as visions of the deceased and dream premonitions. For the ancients there was no such conflict. To them, sleep was a "second life"; as such, the soul was released from the body to be active just as the body is while awake. Dream therapists today talk of "lucid dreaming," a way of retaining a conscious control over the dream state." Many millennia before Sigmund Freud and Carl Jung, the Egyptians considered ways dreams could be used to help people, albeit through magic rather than psychology or psychoanalysis.

Magic was also an integral part of Egyptian medicine[28]; some physicians turned to it with the supposition that illnesses were caused by demons that entered the body. Ancient Egyptian physicians had a twofold task: to administer remedies or perform surgery, and to exhort against evil spirits that caused afflictions.

Physicians also had at their disposal hundreds of herbal medicines, mainly drawn from plants found along the Nile River, including corian-der, anise, and saffron. There were minerals such as arsenic, alum, and sodium bicarbonate, still a popular antacid. One well-known example was the castor bean, a laxative; we know it better as castor oil.

Egyptians were fatalists who believed events were predetermined and therefore inevitable. In order to learn one's destiny, astrologers told people what days were best or worst for various activities; and surviving astrolog-ical writings on papyri show that the Egyptians were expert in "casting horoscopes."

One of the tools of divination that became immensely popular for "self-discovery" in our so-called New Age was tarot, the well-known deck of seventy-eight cards; comprised of four suits of fourteen cards each, and twenty-two symbolical picture cards. Tarot may have origi-nated with priests in ancient Egypt.

Ancient Egypt had its share of apparitions. In the Egyptian belief sys-tem, man had a "double," or duplicate, called the *ka*, that could roam around aimlessly following a person's death. Not unlike modern para-normal and religious beliefs, the ancient Egyptians conceived that man had a physical body and a spirit. The double or ka dwelled in the tomb with the deceased's body; and the spirit could descend from heaven to visit the double.

In about 1334 B.C.,[29] Tutankhamen ascended the Egyptian throne, but died at age eighteen, and so his reign and name would have passed qui-etly into the recesses of history, except for the discovery of his uniquely unspoiled tomb that added greatly to our knowledge of ancient Egyptian life. The tomb may also have been afflicted by a terrible curse.

For centuries the remains of Tutankhamen, or Tut as he was dubbed, lay peacefully. Then in 1922, an amateur British archaeologist named Lord Carnarvon and a colleague, Howard Carter, unearthed the tomb's entrance. However, by opening it, they flouted the command of the orig-inal Egyptian priests who'd sealed it shut. There were clear warnings not to open the tomb and Tut's remains bore a pendant that cautioned anyone who upset its serenity with death; but Carter and Carnarvon ignored the admonition.

To make matters worse, the two men helped themselves to some of Tu-tankhamen's cache of riches, some 5,000 objects, including a wealth of ʾous gems and gold. Not long after, Carnarvon became ill with a fever and died. Did he succumb to the curse by unsettling King Tut's tomb? The English lord's death might be dismissed as coincidence, except that his was but the first of many fatalities. At least twenty-two other deaths were linked to the curse, according to Philipp Vandenberg in *The Curse of the Pharaohs* (1975). Every individual involved in the opening of the tomb was afflicted with some form of sickness, all within a relatively short time, and headlines blared news of the curse.

The only one who did not die was Howard Carter, although many around him met terrible fates, from "illnesses to various misfortunes." But for the remainder of his life Carter faced a barrage of legal woes and adversities that ultimately took their toll until he died in 1939 at age sixty-six.

Had Carnarvon and Carter interfered with a powerful psychic energy? Had they foolishly tampered with divine forces best left alone? By disregarding the tomb's sanctity, had they and others been stricken with punishments meted out by the ancient Egyptian gods? Or had the tomb been sealed with a kind of virus, a bacteria activated upon the opening of the seals? Some have conjectured this because of the suddenness of the onset of Carnarvon's fever and Carter's sickness, but it has not been investigated scientifically.

There's an interesting more recent postscript: on July 14, 1977, Lord Carnarvon's son was asked in a network TV interview whether he believed in the curse. Although he said he "neither believed nor disbelieved it," he added he wouldn't "accept a million pounds to enter the tomb." That evening in New York he watched as the city suffered a major electrical blackout, and reportedly said, "It's again the curse of Tutankhamen."

The Pyramids
Few accomplishments in the history of the world[30] have been met with the continuing awe that greets the Great Pyramid of Giza, constructed during the rule of Cheops around 2530 B.C. It's led to an entire area of study called pyramidology that examines the mathematics, construction, and purpose of the pyramids, and includes inspection of pyramid measurements to determine what connection they may have with biblical prophecies.

There also remains debate about the wondrous construction of the pyramids, an astounding feat of engineering. Were they built by the painful labors of thousands of slave-workers using only "primitive tools?" Or were the pyramids the result of intervention by so-called "ancient astronauts" or some long gone occult knowledge; and if so, why? Traditional archaeologists and scientists, of course, dismiss paranormal theory as myth. But some pyramidologists and parapsychologists tenaciously hold to the belief that only by some supernatural feat of levitation or extraterrestrial help could the Great Pyramid have been built.

The dimensions of the Great Pyramid are amazing. It is composed of some 2,500,000 separate hewn stone blocks, each weighing an average of two and a half tons, and as much as fifteen tons or more; it stands more than forty stories high, and took at least twenty years to build. The accuracy with which the immense blocks were joined so perfectly is a wonder in itself, and its interior is as astonishing as the exterior.

For over thirty years, Max Toth examined the ancient mysteries of the pyramids, and wrote two best-selling books: *Pyramid Power* and *Pyramid Prophecies*.

"No structure in the world has been measured and surveyed as much as the Pyramid of Cheops," Toth explained. But, he added, "The mysteries of the pyramids are many." In fact, experts "cannot agree as to the real reason for the erection of the pyramids, the methods of construction, and the absence of mummies in what were apparently sealed stone coffins called sarcophagi."

The most popular of several theories is that they were tombs for the burial of pharaohs. Another supposition is that the pyramids were a "storehouse for some form of energy."[31] A Czechoslovakian radio engineer,[32] Karel Drbal, developed a theory of "pyramid energy," suggesting pyramid shaped objects could maintain or preserve foods and prevent the dulling of such items as razor blades. In the 1970s, so-called "pyramid power" became a popular fad; and according to Alan Landsburg "some psychics and mediums say they've felt a magnetic force around certain Egyptian pyramids."[33]

Did construction of Egyptian, Mayan, and Peruvian pyramids have extraterrestrial assistance?[34] Why were all of them built "within the same thirty degrees of latitude?" asked parapsychologist Howard Metz. How could cultures separated by thousands of miles, across centuries of time, have used virtually identical advanced "skills and sciences" to build pyramids? Why did all pyramid societies practice mummification? Only from the perspective of outer space could the builders of the pyramids have known where to locate them. Even skeptics are at a loss to answer many of these questions. "Was the Great Pyramid a credit to some superhuman power?" asked Landsburg.[35]

There are enough theories about the Egyptians, the mysteries of their pyramids and magical systems for us to debate endlessly. But to omit the paranormal aspect of their lives, as most traditional historians and even museums have done, is to give only a partial picture of ancient Egyptian culture, belief, and its lasting influence.

The Bible

No paranormal history can ignore the Bible's many accounts of psychic and UFO phenomena, and its profound—some would say stubborn—impact on our thinking, beliefs, and values throughout centuries and to this very day.

Ironically, despite the plethora of paranormal events in both the Old and New Testaments, America's religious conservatives, the so-called Religious Right, or Christian fundamentalists, have found much to criticize and disdain about the paranormal—in and out of the Bible.

Traditional biblical scholars have long regarded psychic interpretations of the Bible as mythological or demonic, or if they're generous, symbolic, or metaphorical. Yet from the Book of Genesis to Revelation, there are accounts of outer-space visitors to earth; angels, mediums, psychics, soothsayers, astrologers, witches, and wizards, as well as dreams, divination, numerology, healings, apparitions, visions, astral travel, psychokinesis, clairvoyance, telepathy, precognition, premonitions, and prophecies—and, of course, the paranormal gifts and miracles attributed to the greatest psychics who ever lived: Moses and Jesus Christ.

For example, consider the "Christian conception of prayer, that man can converse with God (a two-way traffic) without the use of sensory channels," wrote Michael Perry in *Psychic Studies: A Christian's View*.[36] Isn't that paranormal by definition?

The Bible is open to many interpretations and arguments. Passages in the Old Testament strictly condemn consulting mediums and wizards, such as Deuteronomy 18, which warned Israelites against engaging in black magic, calling on evil spirits or practicing as a fortune-teller, medium, or wizard, or summoning the spirits of the dead. Exodus 22:18 states,

"You shall not allow a woman to live who practices sorcery." In Leviti-cus, God warns, "nether shall you use magic, omens, or witchcraft [or predict events by horoscopes or signs and lucky days]." (19:26) "Turn not to those [mediums] who have familiar spirits or to wizards; do not seek them out to be defiled by them." (19:31)[37]

The New Testament is slightly more agreeable to "testing the spirits" to determine if they are from God. The First Epistle of St. John, in the New Testament (Verse 4), states: "Beloved, believe not every spirit, but try the spirits whether they are of God: because many false prophets are gone out into the world." That does not appear to be a blanket denuncia-tion of all spirit contact or communications.

In the Old Testament, I Samuel 28 reveals one of the first written rec-ords of an experience with a medium: Following King Samuel's death, Saul became the ruler of Israel and ordered the expulsion of all mediums and wizards from Israel. The reasons were likely twofold. First, Saul wanted the Hebrew people focused on the One God, rather than oc-cultists. Second, Israel's prophets disliked mediums and considered that they were too familiar with the common people.

But King Saul faced an immediate menace. "The Philistines [had] gathered their forces for war against Israel." He turned first to God for answers through dreams and prophets, but received no reply. Saul then sought a medium for advice from the spirit world. He was told, "There is a woman who is a medium at Endor," a town two miles from where the Philistine enemy was camped.

In seeking a medium King Saul was, of course, violating his own laws. So he disguised himself and at night went to the woman at Endor and asked her to summon up Samuel, whose counsel he'd always respected. The woman was at first frightened of retaliation because of the law against mediums and wizards; not recognizing it was the king who stood before her. The king calmed her and swore there'd be no punishment against her.

The woman said, "I see a god coming up out of the earth!"

Saul asked what he looked like. The woman answered, "An old man comes up, covered with a mantle." Saul realized it was Samuel.

But summoning the dead provoked Samuel to ask, "Why have you disturbed me to bring me up?"

"I am bitterly distressed; for the Philistines make war against me, and God has departed from me and answers me no more, either by prophets or dreams. Therefore I have called you, that you may make known to me what I should do," Saul replied.

"Why then do you ask me, [if] the Lord has turned from you and has become your enemy?" Samuel then gave Saul dreadful news. "The Lord [will] give Israel with you into the hands of the Philistines, and tomorrow you and your sons shall be with me [among the dead]. The Lord also will give the army of Israel into the hands of the Philistines." Hearing this, Saul fell to the floor of the medium's house, terrified.

The predictions from the woman of Endor proved to be true. The Philistines defeated the Israelites and killed King Saul and his sons. Some conservative Christians have translated this to mean God punished Saul for consulting a medium, quoting the New Testament. (I Chronicles 10:13) A more likely interpretation is that Saul's fate would have been unchanged; the medium simply repeated what Samuel's spirit foresaw.

The famed American psychic and seer of the early twentieth century, Edgar Cayce, realized how easy it was to construe the Bible in different ways. When asked if the concept of reincarnation could be found in the Scriptures as some have argued, Cayce wisely answered, "You can read reincarnation into the Bible, and I can read it right out again."[38]

One problem for the paranormal in the Bible is the same semantic difficulty that has plagued psychic phenomena in Western thought and belief for millennia. One person's medium is another's witch, although the two are not the same. The woman of Endor has long mistakenly been called a witch although she was a medium. Conservative theology attributes the words of the biblical prophets to God, but denounces predictions from mediums or seers, often branding them as evil or demonic in origin. The confusion in terminology dating back to ancient times still stirs passions.

Who Authored the Bible?

There is also mystery about who authored the Bible, and its remarkable prescience. Those with strong religious convictions are certain the Scriptures are the inspired word of God. But others go as far as to conjecture input from an extraterrestrial or "superhuman intelligence." There are also scholars who've suggested the Bible contains a hidden or secret code that when translated reveals new meanings, even predictions for our time, as was the contention of the books about the so-called Bible Code and the nature of the mathematics contained in the ancient languages.

Afterlife in the Bible

The Old Testament prophets scorned mediums and considered themselves to be of a higher rank. While mediums claimed their communications came from spirits of the departed, prophets considered the dead to be without any power, dwelling in a place called Sheol "deep below the ground"; similar to the later Greek concept of "Hades," bereft of God's presence.

For the ancient Hebrews, little belief or attention was paid to the afterlife; death was considered "total extinction," wrote Michael Perry. The Jewish religion discouraged interest in mediumship, since it was a reminder of "folk-belief," not unlike "paganism" that Christians despised.

While Christianity developed a strong belief system about the afterlife, with the concept that the soul goes to Heaven, the Hebrew prophets were dedicated to convincing their people that mediums were in contact with "powerless shades," and not with God, Perry explained.

One of the Old Testament's most respected and important prophets, Isaiah, asked, "Should they consult the dead on behalf of the living?" (Isaiah 8:19) The dead, he was saying, were unable to help the living. Who should the Israelites turn to? His answer, of course, was the one God; that was the basis of monotheism.

Unlike the later Christians, ancient Israelites had not developed teachings about the devil. So despite Hebrew criticism of mediums, no denouncement was made that mediums were in league with Satan, as Christians would claim, since no such being had yet been envisioned as God's enemy.

Despite condemnation of mediums and necromancers, Jews did not go to hell for consulting them; the deceased were simply impotent. Later the New Testament contradicted this view about life after death, primarily with its concept and belief in the Resurrection.

The Hebrew prophets believed they brought forth the word of God. Prophecy was not so much about predicting as it was communicating God's message about obedience and trust in the Lord. But prophets could also issue alarming predictions from visions or the word of God. For example, the prophet Joel once forecast a "severe locust plague."

The long history of biblical prophecy dates, of course, from Moses himself, the first prophet whose story is told in the first five books of the Bible, the holy Torah. Later prophets date from Elijah around 875 B.C. to Malachi in about 460 B.C., and although prophets were valued and respected, they offered no personal information to individuals, except to kings, where personal advice had a social and political impact.

Isaiah's ministry around 740 B.C. meant he lived at the same time as several other famed Hebrew prophets: Amos, Hosea, and Micah. Many believe their relevance today is that their messages were not just for their own time but for future generations as well.

The entire book of the prophet Daniel is based on "divine revelation" that appeared to him in dreams and visions, and he also made several specific predictions. When Daniel was captured and taken to Babylonia he gained a high position after telling King Nebuchadnezzar the meaning of frightening dreams the king had about his destiny that royal astrologers, magicians, and soothsayers were unable to decipher.

Did the prophets have psychic abilities? Were they the biblical versions of today's remote viewers? Regardless of how and why certain people were chosen to be God's messengers or prophets, one function they fulfilled through their gifts was critical: their words helped bind the Israelites together as a people through difficult and turbulent times. They were themselves prophesied in the words of Moses in his exhortation to his people as he neared death. Moses warned of the "blessing and the curse" as he counseled the Israelites about their future. Moses said that the Israelites had a choice, they could follow the word of God to the letter or they could fall into their baser instincts. And as successive kings of Israel led their people away from the teachings of Moses, prophets appeared to counsel them back to teachings of the Torah.

The New Testament makes frequent cross-references to Old Testament writings. A fascinating paranormal concept that strengthens the argument for the accuracy of the Hebrews is "fulfilled prophecy." In those instances, later writings confirm predictions made in prior centuries.

As just one example, an angel appeared to tell Joseph to quickly take Mary and the infant Jesus from Egypt where King Herod had ordered the death of "every baby boy two years old and under," after a futile search for Jesus to kill Him. (Matthew 2:2–17)[39] This fulfilled the prognostications made earlier by the Old Testament prophets Hosea (11:1) and Jeremiah. (31:15)

Paranormal Events in the Bible

It is impossible to detail here every paranormal incident or reference in the Bible; there are simply too many. However some highlights will certainly convey that events called paranormal today were familiar to people during ancient and biblical times. One example is the existence of angels or "messengers of God," a word derived from the Greek *angelos* that had its origins in ancient Sanskrit.

During the New Age era of the 1990s, angels exploded in popularity, especially the idea of so-called "guardian angels." But there's nothing new about these celestial beings; there are no less than three hundred passages about them throughout the Bible. In fact, many people first learned of angels from biblical stories, and the concept of angels is accepted by every major world religion. According to the Bible, the "armies of heaven" were comprised of angels who were present to "fight God's cosmic battle."

Jewish religious laws, known collectively as the Talmud, claim that "every Jew has eleven-thousand guardian angels." In fact, according to Jewish tradition, every time a person performs a good deed, such as giving alms to a poor person or doing a righteous or pious act, God creates an angel to intercede for him upon his death. In Judaism, Christianity, and Islam, angels are God's messengers who deliver "inspiration or revelation."

The Old Testament Book of Genesis begins with the story of creation, and angels soon appear. One was sent by God to cast out Adam and Eve from the Garden of Eden. The Archangel Zadkiel appears to Abraham as he is about to sacrifice Isaac, extending God's protection to the child and bestowing upon Abraham the blessing that he shall become the father of his people.

In the Book of Exodus, God orders an angel to guide the Israelites from Egyptian captivity. God also tells of His angel who will "blot out" the enemies of the Hebrew people.

In the story of the "burning bush," the "Angel of the Lord," that may have been God Himself, appeared to Moses "in a flame of fire." The bush burned, "yet was not consumed." (Exodus 3:2)

Once the Israelites fled Egypt and crossed the Red Sea, it miraculously parted. Is there a supernatural explanation? Theories range from God's intervention, to extraterrestrial help, even a natural occurrence such as a change in tides. Once the waters receded, Moses and his followers made safe passage. Then as the Egyptian army gave chase, their chariots became stuck in the mud, and the waters quickly rose and swallowed them.

When the Hebrews once grew very hungry as they wandered through the wilderness, Moses promised that God would provide food, and the next morning the earth around them was covered with a "strange golden crust." Moses explained that it was "manna, the food the angels eat in heaven," considered a miracle from God.

Because Moses was raised in the court of the Pharaoh—he even had an Egyptian name related to Ramsses—he'd been exposed to and learned well "the secrets of Egyptian magic." On at least two occasions Moses used his staff or rod in the Sinai desert to dowse for water underground by striking a rock. His sister Miriam was also a gifted prophet.

How did Moses receive the tablets that contained the Ten Commandments on Mount Sinai? There are parapsychologists who have suggested that God communicated the commandments to Moses through "automatic writing," a process by which "messages are communicated to the living by powerful spiritual beings." There is no evidence that Moses or any other human composed the Ten Commandments.

One the greatest figures in the Old Testament was the venerable Abraham, patriarch of his own family, as well as of the Jewish and Islamic faiths, and angels also came to him. When Abraham's wife Sarah was unable to bear him any children, Abraham followed her instructions and made their servant, Hagar, pregnant. But Sarah became angry, punished Hagar, and the girl ran away.

In the wilderness an "Angel of the Lord" appeared, told Hagar to return, and reassured her that she would give birth to a son who would be named Ishmael (God hears).

Abraham was eighty-six when Ishmael was born, and he would become the ancestor of the Arab peoples. This was the first time, the Bible tells us, God named a person before his birth. (Genesis 16) Others later included Isaac, Josiah, Solomon, John the Baptist, and, of course, Jesus. (Matthew 1:21)

Later, when Abraham and Sarah were both past the age of ninety, a trio of angels announced they would have a child named Isaac. As a test of his faith to God, Abraham nearly sacrificed Isaac, when at the last moment, God sent an angel to stop the killing.

Abraham's grandson Jacob had dreams in which numerous angels appeared moving up and down a ladder to heaven.

The Book of Psalms makes a clear reference to "guardian angels." "For He will give his angels [especial] charge over you to accompany and defend and preserve you in all your ways." (Psalms 91:11)

The stories of Joseph's prophetic dreams and his jealous brothers' treachery are recounted in Genesis. The Bible also tells of Joseph's ability to interpret dreams that predicted seven years of feast, and seven of famine. The Pharaoh, grateful for Joseph's prescience, elevated him to a high position, and so he triumphed, despite adversity, and because of his prophetic dream visions. Joseph's envious brothers, responsible for his Egyptian captivity, when faced by dire famine, had to seek his help to secure food.

The prophet Elijah poses one of the most fascinating individuals in the Old Testament, where paranormal or supernatural events are concerned. In one incident, a group of about fifty Talmudic students gathered on one side of the Jordan River. As they watched, Elijah vanished "in a chariot of fire." Author and researcher Herbert Greenhouse wrote about the event, "Unless it was a collective hallucination, it is one of the most striking cases of psychic phenomena in the Bible."[40]

One day a destitute man, barefoot and in rags, walked along a road fervently praying for God's help; he, his wife, and their five children had scarcely any food. Unexpectedly, he met a younger man who asked what was wrong. The downtrodden man did not know that this was the prophet Elijah in disguise.

Elijah insisted the poor man sell him into servitude, and Elijah was sold to the king. The man now had money to feed his starving family.

Elijah, taken before the king, explained he could build him a "great palace." The monarch offered Elijah immense rewards and his freedom if he could construct the palace within six months. Elijah assured the king it would take far less time. That night Elijah prayed to God for a miracle, and from the heavens came a multitude of angels who completed the task. By daylight the massive construction was done and the angels and Elijah ascended to heaven. The king was in awe when he saw the finished palace. Only then did he realize Elijah was an angel.

Angels also visited Lot and his family to warn them about the destruction that was to befall the wicked cities of Sodom and Gomorrah.

In the Book of Daniel, comprised entirely of that prophet's dream visions, he witnessed thousands of angels. Daniel was the first to call them by name Michael and Gabriel; and when Daniel was trapped in the lions' den, it was the angel Michael who saved his life by calming the lions.

In the story of "Ezekiel's Wheel," traditional interpretations suggest the prophet Ezekiel saw God's throne surrounded by cherubim or angelic beings; but some paranormal researchers suggest that his experience was actually an encounter with outer-space beings, possibly aboard some type of extraterrestrial vehicle. Does it sound preposterous? Consider that even in ancient times there were reports of inexplicable objects and lights flying through the sky both day and night.

In the sixth century B.C., Ezekiel, a young man of about thirty, wrote, "As I looked, behold, a stormy wind came out of the north, and a great fire enveloping it and flashing continually; a brightness was about it and out of the midst of it there seemed to glow amber metal.

"And [then] came four living creatures [and] they had the likeness of a man. But each had four faces and each one had four wings. And their legs were straight and the soles of their feet were like the soles of a calf's foot, and they sparkled like burnished bronze. And they had the hands of a man under their wings on their four sides."

Ezekiel continued, "Their wings touched one another; they turned not out went every one straight forward. And the living creatures darted back and forth like a flash of lightning."

Then as Ezekiel watched he "saw one wheel upon the ground besides each of the living creatures." The wheels "gleamed like chrysolite [a type of yellowish mineral] . . . and their construction work was . . . [like] . . . a wheel within a wheel.

"And when the living creatures went, the wheels went beside them; and when the living creatures were lifted up from the earth, the wheels were lifted up.

"Wherever the spirit went, the creatures went and the wheel rose along with them.

"And when they went, I heard the sound of their wings like the noise of great waters, like the voice of the Almighty, the sound of tumult like the noise of a host [large number of people or things]." (Ezekiel 1:1–24)

In his 1974 book *The Spaceships of Ezekiel*,[41] Josef F. Blumrich, who worked for National Aeronautics and Space Administration (NASA) in the 1960s, noted similarities between the device Ezekiel described, nearly 600 years before the birth of Christ, and NASA's modern designs for a "lunar landing craft."

Blumrich said Ezekiel's description matched that of a modern helicopter. The "wings" Ezekiel referred to might be, in Blumrich's words, "moving rotor blades."

Ezekiel would have had no understanding or recognition of helicopters or rocket engines. Yet he described "metallic wheels" and later "the sound of great tumult." Supporters of the extraterrestrial theory have said that Ezekiel was recounting some type of outer space or aerospace technology.

There is a chilling thought here that all the talk of helicopters and space vehicles such as lunar rovers really mean that what the prophet saw were not space aliens but really human beings from the future. If that's the case, and this is only speculation, does it mean that our very time line itself has already been interfered with by future incarnations of ourselves. Are our past and our very memories being interfered with even as we read this?

Nevertheless, the hierarchy of angels appears throughout the Bible, and they are also significant figures in the New Testament. This is significant because as Flavius Josephus writes, Jesus, and his brother James, were indeed historical figures during the time of the Zealots at the Roman occupation of Israel.

The Gospel of Mark tells of an angel sent by the Lord. According to Luke, the angel Gabriel appeared to announce the forthcoming birth of Jesus. It was an angel who made known to the shepherds in Bethlehem the "good news" that Jesus would be born, followed by a multitude of angels who sang in praise.

Gabriel also came forth to Zacharias, to announce that he and his wife would have a child, who would be John the Baptist, "the herald of the Messiah."

When Jesus was led by the Holy Spirit into the wilderness to be tempted by the devil, He withstood all of Satan's enticements, and when finally the devil retreated, angels appeared to minister to Jesus. (Matthew 4:11)

Following the Crucifixion of Jesus, an angel is said to have moved the huge stone that sealed His tomb. Inside the empty sepulcher the angel told Jesus' followers of the Resurrection, His rising from the dead; another biblical event many consider paranormal.

When the apostles were imprisoned for spreading Christianity in Rome following the death and resurrection of Jesus, "during the night an angel of the Lord opened the prison doors" and led them out. (Acts 5:19)

On another occasion Peter was imprisoned and chained by King Herod who ordered sentries to guard him. "Suddenly an angel of the Lord appeared and a light shone . . . where he was . . . and the chains fell off [Peter's] hands." (Acts 12:7) Following the angel's instructions, Peter "passed through" two guards; an iron gate opened "of its own accord," and Peter was free. (Acts 12:6–10) Later "an angel of the Lord smote [King Herod] and cut him down. . . ." (Acts 12:23)

In Ephesians 3:10, a letter written by Paul around 60 A.D. while he was incarcerated for two years referred to "angelic rulers and authorities in the heavenly sphere."

The last book of the Bible, Revelation, written by the apostle John includes many references to angels, as well as other paranormal phenomena. The chapter is described as "The revelation of Jesus Christ. His unveiling of the divine mysteries." The Bible says, "God permitted [Jesus] to reveal these things to John in a vision" and then an angel was sent from heaven to explain the vision's meaning. "John wrote it all down everything he saw and heard." (Revelation 1)

Even today, many consider Revelation to be apocalyptic in nature, predicting some future cataclysmic event. We'll examine some of that content in a later part of this book. But the paranormal references are undeniable. In addition to angels, Revelation contains dreams, visions, the use of symbolic numbers, and prophecy, as well as admonishing sorcery and demonic powers. Obviously biblical times were rife with angelic and supernatural activity. It's no wonder such phenomena were accepted as a normal part of everyday existence.

The Miracles in the New Testament

According to the Gospel of Matthew, the magi were chosen to "represent the gentile nations in paying first homage to the Christ." Actually, the magi from whom we derive the word "magician" were astrologers. (Matthew 2:1-2) Why astrologers were elected by God to be the first to honor the infant Jesus remains open to debate.

Dozens of miracles were attributed to Jesus Christ during His lifetime. Defined as "remarkable occurrences that can be of a supernatural or unknown origin," they pose the possibility of also being paranormal events; and appear throughout the New Testament. Many are "miraculous healings," by the laying of hands. Among them Jesus cured people with a variety of ailments; healed lepers; made crippled and paralyzed people walk; cured the "blind and dumb," restoring their sight, hearing, and speech; cast out demons from the afflicted; reattached a cut off ear; restored a "withered hand"; and He "[continually] performed on those who were sick."

Among other miracles, Jesus turned water to wine; guided His disciples to catch many fish; from a small amount of bread, He miraculously "multiplied" enough loaves for thousands to eat; walked on water; caused storms to calm; caused a fig tree to wither; and raised the dead, including Lazarus, one of the most remarkable feats attributed to Him. The accounts of these miracles are told in the Books of Matthew, Mark, Luke, and John.

What are we to make of these incidents? Aren't they paranormal; that is, "beyond the scope of normal objective investigation or explanation?" The events of biblical times serve as the basis of belief for millions today, notwithstanding the ongoing debates that often pit theology against parapsychology, leaving many conflicted.

Strengthening the veracity of many accounts are findings by biblical archaeologists that support events in the Old and New Testaments. The Bible's influence has been so profound that serious study of its numerous paranormal references would add greatly to our knowledge of psychic phenomena and the foundation for many of our convictions and misconceptions—as well as cast light on the centuries when the Bible was written.

The Paranormal in Ancient Greece

Around 1600 B.C., ancient Greece began to develop into a complex and sophisticated society. Its contributions to future centuries have been incalculable, from philosophy to the development of democracy, arts, culture, architecture, even physical fitness and fierce athletic competition in the famed and enduring Olympic games, first held in 776 B.C. Greece has also given us some of the most enduring names in history: Socrates,

Plato, Aristotle, Herodotus, Homer, Pythagorus, Pericles, and Hippocrates, to name a few.

Ancient Greece's two great city-states were Athens and Sparta. Athens was more devoted to democracy, the arts, culture, and commerce; Sparta, on the other hand, became known for its emphasis on military readiness and austere living.

However, in retelling the story of ancient Greece, traditional historians typically minimize the role the paranormal played, relegating it to superstition. But it was much more: in no society before or since in Western civilization have oracles—or seers—had such profound influence.

The most famed seer in the ancient world was the oracle at Delphi. At that "sacred site," Apollo, the Greek god, spoke through the oracle, a woman called the Pythia, and people came from near and far for her advice and predictions. But her worth went beyond her psychic gifts. In addition to the oracle at Delphi, there were several lesser ones throughout ancient Greece who had political, psychological and sociological value. When Greece went through periods of turmoil and strife, the Delphic oracle commanded sufficient influence to maintain a sense of stability among the uneasy citizenry.

Other oracles answered questions put to them with a curt "yes" or "no." The Delphic oracle was different; she gave more complete answers. While a lesser oracle was available daily, the famed Pythia was accessible just one day a month.

Questions were asked of the Pythia through a meditating priest, acting as an intermediary. The Pythia seated on a "holy tripod" forwarded her answers in a manner that had to be explained or deciphered by the priest who typically restated the message. There is still debate about how the oracle obtained her gift. Some believe that by hypnotizing herself, she entered a self-induced trance. Another theory is that she inhaled some form of chemical vapors within her temple that served to intoxicate her, producing an altered state of consciousness.

Questions to the oracle were mainly about how best to solve particular problems or what course one might follow; few queries were religious in nature. Often the oracle's advice was sought to explain the meaning of natural disasters and other portents, and how people could better please the gods to regain supernatural approbation.

One persistent and infamous frustration was the oracle's ambiguous responses. Heraclitus put his best spin on this dilemma when he said the oracle at Delphi "neither speaks, nor conceals, but indicates." Mainly her role was to act as an intermediary between the people and the gods, and she was always consulted before changes were permitted in ceremonies or rituals.

Through the oracle, Apollo gave leaders advice for maintaining peace, law, and justice. Government officials often consulted the oracle, and she even had a say in international politics. During the long Peloponnesian War between the Greek city-states of Athens and Sparta, the oracle favored the warlike Sparta, which ultimately won. She also reminded that the gods did not approve of evil doings, vanity, or arrogance. "Know thyself," she admonished, and "Nothing in excess."

During the fifth century B.C., in Athens, a "classical" period of achievements in philosophy, science, and the arts, the oracles' prestige declined significantly, and fewer turned to them for counsel. But for the centuries that the Delphic oracle's influence prevailed, she helped guide Greek society to a higher moral standard.

In the ancient world of Greece and Rome, occult and psychic phenomena were popular. Soothsayers, seers, diviners, and necromancers were easily found, and Greek and Roman governments employed clairvoyants. Many provided the modern equivalent to our therapists and psychiatrists. Magic, scrying or crystal-ball gazing, fortune-telling, and astrology were especially widespread.

The Greek scholar Ptolemy, considered "the father of Western astrology," discovered the "earth-centered" system of astronomy that was accepted for centuries until it was replaced by Copernicus' "sun-centered" view of the solar system. At the time Ptolemy lived (A.D. 100–178) astrology and astronomy were not as far apart from each other as they later became. Ptolemy's fundamental astrological structure has remained largely intact, notwithstanding adjustments over the centuries.

The famed Greek philosophers, writers, and scientists had varying opinions about the psychic or "invisible" world. Socrates believed that his life (469–399 B.C.) was guided by an entity that protected him, even when sentenced to death by drinking hemlock.

The philosopher Plato believed in the immortality of the soul, as well as in visions and precognitive dreams.

The ancient Greek historian Herodotus, and Pliny the Younger, among others, wrote of ghost encounters. The philosopher Athenodorus once lived in a house where he reported witnessing the apparition of an elderly man walking at night. The ghost directed him to the exact place where his remains were buried. Once the bones were given a proper funeral and burial, the ghost never again appeared.

Out-of-body experiences were known in the ancient world. In A.D. 79, Plutarch wrote about a soldier rendered unconscious. When he was revived, the soldier "claimed he'd seen and spoken with a dead relative."

Another early and long-lasting device to receive messages from spirits was invented in the sixth century B.C. by the Greek philosopher and mathematician Pythagoras. This instrument was a type of pointer that identified Greek letters chiseled in stone wedges. The ancient Chinese had also developed a similar device. Centuries later, a modern version of this psychic tool became known as the Ouija board, and the pointer was replaced by a heart-shaped wooden device called a "planchette," that responded to questions supposedly without "conscious control" by the person using it.

Pythagoras is also credited with developing the system of divination known as numerology, "the study of the occult significance of numbers."

The respected Greek physician Hippocrates identified "medical clairvoyance," as the "ability to [psychically] see the internal organs and make diagnoses." In more recent times, Edgar Cayce and later the medium George Anderson had a similar gift to diagnose clairvoyantly.[42]

To most ancient Greeks, dreams were considered communications from the gods. The philosopher Heraclitus (450–375 B.C.) was one of the first dream interpreters; but he hypothesized that dreams came from within man. Also taking a more rationalist view of the origin of dreams was the philosopher Aristotle (384–322 B.C.), who did not believe that the gods sent dreams. In fact, he compared dreams with hallucinations suffered by the mentally ill.

It wasn't until in Rome around A.D. 150 that dream interpretation became a serious endeavor, only to struggle for acceptance again later when the Church discouraged it. Since only God controlled the future, Thomas Aquinas (1225–1274) concluded prophetic dreams might be blasphemous. It seems a contradiction to the Bible's many dreams and visions, but paranormal beliefs often changed depending on the times and culture.

In the *Iliad*, for example, Homer considered the meaning of life and death, but never suggested an afterlife, providing only a vague description of the dead in a state of unawareness. Despite a seeming openness to all manner of paranormal practices, ancient Greek and Roman governments controlled some activities, especially necromancy, that is conjuring the dead, and the private practice of magic. The Roman Twelve Tables, a body of laws, went so far as to exact the death penalty for anyone practicing witchcraft.

Atlantis

In the fourth century B.C. Plato first described a "lost civilization" called Atlantis in two of his dialogues, Timaeus and Critias. Was Plato's story true or merely a fabrication? Did the famed lost continent ever exist? "Atlantis is the world's greatest mystery story," wrote Charles Berlitz in *The Mystery of Atlantis.*

Skeptics consider Atlantis to be mythical, noting that in nearly every ancient culture there was an antediluvian or "great flood" legend and the drowning of civilization. The biblical account, of course, is the story of Noah's ark; and his advance knowledge of the Great Flood proved prophetic. (Genesis 6) Within the paranormal, Atlantis has enjoyed a long reputation as "a great and wonderful empire," in Berlitz's words. It was said to be advanced, sophisticated, energetic, and for a time, Plato claimed, its inhabitants were even immortal.

Plato placed the submerging of Atlantis around 11250 B.C., possibly a victim of floods at the end of the last Ice Age. He described it as an "earthly paradise" until it "disappeared under the sea." His source was likely ancient Egyptian accounts of "a large island continent beyond the Pillars of Hercules [Gibraltar]."

Whether fact or fiction, Atlantis has endured; and may have motivated exploration to the "New World," spurring curiosity about the discovery of uncharted places. Various theories have placed Atlantis in some three dozen different places around the globe.

What explains "flood legends" in places far from each other that had no known contact in the ancient world? It suggests something must have occurred.

In 1882, Ignatius Donnelly wrote a popular book about Atlantis.[43] He too described Atlantis in idyllic terms, and claimed it was destroyed by some horrendous natural disaster that sunk the entire island and killed practically every Atlantean. The few who survived carried the story of its tragic end.

Interest in Atlantis received another boost when famed American seer and clairvoyant Edgar Cayce gave psychic readings in which he referred to Atlantean past lives.[44] In 1940, Cayce predicted Atlantis would be found in 1968 or 1969 in the vicinity of Bimini. Cayce's supporters insist ruins of several buildings were spotted in that area, but no one has determined with certainty their age or origin. One recent credible theory by author Dr. Charles Pellegrino[45] placed Atlantis on an island called Thera, near Crete, in the Aegean Sea, and suggested it was destroyed by a tremendous volcanic eruption around 1500 B.C. That location matches most closely Plato's Atlantis, and it was there in 1969 that a Greek archaeologist found remains of an ancient Minoan city buried in a thick covering of volcanic ash.

Today, past-life hypnotic regressions often suggest subjects once lived in Atlantis, as Cayce claimed. In his version,[46] Atlantean technology was based on energy gathered from the stars in a huge "firestone," or crystal. Cayce said the demise of Atlantis was "the misuse of the crystal's power." "Crystal healing," popular in the recent New Age movement, was motivated by Cayce's writing.

If ever Atlantis is found it may answer many questions about our past and the true nature—and meaning—of the legendary civilization.

Secret Societies

Finally, ancient secret or mystery cults played a significant role in Greek history, including elements of the mystical and occult; some were "dedicated" to certain deities. Because their secrets presumably contained special knowledge or power they were closely protected and surrounded by various rituals and rites. Throughout human history secret societies have played a role in the study of esoteric knowledge.

Greco-Roman classical civilization spanned centuries of European history until about A.D. 500. Wars and invasions inevitably led to the defeat of Greece, but their concepts of philosophy, science, and politics survived, and were then disseminated throughout the vast Roman Empire.

Ancient Rome

To the ancient Romans the practice of magic was essential to their belief in many gods and deities.[47] It was through magic that the Romans defined their thinking and worldview; and it influenced many of their laws and customs. There was also widespread belief in divination such as reading animal entrails and the flight patterns of birds. Roman rulers and nobility often employed fortune-tellers and astrologers; and omens were so accepted that soothsayers read portents before Roman armies went to battle. Virtually every aspect of Roman life was thought under the watchful eye of the deities, summoned by Roman priests when needed. There were also festivals, including one dedicated to the deceased, during which doors to the next world were believed to be open.

Most Romans had a strong conviction in spirits, and a dread that evil specters or phantoms wandered among them; so were cautious not to arouse their wrath. A troubled spirit might steal a person's soul, causing death. Romans were also intimidated by anyone who cast the so-called evil eye, a curse placed on an enemy by a gaze. They also looked to the skies with trepidation; storms were thought to be a result of a vengeful deity. Lightning was particularly onerous; taken to be the god Jove displaying his anger.

Romans had in their midst many practicing witches. Horace wrote about them in frightening terms, as they slinked through the night in cemeteries seeking "bones and herbs" for nocturnal feasts attended by specters. These forbidding sorceresses also employed "image magic," making wax figures of their intended victims to visit evil on them. Even the Roman Emperor Nero and his mother turned to sorcery.

To the Romans dreams were very important, especially prophetic dreams. Virgil wrote that the souls of the departed visited the living in dreams; and learned men such as Cicero sought explanations for them.

Julius Caesar and his wife Calpurnia both experienced dream premonitions in which they foresaw his death. A soothsayer named Vestricius Spurrina also predicted to Caesar that he would be murdered with the warning, "Beware the Ides of March." The predictions proved accurate when Caesar was assassinated in the Roman Senate on March 15, 44 B.C.; a scene later immortalized in Shakespeare's play.

In hindsight many Roman occult practices and fears seem merely superstition; but to the Romans the beliefs were real. Traditional histories and exhibits that today virtually ignore the Roman dependence on magic and occult thinking minimize a significant component of Roman life and culture.

Jesus and Rome

Jesus' public ministry began at age thirty, by thirty-three He had been sentenced to death by crucifixion. His defiance of Roman officials and claim that He was the Son of God resulted in charges of religious blasphemy. Following His resurrection and ascension, followers simply called themselves "disciples," and had not yet created a formal church. Jewish teachings had paved the way for Christianity, and like the Jews, Christians suffered repeated Roman persecutions.

In its early years Christianity attracted few converts. Those who were won over were mostly poor women, slaves, and the disenfranchised, drawn to Christianity by its message that Jesus was a "common man" whose words had made Him a martyr. Outcasts were welcome; no money or education was required. The essence of Christianity was one of hope, no slavery, and sanctuary from "pain and suffering." But to Roman officials, Christianity's growing appeal was a menace to their authority, for Christians did not worship Roman deities, thus the practice of Christianity was outlawed.

For its first three hundred years the Church suffered abuse and oppression. As a result many early Christians were martyred; executed for refusing to renounce their faith. But Roman tyranny failed to discourage converts. Ironically, the stories of martyrs motivated many towards Christianity, eager to learn about this new religion for which people were willing to die.

A significant paranormal event in early Christian history occurred to Saul on the road to Damascus. A Roman soldier of Jewish birth, he was on his way to dissuade followers of Jesus, but as he traveled Saul unexpectedly saw and heard Jesus in a vision. It was what psychiatrists call an "aversion reaction" to his own persecution of the Jewish followers of Jesus. The profound experience resulted in Saul's conversion to Christianity—and he became St. Paul—the very religion he'd been persecuting, and he became an important Church missionary, expanding the word of Christ to gentiles as well as Jews.

Meanwhile, the Roman Empire's power diminished as it faced enemies, notably "warring tribes," while internally its leaders became increasingly decadent. With the Roman government unable to protect its citizenry, the Church became a source of strength and solidity, offering charity and help to the needy, sick, and elderly. "As Rome declined, the

Church grew," wrote Bob O'Gorman and Mary Faulkner in *The Complete Idiot's Guide to Understanding Catholicism* (2000).[48]

The fourth century proved very different for the Church. A paranormal occurrence played a key part, and literally changed not only the Church, but also the history of the Western world.

In A.D. 312, Constantine became the Roman emperor. Although he was not Christian, and only baptized at his death, his mother Helena was a Christian convert. Then Constantine experienced a dream vision. Shortly before going into battle, he saw the image of the cross brightly blazing, and heard a voice tell him if he received Christianity as his faith he would win. Constantine swore he would. He was victorious, and the history of the Church and Western civilization changed for all time when Constantine made Christianity legal in A.D. 313, and the preferred religion in Rome in 324. Once he issued an "edict of toleration," persecutions largely ended.

For the Church, Constantine was both a blessing and a miracle; the Church gained in size and strength. Monasteries, convents, and churches were built, missionaries encouraged converts, and the Church became a safe haven amidst the secular turbulence that led to the Dark Ages.

Unfortunately, as the Church grew it also began to display an imperious and autocratic side. Church leaders, apparently forgetting the unadorned life and principles of Jesus, indulged themselves in luxury and affluence that eventually led to corruption and division.

A highly influential early Church figure was St. Augustine, who wrote *City of God*, a book with immense impact about the relationship between Christianity and the world around it. Augustine's belief was that "only the soul endures forever." His writings had a profound effect on the Church's view of itself, and became the rationale for medieval times, an age that placed more importance on the course of the soul than on the well being of the body.

St. Patrick

One of the most popular supernatural stories concerns the fifth-century Irish missionary St. Patrick, who was said to have driven the snakes out of Ireland. It's likely the story is a metaphor; not meant to be taken literally. St. Patrick's goal was to convert Ireland from Druidism, the ancient Celtic pagan religion, and snakes had been their "sacred symbol."

Patrick experienced profound dream visions in which God summoned him to Ireland. He obeyed, left England, and committed himself tirelessly to missionary work until Ireland was a Catholic country. However, the ancient Druid religion was deeply engrained in Celtic or Irish belief, so certain Celtic "holy days" remained on the Catholic calendar, but they were devoted instead to Catholic saints, and portions of Celtic magical lore became part of the stories of the saints.

The Church in the Middle Ages

The fifth century A.D. marked the fall of the Roman Empire. From then until the end of the Middle Ages in the fifteenth century, when the Renaissance began, the Church went through far-reaching changes in its opinions and positions about virtually everything paranormal and occult.

For St. Paul, St. Augustine, St. Thomas Aquinas, and the major theologians of the early Christian church "occult beliefs and practices ranked among the sins of idolatry as well as false worship, both faithless and sacrilegious," Richard Woods explained in *The Occult Revolution*.[49]

However, there were also contradictions within the early Church about the paranormal.[50] For example, Christians accepted a belief in reincarnation, as Hindus and Buddhists had for centuries before the birth of Jesus. But when the Second Council of Constantinople condemned reincarnation in 553 A.D., the Church rejected the concept as anathema.

Consider the power of the Church to "reinterpret, revise, and dictate religious doctrines and facts instead of reaching some consensus based on the experiences and observations of followers," we wrote in an earlier book, *We Don't Die*.[51]

It appears the Church decried most psychic phenomena not because they were "evil," but because they were remnants of earlier pagan or non-Christian beliefs.[52] The first Christian account of a "pact with the devil" is in a story about St. Basil who lived in the fourth century. But the link between the devil, evil, and the occult[53] didn't become a major issue until 1326, when Pope John XXII proclaimed sorcery a crime; and the Church applied the term "witchcraft" to all psychic abilities, since many witches or sorcerers demonstrated psychic powers.

As the fourteenth century drew to a close,[54] the Inquisition was under way, and anything branded magical or psychic was believed the result of a "vast conspiracy against Christianity." Paranoia spread along with terrible outbreaks of the dreaded plague, the "Black Death," across Europe, killing millions. Perhaps fear, guilt, and epidemics in part motivated witch hysteria as people sought scapegoats. But the Church remained a powerful political and social force and "witch prosecutions became an industry," wrote Kurt Seligmann.[55] It employed many people, no small part of medieval economy in grim times.

In 1484, Pope Innocent VIII issued a papal bull declaring witchcraft a form of heresy,[56] specifically accusing Germans of conspiring with "devils by their incantations, spells, conjurations, and other accursed charms." Later popes also issued edicts that demanded harsh punishments for accused witches. As the fifteenth century wore on witch trials, torture, and executions became a virtual mania within both Church and secular courts.

The most famous victim of the witch hysteria was St. Joan of Arc,[57] who experienced clairaudience among other psychic abilities. Born in 1412, she was only a thirteen-year-old peasant girl living in rural France in 1425, when she first told of hearing voices that she believed were Saints Michael, Margaret, and Catherine, and often they were accompanied by visions of a bright light. *"Sois bonne et sage, et va souvent à l'église,"* the voice said. ("Be good and behave and go often to church.") She also made accurate predictions and demonstrated mental telepathy.

At the time France was fighting the long and draining Hundred Years' War, and Joan's "voices" persuaded her to go to the aid of France. Neither strong nor decisive, the dauphin, heir to the throne, had been unable to gain control of France from the Duke of Burgundy and his English allies.

By 1428, when the English began their siege of Orleans, Joan's "voices" grew louder and more insistent. Somehow she found a way to meet the dauphin, and convinced him that her voices were both genuine and from God. Incredibly, by May 1429, this young girl was leading the large French army, disguised as a male, wearing armor especially designed and fitted to her size. Joan proved to be a brave and fearless warrior; she could fight equal to most men, and under her leadership, the French army freed Orleans from the English, altering the course of the war. That same year the dauphin was crowned King Charles VII.

But in 1430, Joan was taken captive by the Duke of Burgundy; betrayed by the treachery of a Catholic bishop, she was sold to the English.

Deceived into signing a confession, the next year she was put on trial and accused of heresy because of the voices she claimed guided her. She refused to renounce or deny them, and insisted they were godly. Her judges were just as emphatic that the voices were "demonic." Joan was assertive and outspoken when she testified in her own behalf. "*Je suis seulement le messager de Dieu*," she said without hesitation. ("I am only the messenger of God.") She also aroused the wrath of the court by refusing to wear female clothing.

Convicted of heresy she was burned at the stake in May 1431. Her last word was "Jesus." She was only nineteen, according to records, although she may have been slightly older. After flames devoured Joan's body, her executioners examined the remains and found her heart still beating. For several hours they tried to set the heart on fire, but could not. Thus, to their horror, the English realized they'd murdered a saint.

The French were so "inspired" by Joan's life and death that it motivated them to fight until the English were forced from France. It took the Church another twenty-five years to exonerate her. Finally in 1920, she was canonized, officially declared a saint, and became the patroness of her beloved France.

Although much remains unknown about St. Joan of Arc, some trial transcripts survived long enough for historians to gain some insight into one of the most remarkable and enigmatic figures of the Middle Ages.[59] Skeptics argue against her paranormal ability by claiming she suffered "auditory hallucinations" or even "temporal lobe epilepsy." There is no proof of that—but even if Joan was epileptic that does not explain away the accuracy of her psychic gifts.[60]

Around 1486, two fanatical Dominican priests wrote the *Malleus Maleficarum* (*The Hammer of Witches*).[61] With papal approval, the authors became inquisitors, and for the next two hundred years the frightful book was a virtual bible for witch hunters.

During the next several centuries, hundreds of thousands of people were tortured and executed as witches, mainly by burning at the stake, so neither the body nor the soul could survive. Some 85 percent of the accused were women, often elderly, widowed, or unmarried. Anything and everything psychic, magical, or occult were thrown together into an indiscriminate jumble that incredibly persists to this day.

So hysterical had people become[62] that clairvoyance, clairaudience, premonitions, precognitive dreams, visions, mediumship, or any demonstration of so-called "occult powers" were perceived as threats to Christians everywhere. The Church declared it was in a battle for its very survival against the terrible forces of Satan. Therefore anyone in league with the devil—such as a witch—had to be destroyed.

But hypocrisy and contradictions were never far from the war with Satan's army.[63] In the sixteenth century, Catherine DeMedici, queen of France, maintained Nostradamus as both physician to the royal court and her personal astrologer and seer. Without the queen's protection, he would certainly have been fodder for the flames of the Inquisition.

There's an interesting sidelight to Nostradamus's work as a physician during the plagues.[64] Many doctors who'd come in contact with plague victims also became victims of the dread disease. But Nostradamus never succumbed to the plague, despite treating hundreds who suffered from it. One paranormal theory suggested that through his remarkable gift of clairvoyance, he understood the importance of hygiene and sanitation, and by gazing far into the future, avoided contagion. One of his prophecies named the French scientist Louis Pasteur in the nineteenth century—some three hundred years later.

Ironically, those consumed with witchcraft hysteria at the time believed cats and other small animals were capable of carrying out a witch's devilish deeds; so countless thousands of cats were killed. In fact, more cats would have meant fewer rats spreading the highly contagious plague that wiped out much of Europe's population.

During her rule in the sixteenth century,[65] Queen Elizabeth I of England consulted John Dee. She once asked him what omens could be deciphered in the sighting of a comet in 1577. Dee was both a respected mathematician and astrologer, and performed countless tests of scrying, or "crystal gazing," as well as probing alchemy, medieval chemistry that attempted to turn base metals into gold.

The Church has long had conflicts with itself—and others—about the paranormal.[66] On the one hand, psychic events are well known to the Church. On the other hand, the Church hierarchy has never been comfortable unless they controlled the subject. The teachings of Jesus, arguably the greatest psychic ever, are at the heart of Church belief. Yet, when paranormal events were manifested outside the Church, they were soundly condemned as heresy, despite countless miracles and psychic phenomena in both the Old and New Testaments. The division between the miraculous and the paranormal has been a religious issue for millennia, especially in Judeo-Christian thinking.

Among Jews, the ancient system of Kabbalah, or Jewish mysticism, posed a similar problem.[67] To believers, although its teachings provided inspiration and wisdom through occult knowledge, magic, numerology, and symbolism, most devout Jews did not consider it paranormal. Yet, Kabbalah became a major influence on the evolution of modern systems of magical thinking and practice for both Jews and non-Jews.

The subject is too convoluted to detail here[68]; but a paranormal event within religious parameters is a "miracle," a remarkable, but inexplicable event in human terms, and attributed to the work of God. However, if that same miraculous occurrence is manifest by a secular individual, it will likely be condemned by Christian theology. So when is a psychic event acceptable? Is it always of a religious nature or can scientists and secularists also investigate or demonstrate the paranormal?

During his reign in the early seventeenth century,[69] England's King James I ordered the Bible to be revised. Because of his morbid dread of witchcraft, in the King James Version of the Bible, the medium at Endor was purposely mislabeled a witch, a libel that to this day confuses many, although as we said earlier, a medium is not the same as a witch.

In medieval times,[70] *morbus divinus* was the nickname for epilepsy; referred to as "divine sickness" because the fits of epilepsy were frequently confused with the mystical raptures of the saints. Bernini's famed statue, The Ecstasy of St. Therese, has been the subject of centuries of argument about whether it represents a mystical experience or simply a fit of epilepsy.

The fullest Church account about the problem was written by Cardinal Prospero Lambertini, in the 1730s, before he was elevated to Pope Benedict XIV.[71] For centuries it remained the Church's recognized word and criterion on the supernatural. Lambertini was astute and recognized that some events were miracles attributed to God; other phenomena were products of the mind. For example, he said telepathy, clairvoyance, many healings, and some prophecies were not miraculous, while others were. But stigmata, bilocation, certain healings, incorruptibility, the odor of sanctity, Marian apparitions, and "divine images" of Jesus Christ were miracles.

During medieval times,[72] when the Church controlled virtually every aspect of life, because there was room for psychic events if they occurred within the Church, there are centuries of accounts about the paranormal abilities of the saints.

One of the most common and controversial is levitation, "the paranormal ability to rise and float in the air." Throughout history there have been descriptions of many mystics and yogis with the ability to levitate. Levitations have also been reported during some cases of "demonic possession."

A number of saints are credited with levitating, among them, St. Thomas Aquinas, St. Teresa of Avila, St. Ignatius Loyola, and St. Joseph Copertino. One of the most documented of the levitating saints was Joseph of Copertino in the seventeenth century, dubbed the "flying friar." Once, in Rome he levitated before Pope Urban III. Skeptics, of course, deny the accuracy of witness accounts; and some debunkers claim levitations are not paranormal or mystical, but merely "gymnastic feats."

In the Eastern faiths, such as Buddhism and Hinduism, such phenomena are more readily accepted.[73] Yogic practices, dating back thousands of years, may aid in effecting levitation through breathing exercises. Hindu writings from the twelfth century explain psychic abilities that can be accomplished by correctly mastering yoga.

During America's Great Age of Spiritualism in the nineteenth century, levitations by several mediums became a topic of fascination and inevitable controversy.

Rarely do parapsychologists study stigmata, "marks on the body corresponding to the wounds Jesus suffered during the Passion and the Crucifixion," since it is considered miraculous and a "uniquely Christian phenomenon," D. Scott Rogo wrote in *Miracles* (1982).[74] The first to manifest stigmata in the Church was St. Francis of Assisi (1181–1226). Medical explanations fall short of explaining how wounds can open and blood can flow or stream. Sometimes the oozing blood carries a "sweet scent." Often, even serious wounds inexplicably vanish after appearing.

In 1774, St. Alfonso de Liguori was meditating in a chapel in Arezzo, Italy. Suddenly he proclaimed Pope Clement XIV "had just died," although Liguori never left Arezzo, more than a day's ride from Rome. Later, when news of Pope Clement's passing reached Arezzo, there were reports that Alfonso had been simultaneously seen at the bedside of the dying pope. The explanation is a miraculous phenomenon known as bilocation, which is not the same as an out-of-body experience. In bilocation mystics or saints appear in two separate places at the same time, with witnesses in both sites. Church doctrine claims that during bilocation the physical body "is actually duplicated through the grace of God," said Rogo.

One of the most famous bilocators was St. Martin de Porres (1579–1639).[75] There were dozens of witnesses to his miracles—or paranormal feats—that included healings and levitations. The dark-skinned friar was seen in Lima, Peru at the same time he appeared in Japan and China. In another instance, St. Martin was witnessed comforting a Spanish man in an Algerian jail, although St. Martin was in Peru. Many claimed they saw him at the bedside of the sick at times he was observed praying in a monastery. Long known among Hindus and Buddhists, swamis and yogis have also demonstrated bilocating.

A similar paranormal ability attributed to some saints is teleportation, in which the physical body can instantly travel distances through space such as Padre Pio did.[76]

Incorruptibility is a miraculous occurrence in which the bodies of some deceased mystics and saints remain fresh; that is, they do not decay or decompose.[77] One instance was St. Catherine of Bologna, who died in 1463, at the age of fifty, and was buried in convent ground, but not in a casket. A short time later, a beautiful perfume scent exuded from the burial site, a paranormal phenomenon known as the "odor of sanctity."[78] When St. Catherine's body was exhumed weeks after her death, her body showed no signs of decay, the miraculous phenomenon that qualified St. Catherine as an incorruptible. In fact, her body still showed evidence of fresh blood.

Her intact body was honored in 1688, more than two hundred years after her death, in a special chapel built to display her to the public. There is no medical or paranormal explanation for incorruptibility.

The Church officially has long been skeptical of "divine images" of Jesus. The famed—and very controversial—Shroud of Turin purports to show an image, reversed as in a photographic negative, of Christ's body; and is thought by some to be His burial cloth. Others consider it a fraud or hoax created in medieval times.[79]

Consider the miraculous sixteenth-century story of Our Lady of Guadalupe in Mexico.[80] In December 1531, an Indian peasant named Juan

Diego heard the voice of a woman call to him. Then he saw a "radiant and wondrous apparition" of the Blessed Virgin Mary. The stunned man heard her ask him to visit the bishop in Mexico City to have a church built where her vision had appeared. If that wasn't incredible enough, Diego later saw imprinted on his cape "the divine image of the Virgin Mary," in vivid color. Hundreds of years later, the image "has not faded" nor has the coarse cloth made from "cactus fiber" disintegrated. Diego witnessed the apparition three times. When the skeptical bishop saw the image of the Virgin Mary on the cape, he fell to his knees. The church was built, and Diego's cape can still be seen in the Basilica of Our Lady of Guadalupe, in Mexico.

The miracle of Guadalupe has been tested and examined by experts who've agreed the image was not painted on the cape. However the image got there, there's little doubt that it's miraculous, setting aside personal religious beliefs, and a paranormal or psychic phenomenon that science may—or may not—ever satisfactorily explain.

Throughout history, people in many countries have reported seeing "divine images" of Jesus or, in many instances, "Marian apparitions," visions of the Virgin Mary; or "weeping icons" of Jesus and Mary, including some statues or paintings that have shed tears. They have also been reported in the Eastern and Greek Orthodox Churches, inexplicable to scientists and parapsychologists.

To the Church's credit it never accepted every alleged miraculous event until it had thoroughly examined and verified each claim. The process of authenticating a psychic or miraculous occurrence remains as it has always been long, exacting, and tedious. But among many Marian apparitions over the centuries, several have stood the test of time, among them Bernadette's visions of the Virgin Mary at Lourdes, France; and the visions and messages from the apparition to the children in Fatima, Portugal.

The witch-hunting craze in Europe ran from the fifteenth through the seventeenth centuries.[81] But changes in thinking were on the horizon, for the seventeenth century also marked the dawn of modern science. It seems a contradiction that such cruelty against those accused of witchcraft and heresy, often based on the flimsiest of evidence or superstition, could occur at the same time that a new generation of scientific thinkers was emerging.[82]

This was, after all, the age of Sir Isaac Newton, one of the greatest scientists and mathematicians of the English-speaking world, the scientist who developed the basis for traditional physics.[83] There was also Francis Bacon, philosopher and pioneer in "experimental science"; Galileo, the world famous astronomer and physicist; Johannes Kepler, German astronomer and noted mathematician; and Robert Boyle, British physicist and chemist.

How did such intellectually gifted individuals co-exist in a world where demons haunted and witches made pacts with the devil? The answer is deceptively simple: the greatest minds of that time did not dismiss the paranormal or supernatural. Newton, for one, studied the occult, alchemy, and astrology. One of his great interests was to delve into the Bible in search of the meanings of "apocalyptic" verses, hoping to reveal the "innermost secrets of the universe." The creator of the "inductive scientific method," Francis Bacon believed in witchcraft and wrote it could occur "by a tacit operation of malign spirits."

In the seventeenth century there was a strong belief in a "dualistic universe," wrote author Chadwick Hansen.[84] In other words, he explained, there were two worlds: one that was "material or visible." The other was "spiritual or invisible," so few scientists then questioned the reality of heaven, hell, angels, or the devil. They "believed in a world of spirits," Hansen wrote, and many accepted "that spirits can appear in this material world." Of course there were some skeptics, even of witchcraft. The best known was Thomas Hobbes, who wrote that spirits are "nowhere."

One question asked by seventeenth-century skeptics and some scientists was how witchcraft worked: was it by "spiritual or natural means?" Hansen noted. Among the educated, some suspected that many accusations of witchcraft were false. Most of the population was considerably more accepting of the authority of church and state, and more gullible.

The seventeenth century was also a time of unrest among many intellectuals disenchanted with church dogma and domination.[85] In response, a major movement developed known as the Enlightenment, or Age of Reason, influenced by the growth and progress of modern science, and the consequences of bitter religious contention after the Reformation.

Leaders of the Enlightenment were philosophers devoted to so-called "rational inquiry" and secular thinking; they abhorred the intolerance and censorship of Christian churches. Some were atheists or agnostics, while others professed deism or liberal Christianity. They believed that a philosophy "based on reason and human understanding" was the "best method of learning truth," and could improve life and benefit society.

The supernatural was rejected; the "scientific method emphasizing experimentation and careful observation," they hoped, would replace it, and many religious beliefs. There was no place for witchcraft, magic, omens, demons, spirits, or other occult practices for the philosophers of the Age of Reason. Many contributions to science, intellectual freedom, and "human dignity" were made as a result. But, the philosophers also proved naïve; for not everything could be measured "rationally."

The Enlightenment would continue to grow through the eighteenth century, and ultimately spurred both the American and French revolutions. Among its leaders in England, Germany, and France were such well-known figures as John Locke, René Descartes, Thomas Hobbes, Denis Diderot, Jean-Jacques Rousseau, and Voltaire. They were liberal thinkers, to be sure, and their rejection of the occult was to have a lasting effect on the serious study of the paranormal. Once traditional scientists considered the occult "irrational," it would be largely rejected by mainstream science, and tossed back to theologians who did not want the subject, either.

One learned figure of the time felt quite differently about psychic phenomena.[86] Emanuel Swedenborg (1688–1772) was a Swedish visionary and clairvoyant. He'd been a respected scientist and engineer, but surrendered that career to devote his life to "spiritual enlightenment," believing God chose him for the task. He experienced many dreams and visions by which he claimed he'd entered the "spirit world," and described his encounters in several books. "Angels speak from the spiritual world," he wrote about those "conversations," always stressing the importance of "unity with God."

Once when Swedenborg was in Gothenburg, Sweden, he clairvoyantly reported a fierce fire in Stockholm, three hundred miles away. To avoid accusations of heresy, he published some work anonymously, wrote in Latin, and later moved to England where his philosophy became popular, his books translated, and a church created based on his theology.

Meanwhile, in seventeenth-century England, others became disenchanted with the established Church they saw as becoming too ostentatious. These were devout people devoted to the Bible's teachings, and often called "Godly," but their beliefs were unyielding. They came to be known as Puritans, and their unhappiness with the Anglican Church was apparent. Elaborate cathedrals with stained glass windows, statues, icons, and Latin-speaking priests were among their complaints. It led to bitter confrontations with King Charles I who ascended the throne in 1625, succeeding his father, King James I. Neither monarch looked favorably upon the Puritans who wanted simple and unadorned houses of worship.

In 1620, the Pilgrims had traveled to the New World to settle in Plymouth, Massachusetts. Many Puritans looked toward the Atlantic Ocean with the same thought: If they could escape England, they'd be able to worship as they wished. For his part, the king was not unhappy to see them leave; it settled their long-running dispute. So in 1626, the first Puritans sailed across the ocean to the New World, America, where they settled in Massachusetts. By 1630, the exodus from England was underway, and in the next ten years more than 15,000 people, many of them Puritans, migrated to New England.

They brought with them a strict religious faith, a strong work ethic, and many of the Old World prejudices and superstitions that would result in America's first paranormal story, and one of its most peculiar and ugly chapters before the seventeenth century was over. The Puritans named their first English settlement in Massachusetts: Salem.

Colonial America: The Devil in Salem

He who believes in the Devil already belongs to him.
—THOMAS MANN

For us believing physicists the distinction between past, present, and future is only an illusion, even if a stubborn one.
—ALBERT EINSTEIN

Kimberly Padula awoke with a start, shaking uncontrollably.[1] It was that dream again. She'd been having it since 1997, only now it was growing more intense. The faces were sharper, the smells more acrid, the details more frightening. In her vision, this bright and pretty young New York fashion designer saw herself wearing military fatigues as she grabbed and pulled people to safety in what appeared to be a site that had been struck by a bomb. As she looked around her, there were army tanks rolling through the streets, soldiers and other official personnel in blue uniforms, while planes roared through the sky above.

"It was just like a war scene," she recalled. "It looked to me like Armageddon. The dream was so real. Buildings were collapsing and crumbling as if they'd gone through an earthquake. They were just folding and falling. But I didn't seem to be a victim. I was *helping* victims. People were scared and I kept pulling them back into a bombed out area that had already been struck."

Every several weeks the unnerving dream vision returned, sometimes even more vivid than the night before. Kimberly would wake up panting, shaking with fright, the sounds of occasional cars and trucks just below her window only adding to her sense of disorientation. At the time, Kimberly was living in Manhattan's Little Italy, a small enclave of narrow, but crowded, streets and lots of family restaurants. Her small apartment was on the second floor of an old tenement, typical of the buildings that lined the streets in this old neighborhood.

Kimberly was haunted by her recurring dream. So persistent and realistic was that dream that one day she purchased a canvas bag in which she placed green army pants, shirts, boots, flashlights, and other survival gear. "I put the bag behind my bed in the event I had to escape, although I had no conscious reason why I wanted to," she said.

Kimberly's dream was especially ominous because ever since she was three years old she had experienced what she called "psychic feelings," an overpowering sense of intuition. But the predictions she sometimes innocently made in school were not well received by peers. "What are you, a witch?" she was often asked. The frequent taunts caused her to retreat into herself, and so she kept her psychic gifts hidden.

After attending the Fashion Institute of Technology in New York, Kimberly allowed her psychic sensitivity to emerge. By then, close friends were more accepting. "Sometimes they believed me more than I believed myself," she admitted.

By October 1999, Kimberly was convinced her recurring vision of disaster was a premonition. Not certain where to turn for advice, she asked a shaman she regarded as a father figure how he would interpret her dream. "He told me something bad would happen," she said. The shaman added, "You don't belong in New York. You are too sensitive," although outwardly Kimberly gave the appearance of being confident and in control.

"I felt psychically like I was being pushed out of the city," she recalled. "It was as if some bigger force was pushing me out. It was time to go."

Kimberly decided to leave New York, where she'd been born and raised. She packed her belongings, sold some, and shipped the remainder to California, where she'd only visited briefly on several earlier occasions. Her choice to fly to the West Coast was based simply on the fact that a girlfriend in California invited Kimberly to live with her.

"Friends and colleagues were surprised that I was suddenly moving," she explained. "And they were afraid when I told them about my dreams of buildings collapsing. For some reason, the buildings looked like mirrored glass."

Kimberly arrived in Los Angeles in October 1999, expecting whatever disaster she'd dreamed of to take place the next year, in 2000. She assumed because she was in California, the catastrophe would be an earthquake.

Then, while living in Los Angeles, Kimberly had another vision in which she saw two "tower cards," a part of the tarot deck. She paid little attention to the first dream. The second of the "tower card" sent her reeling around Labor Day of 2001. "I freaked out," she said. Was an earthquake coming? Her ability as a clairvoyant or sensitive could go no further in interpreting her persistent vision.

On the morning of September 11, 2001, at about four A.M., Kimberly awoke suddenly with a sharp pang of anxiety. Not knowing what it meant, she uneasily returned to sleep.

She learned of the terrorist attacks on the World Trade Center in New York a few hours later when a neighbor banged on the door, woke her, and told Kimberly of the terrible tragedy, not far from where she'd formerly lived and worked in Manhattan.

At first, Kimberly did not recall her premonition about the terrorist disaster until a friend's phone call from New York that day reminded her. Only then did she associate her recurring dreams with the World Trade Center collapse.

She was, of course, devastated by the news of the many deaths, injuries, and destruction, as all Americans were. "I was also surprised. It was confirmation to me that there was something psychic to what I'd felt and dreamed," she said.

Asked why she thought she had premonitions about the terrorist attack, Kimberly answered, "I don't know. I don't have all the answers, although I've had many psychic dreams."

Today, Kimberly lives in Los Angeles where she has since developed a practice as a professional psychic and sensitive, at the urging of friends who've benefited from her clairvoyant abilities.

Kimberly Padula was not alone in experiencing premonitions about the World Trade Center assault; nor, by any means, was she the first to experience premonitions of disaster, either to individuals or to a collective. In fact, were Kimberly to have reported her premonitions 350 years ago in any of the New England colonies, she would have been declared a witch and sentenced to burn at the stake.

Salem

Life in the small New England village of Salem in the Massachusetts Bay Colony as the year 1692 began was as harsh as the bitter winter winds that howled and beat against the clapboard houses.[2] No Christmas or holiday festivities ushered in the New Year because according to strict Puritan religious belief and law those would have been regarded as frivolous and pagan practices.

Salem had been founded in 1626, only six years after the Pilgrims arrived to settle Plymouth, and before the Puritans set foot there in 1630. With a royal charter received just a year earlier, their home in the New World was now far from England which they'd left in search of a place where they could practice their Calvinist religion as they saw fit; away from the domination of the Church of England with whom they'd had increasing friction. They'd grown disgusted with what they felt were church corruption and a straying from the purity they'd wished to see maintained in the Anglican Church.

The Puritans who settled in New England had no intention of shedding either their unyielding Bible-based religious convictions, including predestination, or occult fears that they tightly wrapped together as one. Democracy, as we know it, was never much of a consideration; and separation of church and state was virtually nonexistent; they were locked in a theocracy in which religious beliefs often influenced civil and political decisions. As God-fearing Christians, the Puritans saw the devil as their archenemy whom they needed to be ever vigilant against, for Satan always lurked, ready to strike anywhere at any time. For the Puritans, fear and superstition held a firm grip.

Life in Salem, as in other Puritan communities was never easy: hard work and prayer consumed most of one's time. There was the genuine dread of insufficient crops and food supplies, illness and epidemics—notably smallpox and infections—Indian attacks, as well as frequent squabbles and disputes between neighbors. For many of the religious—and superstitious—the wrath of God was deemed responsible for nearly anything that went amiss from inclement weather to the miseries of disease. Perhaps God-fearing Puritans needed to be more prayerful to improve their fortunes, went the thinking of the time.

Underlying many of the Puritans' problems was a feeling of helplessness and terror of the unknown. That uneasiness and anxiety created the perfect climate for seeking scapegoats: the eccentric, argumentative, demented, and elderly to whom nearly any affliction could be attributed. It was convenient to accuse them of being witches or sorcerers, in league with the devil and his demons, even if it was irrational. There was no room for dissent. Two well-known instances of voices that spoke up in opposition to Puritan rigidity were theologian Roger Williams and Anne Hutchinson, a courageous woman whose opinions resulted in her being banished from Boston in 1638. She then moved to Rhode Island, founded by Williams two years earlier; "her strange opinions" were not welcomed in the Massachusetts colony, she was told.

While the adults in Puritan communities faced both imagined and genuine stresses, girls and boys were permitted few if any joys or freedoms associated with childhood. Youngsters were to be seen and not heard, "obedient, industrious, and prayerful." Boys were taught the skills they would ultimately need as adults: hunting, farming, and building. They learned to read and write so they could comprehend the Bible, the Holy Word of God. Girls, on the other hand, were not required to be literate; it was sufficient for them just to learn sewing, cooking, and other domestic skills. Little else broke up the monotony of their days and nights. Nathaniel Hawthorne later wrote in *The Scarlet Letter* that Puritan childhood was "grim."

Not surprisingly, the tedious lives of Puritan children encouraged boredom, especially during the long and dreary winters. In turn, the tedium led to mischief that was responsible for America's first major paranormal incident: the witchcraft hysteria of 1692, begun by several young girls in Salem Village, whose apparently innocent curiosity about the occult spun wildly out of control.

The belief in witches, who could carry out Satan's evil deeds, was as real to the Puritans as the constant threat from the devil himself. The Bible admonished, "Thou shall not suffer a witch to live," and the Puritans took the words literally. In England, witchcraft had been a crime punishable by death since 1542; by 1647, witchcraft was against the law in the New England colonies of Massachusetts, Rhode Island, and Connecticut, where there were witchcraft outbreaks at various times. A witch's spell cast on livestock might make an animal ill or die. Witches, in league with the devil, even had the power to deform or kill newborn babies, according to Puritan conviction, ignoring high infant mortality rates; and an inappropriate look, pointed finger, or imprudent word might be construed as an evil curse.

In 1655, Anne Hibbins, a quarrelsome Boston widow, seemed to know that two women were talking about her. Perhaps she'd overheard them—or she had a degree of genuine psychic or intuitive ability. Whatever the explanation, the women were certain that Mrs. Hibbins's prescience represented something occult and, therefore, dangerous. She was charged with witchcraft, tried, found guilty, and hanged the next year.

In Hartford, Connecticut, in 1662, a woman named Ann Cole suffered "strange fits," marked by wild behavior. A minister who observed her wrote that Cole's "bodily motions [were] extremely violent." Cole also confessed she heard "strange voices," a phenomenon that in the seventeenth century was evidence of evil or demonic spirits at work. Today, of course, she would be given psychiatric treatment. But in the words of her day, "She did have familiarity with the devil."

Another of the accused in Hartford, an elderly and uneducated woman named Rebecca Greensmith, confessed to her acquaintance with the devil and acknowledged that he "used my body." Her description of sexual intercourse with the devil was not unusual in the European history of witchcraft. However, her story is rare among New England accounts. The sexual aspects of witchcraft centuries ago were common, especially among those classified as "hysterics." "What is involved is apparently an erotic fit in which the woman actually goes through the motions of copulation and achieves an orgasm; similar fits have been observed in mental patients in the twentieth century," author Chadwick Hansen wrote in *Witchcraft in Salem*.

Found guilty of witchcraft, both Rebecca, and her husband Nathaniel Greensmith, went to the gallows in 1663, an ignominious year in the history of New England witchcraft for there were flare-ups of witch hysteria in several communities; the worst, an outburst that sent panic through Hartford, Connecticut.

What was unique about Salem Village to bring the devil there? For one thing, unlike larger towns such as Boston, which had grown more sophisticated, Salem Village did not have a cosmopolitan or well-educated citizenry, even though it was only about thirty miles north of Boston. Salem Village must also be distinguished from nearby Salem Town, a more tolerant environment. Salem Village (now called Danvers) was, in one historian's words, "a backwater." This small, rural community, with an adult population at that time of 215, was beset by friction and quarrels between various factions, fomenting enough hostility and jealousy for it to become the perfect place to incubate a witchcraft outbreak.

The "Salem witch hysteria," as it came to be called, began, ironically, in the home of the Reverend Samuel Parris. He'd been pastor of the Salem Village Church only since 1689, and although relatively inexperienced, was considered as pious and strict as any Puritan minister could be; and 1692 would prove to be a year unlike any he could have imagined in his worst nightmares.

In the Parris household lived the reverend, his wife, their nine-year-old daughter Elizabeth, his eleven-year-old niece Abigail Williams, and Tituba and her husband John Indian, a West Indian slave couple. The Parris home served as the local parsonage. Elizabeth and Abigail had been fully indoctrinated in the Puritan faith, with its fear of the devil, demons, and witches. How could it be otherwise in such a religious home? The girls were often left in the care of Tituba, and with idle time on their hands and owning young restless minds, the children were eager to hear the tales Tituba told of her culture, so vastly different and unimaginable from their limited Puritan world.

West Indian traditions held belief in voodoo, ghosts, necromancy, and magic—all anathema to Calvinist or Puritan tenets. Tituba's skills, other than as a domestic servant, included fortune-telling, sorcery, and palmistry. So, in secret, Elizabeth and her cousin Abigail huddled in the kitchen of the Parris residence near the hearth, where Tituba would enthrall them with tales of the supernatural and occult she told with such an intensity that the children found them exciting, perhaps all the more so because they were forbidden.

It wasn't long before other girls in the village quietly joined Elizabeth and Abigail to hear Tituba's storytelling and demonstrations of fortune-telling and palm reading. Now the children had something to look forward to that was both secret and captivating. Of course, had their parents discovered what their daughters were learning, they would have been mortified, branded Tituba's behavior as absolute heresy, and punished her severely. Sometimes Tituba's tales of the occult were tinged with evil, something that would arouse the wrath of any responsible Puritan parent. The hidden gatherings generated excitement, but also produced feelings of fright, guilt, and even sinfulness in the children who'd gone way beyond the boundaries of accepted Puritan teachings. Her stories proved difficult for naïve Puritan children to safely absorb in a provincial community in which everything they learned from the young West Indian woman was a contradiction to the indoctrination of home and church.

The first sign of any serious problem occurred when Elizabeth and Abigail began displaying "peculiar" behavior. They gazed emptily at the ceiling above, and seemed to be experiencing strange muscular contractions, twitches, and fits.

What was happening? Reverend Parris and his wife, although shocked and deeply concerned, had not the slightest idea. As quickly as they could they summoned the village doctor, William Griggs, for his advice. While Reverend and Mrs. Parris waited, they resorted to what were then considered traditional solutions in such situations, "prayer and fasting."

Once Dr. Griggs arrived he tried to determine the nature of the girls' distress. It was a while before he solemnly issued his disturbing conclusion. The girls, he said, had been afflicted by witchcraft. "The evil hand is upon them," he stated earnestly.

As troubling as the doctor's finding was, it was not an unusual one in the seventeenth century when most physicians accepted witchcraft as a valid explanation for certain maladies, so it could be blamed for the girls' "fits" and other inexplicable symptoms. Of course, skeptics point out that in addition to misdiagnosing hysterical disorders, medical doctors of that time had limited scientific knowledge, and might explain away any illness they could not understand or treat by conveniently blaming witchcraft or demonic possession.

But *if* one accepted that young Elizabeth Parris and her cousin Abigail Williams were the victims of a witch who afflicted them, then it meant that someone right there in Salem Village was working for the devil. According to popular belief, witches were nearly always women, and they were agents of the devil, agreeing to carry out his evil deeds. This was the same fearful and superstitious mind-set that had convulsed Europe into centuries of thousands of witch burnings and the torture of innocent people. In America, as in Europe, the battle came down to God versus Satan; and the Puritan theocracy never had any doubt about whose side it was on.

But caught now in the grip of fear and guilt were two young girls suffering from the psychological effects of witchcraft and the occult in an age when hysteria was not a well-understood medical condition. Their display of physical symptoms could only be interpreted within the limitations of Puritan thought and belief.

Some would claim the girls were acting, but it is almost certain that Elizabeth and Abigail were highly impressionable and believed strongly in what the devil, magic, and witchcraft could do to hurt them; thus, fright caused them to descend into a genuine state of hysteria. In addition, as news of the girls' mysterious condition galloped through the community, the affliction seemed to spread, and there were soon complaints of similar symptoms reported by several other girls.

Dr. Griggs had inadvertently fanned the flames of fear when he could not provide a better medical diagnosis for Elizabeth and Abigail. His conclusion that "an evil hand is on them" was crystal clear: everyone in Salem Village understood that meant the children were victims of witchcraft.

One "common symptom at the time was a choking sensation in the throat," wrote Chadwick Hansen. "The hideous convulsive fits were thought to be the result of witches and demons wrenching the bodies of their victims into torturous postures," Hansen explained. (Modern medical science recognizes convulsions as a component of the hysterical state.) Senses were also affected—difficulty seeing, hearing, speaking, lack of appetite, even memory loss were all believed to be the result of Satan's evil actions.

The phenomenon of "throat contractions" or globus hystericus was also considered the work of demons to force the innocent to ingest supernatural or "occult poisons." Some victims of witchcraft suffered abdominal bloating. In other instances, demons were blamed for skin eruptions or other external injuries. What caused "hysterical symptoms" may not have been actual witchcraft, but certainly the dread of it.

The Reverend Parris had a copy of Cotton Mather's well-known book about witchcraft, *Memorable Provinces Relating to Witchcraft and Possessions*. It was a topic New Englanders, especially Puritans, spoke about, albeit cautiously, and the Reverend Mather was to play a significant role in the Salem story.

Religious leaders were highly respected and well paid in Puritan New England and "Cotton Mather was the pride of New England Puritanism," wrote H. W. Brands. He was the son of the well-known Reverend Increase

Mather, who led Boston's Second Congregational Church and was the first president of Harvard College. Born in 1663, Cotton, a brilliant child, was only twelve years old when he attended Harvard, and twenty-two when he was ordained. By age twenty-five he was minister of Boston's North Church, the largest congregation in the Massachusetts colony, and became a strong and outspoken proponent of Puritan belief and theology. During his life Cotton Mather wrote prodigiously, publishing a remarkable 450 books and pamphlets, most about religion.

"With his Puritan contemporaries Mather perceived the cosmos as a battleground between good and evil," explained Brands. "That there is a Devil, is a thing doubted by none but such as are under the influence of the Devil." When Salem seemed to fall under Satan's spell, Mather had no cause, by the bounds of Puritan reasoning, to doubt the authenticity of events; the devil and evil entities were genuine. He spent years gathering reports of occult and supernatural incidents, especially those he considered contradictory to his beliefs.

For example, in 1688, the children of John Goodwin, a Boston stonemason, became victims of witchcraft at the hands of a woman named Mrs. Glover whose daughter worked as a laundress for the Goodwin family. When Glover's daughter was accused by one of the Goodwin children of stealing linens, Glover gave thirteen-year-old Martha Goodwin a tongue-lashing laced with profanities. After the confrontation, all four Goodwin children were inexplicably "afflicted with strange convulsive seizures," wrote Alice Dickinson in *The Salem Witchcraft Delusion* (1974). The case drew the attention of the Reverend Mather whose conclusion was that Martha was afflicted by "hellish witchcraft." After he prayed with the girls, the youngest child, age seven, recuperated.

Mrs. Glover's fate was sealed when she confessed to being a witch with "magic powers"; she even spoke to the devil at her trial. Not surprising, she was sentenced to the gallows. But even after Glover was hanged, the Goodwin children still displayed their strange affliction. After more praying with Mather, they seemed to return to good health. That his help proved effective was not surprising; Puritan clergy were considered very successful in healing the demonically possessed. Mather was convinced he'd been a witness to a genuine instance of witchcraft in which the devil "could enter the home of a pious man like John Goodwin," Dickinson added.

In 1689, Mather published his collected findings in a book titled *Memorable Provinces Relating to Witchcraft and Possessions*. The popular book focused largely on the Goodwin story and influenced the thinking of many colonists, especially the Puritans. In Salem Village, Mather's impact reinforced the belief that the occult, black magic, and witchcraft were genuine and negative intrusions into people's lives. The Reverend Samuel Parris was one of those who did not doubt the learned Cotton Mather.

But what else could Parris do for his young daughter and niece now except pray for them? He summoned several other ministers and they also offered sincere and fervent supplication for the afflicted girls. But Elizabeth and Abigail seemed to worsen; their convulsions grew more intense. The girls' bodies became oddly contorted, then stiffened. Their breathing was labored and they cried loudly, complaining of sudden pains. Anyone who saw their torment had no doubt they were observing witchcraft at work; the devil and his handmaidens were obviously busy in Salem, adding another alarm to an already stressed community.

There was an important—and obvious—question that had to be addressed if the devil was to be confronted and thwarted. Who was working for Satan right there in Salem Village? In other words, who'd bewitched Elizabeth and Abigail? Whoever it was, that person had to be caught and stopped.

According to seventeenth-century views of the supernatural and occult, evil entities from the spirit world were invisible to the innocent. However, those who were bewitched could see who afflicted them. To everyone else the "specters," as they were commonly called, were not visible to the naked eye, so the girls were prodded to identify their attackers.

The question of who the witches were in Salem Village was terrifying, for the good and pious citizens might be in grave danger from the devil's agents right in their own community. But the girls were at a loss for an explanation, for they were honestly unable to identify anyone, since they were likely reacting to their fears of the occult, not to any particular individual. Unfortunately, village leaders and the clergy could not allow the situation to continue without finding someone to blame.

One village resident, Mrs. Mary Sibley, "a true Puritan busybody," in author Alice Dickinson's words, decided she'd get to the bottom of the problem. Sibley had apparently located an old recipe that was able to force someone afflicted by witchcraft to identify the sorceress. It was called a "witch cake" and Mrs. Sibley gave the ingredients to Tituba for her to create the concoction: it was to be made of rye meal mixed with the children's urine.

When Reverend Parris discovered Sibley's plan he declared furiously that a witch cake was a form of magical potion. "It is going to the devil for help against the devil," he reprimanded. "The devil has been raised among us and his rage is vehement and terrible!"

Now the children grew increasingly frightened and agitated, for they were in a position where someone had to be identified as a witch if they were to obey their elders, who could be quite intimidating and punishing. So the girls accused not one but three local women as those responsible for their suffering. They were Sarah Good, Sarah Osborne, and Tituba.

Why had Elizabeth and Abigail named these three individuals? Anyone who lived in Salem at that time understood. Sarah Good was poor and disheveled, a rather crude woman who had no real home to call her own, but instead roamed through the streets begging for refuge for herself and her children. To other villagers she was considered unsightly and of poor breeding and reputation. On the other hand, Sarah Osborne's pedigree was not in question, but nonetheless she was looked upon with disapproval because she'd stopped attending church. Accusing Tituba, of course, was easy to explain: the stories of the occult, supernatural, and magic had, after all, begun with her. To make matters worse, she was a woman of color and a slave from the West Indies—sufficient reasons to cast suspicion on her in a white Puritan, backwoods New England community.

Warrants were soon issued for the arrest of the three unfortunate women on February 29, 1692, and they were ordered to present themselves before the local magistrates the next day to face allegations of witchcraft against Elizabeth, Abigail, and two other girls who'd been part of the group around Tituba.

Meanwhile, Reverend and Mrs. Parris, frantic at the turn of events, moved Elizabeth from Salem to live elsewhere with family friends. But his niece Abigail and eight other "afflicted" girls, as they were commonly called, stayed in Salem Village. One of the girls was twelve-year-old Ann Putnam, from a well-to-do Salem family. Another of the afflicted was seventeen-year-old Mercy Lewis, the Putnams' high-strung servant. Mary Warren was twenty and a servant for the John Proctor family. Elizabeth Booth, an eighteen-year-old Salem girl, lived near the Proctors. Another of the afflicted was twenty-year-old Sarah Churchill, servant to George Jacobs's family. There was seventeen-year-old Elizabeth Hubbard, the niece of Dr. Griggs's wife. Susannah Sheldon was eighteen and lived in Salem Village; and seventeen-year-old Mary Walcott's father was the parish deacon.

Salem Village did not have an official courthouse when the legal process began its onerous grind against the accused. So Ingersoll's Tavern was designated as the place where the alleged witches would be officially questioned by two magistrates. Salem Village had never known such turmoil and commotion; most hardworking Puritans put aside their labors for the day to gather at the tavern. Men, women, and children created such a large crush of spectators that the inquiry was forced to move to the village meetinghouse where the accused would be interrogated by two judges, John Hathorne and Jonathan Corwin; there were no female judges in the seventeenth century.

Hathorne took the lead in questioning the unfortunate Sarah Good; and it quickly became apparent that he was not neutral in the inquiry. He had no doubts about witchcraft's dangers, and his tone suggested that he already believed Sarah Good was guilty; all that remained was to force a confession from her.

"Sarah Good, what evil spirit have you familiarity with?" Hathorne asked pointedly.

"None," she answered.

"Have you no contract with the devil?"

"No," Sarah Good replied.

"Why do you hurt these children?" he inquired.

"I do not hurt them. I scorn it," she answered.

"Who do you employ then to do it?"

"I employ nobody."

"What creature do you employ then?" the judge persisted.

"No creature, but I am falsely accused," Good answered.

The alleged victims, the bewitched girls, were present, and now it was their turn to be questioned. Hathorne asked them if Sarah Good was the one who caused their suffering.

Yes, they answered, it was she. Then suddenly they fell into a succession of convulsions, and screamed that they were in pain. Judge Hathorne, who'd watched the outburst intently asked, "Sarah Good, do you not see now what you have done? Why do you not tell us the truth? Why do you torment these poor children?"

But Mrs. Good did not waver in the face of the accusatory nature of the questions or the girls' fits. She repeated she had nothing to do with their affliction, but she did not hesitate to blame Sarah Osborne. Apparently Sarah Good was an unsympathetic presence. In the official record of the proceedings, the clerk who transcribed her testimony indicated that her answers, "were in a very wicked, spiteful manner . . . [and included] . . . abusive words and many lies . . ." and the court transcript also noted that even Sarah Good's "husband said that he was afraid that she was either a witch or would be one very quickly."

Next to be examined was Sarah Osborne, who also pleaded innocence to the accusations. But in insisting she was not guilty, Osborne allowed that it might have been her "specter" that was responsible for the bewitching, or perhaps the devil had disguised himself to look like her, although she'd had no contact whatsoever with the Evil One.

When it was Tituba's turn to be questioned she at first maintained her innocence, then changed her testimony and admitted she'd had contact with Satan. "The devil came to me and bid me to serve him," she announced to the court. She explained how, in exchange for her loyalty, the devil vowed to bestow her with splendid possessions. Tituba also acknowledged that she'd signed the devil's book, "red like blood." Then she implicated both Sarah Good and Sarah Osborne, claiming they also, among others, had made their marks in his book.

"Four women sometimes hurt the children . . . Goody Osborne and Sarah Good, and I do not know who the others were. Sarah Good and [Sarah] Osborne would have me hurt the children but I would not," Tituba explained. She went on to describe the "specter of a tall man dressed in black." According to Tituba, the man told her he'd injure her unless she agreed to afflict the girls. Once the specter commanded, "Kill the children." The apparition was also adept at "shape-shifting": it could change shape from a man to a dog or even a hog. A "yellow bird" accompanied the specter, Tituba added. As well, Sarah Good had a "yellow bird" that acted as her familiar. Sarah Osborne's familiars were a "yellow dog" and "a thing with a head like a woman, with two legs and wings." There was yet another demonic entity: a being that walked erect, covered in hair, and perhaps two or three feet in height. There were also specters of red and black rats that beckoned her, "Serve me."

Tituba confessed that the evil specter attacked the girls, but she hastily added she'd not acted of her own free will; she'd been coerced. She also admitted that she and other witches sailed through the air on wooden staffs or poles to perform acts of sorcery.

Tituba certainly knew how to spin a gripping story. Whether she actually believed everything she was telling the magistrates has long been open to historical debate. More likely, she was shrewd enough to say what she knew her Puritan judges wanted to hear. However, her belief in witchcraft was certainly genuine, notwithstanding her presumed embellishments. It is also possible that Tituba experienced what Alice Dickinson described as "hysterical hallucinations," and was convinced some of what she confessed was factual.

The afflicted girls were present for Tituba's testimony, and they reacted in an outbreak of violent spasms as she began; then they quickly calmed down as she spoke. Meanwhile, those in the crowded meetinghouse listened, as Dickinson wrote, "in fascinated horror." If that was Tituba's goal she certainly succeeded. The naïve and superstitious of Salem were stunned to hear a confession that the devil was doing his nefarious work right in their own village. The magistrates noted that Tituba had said there were *nine* marks made in the devil's book. That meant six more witches were still loose; but who were they?

Meanwhile, the accused women faced more questioning over the next several days about their methods of witchcraft. The afflicted girls swore that the specters of the three had tormented and injured them by "pinching, pricking, biting, and almost choking them to death," in Dickinson's words.

The closeness of living in a small town cut two ways. Beneath the veneer of polite and neighborly behavior, there often seethed resentments, jealousies, and frictions. Under the guise of blaming witchcraft, neighbor could accuse neighbor. In the case of Sarah Good, she had a reputation for uttering foul language and damning those who refused to give her a place to sleep. Now those who'd been accursed by Mrs. Good were able to unburden themselves and gain a measure of vengeance. Several recalled their sheep, hogs, and cattle had fallen sick not long after being cursed by Sarah Good. Was it coincidental—or something more sinister?

In actuality most of the alleged incidents occurred either well before Good's present dilemma or were not related to anything she directly said or did. But that apparently mattered little in court where such incidents were introduced as incontrovertible evidence of witchcraft. Incredibly, the judges simply believed what they were told.

In early March 1692, the three accused women were sent to jail in Boston while their fates were decided. The jail's abysmal conditions took the ultimate toll on Sarah Osborne; she died in the dungeon in May. Meanwhile, Sarah Good and Tituba remained imprisoned.

Salem Village was now abuzz with fear and worry about those among them who might be witches but were not yet identified. The community seemed on the verge of losing its collective mind, gripped by the terror of demons.

March 11, 1692, was a day of prayer and fasting in Salem. It was also the day young Ann Putnam screamed in pain, presumably another victim of witchcraft. Who could be responsible for this newest attack? When Ann Putnam accused a woman named Martha Corey the villagers were shocked, for unlike the dubious reputations of Sarah Good, Sarah Osborne, and Tituba, Mrs. Corey was an upstanding member of the community and church.

But Mrs. Corey had made a serious error in judgment when the witch hysteria gripped Salem. Highly skeptical of the afflicted girls' claims, she neither attended court appearances of the accused, nor did she want her husband Giles to observe them. Word of her inclination to disbelieve the accusations quickly spread through the village. Among some there were already rumors that perhaps Martha Corey was, herself, a witch. But still most in the community and church remained incredulous at the very idea that someone of Mrs. Corey's standing might do the devil's work. Before church leaders would consider such an allegation, they thought it best to speak privately with her.

However, in advance of confronting Mrs. Corey, the churchmen questioned Ann Putnam for further details of what the specter that afflicted her looked like. Ann answered that she'd been unable to witness the apparition's manner of dress because Mrs. Corey momentarily blinded her.

When two church officials, Ezekiel Cheever and Edward Putnam, no relation to Ann, arrived at the Corey house, she acted as if she'd been expecting them. "I know what you come for," she said. "You are come to talk with me about being a witch, but I am none. I cannot help people's talking of me." Mrs. Corey, informed that there had been a complaint made against her, had the presence of mind to ask what her specter had been wearing. Her tone suggested that she was skeptical of not only the hysteria building in Salem, but of witchcraft in general. It's also possible that Martha Corey felt she was in a better position than the three women already tried because of her known piety and loyalty to the church.

What she seemed to overlook, however, was that those who believed in witchcraft could rationalize even exemplary behavior as the work of Satan. The two visiting officials were ready with a quick retort to Corey's defense: even witches could steal their way into the church. The men were not unlike others in the congregation; their suspicions were aroused that she was a witch. On March 21, 1692, Martha Corey was arrested. Only the day before she'd attended Sunday services in church, disregarding whispers about her because she was certain of her innocence. Also in church were some of the afflicted girls. When they saw Mrs. Corey, "They had several sore fits . . . which did something to interrupt my First Prayer," wrote visiting minister Reverend Deodat Lawson, who'd led the church prior to the appointment of Samuel Parris.

This had not been a peaceful weekend for Lawson. On Saturday evening he'd stopped by the Parris family home. There, he later wrote, he'd witnessed twelve-year-old Abigail have "a grievous fit; she was at first hurried with violence to and fro . . . and crying. . . . Presently after, she said, 'There is Goodwife Nurse' and said, 'Do you not see her? Why there she stands!' " Reverend Lawson observed several demonic outbursts that weekend; the one in church also witnessed by the congregation was especially distressing for it interrupted Sunday services, the most solemn occasion of the week. At another point, Abigail screamed out during worship, "Look where Goodwife Corey sits on the beam suckling her yellow bird between her fingers!" Ann Putnam quickly joined in, claiming she saw a yellow bird atop Reverend Lawson's hat placed near the pulpit.

The girls who'd brought the accusations had to be aware that the entire village was watching them in awe and anguish. Never before had these young girls, or for that matter any Puritan children, been the center of such attention; boys and girls in Puritan society were meant to be inconspicuous. The children were "already so frightened and hysterical that they were not wholly responsible for their actions," wrote Dickinson. But these girls were now in an unprecedented spotlight, and with the attention came, as Dickinson explained, "an awful power."

Of course, only the afflicted girls could see the specter of Mrs. Corey and her supposed familiar, the "yellow bird." To everyone else present the specter was invisible. But to the fearful and superstitious Puritan mind that had no doubt about the reality of witchcraft and the danger of the devil, it was nearly impossible to believe these innocent children were lying. Could they have fabricated these events? Historians have long disagreed, and there is no way of arriving at an absolute conclusion about their claims.

On Monday, Martha Corey faced the magistrates and was interrogated at the meetinghouse. She appeared self-assured; her responses were clear. Asked whether she'd tormented the girls through witchcraft she answered without hesitation, "No."

Next she was asked if she was not responsible, who was. "I do not know. How should I know? I am a gospel woman," Mrs. Corey answered.

The afflicted girls present immediately screamed, "Gospel witch! Gospel witch!" Ann Putnam added that now she saw Mrs. Corey's specter and another unidentified woman invoke the devil.

Martha Corey was quick to reply, "We must not believe these distracted children." But the girls showed no signs of calming down. At one point, court transcripts indicated that Mrs. Corey bit her lip, likely from the stress and fright of her predicament. At the exact same time, the girls loudly screamed that they were being nipped. As Corey held her hands so her fingers tightened, no doubt from nervousness, the girls hollered in pain. Then one of them yelled aloud that she saw a "black man" murmur something to Mrs. Corey. Although whatever specter or apparition the girls claimed to see was not visible to anyone else, their cries and contortions were sufficiently convincing that Martha Corey was ordered to join the three other women in jail.

The witchcraft hysteria was gaining strength, and the news that Abigail Williams had seen the specter of Rebecca Nurse quickly made its way throughout Salem Village. Many citizens wondered about the accusation against Nurse; nothing about her fit their conception of a witch. She was liked and respected, a kind woman with a large and loving family; her husband owned a considerable amount of land, and they lived on a comfortable farm. But not everyone approved of the Nurse family; some in Salem were resentful of the Nurses' position and affluence. What also may have worked against them was that they were private people, not given to excess sociability. Worst of all, the Nurses were among the minority of villagers skeptical of the afflicted girls' claims. To many in Salem that attitude suggested a lack of sympathy for the accursed children.

The accusation that the girls had seen Mrs. Nurse's specter was sufficient grounds to bring the elderly woman with poor hearing before the magistrates for questioning. In late March, Rebecca Nurse faced her accusers in the village meetinghouse. The afflicted girls were present and displayed their usual fits, contortions, and shrieks, and blamed Mrs. Nurse for causing their agony. As if the girls' accusations weren't enough, Nurse now faced a new allegation from young Ann Putnam's mother, Ann, Sr.

Both Mr. and Mrs. Putnam swore that Rebecca Nurse had enticed them to wickedness, and also hurt the elder Ann Putnam. Mrs. Nurse must have been bewildered by the turmoil and the charges against her, for she protested, insisting she was not guilty. That only spurred the emotionally unstable Ann Putnam, Sr. to angrily hurl more accusations.

"Did you not bring the black man with you; did you not bid me to tempt God and die?" Mrs. Putnam cried out.

"Oh Lord, help me," Rebecca Nurse pleaded.

Whether truly hysterical or acting for attention, the commotion that ensued in the meetinghouse approached the surreal. The girls wasted no time demonstrating frightening cries as they threw themselves into more contortions and convulsions.

Magistrate John Hathorne chose to accept the girls' performance as evidence of Rebecca Nurse's guilt. "Do you not see what a solemn condition these are in?" he inquired. "When your hands are loose, the persons are afflicted," he said tersely.

Hathorne noted that Mrs. Nurse did not cry. The belief in the seventeenth century and earlier was that witches did not have the normal capacity to shed tears. Nurse replied that she was deeply affected emotionally as others were; however, she preferred not to display her feelings. The magistrate continued his pointed questioning; the implication being that Mrs. Nurse was guilty—unless the girls and Mrs. Putnam were lying.

"I cannot tell what to think of it," Rebecca Nurse answered.

The magistrates again hammered away at the allegation that Mrs. Nurse's specter inflicted harm upon her accusers. "I cannot help it. The devil may appear in my shape," Nurse replied. Meanwhile, the girls stepped up their aberrant behavior. They cried out that they saw a black man talking to Mrs. Nurse, and also claimed they saw birds encircling the elderly woman. Whichever way Rebecca Nurse turned, the girls imitated her movements. Then another of the bewitched, Mary Walcott, spoke up to say she'd also seen Nurse's apparition, and further, Mrs. Nurse had contributed to the deaths of other Salem residents. Those in the meeting-house became so agitated that it was difficult to even hear or follow the proceedings. When the court finally calmed down, Rebecca Nurse was sent to Boston jail.

Fire and brimstone sermons, the fear of lurking demons, and rumor-mongers created a terribly troubled atmosphere in the village. "Satan is representing his infernal forces, and the devil seems to come armed mustering around us," cautioned the Reverend Lawson. In other words, the devil had to be rooted out and that included the witches who were in league with him. "Do all that in you lies to check and rebuke Satan," Lawson exhorted the townspeople about the dangers of the "invisible world." But he added this caution, which apparently few bothered to heed at the time: the villagers should not accuse people lightly. After all, the devil could take the form of someone who was blameless.

Perhaps the most bizarre—and certainly most unjust—arrest on charges of witchcraft was that of a five-year-old child. The people of Salem and the magistrates whose duty it was to determine guilt or inno-cence came dangerously close to the brink of collective insanity with the arrest of Dorcas Good, the daughter of Sarah Good. Little Dorcas "con-fessed" that she, like her mother, was a witch. The child told the court that her familiar was a snake that sucked out her blood, and showed the magistrates a small red mark on her hand, probably an insect bite or blood blister. Once the judges saw the blemish they ordered five-year-old Dorcas Good to jail.

"Fear and suspicion had swept over the village like a wave, and few people had been able to resist it," noted author Alice Dickinson. But what of those who remained stubbornly skeptical of the whole business? One of them was a hardworking farmer named John Proctor. He'd grown an-gry after the public displays by the afflicted girls; and particularly upset that one of them was Mary Warren, whom he'd employed as a domestic. Proctor's solution was to give the allegedly afflicted girls whippings. He remarked sardonically that if the girls were allowed, everyone would be branded "devils and witches." But Proctor's opinion was decidedly that of the minority; and Salem Village was as close to frenzy as a Puritan community had ever come.

Rebecca Nurse's sister Sarah Cloyse was understandably distressed about the accusations against Rebecca. Sarah had no doubts about the reality of witchcraft, but her own sister, a witch? That, she knew, was outrageous and untrue. In early April when Cloyse attended Sunday church services, deeply troubled about her sister's plight, she heard the Reverend Parris make a biblical reference that was clearly an implication about Rebecca being in league with the devil. In a fit of anger, Sarah Cloyse left the meetinghouse, banging the door as she exited so that everyone present heard the noise.

It didn't take long for the afflicted girls to claim they witnessed the specter of none other than—Mrs. Cloyse. Then the girls accused John Proctor's wife, Elizabeth, of bewitching them; claiming they'd seen her apparition. John Indian, Tituba's husband, also alleged Cloyse used sorcery to harm him.

But in court she stood her ground. "When did I hurt thee?" she demanded to know.

"A great many times," John Indian answered.

"Oh, you are a grievous liar," Cloyse replied.

Asked by the Reverend Parris, the girls answered predictably that they witnessed ceremonies in which the devil gave the Eucharist or Holy Sacrament to several sorceresses including Sarah Good and Sarah Cloyse. Hearing the accusations from young Abigail Williams, Mrs. Cloyse collapsed, and the afflicted girls reacted by mocking her. The meetinghouse burst into a commotion while the girls convulsed into fits and spasms. When John Proctor attempted to hurry to his wife's side, the girls also pointed to him.

Inevitably, once the accusations were made, the two women were arrested. By now a panel of five more judges from Boston who'd joined Salem magistrates Hathorne and Corwin questioned the two newest suspected witches. By the time the court session was completed, Sarah Cloyse, and John and Elizabeth Proctor were bound for jail.

Whether intentional or not, the fact that judges from a higher court in Boston came to Salem elevated the controversy to a new level; no longer only a matter of village business, the mania became news that gripped the entire Massachusetts colony.

Later in April, there were four more arrests on charges of witchcraft: Bridget Bishop, Abigail Hobbs, Martha Corey's eighty-year-old husband Giles Corey, and John Proctor's servant Mary Warren, herself one of the tormented girls. The apprehension of Warren raised eyebrows. She'd been one of the afflicted; why would she now be arrested? Likely, she'd been badly shaken by the jailing of the Proctors for whom she'd worked. Her behavior became erratic and confused when she spoke of her own experiences as a victim. "When I was afflicted, I thought I saw the apparitions of one hundred persons," she testified. But once recovered she was uncertain if what she saw was real. When the other afflicted girls got wind of Mary's doubts, they moved quickly to squelch her loose talk by claiming she'd also bewitched them, and, as well, "signed the devil's book."

Mary was brought into court later in April, and it took only a momentary look from her toward the other girls for them to surrender to another round of fits and screams.

When Mary was asked how she went from one who was afflicted to now being accused, her answers were somewhat muddled and contradictory. Seeing John Indian and another woman cry, she became emotionally overwhelmed. This was no act on Mary Warren's part; she was genuinely terrified, and became so hysterical that she was removed from the court and remanded to jail. Several weeks later she was still suffering seizures, and admitted to being a witch, but blamed John and Elizabeth Proctor, among others, for her misfortune. By confessing, Mary probably saved her own life: she was freed and again was considered one of the afflicted. Typically, those who confessed to being witches were spared the gallows, even if they admitted to something they'd never done. Those who maintained their innocence were invariably convicted and condemned to Gallows Hill.

When Bridget Bishop, Abigail Hobbs, and Giles Corey were questioned, both Bishop and Corey insisted they were not guilty of witchcraft. But their pleas were in vain, for when the accused merely glanced at the bewitched, the girls fell into outbursts of fits and contortions. Abigail Hobbs posed an interesting case. Unlike the other defendants, she bragged that she "had sold herself body and soul to the old boy," a reference to the devil. She told the judges that she did practice witchcraft, attended meetings of sorcerers, and drank "red wine [with] red bread." Needless to say, Hobbs was jailed along with the others. During her confession she implicated no less than nine more people. Before April was over, arrest warrants were out for Abigail's parents, William and Deliverance Hobbs, Susanna Martin, and Mary Esty, the sister of Rebecca Nurse and Sarah Cloyse, who were already in jail on witchcraft charges.

Shaken by her arrest and interrogation by the magistrates, Deliverance Hobbs began to question her own sanity. Could she have been a witch and not realized it? Rattled and overwhelmed, she soon confessed to practicing sorcery and offered names of other alleged witches in the village. Her husband, William, outraged by the courtroom spectacle, insisted he was innocent of charges that he was a wizard; that was sufficient to send him to jail in Boston.

Next, Mary Esty was questioned, and although she remained in control of her emotions, her fate was as the others: she was jailed. On the other hand, Susanna Martin apparently did not take the court proceedings seriously, and even chuckled at one point. She doubted the afflicted girls, despite their demonstrations of torment. "They may lie for aught I know," she told the magistrates. As she was being taken to jail she remarked, "A false tongue will never make a guilty person."

When a short time later Esty was freed from the dungeon, her deportment so impressed officials, even they suspected she was not guilty. But her freedom was short-lived. Whether genuinely fearful or simply malicious the afflicted girls grew hysterical, especially Mercy Lewis who became so gripped by fits that she frightened many villagers. When she cried out Mary Esty's name, the poor woman was sent back to jail.

Before April was over, word was that one of the witches was a minister. Ann Putnam, Jr. claimed she'd witnessed a specter of a clergyman who'd tormented and attempted to suffocate her, then enticed her to sign the "devil's book." Who was this diabolical man of the cloth? Ann said the phantom identified himself as the Reverend George Burroughs, once the minister in Salem Village, who in the past had had a disagreement with a relative of the Putnams. Animosity then grew between Ann's parents and the reverend, known to have been abusive to his former wives.

Burroughs's experiences in Salem Village several years prior to 1692 had largely been unpleasant. A number of villagers had not warmed to him; he'd had difficulty receiving salary owed him, and his wife had died. When Burroughs left Salem, he moved to Wells, Maine, took a position as a minister, and also remarried. But Ann Putnam, Jr. certainly remembered him although he'd been gone from Salem Village for some time. Her imagination was apparently in overdrive—or she was genuinely frightened—for Ann now claimed that two ghosts materialized to tell they'd been slain by the Reverend Burroughs. The apparitions were those of the minister's late wives, both long passed on. Ann alleged that other ghosts came to her saying the same thing.

The magistrates issued a warrant for Burroughs's arrest, and he was returned unwillingly from Maine to Salem, and publicly questioned in early May. Despite being a minister, and possibly because he did not demonstrate sufficient Puritan fervor, he received no leeway or special treatment. Young Ann Putnam testified, as did Mercy Lewis, against the reverend; the girls claimed that Burroughs conducted witches' gatherings. Deliverance Hobbs confirmed her friends' version of events, and others in the village agreed. Reverend Burroughs, although physically in Maine, well north of Salem, made his spectral presence simultaneously known miles away in Salem. The testimony against him included the accusation that he induced local witches to bedevil and torment the entire village. He was remanded to jail.

In May 1692, the colony had a new royal governor, Sir William Phips. Although he had not anticipated such widespread hysteria surrounding the witchcraft accusations, he knew he needed to somehow deal with what had become a calamity. This was now a situation not confined to Salem Village; the entire Massachusetts colony was in turmoil. Phips named a special court to bring accused witches to trial and render a verdict in each case with no appeals permitted, and the chief justice would be William Stoughton, from the Boston area, who was also deputy governor. Six other judges were also named: four from Boston, one from Salem, and one from Haverhill.

In June, the first accused witch brought to trial was Bridget Bishop, without the benefit of a defense attorney. For her and the others to be tried in this manner displayed an obviously gaping hole in the legal process, although theoretically the judges were supposed to "protect the rights of the accused . . . this part of their duties was slighted," wrote Alice Dickinson. "The defendants received no more consideration than they had in their preliminary examinations." Adding to the general chaos, the afflicted girls, once in court, were gripped by the behavior spectators had come to anticipate: twisting in pain, wailing, and groaning, an atmosphere in which the accused had little if any chance of escaping a guilty verdict.

Why Bridget Bishop, in her fifties, was chosen first to stand trial for witchcraft is not clear; after all, she'd not been the first accused. It's possible that her dubious standing in the community may have contributed to her dilemma. Mrs. Bishop, twice widowed, was the successful proprietor of a local inn. Loquacious and living alone, she stood out in staid Salem Village for favoring "brightly colored" clothing, abhorred by conservative Puritans who traditionally wore dark dress. For years there were accusations that she was a witch, even by her late husband; and there were suspicions that she practiced "image magic." Bishop's presumed supernatural activities combined with the way she lived, dressed, and prospered made her an easy target for accusers.

If she'd wanted to further displease the judges, she quickly accomplished her goal. She appeared in court wearing a "lace-trimmed scarlet bodice," noted one historian. By Puritan standards, Bishop was a provocative dresser. The evidence against her was mainly gripes by those who blamed her for a variety of problems and ailments, past and present. When women assigned by the court examined Bishop's body they found an "excrescence of flesh," believed to be a teat or nipple used by a witch's familiar to "suckle" or feed from her breast. She did not help herself when she testified that she was not guilty.

"I am innocent to a witch, I know not what a witch is," Bishop protested.

Hathorne attacked her statement. "How do you know that you are not a witch?" the judge asked sternly.

Bishop could not find an adequate response. Not surprisingly she was pronounced guilty and ordered hanged. She was executed on June 10, atop Gallows Hill. Was Bridget Bishop an innocent victim of the hysteria? Clearly she was a victim, but author Chadwick Hansen reviewed "trial testimony" and concluded that Bishop had practiced "black magic." Hansen found that she and several other women had delved into various types of sorcery including curses that were supposed to result in sickness, even the deaths of those they disliked for one reason or the other, as well as image magic. He also contended that some Salem women practiced "white magic" including "fortune-telling and divination." Hansen concluded that the "afflicted girls" were likely victims of hysteria, but their fears were not unreasonable.

In the case against Bridget Bishop, several men claimed in court that they once worked in her house, and had "torn down" a wall where they found several "small images stuck with pins," wrote Alice Dickinson. If that was true, Bishop had engaged in or at least dabbled with image magic, a form of sorcery. In Salem, that was sufficient evidence to send her to the gallows.

During the Salem hysteria the belief in the supernatural went to its most dangerous extreme over the question of so-called "spectral evidence"; in other words, specters or apparitions of witches that tormented and inflicted severe pain on the innocent. But the specters could only be seen by the bewitched. Therefore the important legal question of the time was whether spectral—or invisible—evidence should be sufficient to find someone guilty of witchcraft? And what about the contention that the devil might even take the form of someone innocent? That question was also raised by some of the accused. The concept that invisible or unseen evidence could result in guilty verdicts and executions was mind-boggling to later generations of Americans. However, in the seventeenth century, the "rules of evidence" had not yet been firmly established.

To the detriment of those accused, spectral evidence, unsupported allegations, and hearsay were permitted by the Salem judges. A quarrel, property dispute, or jealousy between angry neighbors could escalate into charges of witchcraft if either party experienced some manner of pain, grief, or damage. The bottom line was that so-called evidence against the accused could be highly questionable. What should be allowed to prove someone was guilty of witchcraft? For the judges in seventeenth-century New England, such questions weighed heavily. If one believed witches and wizards were genuine, how was it to be proven? Was there a means in the Puritan system to safeguard both the victims and those wrongly accused?

One learned individual of the time was the fiery Boston preacher Cotton Mather, whom some judges consulted for advice on such pressing questions, especially as the Salem trials moved forward. He apparently gave the issue a great deal of thought. Although a fervent believer in witches as handmaidens to the devil, Mather answered in a letter that provided considerable insight into his thinking on the troubling question of spectral evidence:

> I must most humbly beg you that . . . you do not lay more stress upon pure specter testimony than it will bear . . . Now first a credible confession of the guilty witches is one of the most hopeful ways of coming at them, and I say a credible confession because even confession itself sometimes is not credible.

Mather also recommended that imposing capital punishment might not always be necessary for some engaged in witchcraft. Other respected ministers throughout the Massachusetts colony were also asked for their input, and there was never any question in their replies that the devil and witches presented a genuine danger and threat to God-fearing Christians. Their suggestions centered only on the means of determining who was guilty of sorcery. They, like Cotton Mather, wanted more than merely spectral or unseen evidence as absolute proof of wrongdoing. But the ministers called on for their advice concluded in a letter that there must be "speedy and vigorous prosecution of such as have rendered themselves obnoxious, according to the direction given in the laws of God, and the wholesome statues of the English nation, for the detection of witchcraft."

About the admission of spectral evidence in witch trials, the judges were not of a unanimous opinion. Chief judge William Stoughton strongly believed spectral evidence should be permitted. He had no doubt, he said, that the devil could take the shape of those who were guilty. Other ministers may have disagreed with some or all of Stoughton's opinions; however, his position was so important that he prevailed: spectral evidence was allowed when the witch trials continued at the end of June 1692.

Also in late June, Sarah Good, Elizabeth Howe, Susanna Martin, Rebecca Nurse, and Sarah Wilds learned their fates. All five were found guilty and would be hanged. In the case of Rebecca Nurse, she'd first been declared not guilty. But the afflicted girls, either acting out of genuine fear upon hearing the verdict, or pretending so as to maintain their newly found power, burst into fits, grimaces, screams, and contortions. Then Nurse was surprised to see Deliverance Hobbs in court as a witness against her.

"She is one of us," Nurse cried out in confusion.

To Judge Stoughton this meant that one witch acknowledged another. Dissatisfied with the "not guilty" verdict, he ordered it to be reconsidered. Not surprisingly, Mrs. Nurse was found guilty.

Stunned, angry, and distraught, Rebecca Nurse's family appealed to Governor Phips who granted a stay of her execution. But the afflicted girls again claimed they were being tortured by Nurse's specter. The judges believed them and sentenced the elderly woman to be hanged. On July 19, Rebecca Nurse and the others who'd been convicted in June went to their deaths on Gallows Hill. Sarah Good's last words were to pronounce her innocence, and in her final moments of life, Mrs. Good rebuked the Reverend Nicholas Noyes who stood there and proclaimed her a witch.

"You are a liar. I am no more a witch than you are a wizard, and if you take away my life, God will give you blood to drink," she shouted. Typically, the condemned asked for God's forgiveness or protection, but not Sarah Good.

Incredibly, Good's prediction eerily came true. Years later, Noyes died after he choked to death on his own blood following a throat hemorrhage. Some recalled Good's words: Could she have inflicted a curse on Noyes, or foreseen his death twenty-five years in the future?

The number of accused witches in Salem Village increased; the effect of the hangings had not served as a deterrent to the madness. Soon the panic moved to nearby communities. An Andover woman named Mrs. Ballard had suffered a lengthy and persistent fever. Since doctors could find no successful treatment witchcraft was blamed. Knowing of the trials in Salem Village, the woman's husband called upon two of the afflicted girls, Ann Putnam, Jr. and Mary Walcott, hoping they'd identify the witches in Andover who had stricken his ailing wife. Ann and Mary agreed, and off they went to Andover where they were warmly greeted. After townspeople and the local minister joined them in prayer, they proceeded to the Ballards' home. True to their word—and Mr. Ballard's expectations—the girls identified those who'd caused his wife's agony. By the time the Salem girls were done in Andover nearly fifty people had been jailed on charges of witchcraft.

The fear of being charged as a witch became so pervasive that many turned on people who'd always lived peacefully near them. It was better to be an accuser than one of the accused, seemed to be the thinking. A number of Puritan communities in Massachusetts were truly in the grip of a "witch hunt." Many of those charged had learned the way to avoid the gallows was to admit to practicing witchcraft—even if they never had. Some fabricated or embellished amazing tales of their involvement with sorcery; although untrue it saved their lives. Those who insisted they were innocent and refused to confess to demonic deeds they had not performed faced relentless examination and questioning, sometimes even torture until they were persuaded to plead guilty, even when they'd done nothing. Then, under intense pressure from officials, they'd accuse others of witchcraft; and so the vicious cycle continued to spin out of control.

There was no doubt that some individuals secretly practiced white or black magic in Puritan communities; however, others were so badly befuddled by the tumult that they could not discern if they were witches, and were unable to distinguish "fantasy from reality," as author Marion Starkey wrote. The combination of fear, superstition, and coercion fed the flames of hysteria so intensely that some—mostly women—became convinced they were in league with the devil, even confusing the physical and spirit worlds.

In July, John Proctor, still in the dismal confines of the Boston jail, wrote to local ministers pleading for the trials to be held in Boston with new justices on the bench. He was certain the witch craze was based largely on falsehoods and intimidation. The fact that Proctor could appeal to the clergy about the course or location of new trials would be impossible a century later when the United States Constitution provided for separation of church and state. However, the Massachusetts colony in the seventeenth century was a theocracy with no clear delineation between clerical and civil authority; often the two overlapped. Technically, accused witches faced magistrates or judges who answered to civil authorities, but religious input was neither frowned upon nor prohibited. Thus the clergy's influence in the Salem trials was not unusual for its time.

Unfortunately, John Proctor's letter had negligible influence. In early August he stood trial, as did his wife, Elizabeth, the Reverend George Burroughs, and three others. More than thirty people from Ipswich, Massachusetts, the town Proctor lived in before Salem, appealed to the judges on his behalf, hoping to save his life. Nearly two dozen Salem neighbors also offered words of support to the judges. Their efforts proved to be in vain: John and Elizabeth Proctor were declared guilty, as were the others. Later, when several of the afflicted girls traveled to Ipswich to ferret out witches, townspeople turned them away, furious at their complicity in John Proctor's hanging. Burroughs, who'd long claimed the devil and witches were genuine, now protested against spectral evidence, insisting that witches could not harm the innocent by use of their apparitions. However, the afflicted girls' words against him were too strong to counter.

George Jacobs, Sr. was convicted on the word of his granddaughter, Margaret. When she'd been arrested on witchcraft charges, she offered his name, as well as the Reverend Burroughs, because she feared she would be tortured and hanged. Although she stated in court that her confession had been coerced, and what she said about being a witch was "false and untrue," it had no effect on the fates of her grandfather or Burroughs; they were condemned to die on the gallows. The only one who escaped hanging was Elizabeth Proctor, who was pregnant. According to Puritan law, executing her would mean killing her unborn—and thus, innocent—baby.

On August 19, John Proctor, George Burroughs, Martha Carrier, George Jacobs, Sr., and John Willard went to the gallows. Just before he was executed, the Reverend Burroughs again proclaimed his innocence and recited perfectly the Lord's Prayer, although witches and wizards were supposedly unable to recite the words, "Our Father who art in heaven, hallowed be thy name . . . ," and so on. Apparently some villagers who'd gathered to watch the hangings noticed the contradiction. But the Reverend Cotton Mather interceded and maintained that Burroughs *was* guilty. He urged those assembled not to be swayed otherwise, because, he said, Burroughs was an ordained minister. That explained why he could perfectly recite the Lord's Prayer—and still be a wizard. "The devil is never more the devil than when he most appears like an angel of light," Mather exhorted the spectators. Burroughs and the others were hanged.

But now there was a faint glimmer of light in the public attitude toward the witchcraft madness; many noticed that Burroughs was able to repeat a prayer he wasn't supposed to if he was really a witch or wizard. Was public opinion shifting? By August, there were a small but growing number of people in the colony who dared to question the type of evidence allowed at the trials. The first stirrings of doubt would hardly be described as an organized challenge to authority. Still, uncertainty and misgivings were slowly emerging.

A magistrate from Salisbury named Robert Pike wrote to Judge John Corwin. Pike was skeptical of both what the afflicted girls claimed and the types of highly questionable evidence permitted to convict someone of witchcraft. His theory was interesting; he did not doubt the reality of witches. However, he suggested that the devil was doing his nefarious work through the afflicted, not via witches. Thus, innocent people were being accused in some instances because the devil was commanding the afflicted to falsely blame the righteous.

The influential Cotton Mather repeated his warning about not depending solely on spectral or unseen evidence. He also spoke against what was called "look and touch" evidence, questioning whether merely the look and touch of a suspected witch was sufficient to sentence them to death. If there was any doubt at all, Mather suggested, it would be more appropriate to consider a less severe punishment.

But the trials and executions continued. In September, fifteen more people were sentenced to death. On just one day, September 22, eight went to the gallows, including Martha Corey. Several of the convicted pleaded to the governor, judges, and clergy for clemency. It was to no avail; their appeals fell on deaf ears.

Giles Corey, Martha's husband, had also been accused of practicing witchcraft. Although the elderly man knew he was not guilty, he also understood that if he claimed innocence, he'd be convicted nonetheless. A proud man, he would not falsely plead guilty just to save his life or satisfy the court. Corey took another approach: he refused to enter a plea; in fact, he would not utter a single word. When questioned by the magistrates he remained absolutely still. Therefore, under Puritan law, he could not be brought to trial. But there was a price to be paid for his bold silence: brutal punishment. The court made no allowance for Corey because of his advanced age. He was laid on the ground while heavy stones were placed on him until he was crushed to death under their weight. It took two days of suffering before he would die. His courage deeply affected Salem residents, as did his composure and resolve. "His firmness and dignity made a strong impression on those villagers who were already becoming doubtful about the summer's events," wrote Alice Dickinson.

Following the death sentences carried out in September, the court recessed with plans to reconvene sometime in autumn. But by October, more than the seasons and colors of leaves had changed in Salem; so did attitudes. More citizens now opposed the witch trials and there was a marked shift in the villagers' perception of the recent hysteria. Even the Reverend Increase Mather, Cotton's father, had delivered an address to his fellow clergy in which he spoke against spectral evidence, and reprimanded those who accepted the unreliable accusations of "confessed witches." He added, "We ought not to practice witchcraft to discover witches. [I would] rather see ten suspected witches go free than execute even one innocent."

Now more people came forward to question the trials. A successful and influential Boston merchant, Thomas Brattle, wrote a letter in which he raised strong objections to the manner in which the Salem trails had been conducted. He noted how cavalierly the magistrates had accepted the words of the afflicted children and others who'd leveled accusations without more deeply probing their testimony and confessions. Brattle, like most people of his time, believed the devil was at work, but much of the girls' claims he thought to be the result of their imaginations. He concluded that some confessions seemed obviously coerced, while others were from the demented or deluded.

When Governor Phips arrived back in Boston he was deeply dismayed to learn that his special court had not found a solution to the colony's witchcraft dilemma. Phips had been visiting western Massachusetts, then unsettled country, where Indian attacks were a constant threat. In fact, the Puritans regarded the natives as "heathens," and also blamed them for doing Satan's work. Meanwhile, the jails in Salem and Boston were packed with many who'd not yet been tried. Still more people—mainly females—were accused every day of being witches. And the afflicted girls showed no signs of being released from the devil's grasp—or their own hysteria and perhaps maliciousness.

In addition to the personal misery suffered by the accused who were locked up in overcrowded, unsanitary dungeonlike conditions, the witch madness created another significant problem for the colony, especially Salem Village. The commotion of the past several months had caused many to disregard their farms, shops, and trades. In other words, the witch craze was taking a financial toll; it also caused many to flee the colony before they would be accused of sorcery. It was not an unwarranted fear; soon allegations were cast against even important and notable individuals whose reputations were beyond reproach, one of them being Lady Phips, the governor's wife. Understandably alarmed, the governor moved quickly to halt this turbulent and troubled environment—or at least slow the panic. In October, Phips ordered that no one else be jailed, except in extreme cases. He also wrote to England requesting counsel about how best to handle Salem's predicament. Before an answer could be returned, in October Phips had in his hands correspondence from many Andover residents pleading for the women of that community whose admissions to witchcraft, neighbors insisted, were forced from them. The letter read, in part:

> We know not who can think himself safe if the accusations of children and others who are under diabolical influence shall be received against persons of good fame.

The special court that Phips named five months earlier, in May, was not permitted to reconvene; instead the governor and lawmakers requested that the Superior Court meet to bring those jailed to trial. The chief justice was still William Stoughton who was joined by four other judges. In January 1693, they began the task of trying those accused and waiting for their long overdue day in court. Conceding that spectral or invisible evidence was specious at best, the court all but disallowed it; that alone resolved most of the cases. Fifty-two people were brought to trial, and the three who were convicted had confessed to witchcraft. Those three were sentenced to the gallows, as were five others who'd been languishing in jail after earlier convictions.

But the royal attorney general ruled the evidence against those to be hanged was insufficient and Governor Phips commuted their sentences. When he did not receive a reply from England as he'd hoped, it was left to him to decide what next to do, without help from the Crown. Phips ordered the jails emptied of suspected witches. In all, 150 people were freed. He also granted amnesty to those who'd run from Massachusetts to other colonies where witchcraft was taken less seriously, even ignored as the ravings of the unbalanced or superstitious in most cases.

Despite the governor's order, before the imprisoned were released, they were first required to pay for the food and expenses incurred during the time they were jailed. That meant they even had to pay for the iron shackles they wore, hand and foot, while incarcerated. For the poor who'd been imprisoned it was an immense strain to find the funds necessary to secure their release. It was an added insult to the injury many innocent people already suffered, and some never overcame the hardships and costs—physically, emotionally, and financially. Under the law at the time, those jailed had their property confiscated and never returned; so many spent the rest of their lives destitute.

Gaining Tituba's freedom posed a problem; since she was a slave, she could not legally own any property and was considered otherwise without any resources. The Reverend Parris, in whose home and parsonage the witch hysteria had begun, wanted no part of her. Not until a man came forward and paid jail costs for Tituba's release was she freed; she then became his "indentured servant."

By 1693, the witch hysteria had calmed, but the acrimony it created between villagers would linger. The accusations and harsh words were bitter memories that would not be forgotten for years to come. Those who'd been badly hurt were not able to quickly forgive and forget, and some who had fled Salem during the craze chose never to return. Unlike Europe, New England's encounter with the devil had not been lengthy, but it left an ugly mark, especially on Salem.

When Salem returned to something resembling normal, the governor asked the Reverend Cotton Mather to write a book both explaining and legitimizing the court's actions during the crisis. Mather wrote *The Wonders of the Invisible World*, which provided, author Robert C. Fuller explained, "a theological rationale that made [the] trials and execution of the 'guilty' appear as an exercise in righteousness."

What happened to the "afflicted girls"? Once public sentiment shifted from them, they withdrew from sight. Only Ann Putnam, Jr. publicly admitted the wrong she'd taken part in. In 1706, she requested to be allowed back as a member of the church in Salem Village, and the Reverend Joseph Green read her apology from the pulpit. In the spirit of healing, she was forgiven and accepted back into the congregation.

Many in the church were angered at the Reverend Parris for his rush in demanding that the children accuse others for supposedly bewitching them. The most furious, of course, were the loved ones of those jailed, tortured, and executed. Parris was forced to leave Salem by 1697 and he never returned, although he carried always the stigma of Salem events; a heavy weight he bore the remainder of his life. The minister who followed, the Reverend Joseph Green, devoted considerable time and effort to easing hostilities and tensions that remained from the madness. No one was blameless; for those who'd lost their lives, no compensation was possible.

Eventually, with hindsight, the good citizens of the colony realized that the Salem insanity was a deception instigated by fear and extremism. Throughout the Massachusetts colony, January 4, 1697, was a day devoted to fasting and prayer, and to asking "God's forgiveness" for the tragedy of 1692. One of the witch trial judges, Samuel Sewall, wrote a letter that his minister read to the congregation. Sewall acknowledged his terrible mistake when he condemned innocent people to death. All he could do now, he said, was plead for absolution by God and his fellow men and women. Also on that day of repentance, former witch trial jurors admitted their transgressions, especially in allowing spectral evidence to be used to hang people. The jurors begged for forgiveness and deeply apologized, saying they'd fallen "under the power of a strong . . . delusion."

Although no amount of apologies could erase the damage done it was still extraordinary for that time. By contrast, after Europe was swept by centuries of witch hysteria there was barely a word of regret or apology from secular or clerical authorities, despite hundreds of thousands of deaths. But in New England, many who'd taken part in the misguided and tragic events at least displayed a modicum of decency by sincerely asking God and their fellow citizens to forgive them. Interestingly, one of the most significant figures during the witchcraft mania chose not to apologize: the chief judge at the trials, William Stoughton.

Some things moved too slowly. It wasn't until 1703—eleven years after the trials—when the Massachusetts General Court pronounced the Salem witch trials illegal and spectral evidence as something that should not have been permitted. But the names of the accused and convicted remained officially on the record, despite appeals from families of those wronged to have their names cleared. Eventually, in 1711, the General Court, as it was called, approved some monetary restitution, albeit small, for the families of those put to death, and the condemned who escaped the gallows. The wheels of justice crawled but ultimately the names of all those who'd been charged, convicted, and executed were, at last, exonerated.

In all, twenty people went to their deaths: nineteen of them hanged, and one crushed. More than 150 had been jailed. Of those accused, fifty confessed to practicing witchcraft, likely most under the threat of torture. Several died in jail; no doubt the deplorable conditions were a contributing factor. Remember little Dorcas Good, the five-year-old sent to jail on witchcraft charges along with her mother? She nearly went insane from the experience and subsequent trauma, and remained mentally ill all her life.

Ever since the horrific events of Salem Village in 1692, historians, parapsychologists, psychologists, and sociologists have been among the many experts and researchers who've attempted to unravel what really occurred in the Puritan community, and what caused the mania. The following is compiled from several books and other sources, and represents some of the leading theories about the "afflicted girls" advanced over the years:

Hoax. Unlikely at the beginning of the afflicted girls' episodes of seizures, contortions, and crying. Historic records from early witnesses suggest the children's suffering was genuine.

Fear. A theory that has possibility, since the girls, not well educated or sophisticated in their time, had been fed stories of the occult that were not only frightening, but were also in marked contradiction to their strict Puritan upbringing.

Attention. Puritan children received little notice from their elders; to "be seen and not heard" was the rule for boys and girls. Once the "afflicted girls" realized they were the center of attraction, they may well have continued their abhorrent behavior for both the attention and rare power it gave them, especially over the adults in the community.

Malice or spite. The girls may have offered a few names of elderly or poor women they disliked, but they'd been prodded to give names when they were first stricken. Later, jealousy clearly caused some of the false accusations neighbors brought against neighbors, and there was hostility between social classes.

Hysteria. It would be consistent with the fear and guilt the girls experienced as a result of Tituba's stories and fortune-telling demonstrations that well may have produced a "functional disturbance of the nervous system." Hysteria as a medical condition of "psychoneurotic origin" was poorly understood in the seventeenth century.

Ergot poisoning. A disputed theory held to by some historians who argue that ergot, a fungal disease of rye and other cereals, may have caused hallucinations in the children, and even in some of the adults who confessed to seeing demons and other apparitions.

Sexual repression. A theory held by some experts, since Puritan females were allowed so little freedom; pent up frustration and abuse led to their "acting out" behavior.

Superstition. Puritan religious zealotry was steeped in superstitions such as the absolute belief in the power of witches to inflict harm by magic.

The role of the clergy in Salem Village. The influence of the Reverend Cotton Mather was especially strong in a backwoods community such as Salem. His fanaticism about witches and the evil they could cause certainly fueled the mania.

Delusion. Since the afflicted girls reported witnessing countless specters, they might have suffered from hallucinations brought on by anything, from hysteria and fear to overactive imaginations or ergot.

Power of suggestion. If the girls were susceptible to what they'd heard at home, in church, and from Tituba, they may have reacted to the confusing combination and believed what they'd been told.

Genuine witchcraft or sorcery. This possibility is traditionally given little credence. But if there is any truth that image magic, spells, charms, and incantations work, as many claim, it is has to remain a possibility that Tituba had occult powers associated with West Indian religion and culture. Some women—and men—practiced black magic in Salem and other Puritan communities; Bridget Bishop and Sarah Good both practiced witchcraft. Could the girls have been demonically possessed? Larry Dossey, M.D., the nation's leading authority on healing prayer, suggested that if one can pray for good, one can also pray—or invoke a curse—to inflict evil or harm. "If there is power in positive prayer, as most believe, why wouldn't there be power in negative prayer, and by extension power or energy in curses and spells?" Dossey asked. Could some in Salem have called on demonic or evil forces?

Likely no one explanation suffices; more probably some combination of causes was responsible. Salem marked an important turning point in the history of centuries of witchcraft persecutions. Once people took responsibility for the destructive craze, its days were numbered in New England. The Age of Reason, or Enlightenment, that emerged in the eighteenth century brought a more rational and reasoned view of the world; spectral or invisible evidence would never again be allowed in a trial. But unfortunately the rationalists who correctly criticized Puritan excesses went too far in their thinking about the paranormal. For many, all spirit or psychic phenomena was disregarded as the belief of the naïve, uneducated, or superstitious. That attitude, a reaction to Calvinist extremes and centuries of church dogma, combined with the new "enlightened" thinking, left little room for a serious study of the paranormal in the eighteenth century. America's Puritan heritage cast a shadow over the history of this country and influenced many of our opinions and fears, to this day, about the so-called occult.

Unfortunately, the dark and odious side of the supernatural was America's first major paranormal event. Yet it provided later generations with a cautionary tale never to be forgotten. Its legacy remains a powerful one: witch hunts can take many forms. In 1953, Arthur Miller's play *The Crucible*, about the Salem trials, became a metaphor for the political "witch hunt" that ferreted out Communists in America during the dark days of the House Un-American Activities Committee (HUAC), and the Senator Joseph McCarthy era of the early 1950s. Then, too, many innocent people lost careers and reputations; some even their lives as suicides. The term *witch hunt* forever entered the American psyche as a "campaign directed against a particular group holding unpopular or unorthodox views."

The famed nineteenth-century American author Nathaniel Hawthorne was a Salem native and a direct descendant of witch trial judge John Hathorne. Hawthorne purposely changed the spelling of his name because he always feared the taint of his ancestry—and perhaps its karma. Sarah Good's curse on the Reverend Noyes formed some of Hawthorne's classic, *The House of Seven Gables*.

While the excesses of Salem proved disastrous, evil does exist in many forms, and summoning it, as did those in Salem, can be dangerous in many ways: psychologically, politically, physically, and psychically. Is the supernatural genuine? For both the accused and accusers in Salem it proved very real. What people are able to do with negativity and misguided beliefs can be more potent and dangerous than anything the spirit world can manifest or conjure. "In manners of malice the devil suits his actions to [people's] beliefs about them," author Chadwick Hansen concluded.[3]

2

Whig, Tory, and Spiritualist

Often do the spirits of great events stride on before
the events/And in to-day already walks to-morrow.
—SAMUEL TAYLOR COLERIDGE

The Salem witchcraft madness drained America of its fervor for the supernatural by the early years of the eighteenth century, producing something of a backlash. None of the other colonies had ever taken witchcraft persecutions to the extreme the New England colonies had; in fact, elsewhere the idea was never considered the incipient menace that the Puritans considered it to be in Massachusetts. But now even those who held tenaciously to Puritan or Calvinist beliefs realized that people had made a terrible error in Salem, and organized interest in the "occult," as it was often called, declined sharply. While many people still quietly practiced divination and sorcery, serious scientific interest in alchemy all but disappeared.

As decades passed and the furor of the witchcraft craze died down, the severe Puritan approach to life changed as well, largely a victim of its own excesses. American thinking and culture were changing with the dawn of the eighteenth century and advent of the Age of Reason in Europe, which brought about a growing divide between science and religion. In fact, "faith and science" had been drifting further apart since the time of Galileo in the seventeenth century when, with the help of the newly invented telescope, Galileo postulated that the Earth orbits around the Sun, seconding Copernicus's theory. However, the Church had long held to an opposite theory advanced by Ptolemy in ancient times that the Earth was the center of the cosmos. They attacked Galileo's teachings and forced him to declare that he agreed with the official—if erroneous—Church position.

The rift between science and the Church never fully healed, and in the eighteenth century, a new philosophy emerged, the so-called "rational thinking," which became the basis of the Enlightenment. Catholics were ordered not to read about Enlightenment concepts under penalty of sin, and the writings of Voltaire and John Locke were banned. Where did this leave the paranormal? For those who held fast to biblical beliefs, the occult remained anathema. It was not in the interests of Christian churches to consider supernatural events useful or spiritual; it behooved the clergy to cast them negatively, so as to maintain ecclesiastic control. For those newly immersed in rational and scientific thinking, the occult and magic were medieval superstitions—best ignored, and no more welcomed than repressive church dogma. As far back as the sixteenth century, the respected astronomer Johannes Kepler had wrestled with the frustrating problem of trying to make astrology and astronomy compatible.

In America, religion remained an important part of colonial life; by 1740, Protestant faiths continued to lead the way: Congregational, Anglican (Episcopalian), and Presbyterian ranked as the largest denominations. At the same time, however, new views of the cosmos based on science and reason had emerged, and as was so often the case, the paranormal was neglected.

"No significant occult literature was printed in eighteenth-century England or America," noted Jon Butler, who titled the period between 1760 and 1848 "the Dark Ages of American Spiritualism."[1] Yet events were occurring, albeit quietly, that would prepare future generations of Americans for a renewed and powerful interest in psychic and supernatural phenomena. It may seem at first that whatever paranormal activity took place then was in "bits and pieces," with one event not connected to another. But taken in its totality, supernatural and mystical phenomena in the eighteenth century was very much a part of many lives and the emerging American culture.

Although this was the New World, colonists still frequently looked toward Europe for intellectual and scientific ideas, as well as tastes, trends, and fashions for those able to afford them. One leading figure of the age who piqued interest in the supernatural was Emanuel Swedenborg, a Swedish mystic whose influence was felt among the educated and curious in Europe and America for his lucid accounts of visionary experiences and travels to "higher spiritual realms." For centuries, Western civilization had only church teachings and the Bible to depend upon for explanations of the supernatural. But Swedenborg was not a theologian; he came from the secular world and it was to this audience that his writings made the deepest impression. It was the first time in Western history that a nontheologian wrote so prolifically about the metaphysical for a popular readership.

Born in Stockholm, Sweden, in 1688, Swedenborg was initially a scientist who specialized in metallurgy and mining. Although his father had been a professor of theology, it wasn't until 1743, when, in his mid-fifties, Emanuel developed a curiosity about religion and spirituality after he experienced a vivid dream that purported to show him the spiritual realm. By then he'd traveled extensively throughout Europe, studied "natural philosophy," as science was then often called, and was influenced by the recent discoveries of Sir Isaac Newton and Edmond Halley.

Following Swedenborg's initial vision he experienced many more during which he claimed to meet Jesus Christ and such notable historic figures as Plato, Aristotle—and even God. He wrote that in his journeys to other planes he communicated with spirits of the deceased, which he described as angels, and explained it was through these experiences that he came to understand the "true nature of the universe." Disseminating "spiritual enlightenment" then became his life's work.

No matter what opinion one draws about Swedenborg's otherworldly excursions, there's no question he possessed genuine psychic ability, including "second sight." In a well-known and documented incident that occurred in 1759, he clairvoyantly saw a raging fire taking place in Stockholm, some three hundred miles from Gothenburg where he was at the time. It was many hours later when Swedenborg's vision was confirmed as entirely accurate. Some researchers have suggested that he may have witnessed the Stockholm blaze during an out-of-body experience.

Whatever the cause, the German philosopher Immanuel Kant verified a number of Swedenborg's psychic encounters, and wrote about them in *Dreams of a Spirit-Seer* in 1766. Swedenborg could hardly have been displeased for he considered himself a "divinely appointed messenger," whose responsibility was to share the knowledge he received with others. The mystic put aside all his metallurgy and mining activities, and instead wrote prolifically, based on his spirit communications. Rosemary Ellen Guiley wrote that he believed that "the spiritual realm" had a strong impact on human life, and that "God created man to exist simultaneously in the physical and spiritual worlds."[2]

His "doctrine of correspondences" considered the two planes of existence: the physical and the spiritual. Accordingly, once the soul leaves the physical body, deceased family and friends meet it in heaven. Then, following a period of introspection by the deceased, the departed soul moves on to the world beyond, whether "heaven or hell," depending on what the person's mind conceived while in the physical body. Hell is occupied by "demons," while heaven is populated by souls that are righteous and worthy, those Swedenborg called "angels."

Swedenborg's description of the afterlife includes many familiar activities and "social structures," even government, war, and crime. His version of the hereafter allows for souls to advance through different planes, although once the soul is in heaven or hell that is where it remains.

Reception to his teachings was not always positive. Church leaders and theologians vigorously disputed him and, gaining recognition as he did during the Age of Reason, he was considered by some to be "anti-Enlightenment." Still, he continued to draw attention and interest in both Europe and America, and at various times lived in Sweden, Holland, and London. The latter afforded the greatest amount of intellectual freedom and popularity. Some of his friends had a simple explanation for his ideas and visions: he'd lost his mind. It apparently never dawned on many religious and scientific leaders and thinkers to consider that Swedenborgian beliefs represented an alternative form of spiritual growth.

Undeterred by critics and detractors, he learned to self-induce lengthy trancelike states of rapture. He also became a medium and recorded spirit communications through automatic writing; his best-known book, *Heaven and Hell*, described the afterlife with information he maintained was received from the spirit world. "Angels speak from the spiritual world according to individual thought . . . but when angels speak spiritually with me from heaven, they speak just as intelligently as the man by my side," he wrote.

Swedenborg continued his metaphysical work unrelentingly until his death in London in 1774, at the age of eighty-four. In 1778, the Church of the New Jerusalem was founded to advance his teachings. In 1792, one was started in the United States, and in 1810, a society named for him in London began to publish his writings; it remains in existence.

Swedenborg never developed a large number of adherents in the United States. His greatest influence in America was yet to come; it would be felt most strongly about seventy years after his death during the Great Age of Spiritualism from the 1840s onward. He is "generally credited with providing a focal point around which coalesced the quasi-religious belief that living persons could converse with the spirits of dead persons," wrote Richard S. Broughton in *Parapsychology: The Controversial Science*. In other words, his ideas formed the basis for spiritualism, a far cry from what Christian churches preached. A number of current New Age ideas are remarkably similar to those advanced by the Swedish mystic.

Finally, for those who wonder how he avoided the wrath of both church and state for what were then considered by many "heretical ideas," Swedenborg first published anonymously until, eventually in 1760, his name appeared on a published work. He also purposely wrote in Latin so the average person was unable to read his books; it was left to educated colleagues and church leaders to decipher his writings. Once his teachings were translated into English, they had a major impact on spiritualism in America. We will talk more about that influence later.

The strict Calvinist doctrines had served seventeenth-century New England, bringing together settlements that grew and thrived despite immense hardships and obstacles. But the Puritan model of life eventually became outdated and too restrictive in an expanding and increasingly diverse country.

By the 1730s, American religion—mainly Protestant denominations—had settled into a comfortable routine. Some historians have even said they'd become complacent, and their practices less relevant. Then, to fill the void left by the lapse of religious zealotry, came the Reverend Jonathan Edwards, a Puritan minister from New England whose Calvinist fervor translated into a period of American history dubbed the Great Awakening. It was a time of religious revival when Edwards's stirring sermon, "Sinners in the Hands of an Angry God," delivered in Connecticut in 1741, motivated many to convert after he'd struck a chord with his passionate emphasis on the "depravity of man and the sovereignty of God." Revivalists stressed faith "rather than good conduct as the means to salvation."

There was no resemblance to the Enlightenment teachings that were a virtual polar opposite from the Calvinist beliefs Edwards articulated in his powerful sermons about God and predestination. Edwards's genuine zeal "expressed his sincere spirituality but the Puritans demanded control and strict conformity," Robert C. Fuller wrote. He noted the Great Awakening resulted in conversions, but the Calvinist purpose was to hold tight to Puritanism's "theological and social boundaries, not expanding them." By the 1750s, the Great Awakening had waned, but the divide between "rationalists" or "liberals," and "Calvinists" or "evangelicals," separated opinion in the years prior to the American Revolution. Some historians have spoken well of the Great Awakening, claiming it fostered religious tolerance, and perhaps even the ideas of "independence and rebellion," while others reviled it for its "anti-intellectual bias."

By the next decade Americans were caught up in the debate about whether to seek independence from England. By no means were the colonists of one mind politically, any more than they were all of the same religious belief. About a third of the colonists, mostly in New England, favored independence; another third opposed it; and a third did not seem to care one way or the other. When the decision was made to fight for American liberty, the revolutionary mood brought with it a new freedom of thought that attracted many of the Founding Fathers and stirred patriot leaders.

Prior to the American Revolution in 1775, the ideas of the Age of Reason or of Enlightenment continued to gain in popularity, especially among the scholarly drawn to its rational outlook on life. One of those who had the most impact was the great British physicist, Sir Isaac Newton (1642–1727). His remarkable achievements in science and mathematics concluded the universe operated by "laws," and that resulted in his creation of a new scientific approach to make sense of these "laws of nature." "The universe could now be understood as a vast machine—lawful, harmonious, and comprehensible by the human mind," wrote Robert C. Fuller, who added that Newton developed "a widespread faith in reason," and also recognized the significance of rigorous experiments to test his theories.

Such important eighteenth-century American figures as Benjamin

Franklin and Thomas Jefferson drew inspiration from Newton. Often overlooked, however, by rationalists who claimed Newton as one of their own was the fact that Sir Isaac also had a deep curiosity about religion, prophecy, and the occult. To the Anglican Church, he was a heretic who "denied the divinity of Jesus and of the Holy Ghost," but was clever enough to keep secret those ideas that might provoke confrontation with church authorities.

This man who took credit for inventing calculus, also found time to delve into alchemy—medieval chemistry that sought to turn base metals into gold. He read books about astrology, and closely studied the Scriptures; there was no question that he believed in God. "In theology as in alchemy, he felt himself to be questing for ancient truths," author James Gleick explained. The implication for the paranormal was clear: if intellectuals focused only on Newton's so-called "rationalism," then any supernatural or psychic interests he had could easily be disregarded, even if that meant omitting his curiosity about the occult. On the part of rationalists it was, to say the least, disingenuous.

Newton had long been curious about planetary movements. It was his observance and calculations of the comet in 1680–1681, which helped his friend Edmond Halley formulate the theories about the orbit of the comet that would later be named for him. In 1687, Newton wrote his masterpiece about physics, *Principia*, generally regarded as ushering in the Age of Reason; it was translated from Latin into English in 1729. The irony in his discovery of gravity was that science wanted to obliterate anything it considered occult or magical; yet there was Newton claiming the existence of an unseen force called gravity and arguing that the moon influences tides. To some of his critics, that sounded much like the supernatural they scorned.

"The new mechanical philosophers [scientists] striving to create a science free of occult qualities, believed in matter without magic," Gleick wrote. He added, "They wanted . . . to build all explanations from reason and not miracles." But magic survived, and astronomers were also astrologers. Even Galileo had drawn horoscopes. Newton eventually realized he could not explain everything by a "purely mechanical world view," and so he dug deeply to find the "mystical force" that gave movement to the universe, and discovered that force was "gravity." But alchemy remained a passion, and Newton's many notes and research about it were not fully discovered until after his death.

"Sir Isaac Newton was not a believer in the doctrine of alchemy," biographer Sir David Brewster insisted in 1831.[3] Of course, any claim could be made for or against Newton a hundred years after his death. But in his life, "He never purged occult, hidden, mystical qualities from his vision of nature," Gleick noted.

Several historians, including Gleick, have suggested that some of Newton's discoveries may have originated from a "supernatural, super-human intuition." In helping to create the "modern world," did Newton have some "otherworldly insight"? This question cannot be answered with certitude. However if it were so, it would be the ultimate irony for the rationalists so influenced by him, and yet so myopic when considering his supernatural interests. It is as if the Sir Isaac Newton whom traditional science and history have taught us about was a creation of later generations, not the man whose curiosity spilled into the mystical.

Another major influence on the Age of Reason was the English philosopher John Locke (1632–1704). His writings strongly refuted the Calvinist mistrust of logical thinking. While for Enlightenment intellectuals "experience and reason" formed the basis of "human knowledge," wrote Robert C. Fuller, Locke took issue with "divine revelation," although he claimed to be a Christian, because he considered revelation to be "extrasensory," a contradiction to his thesis that "ideas come from sensory experience." Locke wrote, "Reason must be our last Judge and Guide in every thing."

Enlightenment thinkers encouraged people to spend less time dwelling upon "heaven and eternity," and more time considering "the here and now." According to Locke, rational thought required skepticism and mistrust of power and control by political and religious authorities. His philosophy was his "commitment to individual freedom and political equality," Fuller noted; and "rational thinking" has long been the mantra of skeptics and debunkers to reject psychic phenomena as "pseudo-science" or superstition.

Those certain that "reason" was the road to travel in life also began to rethink long-accepted religious dogma. Some noted French philosophers, including Denis Diderot and Voltaire, turned to atheism. But other

Enlightenment figures weren't so quick to discard religion; many were attracted to a faith called *deism*, which developed from the Enlightenment with a definite liberal bent in the eighteenth century, and was imported to America from England. One could be a deist and yet remain a skeptic of dogmas, rituals, and miracles, although they acknowledged a belief in the existence of God. To a deist, the most important religious tenet was morality: the concern with doing right in this physical life. Deism, however, did accept the principle of the afterlife where righteousness would be requited, and villainy or wrongdoing penalized.

Deists raised too many questions and doubts about Christ, the Scripture, miracles, and mystery; therefore "Christianity has always opposed [it]," explained John J. Heaney, author of *The Sacred and the Psychic* (1984). If one sought personal guidance or direct intervention from God, deism definitely was not the way to go; its main purpose was to declare a "rational faith."

Many colonial leaders and Founding Fathers were drawn to deism; it fit the "forward-thinking" spirit of the times. Deists could count among their numbers such American patriots as Thomas Paine, Samuel Adams, John Adams, Thomas Jefferson, and James Madison. Then there was Benjamin Franklin, who distanced himself from organized religion, but who formed his own convictions based on deist principles, and Ethan Allen, who openly disputed traditional Christianity even though he captured Fort Ticonderoga from the British in the name of Jehovah. George Washington remained an Episcopalian. However he, like many other patriots, was highly tolerant in regards to religious faith.

When Newton removed much of the mystery from his view of the universe, a number of critics complained that he'd also tampered with their religious beliefs, and when he postulated scientific answers he expunged metaphysical explanations. Unfortunately, by rejecting as superstition anything that smacked of the occult or magic, these scientific and rationalist thinkers ignored a wealth of psychic phenomena that might have been more closely and seriously studied. The paranormal swung like a pendulum from one extreme to the other in colonial America. Reviled by Puritans in the seventeenth century, now in the eighteenth century, the supernatural remained scorned by Christianity, while those who were liberal thinkers and rationalists wanted nothing more to do with it than its traditional religious enemies.

The mind-set of that time took such a firm hold, that many of the attitudes and opinions toward the paranormal today by skeptics and fundamentalists—two extremes—still reflect some of the thinking of centuries ago when Newton was a college professor in his native England. The Bible was the ultimate word, and God the supreme authority. While Enlightenment thinkers such as Locke and Voltaire influenced America's Founding Fathers, psychic practices were relegated to astrologers, fortune-tellers, and assorted healers, again left to drift aimlessly, and to serve mainly the "lower classes," although anyone who has researched the paranormal knows only too well that psychic experiences cut across all socioeconomic, racial, ethnic, and religious boundaries. Perhaps because of the Enlightenment, the educated and elite did not want to be associated publicly with a belief in the supernatural; an attitude that many stubbornly cling to today.

During the eighteenth century, the paranormal in America also suffered from a lack of organization and leadership. No notable names arose to guide it, as would happen in the nineteenth century. But if you wandered through the colonies you'd find evidence of supernatural belief and practice. For example, almanacs were popular in virtually every town and city, and many were published that offered calendars, bits of useful advice, proverbs, astronomical data, and astrological information. Arguably the best known and most successful of the genre was *Poor Richard's Almanack*, which Benjamin Franklin began publishing in 1732. In almanacs one could look up astrological birth signs and forecasts, not unlike newspaper horoscopes today. Strangely, however, it is difficult to locate names of practicing astrologers in colonial America. Perhaps it was more a matter of poor record keeping than a lack of those who could interpret the influence of celestial bodies on human affairs. Similarly there are few surviving documents telling us the names and locations of mediums and fortune-tellers in the colonies during the eighteenth century, although they also were present.

One name not lost to history is "Mother" Ann Lee (1736–1784) who, although a religious figure, earned a reputation for communicating with the souls of the departed. In 1747, the Quakers in England experienced a religious reawakening from which a new sect came into being, the Shakers who, seized by the Holy Spirit, literally trembled and shook when they sang and worshipped. When the leadership fell to a blacksmith's daughter named Ann Lee, she acted on a psychic vision or revelation she experienced. The result was that "Mother" Ann and her followers moved to America where they founded a Shaker community near Albany, New York. She was also considered an accomplished faith healer as well as one of the better-known mediums of the eighteenth century. The Shakers held that God was male and female, and some followers believed her to be the Second Coming of Christ; following her death, the Shakers founded several self-sufficient communities in America. Lee's story represents an interesting overlap between religion and the paranormal, one that is more common than most people realize, and is long a bone of contention. Her gift to receive spirit communications was acceptable to Christians when placed in a religious context. However, defined as a psychic ability it was, at best, unwelcome, or even possibly of evil origin.

Some centuries-old occult beliefs remained present in the eighteenth century, despite the Enlightenment. In one incident, before the American Revolution, an anonymous Philadelphian, angered at the British-imposed Stamp Act, wrote a critical broadside that included a hex or curse on the commissioner who administered the hated law, wishing him painful illness if he continued issuing the stamps. In another incident in 1787, also in Philadelphia, a crowd stoned a woman whom they believed to be a witch. In the Southern colonies, many whites turned to magic, conjuring spirits, and herbal remedies learned from black slave healers.

Surprisingly, slavery, one of America's most hideous and onerous institutions, kept interest in the occult alive and purposeful as a result of African traditions brought here. It's likely that the first African slaves to America numbered about twenty and were brought on a Dutch ship to Jamestown, Virginia, in 1619. Slavery did not grow quickly in the seventeenth century; but by the eighteenth century, the "system of Negro slavery" developed rapidly, especially in the Southern colonies "where it became an integral part of the emerging plantation economy," Tom Cowan and Jack Maguire explained in *Timelines of African-American History* (1994).

By 1700, there were nearly 28,000 slaves in America, about 22,000 of that number in the South, out of a total population in the colonies of 250,900. Slavery was a "moral travesty," wrote Joseph J. Ellis, "an institution clearly at odds with the values of the American Revolution."

In his highly regarded 1968 book, *White Over Black: American Attitudes Toward the Negro, 1550–1812*, author Winthrop D. Jordan said "that racism had infiltrated the American soul very early in our history."

Conditions for slave transport to America were horrendous and unsanitary. Most slaves had been captured or kidnapped from Africa's west coast. Chained, branded, and packed into slave ships for journeys, many captives did not survive. To add to their misery, they were often forced by slave masters to exercise by dancing on the ships, a debasement of ancient African religious traditions meant to honor spirits; if they refused, they were flogged. The destruction of African belief systems and heritage were hastened by these viciously cruel voyages to the Americas, known as the Middle Passage.

The black men and women who lived through this humiliation and agony found themselves in a strange land, torn from their families, communities, and culture. Before the end of the seventeenth century, the standing of Africans in America had actually worsened. "They'd been reduced to the status of chattel," Jordan explained. Conditions for slaves were stark at best, subhuman at worst. "The slave was treated like a beast," Jordan wrote. "Enslavement was captivity; slaves were infidels or heathens."

Unlike Christianity practiced by whites, native African spiritual beliefs first brought here by slaves centered on occult and magical practices and rituals. As mentioned in a previous chapter, the West Indian slave, Tituba, was blamed for initiating the Salem witchcraft hysteria of 1692 by telling supernatural tales and demonstrating fortune-telling and sorcery to Puritan girls.

While it's true many slaves later converted to the Christian beliefs of their owners, most initially looked to their own native religions for faith and resolve. At the center of the religious system that African slaves held close to through their suffering, especially on Southern plantations, was the "medicine man" or healer, sometimes referred to as a "witch doctor." It was not unlike indigenous or Native American people whose tribal communities had shamans. The healer, like the shaman, represented a powerful figure who practiced sorcery, and used magic spells, potions, powders, and herbal remedies, often quite effectively. So-called traditional medicines and treatments that whites received at the time were frequently rather primitive and sometimes dangerous.

Witch doctors or "black conjurers" also were adept at calling upon spirits. The noted nineteenth-century African-American scholar W. E. B. DuBois wrote that conjurers were at the heart of the black culture because they were critical to preserving the physical health of slaves. He explained that the conjurer or medicine man "appeared early on the plantation, found his function as a healer of the sick, the interpreter of the unknown, the comforter of the sorrowing, the supernatural avenger of the wrong, and the one who . . . expressed the longing, and disappointment of a stolen and oppressed people."

Jon Butler wrote that in examining slave cemeteries of that period, "evidence of African occult practices" has been found. As well, Butler said, "in slave narratives" there were many references to the use of amulets to fend off illnesses; to voodoo, which employed casting spells and image magic; and to the conjuring of spirits to resolve disagreements between slaves.

Black healers often treated both blacks and whites—a seeming contradiction in a time of unspeakable inequality and unbridled brutality against slaves. But foremost, these "black occult practitioners" helped their people bear the burden of captivity with all its abuses. They provided survival skills, a sense of belonging, and the promise of a better life in the next world.

Two centuries later, during the 1920s in Harlem, New York, Gilbert Osofsky wrote that there were many "spiritualists, herb doctors, medicine men, faith healers, palmists, and phrenologists," all practicing skills that could be traced back to African and slave cultures.[4]

In their book, Cowan and Maguire recount the story of Onesimus, the Reverend Cotton Mather's slave, who in 1721 told the minister about "medical inoculations performed in Africa by tribal healers." In turn, Mather told a Boston physician, Dr. Boylston, who performed the first smallpox inoculations in North America on his son and two slaves.

By 1743, the year Thomas Jefferson was born in Virginia, that colony had a population of 42,000 African slaves. By 1750, twenty percent of the population in the colonies was of African origin. The total slave population was about 236,400; of that number, 206,000 were in the South. Throughout the eighteenth century, the rapacious slave trade from Africa to America numbered some 50,000 to 100,000 slaves brought here annually. By 1776, the year the Declaration of Independence was signed, there were a half-million slaves in America, out of a total population of more than two million.[5]

The recently arrived slaves, and the black people who remembered the African roots of their religion, believed in and feared the power of witches and sorcerers. African occult traditions comprised the early belief systems that sustained the slave population, although some slaves committed suicide as a way of paying homage to their native religions—and escaping bondage.

Not a great deal is known about the specific religious practices of slaves, especially prior to about 1760 because few written records were kept. But "African occultism usually reinforced rather than contradicted Christian practice, and Christianity also helped sustain some African beliefs and practices," Jon Butler wrote. Eventually the slaves' religion became a combination of African and Christian convictions, as Christianity expanded among slaves in the late eighteenth century.

After 1760, there were significant efforts to convert slaves to Christianity. Both "Black Christianity" and "African occultism" helped develop and shape African-American culture. By 1800, there were more than one million blacks in the United States, about 19 percent of the population of the country. And the first African Methodist Episcopalian Church had been founded in Philadelphia by 1794. But as slaves developed "kinship and family systems," African religious traditions that might have been forgotten were reintroduced with each new shipload of slaves. Thus, later generations of slaves came into contact with African occult beliefs they otherwise would not have known.

Lawrence Levine wrote, "Conjurers could be pictured as exotic Old Testament type prophets or magicians . . . who commanded great respect."[6] In fact, as slaves learned from biblical accounts of the enslaved Hebrews and their later deliverance from captivity, they were provided with hope of eventual freedom.

Butler described one incident in the early eighteenth century when a slave revolt was in the making. Leaders were given some kind of magical powder by a "black sorcerer." The powder, sprinkled on clothing, was supposed to make the rebellious slaves impenetrable to the white man's weapons. There was also a blood ritual between slaves bent on revolt in which they "sucked blood" from one another's arms to symbolize a "ritual bond" between them. Butler also told of a white planter in South Carolina who grumbled about the "rites and revels" his slaves practiced, and throughout the colonies white owners labeled slaves "heathens and pagans." By comparison, of the many daring slave rebellions in the nineteenth century, those fomented by Denmark Vesey in 1822, and Nat Turner in 1831, were based in "black messianic Christianity."

The stereotype that African occultism was "something dark, hidden, and secret" was untrue, wrote Lawrence Levine.[7] Unfortunately, neither Christianity nor African occult religions and practices helped foster better relations between or united the races. The expectation that the mingling of black and white spiritual beliefs might lead to integration or improved conditions for African-Americans never came to fruition. In the North and South, white churches prohibited blacks or required segregated seating. Black churches developed on their own as unique—and separate—institutions.

By the 1760s and 1770s, patriot leaders were consumed with plans for independence from England, and political strategies commanded far more attention than did miraculous or metaphysical phenomena. Colonists who favored liberty and the Revolutionary War supported the Whig Party. Those who remained loyal to the British Crown were Tories. For as long as Enlightenment philosophy held sway and the Revolutionary War preoccupied Americans, the occult and supernatural were overshadowed.

One of America's most remarkable men of the eighteenth century was Benjamin Franklin.[8] Born in Boston in 1706 to a devout Calvinist family, as a child he obediently attended church. However, in his teens, he began to feel differently about his parents' unyielding religious beliefs, finding them intellectually confining. An avid reader, he'd studied the science of Newton, and the "social philosophy" of Locke; he found deism more rational and appealing than the constraints of Christian dogma. As a young man, Franklin set about creating his own ideology, based largely on deist principles, and always maintained a belief in God or, as he sometimes referred to Him, the "Grand Architect or First Cause." Although never dogmatic or rigid, he recognized the need for a faith or creed to direct and bind people toward productivity and performing good deeds for others, even as he strongly advocated religious tolerance. He even had a friendship with a well-known revivalist preacher, George Whitfield, although the two men could not have been further apart theologically.

What has unfortunately been omitted from most traditional accounts of Franklin's life was his curiosity about mysticism and interest in reincarnation, despite some historical interpretations that Franklin did not believe in the "immortality of the soul." We know him as a scientist, an inventor, a printer, and a statesman, but we know far less regarding his religious and metaphysical beliefs, which he kept as private as he could. The story of his move from Boston to Philadelphia as a young man to become a printer is familiar, as are his experiments with electricity, and his rise to fame. Less known is the fact that when Franklin was only twenty-two, he composed one of the most noted—and unusual—epitaphs in American history that suggested the idea of reincarnation[9]:

The body of B. Franklin,

Printer,

Like the cover of an old book,

Its contents torn out

And

Stripped of its lettering and gilding,

Lies here

Food for worms,

But the work shall not be wholly lost,

For it will, as he believed,

Appear once more,

In a new and more perfect edition

Revised and corrected

By the author

Here, Franklin's belief in reincarnation is obvious. "Observing the 'great frugality' of nature, which the Deity had designed so as to ensure that nothing once created was lost, Franklin supposed that something similar applied to souls," wrote H. W. Brands in *The First American* (2000).

"When I see nothing annihilated, and not even a drop of water wasted, I cannot suspect the annihilation of souls, or believe he will suffer the daily waste of millions of minds ready made that now exist, and put himself to the continual trouble of making new ones," Franklin wrote.[10] "Thus finding myself to exist in the world, I believe I shall, in some shape or other, always exist; and with all the inconveniences human life is liable to, I shall not object to a new edition of mine; hoping however, that the errata of the last may be corrected."

Franklin apparently understood the controversy his reincarnation beliefs might engender, for he was careful whom he told, and warned others with like opinions to apply the same wariness.

Toward the end of his long and remarkably productive life, Franklin was asked by an acquaintance what his religious beliefs were. He wrote back that he indeed believed in "one God, creator of the universe." About Jesus, Franklin offered, "I think the system of morals and his religion, as he left them to us, is the best the world ever saw or is likely to see." Franklin also said he considered "that the soul of man is immortal," a marked change and contradiction to his earlier beliefs. Touching upon the question of an afterlife, the great American patriot had this to say: "I shall only add, respecting myself, that, having experienced the goodness of that being in conducting me prosperously through a long life, I have no doubt of its continuance in the next, though without the smallest conceit of meriting such goodness."

These thoughts were not his only venture into the so-called occult or supernatural. While still in college, Franklin understood astrology well enough that he charted a horoscope for another student, even predicting the precise time of the fellow's death.

In 1731, he became a member of the Freemasons[11]; the Philadelphia lodge he joined was believed to have later influenced the French Revolution. In Franklin's lifetime, the Freemasons was a fraternal organization useful for someone with political aspirations or seeking upward mobility. The Masons would attract many who wanted independence from England, including a number of the Founding Fathers, and there, young Franklin, only twenty-five, would meet some of the city's better-known and more influential citizens. But the Freemasons also included occult elements, as did other secret societies.

Franklin also explored the ancient mystical beliefs of the Rosicrucian movement. At one time, when Franklin was a Philadelphia printer, he worked for the cloistered religious community at Ephrata, Pennsylvania, "whose zealous teachings combined Christianity with mysticism."[12] With access to the sect's library, he learned occult concepts he later shared with George Washington, who was in contact with the group's leaders as well. "Astrological medicine" had been practiced at Ephrata, while healers taught at the "mystical Rosicrucian" community near Philadelphia.

In 1784, Franklin was named to a committee of the Academie des Sciences in Paris[13] to investigate animal magnetism, the forerunner of modern hypnotism, first discovered by Austrian physician Franz Anton Mesmer. It supposedly was a method of healing produced by a newly discovered "physical force." But the committee concluded there was no evidence of any such energy as "animal magnetism," and attributed healing effects in patients to their own imaginations. It was a serious blow to Mesmer's work and reputation at the time.

Is it possible the great American patriot and thinker, Benjamin Franklin, possessed psychic ability of his own? It's unlikely he ever would have admitted it, given his penchant for holding closely his personal beliefs. But consider that many of his so-called scientific "guesses" bordered on clairvoyance. For example, "the shifting of the earth's magnetic and geographic poles, about the fluid nature of the earth's interior and its relation to surface structure were remarkably prescient, identifying a research agenda that would keep geophysicists busy into the twenty-first century," wrote H. W. Brands. In his own lifetime, Franklin's far-reaching ideas encouraged considerable dialogue among scientifically minded peers. His great mind was stilled—on earth, at least—when he died on April 17, 1790, at the age of eighty-four, with several family members at his bedside.

We mentioned a little earlier that in 1731, Benjamin Franklin joined the Freemasons in their Philadelphia lodge, newly started in 1730. He later became its grand master, and then grand master of all Masons in Pennsylvania. Freemasonry had considerable influence on fomenting the American revolutionary spirit, attracting many patriots as members.[14] It was a fraternal organization as well as a secret society; its principles were based on an acceptance of God coupled with ancient mystical elements. No one can say with certainty what the origins of Freemasonry were or its age, but it's generally believed it developed from the stonemasons' guilds during the Middle Ages that constructed magnificent cathedrals and castles.

In order to survive, secret societies in Europe presented an outward demeanor that conformed to established church teachings. Privately, it was another story, however; the societies held to ancient mystical and occult traditions and doctrines, some that dated back to pre-Christian pagan beliefs. Many people were likely attracted to these societies, intrigued by "the art and power of magic" they professed to offer. No one can say with certainty how the "Craft," as Masonic practice is called, was able to transmit Ancient Mysteries or how its traditions remained hidden from the Church through the Dark Ages and the Inquisition, according to W. Kirk MacNulty in *Freemasonry: A Journey Through Ritual and Symbol* (1991).

The working masons of medieval times often left small carvings in the stone buildings and cathedrals they constructed. The best speculation is that the carvings represented demons or "imaginary" spirit beings possibly associated with afterlife beliefs. There has long been speculation about the origins of Freemasonry symbolism. Some date it back to the Old Testament given the "many biblical references such as the symbolic use of Solomon's Temple." Freemasonry "also takes many of its symbols from Renaissance mystical tradition," MacNulty wrote. In seventeenth-century England, the first important Masonic leader was Elias Ashmole, an astrologer; and the first Grand Lodge was formed in London in 1717.

The Freemasons became the most influential secret society in colonial America. Many of the Founding Fathers and leaders of the American Revolution, including George Washington, were Masons and a number of them were also deists or "freethinkers." Masons were in the forefront of the revolutionary cause and were largely responsible for guiding America to victory. According to historian Bernard Fay, "Benjamin Franklin established a network of Masonic newspapers throughout the colonies" as the Freemasons became increasingly popular. "Franklin did more to establish Freemasonry in America than any other man of his time," wrote J. Hugo Tatsch, author of *Freemasonry in the Thirteen Colonies* (1995).[15]

In addition to Franklin and Washington, other prominent early Americans and patriots who were Freemasons included Paul Revere, John Singleton Copley, Joseph Warren, General Henry Dearborn, William Franklin, John Hancock, Marquis de Lafayette, James Madison, John Marshall, James Monroe, James Oglethorpe, General Israel Putnam, General John Stark, Major General John Sullivan, John Paul Jones, Lord Baltimore, the Sons of Liberty, at least seven signers of the Declaration of Independence, thirteen signers of the United States Constitution, no less than a dozen of George Washington's generals, nearly half of all officers who served in the American Revolution, the majority of the Continental Congress in 1776, and even Benedict Arnold—before he turned traitor to the American cause.

It was the Freemasons who carried out the legendary Boston Tea Party on December 16, 1773, to protest the imposition of a British tax on tea.[16] The so-called party likely originated in a Boston tavern where the Masons regularly met. Dressed as Native Americans, they were seen leaving the tavern before the Tea Party commenced; however, no one claimed to see any of them enter the tavern. In their disguises, the patriots hurried to the docks where the British ships were berthed, and dumped the cargo of tea overboard. Then the band headed back to the tavern from where they dispersed; again, without being seen by any witnesses, according to historian Bernard Fay.[17]

Critics of Freemasonry mainly based their attacks on the secret nature of the Craft, and insisted it was "an occult religion of Cabbalistic Gnosticism," wrote author Paul A. Fisher in *Behind the Lodge Door*.[18] Masons were not adverse to revolution; they were more than merely a fraternal organization, they constituted "a government in itself," Fisher explained. During the eighteenth century, Freemasons embraced Enlightenment principles, such as support for a democratic government and opposition to the English Crown.

Masonry's mark is embedded in the Great Seal of the United States,[19] which, among other places, appears on the back of the dollar bill. There is the depiction of the "divine" or "all-seeing eye" atop the pyramid, a symbol of Masonry; and the phrase NOVUS ORDO SECLORUM that translates to "New Order of the Age," is a reference to "the realities of this world as distinguished from divine realities."[20]

Above the all-seeing eye of the pyramid is the phrase ANNUIT COEPTIS, meaning, "He is the Divinity looking favorably on the new but incomplete nation." Both quotations were taken by the Founding Fathers from the Roman poet Virgil. On the banner being held in the eagle's beak are the words E PLURIBUS UNUM, Latin for "Out of Many, One," an original phrase created by the designers of the Seal.

Why does the Great Seal of the United States depict a pyramid?[21] "The enigma of the Great Pyramid has long captured the imagination of countless students and masters of metaphysics," explained Max Toth, author of *Pyramid Prophecies*, and a longtime Freemason. "It is obvious that the ancients conveyed one simple fact through their construction—that is, their knowledge is still superior to our present-day technology." He added, "We stand in awe of their amazing mental prowess. . . . A tremendous amount of cabbalistic and occult symbolism have been attached to and derived from the Pyramid. The Masons as well as the Rosicrucians have embodied the Pyramid within their mysticism and secret rituals."

By 1776, when the Continental Congress of the United States decided to create the Great Seal, the designers already had in mind a plan to include the Great Pyramid. To achieve the task, the Congress appointed three committees that met between 1776 and 1782. Significantly, all the committees included Freemasons; as a result all three designs submitted showed "Freemasonry's influence—in symbolism such as the eye of providence, a triangle, a Pharaoh, Moses, clouds, stars, constellations, olive branch, and phoenix," Toth noted.

In 1782, the Congress approved a design for a seal that included an American eagle on one side, representing the phoenix, the mythical bird that rose from the ashes to live again.[22] In its beak is a parchment with the saying, E PLURIBUS UNUM and thirteen "tail feathers." On the eagle's breast is a shield containing thirteen stripes. The eagle's wings are spread and it is carrying an olive branch with thirteen leaves in its right talon or claw, while in its left is a cluster of thirteen arrows. Above the bird's head is an emblem in which there is a group of thirteen stars shaped as a figure of a "Mogen David" bursting through a cloud.

On the other side of the Great Seal is the incomplete pyramid. The "eye of providence" is in a triangle that appears to hover at the top of the pyramid; and from the eye a light radiates. The words ANNUIT COEPTIS are above the pyramid's top or "capstone." The pyramid contains thirteen horizontal layers of brick. At the pyramid's base—the bottom row—are the Roman numerals for 1776: MDCCLXXVI. At the bottom of the seal is a scroll or banner with the saying NOVUS ORDO SECLORUM.

When George Washington was sworn in as the first president of the United States on April 30, 1789,[23] he was administered the oath by Robert Livingston, a Masonic Grand Master who borrowed a Bible from a nearby Masonic Lodge in New York City, then the capital of the country. The Bible was opened to the Old Testament Book of Genesis 49; and Washington placed his hands on verses 13 to 33.[24]

What's significant about the Masonic influence on the founding of the

United States is the spiritual and mystical knowledge borrowed from various "ancient schools and philosophies," including the Bible, the teachings of Plato, Pythagoras, Rosicrucianism, and Kabbalah. According to Toth, "Cabbalistic influence appears to be greatest in Freemasonry and reveals itself very dramatically in the Great Seal of the United States."

Kabbalah, ancient Jewish mysticism, contains elements of numerology and true to its belief in the occult significance of numbers is the frequency with which the number "13" appears, and is repeated in connection with the founding of the country. Here are just a few examples:

- The phrase E PLURIBUS UNUM has thirteen letters.
- The phrase ANNUIT COEPTIS has thirteen letters.
- "July the Fourth" contains thirteen letters.
- "American Eagle" contains thirteen letters.
- The numbers "76," the year the Declaration of Independence was signed, adds up to thirteen in numerology ($7 + 6 = 13$).
- The motto IN GOD WE TRUST adds up to 13 if numerology is applied. Each letter has a numerical equivalent, so that $I = 9$, $N = 14$, $G = 7$, and so forth. Added together the sum of the phrase is 175, and when $1 + 7 + 5$ is totaled, it equals 13.
- At his inauguration, George Washington placed his hand on the Bible, and opened it to Genesis 49. In numerology, 49 or $4 + 9 = $ equals 13.

Those who do not accept numerology, or deny its relevance to the founding of the new nation, miss the point.[25] It makes no difference whether we believe in the occult meaning of numbers; what matters is that some of the Founding Fathers did, and they applied it to the creation of the Great Seal of the United States. In addition to the above examples, remember the frequency with which the number "13" appears in the Great Seal on the dollar bill:

- There are 13 tail feathers on the eagle.
- There are 13 stripes on the eagle's breast.
- There are 13 arrows in the eagle's left claw.
- There are 13 horizontal rows in the pyramid.
- There are 13 stars above the eagle's head.
- There are 13 leaves on the olive branch in the eagle's right talon.

Researchers have concluded that the designers of the Great Seal definitely emphasized the number "13." It appears their primary intention was "to commemorate the thirteen states forming the new nation." In doing so the planners, including Benjamin Franklin, for all their arguments about rational thinking and reason, drew from Freemasonry and the occult in their hopes for the new country. Some think that numerology was not the only occult system that showed itself in the founding of the United States. Astrology also may have figured in the beginning of the country, believed nationally recognized astrologer William Marshall.

"The horoscope for the Declaration of Independence reveals the sun in thirteen degrees of the sign Cancer and makes thirteen degrees ascendant of the sign Scorpio, which sign is also represented by the number 13 in the ancient Rosicrucian and Masonic tarot keys," Toth explained. Whether it is coincidence or superstition, as skeptics maintain, or there was some occult intent in the founding of the nation cannot be answered, it depends on which view one holds.

Considering how often the number 13 appears in the Great Seal of the United States it's conceivable that Masonic influence may also have had as its goal "a possible key to the destiny of the United States, which in turn will affect the destiny of the rest of the world," Toth concluded.

If the Founding Fathers did, in fact, employ occult ideas and symbols in creating the new nation it seems that their so-called "rationalist" thinking stopped at the doors of the Masonic lodge; or they considered mysticism compatible with Enlightenment and deist philosophy. Either way, their positions appear contradictory and puzzling, and their relationship to the occult open to many questions. What we do know is that their actions helped them arrive at the founding of a democratic system of government and the overthrowing of the British monarchy in America.

For those brought up with the belief that the Founding Fathers were Christians, part of their story has been expunged from American history. While acknowledging the United States as a Christian nation in their day, most patriot leaders were deists, religious liberals, freethinkers, or Freemasons—not fundamentalist Christians.

One of the eighteenth century's most brilliant American thinkers and "political leaders" was Thomas Jefferson (1743–1826). A Founding Father, almost without equal, he was the principal author of the Declaration of Independence, one of America's first foreign ambassadors, the new nation's second vice president, and then the third president of the United States for two terms. Lest we paint him as some colonial superhero, Jefferson was not without faults and controversy. He faced criticism and derision because of his long relationship with a pretty black slave named Sally Hemings, and with their offspring. There was also the obvious contradiction about the man who could write the eloquent words, "All men are created equal," in the Declaration of Independence and, at the same time, own an estimated two hundred slaves on his Virginia plantations. Although he spoke and wrote against slavery, he never engaged in political leadership against it; and a condemnation of the slave trade was deleted from the Declaration.

Jefferson was also severely criticized for his deist beliefs.[26] He was often branded an atheist by clergy of other denominations who feared his influence might take America on a road away from Christianity, to the point where he'd demolish churches, and do away with the Bible. Supporters, of course, praised his "rational religion." Clearly, Jefferson was the epitome of an Enlightenment thinker; to him every religion needed a "rational component." Needless to say, for Jefferson, supernatural events did not seem to fall within his definition of "reason."

Once, when called an infidel by a minister who vehemently opposed his political aspirations, Jefferson's answer was succinct and wry: "My opinion is that there would never have been an infidel, if there had never been a priest."

Yet he wrote to fellow patriot John Adams that he could not comprehend how anybody could dispute there is "a Creator of the World, a being whom we see not and know not." But Jefferson apparently had problems accepting how "miracles" might occur; he could not believe that the laws of nature would be interrupted or deferred to permit miraculous events. While, on the one hand, he fought for "religious liberty," he carefully studied the Bible, and concluded that much of the Scriptures were irrational, even preposterous. In opposing the establishment of an official church, Jefferson was the designer of the constitutional concept of separation of church and state, an issue as contentious today as it was in his time.

At the end of his life Jefferson had one of the most curious psychic incidents in American history.[27] Once political adversaries, after Jefferson and his predecessor John Adams both left the White House, they became close friends, and engaged in a long correspondence in which they shared many opinions and thoughts on the great issues of their day. Jefferson retired to his home at Monticello, Virginia; Adams returned to Quincy, Massachusetts.

It was at his home in Quincy that John Adams died at the age of ninety on July 4, 1826, the fiftieth anniversary of the signing of the Declaration of Independence. Among his last words were, "Thomas Jefferson still survives!" Unbeknownst to Adams, in an era before instant communications, his dear friend Jefferson, at Monticello, on that very same day, and only hours before Adams's passing, also departed this physical world. On his deathbed, Jefferson asked, "Is this the Fourth of July?" Yes, he was told. Then he passed on, at the age of eighty-three.

Rationalists and skeptics dismiss as coincidence the deaths of two of America's great patriots and presidents, as well as dear personal friends, on the same day—the nation's birthday. But was it something beyond that? Carl Jung, founder of analytical psychology, advanced the theory of synchronicity to explain "meaningful coincidences," which are not obviously connected by cause and effect. An incident of synchronicity is a chance occurrence that is so unlikely it is reasonable to assume it is founded on some as yet unexplained precept. What might be responsible for synchronous events? Is there a supernatural component? Might there be an element of premonition involved?

Adams and Jefferson had developed a strong emotional bond, the result of their long and close association, and prolific exchange of many deeply felt thoughts. Therefore, it is not unreasonable to conclude a psychic link or connection existed between them. Had Jefferson's spirit materialized to help his friend ease the transition to the afterlife? Had Adams chosen to make the transition to the next stage of life with his esteemed friend? Far from coincidence, people on the brink of death often sense or experience visions of predeceased loved ones or individuals close to them. If the deaths of the two famed patriots and former presidents on the Fourth of July in 1826 were beyond chance, it would have been the ultimate irony for them as "rational thinkers."

The story of George Washington's vision at Valley Forge is one of the greatest tales of prophetic visions in American history.[28] It was there, if the story is true, that a new era in modern history began when Washington was visited by an angel prophesizing the victory of America and establishment of a new moral force in the world.

The bitter conditions that General Washington and his tattered troops found themselves at Valley Forge when they arrived on December 19, 1777, could have weakened any soldier's spirit, after they'd been forced to retreat from New York. Now the freezing rain and biting winds that greeted them was the darkest hour Washington had experienced as commander of the American Continental Army. Only miles away, the powerful and far better equipped British Army occupied Philadelphia. The War for Independence was not going well if Valley Forge was any indication. The hard frozen ground was covered by sheets of ice that cut into the frostbitten feet of the sentries guarding the general. Dangerously low on provisions and other supplies, the Americans could not have moved if they wanted to; their escape routes had been blocked by the British garrison.

Washington was alone in his command. His own staff had become demoralized, adding to the misery his threadbare and hungry soldiers were suffering, unprotected from the harsh winter wind, and with no hope of reinforcements. The general knew he needed help and some way to keep his army together. But from where would aid come? Although publicly stoic, he agonized privately for his men in what seemed to be utterly hopeless circumstances. He implored the Almighty for help and comfort. Often his prayers and meditations were offered secretly in a thicket, where, with bowed head, he appealed for strength and guidance.

He'd written to the Board of War, but his complaints largely fell on deaf ears. On December 31, 1777, Washington wrote to Governor William Livingston: "A dreadful year. Our sick naked, our well naked, our unfortunate men in captivity naked." Washington angrily called upon Congress for help, predicting the army would be forced to "starve, dissolve, or disperse in order to obtain subsistence." But Congress, already critical of Washington's leadership, had fled from the nation's capital in Philadelphia before the advancing British; thus they were unwilling or unable to provide any aid.

There was little food to be found. Supplies of beef and pork were nearly depleted. In addition, the American soldiers had not been paid for several months. The conditions grew so severe that pieces of clothing from those who died of illness and disease were reissued to the living.

There would eventually be four thousand soldiers in these deplorable circumstances. Against the background of this desperate situation, General Washington was prepared for his soldiers to mutiny.

The general himself wrote on April 21, 1778, "To see men without clothes to cover their nakedness, without blankets to lie on, without shoes—by which their marches might be traced by the blood from their feet—and almost as often without provisions as with, marching through frost and snow at Christmas taking up their winter quarters within a day's march of the enemy, without a house or hut to cover them until they could be built . . . in my opinion scarce can be paralleled."

Despite his devotion and respect for the troops, Washington feared his army was on the verge of collapse. To his surprise and relief, however, the men remained steadfastly loyal, despite some anger and grumbling. They neither mutinied nor deserted, and their devotion in the face of terrible deprivation brought tears to Washington's eyes. He thanked them deeply for their unswerving loyalty. "Naked and starving as they are, we cannot enough admire the incomparable patience and fidelity of the soldiery," he wrote.

Throughout the misery at Valley Forge, Washington maintained his composure and steel-like courage. His officers described him as "calm and firm," despite the brutal conditions. During this period, he often called upon his deep faith in God. Washington believed that the American people were under the direct protective care of God, and that he had been personally directed and shielded by the Almighty.

One cold gray day in early 1778, when all seemed lost, General Washington sat at a crude wooden table in his headquarters. He was preparing a dispatch, when he glanced up. To his surprise, before him was, according to his own description, an "apparition of a beautiful woman."

He said he was riveted by her gaze and unable to rise from his seat. "My thought itself became paralyzed!" he later recalled. "So astonished was I that it was some moments before I found language to inquire the purpose of her presence, for I had given strict orders not to be disturbed.

"I felt strange sensations spreading through me. I assayed once more to address her, but my tongue had become useless!"

Washington recalled that for a moment he thought he was dying, believing the presence of an angel was a sign that he was about to make the transition to the afterlife.

"Gradually the surrounding atmosphere seemed filled with sensations, and grew luminous. Everything about me seemed to rarefy; the mysterious visitor herself becoming more airy and yet more distinct to my sight than ever.

"I did not think, I did not reason. I did not move. All that was impossible. I was conscious only of gazing fixedly, vacantly at my companion."

Washington continued, "Presently I heard a voice saying, 'Son of the Republic, look and learn!'" Now the visitor extended her arm eastward, and Washington saw a heavy white vapor rising at a distance. "This gradually dissipated, and I looked upon a strange scene," he said. "Before me lay spread out in one vast plain all the countries of the world—Europe, Asia, Africa, and America.

"I saw rolling and tossing between Europe and America, the billows of the Atlantic. And between Asia and America lay the Pacific. 'Son of the Republic,' said the mysterious voice, as before, 'look and learn.' At that moment I beheld a dark shadowy being, like an angel, standing or rather, in midair between Europe and America.

"Dipping water out of the ocean in the hollow of each hand, he sprinkled some upon America with his right hand, while with his left hand he cast some on Europe. Immediately a cloud arose from those countries, and joined in mid-ocean. For a while it remained stationary, and then it moved slowly westward, until it enveloped America in its murky folds.

"Sharp flashes of lightning gleamed through it at intervals; and I heard the smothered groans and cries of the American people. A second time the angel dipped water from the ocean and sprinkled it as before. The dark cloud was then drawn back into the ocean, in whose heaving bellows it sank from view. A third time I heard the mysterious voice say: 'Son of the Republic, look and learn.' I cast my eyes upon America and beheld villages and towns and cities springing up, one after another, until the whole land [was] dotted with them. Again I heard the mysterious voice say: 'Son of the Republic, the end of the century cometh, look and learn.'

"And with this the dark shadowy figure turned its face southward, and from Africa I saw an ill-omened specter approaching our land. The inhabitants presently set themselves in battle array against each other. As I continued looking at the bright angel, on whose brow rested a crown of light on which was traced the word UNION, I saw the angel place an

American flag between the divided nation, and say, 'Remember, ye are brethren.' Instantly, the inhabitants, casting from them their weapons, became friends once more, and united around the National Standard."

Washington described his angelic encounter further. "And again I heard the mysterious voice saying, 'Son of the Republic, look and learn.' At this, the dark shadowy angel placed a trumpet to his mouth and blew three distinct blasts; and taking water from the ocean, he sprinkled it upon Europe, Asia, and Africa. Then my eyes beheld a fearful sight: From each of these countries arose thick, black clouds that were soon joined into one.

"And throughout this mass there gleamed a dark red light, by which I saw hordes of armed men, who moving with the dark cloud, marched by land and sailed by sea to America; which country was enveloped in the volume of clouds. And I dimly saw these vast armies devastate the whole country and burn the villages, towns, and cities that I beheld springing up.

"As my ears listened to the thunder of the cannon, the clashing of swords, and the shouts and cries of millions in mortal combat, I again heard the mysterious voice saying, 'Son of the Republic, look and learn.' As the voice ceased the shadowy angel, for the last time, dipped water from the ocean and sprinkled it upon America. Instantly the dark cloud rolled back, together with the armies it had brought, leaving the inhabitants of the land victorious.

"Then once more I beheld the villages, towns, and cities, springing up where I had seen them before; while the bright angel planting the azure standard he had brought in the midst of them, cried with a loud voice: 'While the stars remain in the heaven [and] send down dew upon the earth, so long shall the Union last.' And taking from his brow the crown on which was blazoned the word UNION he placed it upon the standard, while people, kneeling down said, 'Amen.' "

Finally, General Washington concluded, "The scene instantly began to fade and dissolve, and I at last saw nothing but the rising, curling vapor I at first beheld. This also disappearing, I found myself once more gazing upon the voice I had heard before, [and it] said, 'Son of the Republic, what you have just seen is thus interpreted: Three great perils will come upon the Republic. The most fearful for her is the third; but the whole world united shall not prevail against her. Let every child of the Republic learn to live for his God, his land, and his Union.'

"With these words, the vision vanished. I started from my seat, and felt I had seen a vision wherein had been shown to me the birth, progress, and destiny of the United States."

Could George Washington actually have had an encounter with an angel? Might a messenger of God have come to Washington to help him survive the miseries of the terrible winter at Valley Forge? Had the angelic being truly provided the general with a vision of America's future?

Washington certainly thought so. Some time after his remarkable encounter, he shared the experience with a close aide, a young man named Anthony Sherman, who years later, in 1859, retold the account to reporter Wesley Bradshaw, who then published it in the *National Tribune* in 1880.

Portions of Washington's prophetic vision seemed to refer to slavery in America, the divided opinions people had about the insidious issue, the eventual Civil War, and the ultimate reuniting of the nation as one. The apparition had warned that "three great perils" would befall the Republic. The most fearful, the angel warned, would be the third. Were these future wars that America was destined to win? Which wars? Though there have been different interpretations, the likeliest is that the apparition predicted the outcome of the American Revolutionary War, the Civil War, and World War I.

Washington told confidants he was deeply inspired by the angelic visitation, whose appearance restored his faith in the cause for American independence. He was certain the angel's message had meant he would see victory, despite the hardships. When spring arrived, the muddy, impassable roads dried, and fresh supplies were delivered. The American troops had not only survived, they'd emerged a stronger and better-organized Continental Army, more ready to face the British and their paid Hessian confederates.

The American cause also received help from two renowned European military experts: the skilled Prussian Baron von Steuben, and the brilliant young Frenchman the Marquis de Lafayette, who ultimately convinced France to send troops and supplies to aid the Americans. Eventually, Washington led his troops to victory over the British at the battle of Yorktown, Virginia, in 1781, where the surrender of British general Lord Cornwallis effectively ended all hostilities. It had been an astounding turn of events for Washington.

Was this purely a supernatural vision or, in fact, a messenger from God in answer to Washington's devout prayers? Angel or apparition, the vision comforted and inspired Washington when his situation seemed absolutely hopeless. Thus, even before there was a president of the United States, even before there was a United States, the supernatural had intervened.

It is a belief as old as humankind: Every person on earth has a guardian angel charged with the responsibility to watch over and protect them. Washington's angelic visitor, of profound importance to the destiny of the new nation, may have altered the course of events. Such visitations have been reported throughout history, in virtually every culture and religion, and centuries before the birth of Christ. Millions have experienced the effects of angelic interventions.

It is common during wartime for soldiers to accept a deeper connection with religion and God, because of their proximity to battle and potential death. Paranormal researchers have also noted that psychic experiences are more frequent in times of war. Thus, it is not unusual for soldiers to claim they have witnessed angelic beings or other apparitions, which often provide protection in the face of combat.

Protective "angels on the battlefield," as they have been called, have played a significant role in many struggles throughout history, most notably in the case of Joan of Arc. George Washington's vision at Valley Forge qualifies as a meeting with an angel on the battlefield.

Although skeptics would argue that angels on the battlefield are a product of stress or hallucination produced by the dangers of war, there is ample evidence to suggest otherwise. In many instances, angelic visitations have communicated information unknown to the recipient at the time of the encounter. As well, in some experiences, there have been multiple witnesses, suggesting that hallucination or imagination is an unlikely explanation.

One question asked by some is why no mention is made of Washington's angelic vision in his well-known diaries.[29] Although Washington kept diaries for many years that reveal much about his activities and private thoughts, he did not keep a journal during most of the Revolutionary War. His necessary preoccupation with the demands of war made it difficult to maintain a diary. Thus, with no personal written record for the period from June 19, 1775, to January 1780, we have no entries about the angelic visitation at Valley Forge. Washington did not resume his diary until 1781.

Historians and parapsychologists are left to ponder the role of the supernatural in the course of General Washington's leadership. Many traditional historians ignore the story altogether. In fact, some make no reference whatsoever to Washington's religious or spiritual side. For example, in 2004, a highly touted biography about George Washington was written that ignored Washington's religious beliefs and the angelic vision because the author was an atheist. Although Washington was nominally an Episcopalian, he was more a man of deep personal faith than a blind follower of organized religion.

What was on Washington's mind when he wrote to a friend named Thomas Nelson in Virginia in August 1778? Washington's letter reflected on the bitter winter at Valley Forge he and his men survived, and suggested a supernatural force had saved them:

> The hand of Providence has been so conspicuous in all this that he must be worse than [an] infidel that lacks faith, and more wicked that has not gratitude to acknowledge his obligations . . .

Did the mysterious apparition so profoundly affect Washington that the experience influenced his thinking, even in future political philosophy?

After serving two successful terms as the first president of the United States, Washington retired to his home at Mount Vernon, Virginia, where he died on December 14, 1799, at the age of sixty-seven.

Typically, ghost stories about the presidents have not found their way into traditional American history; they are largely relegated to folklore and legend. However, in the case of George Washington's spirit, the credibility of the witnesses and situations in which his apparition was encountered long after his death deserve mention. There is also the degree to which the apparition influenced those who saw it.

One evening in 1850, John C. Calhoun of South Carolina, long one of America's most prominent and influential politicians, then in his late sixties and ailing, glanced up from where he sat in his Washington, D.C., home to notice a visitor standing before him. He soon realized it was an apparition, specifically the spirit countenance of George Washington. Why would Washington appear to John Calhoun?

Calhoun soon learned the purpose of Washington's ghostly return. The Father of His Country had come to warn Calhoun about the danger to the nation of secession. As the antislavery movement gathered momentum in the North, Calhoun had stubbornly defended the evils of slavery, although he worried openly about secession as a result of the divisive issue.

Shortly after the visitation, Calhoun accurately predicted that secession would occur in the next decade. He cautioned ominously in an emotional address to Congress that, "The dissolution of the Union is the heaviest blow that can be struck at civilization and representative government."

Many criticized Calhoun's dire prediction. Unfortunately, his admonition was ignored and a decade later, the United States was in the throes of the bloody Civil War. But few likely realized that Calhoun's all too accurate warning to Congress was inspired by the vision of George Washington. On the day he died, March 31, 1850, Calhoun's last words were: "The South . . . the poor South."

Perhaps Calhoun's experience with George Washington was merely a dream. Then again, maybe it wasn't.

Union Army General George McClellan also reported an encounter with the apparition of George Washington.[30] Lincoln had appointed him, but McClellan had not moved his army into position to defend Washington, D.C., as Lincoln urged. One night the dashing young West Point graduate was deeply engrossed in military maps and reports. It was about two in the morning when McClellan fell asleep. He said his brief nap was interrupted when he heard his room door open, and then felt a hand on his shoulder. Next he heard a "solemn voice" say, "General McClellan, do you sleep on your post? Rouse you, or ere it can be prevented, the foe will be upon Washington."

McClellan next saw what he described as a "living map" that showed him a vast part of the United States. When the general turned in the direction of the mysterious voice, before him was an apparition that at first he did not recognize. The mysterious voice repeated to him, "General McClellan, your time is short. Look to the southward." The general obeyed and turned to look at the living map. In it he saw cities, villages, fortifications, tents, bodies of soldiers, hills, valleys, cannons, and many other details.

McClellan interpreted the vision to mean that he was being given knowledge that "would insure a speedy and happy termination of the war." The voice again warned him, "Tarry not, your time is short." McClellan said he felt a chill as he realized he was seeing "masses of enemy forces being hurried to certain points . . .

"Ruin and defeat seemed to stare me in the face," McClellan reflected. The voice repeated its warning. Then he noticed a "shining light" had accompanied the apparition. When McClellan looked again, the apparition was no longer a shadowy figure. It was George Washington. "Were I to live forever, never . . . should I forget what I saw." McClellan watched and listened in awe as Washington's apparition raised his hands above the Union commander's head. McClellan had the feeling Washington blessed him.

Then there was a clap of thunder. The apparition had ceased speaking and McClellan watched the figure in awe until it disappeared. Now McClellan noticed that someone had "literally covered his maps with a net of pencil signs and figures." The detailed military information it provided would have taken McClellan years to gather and record.

McClellan interpreted the message from George Washington's spirit to mean: "The American Union is saved."

While that communication proved to be prophetic, McClellan's personal fortunes were not as successful. He did not heed the apparition's warning, "Tarry not, your time is short." Within a year of his appointment as commander of the United States Army, President Lincoln realized McClellan could not lead the Northern Army to victory. McClellan's hesitant approach to battle finally frustrated the president, and after several unsuccessful attacks in Virginia, Lincoln removed him from command. General Ulysses S. Grant eventually led the Union Army to victory.

What should history make of McClellan's obvious paranormal experience? Many psychic experiences take place in a state somewhere between sleeping and being awake. Was McClellan's encounter merely a dream or hallucination? Such glimpses of future events often reveal themselves through clairvoyance or second sight. Another paranormal theory is that McClellan had astral traveled, meaning his spirit left his body during the time he was asleep, and thus witnessed details he could not otherwise have known. Today we sometimes call these out-of-body experiences by the term *remote viewing*.

The most startling apparition reported of George Washington occurred in 1863, nearly sixty-four years after his death.[31] The place was the Battle of Gettysburg, dubbed "the greatest battle ever fought on the North American continent." It began on the morning of July 1, 1863, in the small Pennsylvania town where several major roads from different directions all came together.

By the next day, 85,000 Union troops faced 75,000 Confederate troops, under the leadership of General Robert E. Lee, as he tried to break through to the North. Eventually the two armies totaled more than 170,000 men in and around Gettysburg. One of the Union Army regiments was a contingent from Maine, under the command of Colonel Joshua Chamberlain. His exhausted men had marched all night from Maryland on dismal and fog-shrouded roads, and without precise maps to tell them if they were even heading in the right direction.

Eventually they came to a fork in the road but were not certain which road to take. While they considered what direction to go in, the clouds inexplicably broke, and by the light of the moon, the men saw the outline of someone on horseback. The figure, dressed in a bright coat and tricorn hat, sat atop an imposing light-colored horse. The horseman galloped in the direction of one of the two diverging roads, waving for Chamberlain's soldiers to follow. Some of the men thought General George McClellan had returned to lead them. They cheered wildly with excitement, and despite their obvious exhaustion, followed the figure on horseback.

However, the figure was not General McClellan, who the puzzled men finally figured out was nowhere in the vicinity of Gettysburg. Then one of the soldiers recognized the towering figure on horseback as none other than General George Washington!

Word spread quickly that General Washington's spirit had returned to lead them in the right direction. Despite their fear and exhaustion, the regiment marched with renewed confidence along the dark road. The sight of Washington's apparition seemed divine intervention.

Once they arrived at Gettysburg, the 20th Maine Regiment was ordered to defend a rocky hill known as Little Round Top, which they were instructed to hold "at all hazards" even though Union forces were out-numbered by the Confederates. Little Round Top didn't look like much, but it was critical to a Union victory, and Chamberlain's men were in the best position to defend the strategically important hill.

Meanwhile, all around them, the fighting raged. There were ground-shaking artillery explosions, and blasts of smoke and fire above the treetops. The three-day battle with the Confederates, which began on July 1, 1863, was ferocious. The Rebels from the 4th Alabama Regiment overwhelmingly outnumbered the 20th Maine. Chamberlain's soldiers were also desperately low on ammunition. Surrounded by the Confederates, Chamberlain real-ized it would only be a matter of time before his men would have to surren-der the hill. It was a dangerous and frightening situation.

But Chamberlain made a bold decision not to retreat. Instead he bellowed above the sound of exploding gunfire, "Fix bayonets. Charge!" It was an order tantamount to virtual suicide. He was not even certain his men would obey the command.

Then something happened that could only be described as miraculous or supernatural. The same enigmatic specter on horseback that led the soldiers to Gettysburg again inexplicably materialized. Glowing and with raised sword, the specter urged the soldiers to follow him into bat-tle. The sight of the ghostly figure on horseback inspired the 20th Maine to attack. Charging down the hill into enemy fire with the taste of victory in their mouths, they completely overwhelmed the Confederates who broke and ran for their lives. Both sides suffered heavy casualties.

Little Round Top proved to be one of the most unexpected victories of the Civil War, and one of the most important at Gettysburg. Chamber-lain's daring attack saved Little Round Top and helped maintain the Union defense; many considered his accomplishment nothing short of a miracle—and perhaps it was. The Battle of Gettysburg was a major turn-ing point of the Civil War. The Union victory thwarted the Confederate effort to penetrate the North.

After the Battle of Gettysburg, accounts of Washington's apparition witnessed by hundreds of soldiers resulted in Secretary of War Edwin Stanton's asking the Union Army to investigate. At least one general, in addition to other officers, swore the ghostly image was that of George Washington's face.

Chamberlain later achieved the rank of general, and was awarded the

Congressional Medal of Honor. He also served as president of Bowdoin College, where he had once taught. Afterward, he became governor of Maine, and the incident of Washington's appearance seemed to fade into memory.

Many years after Gettysburg, Chamberlain was asked by a reporter about the story of Washington's ghost leading his troops. Upon hearing the reporter's question, Chamberlain grew pensive, then answered, "Yes, that report was circulated through our lines, and I have no doubt that it inspired the men. Doubtless it was a superstition." Then after a pause, the elderly soldier added, "Who among us can say that such a thing was impossible? We have not yet sounded or explored the immortal life that lies out beyond the Bar. We do not know what mystic power maybe possessed by those who are now bivouacking with the dead. I only know the effect, but I dare not explain or deny the cause. I do believe we were enveloped by the powers of the otherworld that day and who shall say that Washington was not among the number of those who aided the country he founded?" Chamberlain added a final thought, "You could not say from what world they came, or to what world they go."

Gettysburg, where more than 50,000 men lost their lives, and many more were wounded in three days of brutal and bloody fighting, has been called the most haunted battlefield in the nation. And it seems George Washington, who himself was inspired by an apparition at his army's darkest hour, was its most celebrated and important ghost at what could have been the darkest hour of the Union Washington fought so hard to defend.

Adams is a tiny town on the banks of the Red River in north-central Tennessee.[32] In the early nineteenth century, it was home to a wealthy farmer, John Bell, his wife, Lucy, and their children. The Bells were God-fearing people, well liked and respected in their small Baptist community, where they lived comfortably on their thousand-acre farm in the peace and prosperity that followed the Treaty of Ghent that ended the War of 1812.

One especially hot summer day in 1817, as John Bell walked through his cornfield he was stopped short by the sight of a strange creature that he at first mistook for a dog. He'd never seen anything like it before. The animal just sat there motionless and calmly stared at him. It had unusual, almost human-looking eyes. Bell raised his rifle ready to shoot the beast if it attacked him. But suddenly the strange creature began to dim until it disappeared. Bell was incredulous. However, despite the disturbing nature of the incident, he decided not to tell his family so as not to alarm them.

Several days later Bell cautiously returned to the cornfield and was relieved that the odd creature he'd earlier encountered there was gone. But then Bell noticed a large bird perched on a split-rail fence. He stared in astonishment at the gigantic fowl. He'd never seen a bird that size before. Bell realized the strange bird's eyes were identical to the bizarre-looking animal he'd witnessed days earlier. Bell wasted no time firing a rifle shot at the horrific creature. But he missed and the bird spread its massive wings and flew overhead, casting a gigantic shadow on the ground as Bell shivered in terror.

From that moment, never again did the Bell family have any peace. For the next three years, they were haunted and cursed by a sinister and demonic spirit, an evil force that came to be popularly known as the Bell Witch. Actually, from its behavior, it was not a witch at all, but rather a poltergeist or noisy spirit, capable of moving objects and people, even sending them flying. However, unlike most benign or mischievous poltergeists, the Bell Witch proved to be an angry and dangerous force.

Shortly after the encounters in the cornfield, the Bells heard a terrible noise outside their home that sounded as if an animal was scratching at the door. Then the noise grew louder. Someone or something was banging fiercely on the doors and windows. The Bells typically went to bed nightly at nine o'clock, but every night at about ten an incessant thumping began. Whenever Bell would go to the door and open it, the terrible banging ceased, but it resumed when he returned to bed. Usually it ended around midnight. Not surprisingly, the Bells became frazzled.

One day, the inexplicable noise moved indoors. It sounded as if hundreds of little animals were scratching on every surface of the house; the clatter was nerve-racking. Sometimes it seemed as if rodents were gnawing; other times there were choking noises, and the sound of lips smacking. Family members heard chains being dragged, furniture being moved about, and invisible stones pelted at the roof. Might it have been the work of pranksters? Bell and his son kept watch at night, but found no prowlers or anyone lurking about. Bell demanded that family members keep their bizarre supernatural experiences a secret, no matter how frightened or disturbed they were.

A year later, the events grew worse. Even though the scratching noises ceased, the whole house now shook on its foundation as if struck by an earthquake. Some nights the invisible evil force tore covers from the beds as family members slept, striking terror into the children. The Bell family found it increasingly difficult to live normal lives with the presence of the force in and about the house. Then, inexplicably, the witch became even more aggressive and cruel. One night, something struck seven-year-old William Bell, and the boy screamed in pain from blows by the unseen force. He later described the attack as if someone was trying to tear his head off.

The witch seemed angriest with thirteen-year-old Betsy Bell, the only daughter of the eight Bell children still living at home. At first, the poltergeist dragged the terrified child out of bed by her hair. Then the apparently demonic entity cast spells on the pretty little girl, which sometimes lasted up to a half-hour. With each attack, Betsy momentarily lost her breath. The episodes became so severe that she would gasp for air, and then faint. Other times, the invisible force smacked Betsy's face hard enough that red marks appeared where she'd been hit.

Finally the Bells realized they could not keep secret their encounters with the sinister being. Obviously they needed help, so Bell shared his family's ordeal with a trusted friend and lay preacher, James Johnson. Johnson's concern for the Bells' safety was increased after he heard the unearthly noises for himself. This was no tall tale; it was a real demonic possession. His immediate course of action was to call upon God's help, so he conducted an exorcism, read from the Bible, and commanded the evil entity, "Stop, I beseech you, in the name of the Lord!"

The exorcism appeared to work. Incredibly, for a time, the commotion stopped. Relieved that their home was once again peaceful, the Bells gave thanks to God. For the next several weeks, they enjoyed the calm and quiet, free from the frightening and relentless tumult of the past year. The Bells assumed the witch was gone from their lives.

To their dismay, they were wrong. When the unseen entity returned, it was even more enraged. The Bells again called upon the preacher for assistance, and once again, the witch seemed to respond. It was as if the demonic spirit calmed when prayers were offered. However, the poltergeist soon resumed its unceasing noises and assaults, especially against young Betsy Bell. In one incredible incident, Betsy threw up after she drank a foul medicine given to her to combat the witch's spells. The child's vomit contained sharp needles and pins. Mrs. Bell and the family physician both witnessed the event, and were appalled and repulsed. The witch, however, laughed and goaded Betsy to consume more of the putrid tonic so that she might retch again. Lucy Bell gathered the pins and needles, placed them in a closed glass jar, and kept them for the remainder of her life.

The Bells next invited a committee of local citizens to visit and witness the terrible incidents for themselves, and perhaps suggest a solution to free the family from their affliction. This made the witch even more incensed; again, the attacks against Betsy became even harsher. Fearing they could no longer protect her, the Bells sent Betsy to live with neighbors. However, wherever she went, the persistent spirit followed. There seemed no escape from the relentless being who continued to harass other family members, even as it tormented Betsy.

Eventually, as news of the entity spread, the Bell house drew the curious from throughout the region, who came in droves to observe for themselves evidence of the witch. There were times when the spirit complied. One night it whistled and then began to speak in a whisper that became a low female voice. At first, the words were inaudible; then they became clearer. The entity even debated the Bible and the Scriptures with visiting clergy, but when asked to identify itself and its purpose, the witch refused to answer. There were skeptics of the phenomena; some blamed Betsy, claiming the entity's voice was really manufactured by the child. Was Betsy capable of ventriloquism? When a visiting doctor placed his hand over the girl's mouth, the witch's mutterings could still be discerned.

By the summer of 1820, the story reached all the way to Nashville, and newspapers told of the family's troubles. One of those who heard about the witch was none other than General Andrew Jackson, hero of the Battle of New Orleans. Like many others, he was curious about the tale of the elusive and troublesome spirit. After defeating the Creek Indians, facing down the Seminoles, and driving the invading British to the Gulf of Mexico, General Jackson considered himself well equipped to face the Bells' witch.

Jackson, accompanied by several friends, one of them a self-proclaimed "witch-slayer" or exorcist, set out from the Hermitage, his home in Nashville, to the Bell farm to personally witness the bizarre events. Jackson was a skeptic; he even wagered a gallon of "good Tennessee whiskey," insisting the witch did not even exist, let alone engage in all the terrible acts of which it was accused. Jackson reasoned the entire story was either a hoax or a result of some perfectly rational and natural phenomena. Events soon changed Old Hickory's opinion.

Jackson's wagon was within a mile of the Bell home when inexplicably its wheels locked. The wagon stopped dead in its tracks and would not move so much as an inch. The men attempted to get the wagon going again, but they could not budge it or force the horses to advance even though the road was smooth and dry. Jackson himself personally inspected the axle and wheels. The men again struggled to push the wagon, but it still refused to move. Jackson found the predicament amusing. "What else could it be but the Bells' witch?" he asked. Then the group was surprised by a female voice that seemingly came from nowhere. "I'm glad you understand, General. Now you can go on. I'll speak with you tonight," the dismembered voice snickered.

Jackson immediately knew he'd heard the entity. "By the eternal, boys, it's the witch!" he exclaimed. Then as suddenly and incomprehensibly as the wagon wheels had frozen, they unlocked. Jackson and his band continued their ride to the Bell home, wondering if the witch would be waiting there as she promised.

John Bell played host to Jackson and his party that evening. The men sat around the fireplace talking, telling stories, and drinking rum, as they nervously anticipated the arrival of the witch. One especially brazen member of the group who fancied himself a witch slayer claimed he could rid the house of the noxious entity. To prove it, he took his pistol, loaded with a silver bullet—which, legend says, is one way to kill a witch, ghost, or devil—then screamed at the Bell Witch, demanding it show itself.

Jackson, not amused by his boastful crony, declared, "I wish the spirit would appear to show this braggart's true colors." Moments later, the stunned group heard heavy footsteps, and a voice announced, "Here I am as promised, General, and ready for business."

Jackson and the others were speechless as the spectral voice turned to the boastful man and declared, "And that business would be this bag of hot wind." The man fell silent. But the entity continued. "Here I am. Go on and shoot. I'll make it easy. Go on and shoot, for Christ's sake!" The others moved aside cautiously. The braggart pulled the trigger of his pistol, but the weapon wouldn't fire. "I can't wait forever. Try again. Hurry up!" the Bell Witch demanded. Once again, the gun refused to fire. "Now it's my turn," the entity angrily retorted.

Within the next moment, the boastful witch slayer was lifted off his feet by an invisible force, and as he fell, the unseen spirit slapped and dragged him by one leg, crashing him into furniture, walls, and dishes. Then the witch grabbed the horrified man by the nose, causing him to scream in pain. Amused by her accomplishment, she began laughing, and her eerie cackle filled the room. The man who'd experienced the unearthly wrath fled screaming in terror, and never returned to the Bells' house.

Jackson had watched the remarkable supernatural demonstration in rapt attention, and when it concluded, he laughed. "Double-dee-damned, that was the most fun I've had in my life. I'm glad I said nothing against the witch!" he exclaimed. "I vow I'd rather fight the entire British Army single-handed than face this witch."

The witch also chuckled. "I'm pleased to entertain you, General," she declared. "I'll wager this is the last we'll see of that coward. But there is another in your company who is a fraud. I will attend to him tomorrow night, as the hour is getting late."

But the entity could not depart without a swipe at Rachel Jackson, the general's wife. The witch howled, "How's that fat old wife of yours? Think you'll ever get Rachel's swollen carcass into the White House?" A stunned Jackson claimed he felt the witch brush his chin. Then the evil being vanished into the night, leaving Jackson, who'd once shot a man for insulting Rachel's name, angered by the unexpected and vulgar outburst.

Despite the spirit's promise, the next morning Jackson was convinced by his men to leave the Bell farm. Although several insisted the witch could not go beyond her chilling demonstration of the night before, likely they were frightened about what she might conjure next. Jackson appeared exhausted as he and his group departed and headed back for Nashville.

Curiously, in future years, Jackson said little if anything to others about his encounter with the witch. If he ever spoke publicly about having faced the entity, there is no record. Nor did he ever again visit the Bell farm or urge others to go there. His last known words on the subject were: "I wish no more dealings with that torment." Jackson went on to a successful political career, and was elected the seventh U.S. president, serving from 1829 to 1837. His wife Rachel died in 1828, shortly before she would have lived in the White House.

The entity did visit others in Robertson County, Tennessee, from time to time, often spewing crude and obscene remarks. There is no question, however, that the visit to the Bell farm by the famed general added to the notoriety and veracity of the story. That Andrew Jackson, a respected national figure, witnessed the haunting added immensely to the credibility of the Bells' claims.

What eventually happened to the witch? Her malevolent and demented antics continued unabated. She especially despised John Bell, though curiously, she never bothered Mrs. Bell. The entity finally revealed itself to be someone named Katie Batts. There were various theories about who she might have been, but her identity was never determined with certainty. Old Kate, as many called her, promised to haunt John Bell until he was "dead and buried."

In the autumn of 1820, John Bell took ill. He'd felt "strangeness" in his mouth. Then his tongue stiffened and became badly swollen, and he was unable to speak or eat for hours at a time. He also developed an uncontrollable facial twitch. He knew the cause of his affliction. "This terrible thing, the witch, is killing me," he told his son.

Finally, on December 19, 1820, Bell lapsed into a coma, and the vindictive entity was ecstatic. "It's useless to try and revive Old Jack," the witch said. "I've got him this time. He'll never get up from that bed again!" She even bragged she'd converted a tonic he was prescribed into poison. When the cat was given a taste of the medicine, the animal quickly dropped dead. The next day, Bell died. The witch, who could not contain her joy, was heard laughing and singing, even as family members grieved and buried John Bell.

The Bell Witch pronounced her work done. She threatened to reappear in future years, but one later visit, in 1827, was brief, inconsequential, and largely ignored. However, many Bell descendants met violent or untimely deaths.

True to the behavior of most poltergeists, the Bell Witch had centered her attention on a child, Betsy Bell. While ghosts generally cling to a single location, poltergeists are capable of attaching to a person or family, and they even have the ability to move with them from one place to another. Unlike ghosts, who often remain for years in a familiar earthly haunt, poltergeists seem transient and ultimately dissipate and leave.

Was young Betsy the "poltergeist agent" whose own telekinetic energy caused some of the horrific activity in her family's home? Some researchers have theorized that Betsy, under emotional stress, may have acted out of subconscious resentment of her father that manifested itself in the form of psychic energy responsible for creating the poltergeist's havoc. Skeptics blame Betsy, accusing her of fabricating the Bell Witch phenomena. However, no one ever proved that, and Betsy never again spoke of her family's "troubles."

Once the Bell Witch vanished as mysteriously as she'd first arrived, people were left to wonder why she'd so vehemently attacked the Bell family. No definitive answers have ever been established. Although poltergeist phenomena have been reported since ancient times, the Bell Witch holds the distinction of being the only poltergeist to ever speak to—and kill—someone. Poltergeist activity typically results in mischief, rather than serious harm. The Bell Witch proved the exception to that rule. Andrew Jackson had been one of the best-known and most credible witnesses to America's most infamous ghost story.

Eventually, the Bell house was torn down. However, some believe the area remains haunted. There have been reports of "ghostly lights" where once the entity made her vengeful presence felt, and a cave on the former Bell property is believed to be plagued by strange sounds of rattling chains, unearthly screams, and the sight of mysterious apparitions.

On U.S. Highway 41, a marker placed by the Tennessee Historical Commission briefly tells the story of the infamous haunting. Close by is a monument dedicated to the Bell family, the only official monument to a ghost in the United States.

While little formal or organized study of the paranormal occurred in America, during the eighteenth century there was at least one place where the "scientific" pursuit of psychic phenomena was seriously considered; it was being carefully studied by a prelate of the Roman Catholic Church named Prospero Lambertini (1678–1758), later to be known as

Pope Benedict XIV.[33] It may seem ironic that a man who rose from priest to bishop, cardinal, then archbishop should engage in the investigation of the very topic the Church so long claimed to detest.

Lambertini was born of noble lineage in Italy and was unusually well educated for his time; he earned doctorates in theology and law. For twenty years, from 1702 to 1722, he was the "devil's advocate," an important Church position in cases of people being considered for canonization, that is sainthood; a process the Church weighed very seriously. An individual had to first be beatified or "blessed" before sainthood could be declared, and the investigative process was exhaustive. If claims were made of supposed miraculous events on behalf of a deceased candidate, the initial position of the Church was skeptical until there was sufficient evidence to satisfy ecclesiastic officials. In other words, the Church did not accept unsubstantiated supernatural claims.

Few people think of the hierarchy of the Roman Catholic Church as psychic researchers; but, in fact, Church experts were arguably the first serious and most exacting investigators of paranormal phenomena. Lambertini, in two decades on the Church's commission investigating supernatural claims of candidates for sainthood, held a remarkably thoughtful and enlightened position for his time. Even as he earned a reputation as a skeptic, he recognized that "miracles" could and do sometimes occur.

He showed his intelligence and sensitivity regarding the controversial issue of what is—and isn't—paranormal. If a psychic incident might result from "natural phenomena," Lambertini discounted it as a "miracle." He undertook his own examination of such experiences as healings and what is now known as ESP or extra-sensory perception; then he concluded that ESP was a "natural phenomena neither spiritually or diabolically based," according to the *Encyclopedia of Occultism and Parapsychology* (1990).

His thinking and conclusions were far ahead of his time in an age of fear and superstition. Between 1734 and 1738, he published his findings in a four-volume work, *De Canonization Santorum*, that had a profound influence on the Church attitude toward miracles at a time when virtually anything could be mistaken as the occult.

In 1740, Lambertini became Pope Benedict XIV, a position he held until his death in 1758. His tenure earned him respect for his quick intelligence, and even praise from Enlightenment writer Voltaire, no small feat.

He is acknowledged with making "the first modern objective scientific studies of the paranormal in Italy."

There are scant records of whether the leading minds of colonial America studied Lambertini's conclusions about the paranormal. But it is likely that Benjamin Franklin, at least, was familiar with his writings. Franklin was a voracious reader, interested in the supernatural, and prided himself on keeping abreast of current affairs. Unlike many of his time, he would not have resisted perusing Catholic documents. Most Protestant denominations feared and abhorred the influence of Roman Catholicism in the colonies, regarding it as "papist" and a foreign incursion. Nonetheless, Maryland was settled in 1632, and only two years later a large number of Roman Catholics arrived. It is inconceivable that later generations of Catholics were unfamiliar with the writings about the supernatural by their liberal pontiff, Benedict XIV, who reigned about the time Ben Franklin was a middle-aged man.

Born in Germany in 1734,[34] Franz Anton Mesmer went on to earn a medical degree from the University of Vienna. He theorized that "a magnetic fluid surrounds or links all things and beings on earth and in the heavens," James R. Lewis explained.

He believed that this "universal fluid" in the human body could be influenced to treat and heal illnesses. Mesmer called his new method *animal magnetism*, and in Paris he attracted a huge following. In 1773, he produced his first cure when he applied "magnetic plates to a patient's limbs." His fame grew after he cured a blind girl in 1778.

Actually Mesmer's theory was not entirely new. It was roughly equal to the ancient Chinese concept of the *chi* or the Hindu belief in *prana* that suggests an energy or "vital force" circulates through the body.

In Paris, people claimed to be healed after sitting in Mesmer's famed *baquet*, a large circular tub filled with water that contained a variety of "magnetic" substances. Iron rods containing magnetic properties from the water were applied to the patient's body in order to affect a cure.

There was sufficient controversy that an official French scientific commission, led by Benjamin Franklin, was asked to investigate Mesmer's claims. The group, however, said it could find no evidence of this mysterious new physical force" or "magnetic fluid." Franklin chalked up the successful healings largely to the imagination of patients. As a result, public interest declined, and Mesmer was branded a fraud. But in 1823, a French doctor, Alexandre Bertrand, was curious about Mesmer's work—and cures—and so there was renewed interest in animal magnetism.

While most early experiments took place in Europe, it was discovered that what were later called "hypnotic trances" were the result of the "power of suggestion." Franklin had not been so far off the mark. But most of traditional science and medicine at the time rejected animal magnetism or mesmerism, as it came to be called. No one thought to consider how mesmerism was affecting human minds and imaginations. Even Thomas Jefferson was highly skeptical of animal magnetism, and discouraged its use in America, because he could not fit it into his "rational" approach to thinking.

Those who delved into mesmerism believed they discovered something unusual. While many patients were in trance they could demonstrate psychical abilities they otherwise could not have, such as telepathy or mind reading; seeing objects or articles even while their eyes were closed; clairvoyant abilities; even precognition or peering into the future; and speaking in voices other than their own. Traditional physicians and skeptics rejected the claims, but another French commission in 1836 was more favorably inclined to mesmerism.

Mesmerism arrived in America at a propitious time. In the first half of the nineteenth century, Americans were seeking and exploring new religious and spiritual ideas. Demonstrations of mesmeric abilities became popular with the public in the 1830s and 1840s. There were as many as thirty mesmerists on the lecture circuit just in New England; in Boston alone, there may have been as many as two hundred practicing mesmerists.

In one widely reported experiment at the time, a blind girl was able to "psychically discern" the contents of sealed envelopes while she was mesmerized. Skeptics blasted the demonstration as a fraud. Even if the effects of mesmerism were genuine, one valid criticism they had was, What caused enhanced psychical abilities to occur while one was in a trance?

The noted author of the time, Nathaniel Hawthorne, was fascinated by mesmerism; but in his 1851 classic, *The House of the Seven Gables*, a mesmerist fails to find a missing paper. He employs his ability to control a young woman until he causes her to die.

Edgar Allan Poe also found mesmerism a useful contrivance in at least one short story he wrote in the mid-1840s, in which a character wishes to live forever.[35] The story caused a storm of public controversy, for if mesmerism could help accomplish immortality, it was equal to blasphemy. Although Poe, the master of the macabre, after witnessing demonstrations of mesmerism, had written a fictional story, many worried that such a possibility might actually occur.

The noted literary figure Ralph Waldo Emerson wrote in 1837 that he was concerned that someone—even he—might be mesmerized against his will.[36]

Mesmerism, as with so many other areas of the unexplained and supernatural, at first provoked people's curiosity, and at the same time frightened them. Some even linked it to the satanic. But to their credit, mesmerists quickly learned to answer their critics and detractors, and thus corrected misconceptions.

The trance state induced when one was mesmerized was embraced by spiritualism in the United States by the late 1840s and became a very important part of its growth. Although Mesmer never showed any interest in the use of his technique for psychical purposes, mediums claimed that when they were induced into a trance state, they could communicate with the spirits of the departed. So at spiritualist séances throughout the nineteenth century in the United States, it was typical for participants or sitters to join hands while the medium entered into trance, and then wait as the medium brought forth messages from the spirit world.

The trance state, which dated back to ancient times and was widely employed by shamans, had found a new home in America, embraced by spiritualist mediums, who insisted that trance states made possible their ability to communicate with spirits in the next world. One of the first to be known as a trance medium was Mrs. W. B. Hayden.[37] In 1852, the Boston woman utilized metal disks to induce a trance state that allowed her to provide some highly accurate information for her audiences about their departed loved ones.

Ultimately, what was first called animal magnetism, then mesmerism, evolved into what we today call hypnotism. But while the mesmeric movement was folded into spiritualism, hypnosis eventually became an accepted "medical technique." It was a far cry from the time when it was labeled part of the "occult," and the scientific and medical establishment shunned mesmerists.

Altered states of consciousness—such as trances—have played a significant role in the paranormal. The rapid growth of spiritualism in nineteenth-century America owes much to animal magnetism or mesmerism, for the mediumistic trance—a form of self-induced hypnotism—greatly enhanced the popularity of psychic abilities.

America in the early nineteenth century was undergoing wide-ranging social changes, and the paranormal would soon play a significant part in the way Americans thought and what they believed, far beyond mesmerism. Long-established Christian denominations now faced competition from emerging new "religious sects and utopian social movements," Robert C. Fuller wrote, as Americans sought alternative ways of expressing their spirituality.

There was also a steady stream of immigrants arriving. America, with its wide-open spaces, offered them unprecedented freedom and opportunity. The immigrants also brought with them their own religious and cultural beliefs. In addition, many people were moving westward from the burgeoning but older towns and cities that hugged the Atlantic coast in order to find more room on such new frontiers as western New York State, Ohio, and even beyond. By 1800, the nation's population had grown to more than five million people; it had been under four million in 1790, and the Louisiana Purchase in 1803 added more than 830,000 square miles to the country.

In western New York, the Erie Canal opened in 1825 providing a direct east-west water route across the state from Albany to Buffalo. Better transportation meant improved services, more commerce, and growing towns and cities. One of the thriving communities was Rochester, New York, which would become known as the Flour City, for its mills. It would also be a region for immense psychical and social changes, including spiritualism, abolitionist activity, and the women's movement, as well as the birth of several new religious sects such as Mormonism and Adventism.

As towns became populated, the clergy followed. Traveling preachers had found fertile territory to convert many to evangelical Christianity in newly settled communities. These were ministers whose emotion-filled sermons rang with fire and brimstone. Thus was born the country's "Second Great Religious Awakening." Eventually, so much fiery evangelical oratory was preached that it seemed there was no one left to convert, many people remarked, and western New York became known as the "burned over region."

The mesmerists were also out and about, and their lectures in the 1830s and 1840s were immensely popular with the public, if less so with scientists. Those decades also had their version of a "self-help" movement. Unlike modern times when we target one specific problem area at a time, such as weight loss or quitting smoking, at that time "self-improvement" had a broader definition; the idea then was to create a completely fresh perspective on life.

And there to help the willing find this new mental and spiritual attitude were the mesmerists who claimed they could restore a deeper sense of balance and understanding between people and the unseen spiritual realms. Mesmerism, in its efforts to restore "health and virtue," was not unlike the religious revival that had been sweeping America.

Mesmerists were utilizing, whether or not they understood the term, psychology, coupled with the Word of the Bible. In fact, it would be another half-century before any American university would formally recognize a Department of Psychology.

Christianity had long taught the way to betterment was God. America's religious teachings had always raised mistrust about the extent to which people could make personal improvements unless they did so through the intervention of the Holy Spirit. The revivalists offered the opportunity for converting to "born-again" or fundamentalist Christianity, and maintained that people could "take responsibility" for seeking their own deliverance from sin and damnation, unlike Puritan or Calvinist belief. Of course, anything that strayed from the fundamentalist definition, such as the occult and supernatural, remained anathema and likely the work of the devil.

The 1820s and 1830s marked a time in America of "expansion and discovery that reached its apex by the end of the 1830s," wrote Robert C. Fuller. It was an era of "religious fervor," he noted. At the same time, scientists were making exciting new discoveries about the uses of electricity and magnetism.

In upstate New York in 1830 a young man by the name of Joseph Smith founded a new religious faith called Mormonism or the Church of Jesus Christ of Latter Day Saints. Smith said he'd received communications and instructions from an angel named Maroni. Other new belief systems such as Adventism and Shakerism also took root. Deism had lost much of its appeal by the early nineteenth century; but now there was Transcendentalism, Unitarianism, and Universalism, all liberal ways of seeking spirituality. Mesmerism could fit comfortably with any of the new belief systems, yet it never was associated with any particular religious denomination.

Mesmerists believed they could bridge the traditional divide between science and religion. "Mystical illumination and ecstatic revelations needed no longer be dismissed as fanciful irrationalities," wrote Robert C. Fuller. Mesmerism found itself welcome especially by "Swedenborgians, Spiritualists, and Universalists" for it provided "scientific underpinnings for spiritual beliefs," he explained. For those with a scientific bent, mesmerism was evidence that "the abilities of the mind could go beyond the limits of the physical organ we call the brain."

One of the most important early figures to encourage the growth of spiritualism in the nineteenth century also came out of upstate New York. His name was Andrew Jackson Davis (1826–1910) and he was to become a medium, channeler, and one of the founders of modern spiritualism. The son of a poor shoemaker, even as a child Davis had clairvoyant and clairaudient abilities.

The Davis family moved to Poughkeepsie, New York, and it was there when Andrew was about sixteen that he attended a series of public lectures about mesmerism presented by Dr. J. Stanley Grimes. After watching the demonstrations of mesmerism, Davis volunteered to be a subject but was unable to go into trance. However, he'd become intrigued by the subject and later tried again with the help of a local merchant. This time he became "entranced," and to his surprise, discovered that he could offer "clairvoyant medical diagnosis" while in the trance state.

A year later, in 1844, eighteen-year-old Davis one day roamed away from Poughkeepsie and walked some forty miles into the mountains where he received spirit visitations from the ancient Greek physician Galen, and the Swedish mystic, Emanuel Swedenborg. The experience motivated Davis to write and teach about "spiritual subjects," particularly mesmerism or magnetism, as it was still sometimes called.

Davis attracted a group of followers and while in trance he dictated a book with the lofty title, *The Principles of Nature, Her Divine Revelations, and a Voice to Mankind*. It quickly became popular when it was published in the summer of 1847. Its language and philosophy were both erudite and inspirational, especially for a young man with no formal education.

At first Davis required a mesmerist's help to induce a trance state. His trance writings, most agreed, were "inspired," and he soon earned the title the "Poughkeepsie Seer." He was fortunate to receive support from George Bush, a highly regarded professor of Hebrew at New York University. Bush confirmed that Davis's trance was legitimate and lauded the young man's book. The professor called it a "work [of] profound and elaborate discussion of the philosophy of the universe." The book, totaling almost eight hundred pages, was separated into three parts. Here is an example of the lively style and the concepts Davis presented in describing the origin of the universe:

> In the beginning the Univercoelum was one boundless, undefinable, and unimaginable ocean of liquid fire! The most vigorous and ambitious imagination is not capable of forming an adequate conception of the depth and length and breadth thereof. There was one vast expanse of liquid substance. It's [sic] inconceivable magnitude and constitution were such as not to develop forces, but Omnipotent Power.

Davis faced criticism when predictions or prophecies he made in trance did not prove true. As well, critics noted some obvious scientific errors that seemed inconsistent with trance dictations supposedly received from spirit realms. But overall, Davis apparently was offering "a broadly evolutionary view of this planet," wrote Georgess McHargue in *Facts, Frauds, and Phantasms.*[38]

3

Is That You, Mr. Splitfoot?

The Great Age of Spiritualism Begins

And now 'tis said, by some of late of Hydesville, in this town and state; that apparitions do appear, and people gather far and near.

—*Newark* (New York) *Herald*,
May 4, 1848

The winter of 1847–1848 was one of the worst in memory in western New York State.[1] Biting winds, frigid temperatures, and snow battered the area. On December 11, 1847, exactly two weeks before Christmas, John and Margaret Fox and two of their daughters, ten-year-old Margaretta, and seven-year-old Catherine (called Kate), both pretty girls with dark hair and eyes, moved into a small wooden-frame house in the village of Hydesville, really just a group of homes, several necessary stores and mills—typical of the farming communities that dotted the country.[2]

Mr. and Mrs. Fox were both past fifty. Their older children were all married and lived on their own. A son, David, resided nearby with his family, and there were three other daughters. One of them, Leah, was a piano teacher, who made her home in Rochester, the nearest large city in western New York. She was about twenty years older than her two youngest sisters. The Foxes were a close family, although John, a blacksmith, was stoic and introverted; Mrs. Fox was by far the friendlier of the two. Both were devout Methodists who prayed daily, and their lives were typical of many struggling and striving rural Americans in the first half of the nineteenth century.

Hydesville may have seemed an unlikely place for the birth of an enormous national movement that would attract millions and dramatically change the way many Americans would come to view life and death. But it was in that tiny hamlet where the Great Age of Spiritualism was born on a cold and blustery night, March 31, 1848. The country would never again be the same.

The first three months that the Foxes lived in their new rented home, life was fairly normal, and although the house had a reputation for "mysterious rapping noises," the family did its best to ignore the stories and even the fact that the sounds caused the previous tenants, the Michael Weekman family, to move out after living there in 1846–1847. Weekman said he was often bothered by "loud rapping" at the house door, although no one was ever there. One night, Weekman's eight-year-old daughter "felt a cold and clammy hand pass over her face."

But by March, the Foxes began hearing a clamor they could not identify. When they searched the house after dark by candlelight they found nothing to explain what might be causing the disturbances. Mrs. Fox admitted she was upset by the inexplicable jarring sounds and mysterious footsteps. She concluded some "unhappy restless spirit" was haunting the place.

Mrs. Fox wrote: "On Friday evening, March 31, 1848, we concluded to go to bed early and not permit ourselves to be disturbed by the noises, but try and get a night's rest. My husband was here on all those occasions, heard the noises and helped in the search. It commenced as usual. I knew it from all the other noises I had ever heard before. The children, who slept in the other bed in the room, heard the rappings and tried to make similar sounds by snapping their fingers.

"My youngest child, Katie, said: 'Mr. Splitfoot, do as I do,' clapping her hands. The sounds instantly followed her with the same number of raps." [They'd named the unseen entity Mr. Splitfoot because of Mrs. Fox's fear that the disturbances were "the work of the devil."] "Then Margaretta said in sport, 'Now, do just as I do. Count one, two, three, four,' striking one hand against the other at the same time; and the raps came as before.

"Then Katie said, 'Oh Mother, I know what it is. Tomorrow is April Fool's Day and it is somebody trying to fool us.' I then thought I could put a test that no one in the place could answer. I asked the noise to rap my different children's ages successively."[3]

The answers were correct.

"I then asked: 'Is this a human being that answers my questions so correctly?' There was no rap. I asked, 'Is it a spirit? If it is, make two raps.' Two sounds were given as soon as the request was made. I then said: 'If it was an injured spirit, make two raps,' which were instantly made causing the house to tremble. I asked: 'Were you injured in this house?' The answer was given as before."

Mrs. Fox summoned neighbors. The first was Mrs. Mary Redfield, who was blunt and dismissive about spirit presences; she assumed the girls were playing a prank. She soon changed her mind and became frightened after questioning the spirit and receiving correct answers. Mrs. Fox also sent for another neighbor, William Duesler. He may have been the first to determine through questioning the spirit raps that a peddler, Charles Rosna, was killed in the house sometime during 1843–1844, for the money he carried: five hundred dollars, a large sum at that time. If the spirit raps were correct, the peddler was murdered, his throat slashed, and buried in the cellar by a former tenant named John Bell who'd since moved away.

A search was first made of the cellar the next day by several of the men, and by summer, as the searches continued, several human bones and some hair were discovered. They appeared to have been buried in charcoal and quicklime to quicken the body's decomposition.

Soon, news of the spirit rappings attracted so much attention that a great many of visitors sought entry to the Fox house, as many as five hundred in a single day. "It caused a great deal of trouble and anxiety," Mr. Fox complained. "I am not a believer in haunted houses or supernatural appearances." Still, the Foxes could not account for the noises, which not only grew worse, but were also transformed into other physical manifestations. In addition to the mysterious rappings, other inexplicable phenomena—including slamming doors, shaking beds, "etheric hands" seizing the girls, the ghostly sounds of a struggle, someone being dragged down a flight of stairs—occurred in the house, and gossip about it excited neighbors even more. By early April, raps were heard during the day as well as at night.

The startling revelations spread quickly beyond Hydesville and attracted curiosity from both believers and skeptics. In an era before instant communication, the information spread so rapidly that it was as if another world had been discovered, one that both skeptics and believers wanted to know more about. It seemed a path had opened between the Fox sisters and the alleged unseen entity that touched a nerve in a population eager to look beyond the physical limits of everyday existence and the mysteries of death.

The local newspaper, the *Western Argus*, quickly reported the story; and it wasn't long before E. E. Lewis, an enterprising writer from a nearby town, published a pamphlet, *Report of the Mysterious Noises*. Then, Lucretia Pulver, a girl who'd worked as a maid for the Bell family in 1843–1844, came forward to claim she heard "knockings in the bedroom and sometimes unaccountable footsteps" in the house at night. She also said she'd discovered that part of the cellar was dug up. Some time later, evidence revealed that a peddler had vanished about the time Lucretia first heard the inexplicable knocking noises. Another locally written book told about the Weekman family's "unpleasant experiences" in the house.

In April, Mrs. Fox wrote about the events of March 31:

> I am not a believer in haunted houses or supernatural appearances. I am very sorry there has been so much excitement about it. It has been a great deal of trouble to us. I cannot account for the noises; all I know is that they have been heard repeatedly as I have stated.[4]

With the ability to receive a response from the spirit inhabiting their house, the young Fox sisters had tapped into the public's enthusiasm for the supernatural. Within a matter of months, what began in Hydesville spread to surrounding communities, and from there, via newspapers, to the large cities; it was as if a "new age" was dawning wherein people would find confirmation of the spirit world's ability to communicate with the physical world.

As the public's fascination with the sisters' paranormal abilities grew, Mrs. Fox sent them to visit their older sister, Mrs. Leah Fish, in nearby Rochester. But if the Foxes thought that would end the tumult surrounding their house they were greatly mistaken. The spirit rappings followed the two young girls from Hydesville to Leah's home where they and the spirit actually attracted more attention, and Margaretta soon became the center of a faithful "spirit circle," which allowed participants to come together to receive spirit communications. Meanwhile, Kate was sent to live in nearby Auburn, New York, with her brother. There, her parents hoped, she would be free of the spirit that had followed them to Rochester.

But many curious people who believed in what they called the "rapping telegraph" eagerly gathered in Leah's home to witness for themselves Margaretta's paranormal abilities. They even worked out a more manageable code to communicate with the spirit: one rap indicated "no," two raps that the spirit was unable to answer a question, and three raps signified "yes."

When Leah saw the effect her younger sister's contact with Mr. Split-foot had on large numbers of people she did the arithmetic and realized she was sitting on a gold mine. She told friends she'd suddenly become aware of the financial possibilities inherent in Margaretta's psychic talents because, she said, "all western New York was excited by the reports and doctrines of Spiritualism."

About that Leah was correct. This was a part of the country that had been unusually open to new religious sects and social movements such as abolition and women's rights. In fact, two close friends of the Fox family were Isaac and Amy Post, both Quakers and active in Rochester's anti-slavery movement. Isaac also became known as a medium. The Posts, open to spiritualism, were supportive of Kate and Margaretta.

It had only been a few years since Samuel Morse first successfully demonstrated the miracle of the telegraph in 1844. If electricity could provide virtually instant communication between distant places, why then wasn't contact possible between the living and the spirit world? Perhaps the marvel of electricity played some role in the spirit contact process, some suggested, hence the term the *rapping telegraph*.

But Leah realized the need to tread softly because Margaretta's spirit communications produced sharply differing positions. There were some, especially Christian fundamentalists, who denounced the girl for "heresy and blasphemy," while at the other end of the spectrum were those positively elated by contact with spirits. In addition, there were outspoken skeptics who dismissed the doings entirely, and wanted it exposed as fraud.

In Hydesville, only the murdered peddler's ghost had given messages; now, in Rochester, many other spirits allegedly came forth to rap out messages to Margaretta, who would henceforth be known professionally as Margaret; or Maggie to friends and family.

Leah wasted no time in capitalizing on her young sister's abilities. She organized a public lecture and demonstration on the evening of November 14, 1849, in Rochester's largest auditorium, Corinthian Hall, at one dollar a person, which at that time was a steep price for admission. The audience was comprised of people who ranged from the merely curious to those who thought they were witnesses to a spiritual revolution in the making, and they filled the auditorium to capacity. It was a sell-out crowd of about four hundred and Leah profited handsomely, while Margaret's career as a medium was launched.

One circulating rumor had the spirits suggesting that after more than a year and a half of small circles or gatherings, it was time for the public to witness the rappings in a venue larger than someone's private home. That explanation obviously sounded more appealing than the likely truth: it was Leah's idea to profit from her sisters. It was around this time that Leah discovered that she also had the "powers of a medium."

Of those who attended the demonstration, many were certain they'd witnessed genuine communication with the spirit world, while others were just as sure they'd seen a fraud. However, no one could explain what caused the rappings, and Margaret's performance received positive reviews in the local newspapers. All agreed, "The effect upon . . . guests was great."

As a result of the demonstrations at Corinthian Hall, many of Rochester's most prominent citizens organized into several committees to investigate and test Margaret and, if possible, determine the source of the raps. Some thought that if they could prove this entire episode was nothing more than a "parlor trick," the public fascination would dissipate. However, they also ran the risk of being unable to debunk the demonstration, and that would only strengthen the belief that Margaret was a gifted and genuine medium, one who'd actually made contact with the spirit world.

The investigators tried their best, but they were unable to explain the girl's performance. Some suspected she was a ventriloquist and was therefore only answering herself. They studied her carefully but could not prove that theory. If she was engaging in ventriloquism, she was excellent at it. If the rappings were a ruse, no one who investigated her could prove it. Therefore, the examination seemed to confirm what Margaret had claimed: the spirit raps were real. It was not the answer skeptics had hoped for, since some angrily insisted from the start that the sisters were frauds who somehow were responsible for creating the noises themselves. In all, three separate committees of learned men tried—and failed—to locate the source of the knocking sounds.

At the last Corinthian Hall demonstration Margaret gave, some in the audience became so frustrated and outraged that a disturbance erupted. There was yelling, firecrackers were thrown, and police had to be called for fear that some people might rush the stage and hurt Margaret. A phalanx of Rochester police intervened to escort her and Leah home.

Kate soon rejoined her sister, and the two girls quickly became the talk of Rochester and were also receiving publicity throughout the entire state. While Kate had lived in Auburn she hadn't been idle. She'd conducted séances there that attracted many "believers" to her spirit circles.

It wasn't long before news of their demonstrations was being reported in other large cities, and the girls were becoming nationally known, unusual in an era when such celebrity was rare. A few months later, with their popularity on the upswing, they were traveling throughout the country and demonstrating spirit raps for huge audiences, as well as offering exclusive private sittings for the wealthy and famous.

The Age of Spiritualism had begun and was already generating money. Skeptics, to their chagrin, were powerless to curb the enthusiasm of millions who sought contact with the spirit world. There was suddenly a demand for spiritualist mediums, and although the Fox sisters were there first, they soon had competition that would force them to vie for a place in an increasingly crowded market. Other self-proclaimed mediums came forward for their share of the limelight.

The skeptics and detractors had actually done a favor for the sisters, for if the girls couldn't easily be exposed as frauds then many people concluded they must be genuine. Some of those who attended private sittings with Margaret were far from ordinary or average: they were the celebrities of that era. Among them were the famed writers Harriet Beecher Stowe, James Fenimore Cooper, and William Cullen Bryant. Another important figure to show great interest in the sisters was the distinguished editor of the *New York Tribune*, Horace Greeley; he'd been the first to call on them personally when they visited New York City.[5]

When the Fox sisters arrived in New York to demonstrate their abilities during the summer of 1850, they stayed at hotels and private residences.

One of the places they were invited was Greeley's Manhattan home, where they remained as guests for several days. His initial interest was largely motivated by the recent death of his son. Greeley and his wife Mary had lost four of their five children. Throughout its history, spiritualism was closely related to bereavement, and Greeley's reaction was not unusual among those who'd suffered loss.

After Greeley witnessed the "rapping phenomena" several times, under what were described as "test conditions," he pronounced himself perplexed by what he saw. He wasted no time in writing an editorial in the *Tribune* titled "The Mysterious Rappings." Greeley said that he believed the raps were genuine, if inexplicable, but initially had doubts that spirits were responsible. He wrote:

"Whatever may be the origin or cause of the rappings, the ladies in whose presence they occur do not make them: we tested this thoroughly and to our entire satisfaction.

"Mrs. Fox and her three daughters left our city yesterday. They returned to Rochester, after a stay here of some weeks; during which they have subjected the mysterious influence, by which they seem to be accompanied, to very reasonable test, and to the keen and critical scrutiny of hundreds who have chosen to visit them or whom they have invited to visit.

"The rooms which they occupied at the hotel, have been repeatedly searched and scrutinized; they have been taken without an hour's notice into houses they had never before entered; they have been all unconsciously placed on a glass surface under the carpet, in order to interrupt electrical vibrations; they have been disrobed by a committee of ladies, appointed without notice and insisting that neither of them should leave the room until the investigation had been made; yet we believe no one, to this moment, pretends that he has detected either of them in producing or causing the rappings, nor do we think any of their condemners has invented a plausible theory to account for the production of these sounds, nor the singular intelligence which (certainly at times) has seemed to be manifested through them.

"Our own dwelling was among those they [the Fox family] visited; not only submitting to, but courting, the fullest and keenest inquiry with regard to the alleged manifestations from the spirit world, by which they were attended.

"We devoted what time we could from our duties, out of three days, to this subject; and it would be the basest cowardice not to say that we are convinced beyond a doubt, of their perfect integrity and good faith in the premises.

"Their conduct and bearing is as unlike that of deceivers as possible and we think no one acquainted with them could believe them at all capable of engaging in so daring, impious and shameful a juggle as this would be if they caused the sounds.

"And it is not possible that such a juggle should have been so long per-petrated in public. A juggler performs one feat quickly, and hurries on to another; he does not devote weeks after weeks to the same thing, over and over, deliberately, in full view of hundreds who sit beside or confronting him in broad daylight, not to enjoy, but to detect his trick.

"A deceiver naturally avoids conversation on the subject of his knav-ery, but these ladies converse freely and fully with regard to the origin of these 'rappings' in their dwellings, years ago, the various sensations they caused, the neighborhood excitement created, the progress of the developments—what they have seen, heard and experienced from first to last.

"Of all this we know nothing, and shall guess nothing. But if we were simply to print (which we shall not) the questions we asked and answers we received, during a two hours, uninterrupted conference with the 'rap-pers,' we should at once be accused of having done so expressly to sus-tain the theory which regards these manifestations as the utterances of departed spirits."

There is no question that Horace Greeley's support for the Fox sisters did a great deal to boost their fame and credibility, as well as that of the entire spiritualist movement. With national attention and press coverage the scrutiny of the girls intensified along with the public's interest.

Controversy was always present. Were the raps evidence of spirit communication, and therefore an afterlife? Or was this all a clever hoax to deceive a gullible public? Every time a skeptic failed to expose the Fox sisters, their credibility was enhanced. But their corner on the spiritualist movement would be short-lived. It wasn't long before thousands across the country were claiming to be mediums in virtually every town and city. Still, the girls became so famous that their reputations reached all the way to the White House.

On January 6, 1853, only two months before Franklin Pierce was to be inaugurated the nation's fourteenth president, tragedy struck him and his wife Jane.[6] The Pierces were traveling by train with their only child, eleven-year-old son Benjamin, when not far from Boston, the car they were in uncoupled and derailed. The train tumbled, split apart, and crashed down a rocky ledge. President-elect and Mrs. Pierce suffered only minor injuries. However, there was one fatality in the accident: young Benjamin Pierce, whose head was struck by a large rock so violently that the impact cracked open his skull as his horrified parents watched helplessly.

For the frail and introverted Mrs. Pierce, the gruesome sight was so traumatic that she never recovered emotionally. She was inconsolable for many weeks, and so paralyzed by grief that when her husband was inaugurated in March 1853, she was unable to attend. Benjamin's death cast a pall over their lives and the presidency. Jane became "one of the most tragic figures" to ever occupy the White House. Those who saw the once beautiful young woman described her "woebegone face, with its sunken eyes and skin like yellowed ivory. . . . Her life was over . . . from the time of that dreadful shock of her son's death."

She remained in solitude in the White House family quarters, where she wrote lengthy letters to her deceased son, whom she never stopped mourning. Servants said they could hear her call to Benjamin, while at other times she was heard playing with her three departed children: Benjamin, also a first-born son who'd died as an infant, and a second son who succumbed at age four.

To skeptics, her behavior was evidence that the poor woman had descended into "fantasy." But who could say with certainty that she'd not actually made contact with her deceased boys? Millions of bereaved parents have reported similar experiences over the centuries and right up to the present time. Might she have glimpsed the apparitions of her sons in the gloom and quiet of her private rooms? Such encounters with spirits have been recorded in every age and culture, throughout human history.

But parents then, not unlike those today, desired to find some way to make sense of the tragic loss of their children. Jane had been raised in a strict religious family and inculcated with Calvinist beliefs. Not surprising, she arrived at the erroneous assumption "that Bennie's fate was a divine punishment for [her husband's] political ambition." Franklin Pierce also concluded that his son's horrific death was "a judgment of God on him." Both parents were in serious error in their thinking. Nowhere does Christianity or spiritualist belief suggest that God kills innocent children as retribution for the sins of their parents. No responsible minister or medium would make such a claim.

Jane Pierce ached for contact with young Benjamin's spirit. She had heard of the Fox sisters, now nationally known as spiritualism swept the nation. So for the first time in American history, mediums were invited to the White House to conduct a séance at which the Fox sisters would attempt to receive spirit raps from Benjamin in the afterlife.

Exactly what occurred at the sitting is unknown, for no record exists to tell us exactly what spirit messages were given to Mrs. Pierce. The sisters never revealed any details of their White House experience, but rumors circulated that it was successful.

Still most major press branded spiritualism a "swindle." For millions of Americans the criticism was largely ignored as they enthusiastically sought mediums to contact the spirit world. To make a modern analogy, the popularity of spiritualism at its height in the mid-nineteenth century is equivalent to a motion picture that garners nearly universal negative reviews, yet rakes in a huge box office. Similarly, skeptics might rant from the rooftops against spiritualism, but a huge number of Americans weren't listening. What many preferred to hear was a message from their Aunt Emma or Grandpa Jeb, in the next world.

Later in her life, Kate Fox achieved another milestone for spiritualism when one of the attendees at her séance was former first lady Mary Todd Lincoln. Mrs. Lincoln, an avowed spiritualist, was there in the hope that she'd make contact with the spirit of her murdered husband, President Abraham Lincoln and their deceased sons.

Notwithstanding the genuine problem of fraud and chicanery in the spiritualist movement—and there was plenty—people were anxious for a sign from a departed loved one or some demonstration from the spirit world. A significant change in the American attitude toward death was taking place, for spiritualism was encouraging a new mind-set.

"The modern idea of a personal death, of 'my death' is a product of the European Middle Ages," explained historian Caroline Walker Bynum. "In the later Middle Ages death became increasingly personal. [It] was seen as the moment at which the individual, alone before his personal past, took stock of the meaning of his life."

Not surprisingly, spiritualism polarized public opinion. There were millions of adherents and believers who had little or no doubt that the Fox sisters were in contact with the spirit world. On the other hand, many were quick to debunk even the possibility of communication between the living and the deceased. Traditional clergy promptly denounced spiritualism as a manifestation of evil, not unlike the first spirit raps that were heard by Mrs. Fox, and named "Mr. Splitfoot," a religious allusion to the devil's cloven hooves, since from their Methodist perspective, the rappings were considered "evil." Conversely, others interpreted the spirit raps as a corroboration of "church teachings."

Many spiritualists insisted that what was learned at séances was "the evidence of things not seen," explained author Georgess McHargue in *Facts, Frauds, and Phantasms*. The question was from where did the raps originate? The bottom line was that spiritualism could be viewed in very different ways: to some it was a "devil's tool," McHargue noted. To others, it was the herald of a new age; while for many there was great uncertainty about the source and meaning of spirit raps.

There were a sufficient number of the curious at the beginning of the spiritualist craze determined to find an answer—one way or the other. In February 1851, a committee of three medical professors from Buffalo gathered to ponder the question. They decided their best hope of arriving at an answer was to closely examine the Fox sisters. For about an hour, the three placed themselves in a soundproofed room where they held Margaret's legs. It was definitely unusual behavior in Victorian times for a man to behave this way with a young girl. But these were doctors who'd decided to ignore social propriety in the interests of scientific investigation. Their conclusion was that the spirit raps were audible only when Margaret's legs were freed or at least not held tightly.

The professors reached the conclusion that spirit raps were caused by Margaret snapping the joints of her knees. What's more, she could so without any discernable physical movement. To the committee's chagrin, its findings were not well received. It seemed the Fox sisters had already garnered considerable support, and their defenders were willing to take up the cause of spiritualism on their behalf. So many people believed in the possibility of contact with the spirit world that attempts to discredit it were often met with anger. To doubt the Fox sisters was to disbelieve in an afterlife and communications between here and hereafter. Besides, who was able to say with absolute certainty that no spirit world existed beyond death?

One committee member, Dr. Charles Lee, thought he'd found a way to absolutely debunk the Fox sisters. He went so far as to find a man who could crack his joints to imitate spirit raps. Lee believed this would bring a quick end to the rapidly growing spiritualist movement. But his public appearances with the man badly backfired. Instead of concluding the sisters were frauds, Lee's efforts only created greater interest in spiritualism. "The Fox sisters had apparently aroused a determination to believe that simply could not be undermined," author McHargue concluded.

In fairness to the sisters, supporters pointed out several inconsistencies and omissions in the doctors' tests. One unanswered question was how the spirit rappings responded accurately however the noises were created. Many questions were even asked mentally and answered correctly. Skeptics neglected to address that issue.

In 1853, the sisters demonstrated what was described as "their most powerful early manifestations." It consisted of a table levitating with a well-known politician, Governor George Talmadge, seated atop it. Talmadge also claimed he'd received a message through automatic writing from the spirit of another noted political figure, John C. Calhoun.

By 1854, it appeared the Fox sisters' popularity was on the wane. For one thing, the public wanted more exciting spirit demonstrations than merely rappings; also the girls were facing competition from many other mediums, even as the skeptics and doubters persisted. In 1857, the *Boston Courier* arranged for a committee of four learned Harvard professors to examine a number of mediums. Among those who accepted the invitation were Kate and Leah Fox. The group of skeptical academicians was not easy to please. The committee promised to issue a report of its findings and conclusions but never did.

Newspapers at that time, like today, were generally hostile or snide in reporting about the Fox sisters or other spiritualist phenomena. Only Horace Greeley, editor of the *New York Tribune*, remained steadfast in the girls' defense.

Later in their lives, Kate and Margaret fell on hard times, after years of séances, public appearances, tours, tests, and scrutiny, much of it antagonistic. Those who knew the sisters felt they were physically and emotionally drained from their grueling schedule. They also were not sufficiently sophisticated when they were younger to realize they'd been exploited. Nor did they fully comprehend the depth and hostility of the religious and scientific controversy that surrounded spiritualism.

There were some bright spots before their world fell apart. Margaret married a noted Arctic explorer and physician, Dr. Elisha Kane. Although he remained a skeptic about spiritualism, he was certain that Leah had taken advantage of Margaret. Perhaps Margaret's life would have taken a different and better turn with Kane's advice. However, he died in 1857 during one of his frequent trips. Leah, meanwhile, married for a third time in 1858 to Daniel Underhill, a successful insurance man. Following their marriages, both Leah and Margaret withdrew from practicing mediumship.

Kate, however, continued her career. In 1861, she went to work as a medium for a wealthy New York banker named Charles Livermore whose wife Estelle had died the previous year. Over the next five years, Kate provided Livermore with close to four hundred "sittings" or séances in his home. There were witnesses to many of the sessions, and written documentation was kept.

Eventually, at the forty-third sitting, the spirit of Estelle Livermore "materialized," and was seen bathed in what was described as a "psychic light." The spirit communicated to Kate via rappings and automatic writing. According to an account by psychic researcher and author Nandor Fodor, "Estelle and another spirit, calling himself Benjamin Franklin, wrote on cards brought before [Charles] Livermore. While she [Estelle] wrote, the hands of Kate Fox were held. The script was a perfect reproduction of the characters [Estelle] used when on earth."

Finally, at the 388th psychic sitting or séance, Estelle's spirit made it known that she would no longer materialize. True to the communication, Livermore never again saw his late wife's spirit. But because he was grateful to Kate Fox for the comfort she'd brought him during his grief, in 1871, he arranged for her to travel to England where she continued to work as a medium.

In England, her career thrived and she often gave sittings for well-known figures of the day. Kate also made herself available for testing by British scientists such as Sir William Crookes, one of the greatest physicists of his time, and one of the first advocates of serious inquiry into psychical experiences. She also shared a number of sittings with the famed medium of that era, Daniel Dunglas (D. D.) Home, and the medium Agnes Guppy-Volckman.

In 1872, Kate married an attorney named Henry D. Jencken who died in 1881. The couple had two sons, both of whom showed evidence of psychic abilities when they were quite young. Kate's reputation as a medium earned her a visit to Russia in 1883 where she demonstrated her psychic gifts for the czar.

There was a lesson to be learned from Charles Livermore's earlier employment of Kate Fox that many scientists, clergy, intellectuals, and so-called rational thinkers of that time overlooked in their zeal to debunk or expose spiritualism. The fact was that millions, similar to Livermore, regardless of their social or economic status, were seeking a way to cope with death and the resulting grief. Spiritualism, for all its flaws and frauds, offered a connection between here and hereafter, and the promise that loved ones would someday be reunited in the afterlife. The spirit world offered hope that death was not a termination, but rather a transition to the "next stage of life." Many scientists, skeptics, and rationalists never quite grasped the value of spiritualism and the need it fulfilled for millions. Nor did the skeptics with their "cold" logic offer a means or alternative for easing the fear and mystery of death.

Like it or not, spiritualism in the nineteenth century produced a critical shift in the way millions of Americans thought about the nature of life and death. All mediums were *not* proven to be fraudulent, and many who investigated them, including some of the most learned minds in America and Europe, concluded that there was sufficient evidence to make a case for discarnate communication.

For the dying and the bereaved, spiritualism offered something more tangible than unyielding and sometimes impersonal religious dogma, which may explain why it attracted adherents from many denominations. Although fundamentalist clergy strongly disapproved, some people found that the message and hope of spiritualism was similar to Christian teachings. When the New Testament declared, "And this is the promise He made us: eternal life." (1 John 2:25), it came close to the spiritualist belief in the afterlife. However, traditional Christianity would continue to rail against spiritualists reminding the faithful that the Old Testament prohibited and condemned consort with mediums, fortune-tellers, necromancers, and the like.

Those in nineteenth-century America had closer contact with death in many ways than recent and present generations. More people died at home, and typically were laid out in the parlor, hence the term *funeral parlor* remained in use even when ceremonies and rituals surrounding death were moved from the home. Statistically, life expectancy was far shorter than it is today. Infections, epidemics, high infant mortality rates, childhood diseases, and unsophisticated medical treatments had long been ominous shadows cast over people's lives. Denying death, common in our youth-obsessed culture, is a relatively new and unrealistic way of facing our mortality.

By comparison, when the Fox sisters were growing up, death was not an unusual topic, even in public schools. Here are just a couple of examples from one of the country's most popular schoolbooks in the 1840s and '50s, the *Sanders' First Reader*, published in 1846:

THE DYING BOY
It must be sweet, in childhood, to give back
the spirit to its maker.

Then there was this:

Mother, I'm dying now!
There's a deep suffocation in my breast,
As if some heavy hand my bosom pressed,
And on my brow
I feel the cold sweat stand . . .
My lips grow dry, and tremulous, my breath
Comes feebly up. Oh tell me,
is this death?

By our contemporary standards, these examples probably seem morbid and inappropriate for young children to read in classrooms. But, as we said a bit earlier, death was ever-present in the nineteenth century and before, and being prepared for it, even at an early age, was both practical and responsible on the part of parents and schools, as well as churches. Spiritualism's nearly instant popularity added a measure of comfort and acceptance of death, and offered hope of what lay ahead once we left our physical body.

"In contrast to prevailing rigid traditional belief, spiritualism offered the possibility of the individual's direct access to divine truth, attracting adherents who rebelled against death and temporal authority," wrote Ann Braude in *Radical Spirits* (1989).

Meanwhile, Margaret visited England in 1876, and then returned home to the United States. She was still a medium, albeit reluctantly, forced by her dire economic situation. Those who knew her said she lived in virtual poverty in her last years.

Then the lives of the Fox sisters took another unhappy turn. While the reasons are unclear, the three of them became embroiled in disputes and quarrels with each other that were apparently instigated by Margaret. Their later years were mired in public controversy and personal difficulties, not the least of which was a lack of money. Only Leah had prospered from mediumship.

Still, the Fox sisters remained known,[7] and in 1884, Margaret appeared before the Seybert Commission in Philadelphia. The commission had been the brainchild of a Philadelphia spiritualist named Henry Seybert who bequeathed some $60,000 to the University of Pennsylvania for "a thorough and impartial investigation of all systems of morals, religion, or philosophy, which assume to represent the truth, and particularly of modern spiritualism."

Among the psychic phenomena the commission looked into were slate writing, spirit materializations, spirit photography, and spirit rapping. They also found time to examine telekinesis, and "direct voice" phenomena.

When Margaret demonstrated the rapping noises, she did so while standing upon "four glass tumblers." Commission members, however, were unable to arrive at any definitive conclusions about the nature of the rappings. One member, Horace Howard Furness, commented after hearing the raps, "This is the most wonderful thing of all, Mrs. Kane [Margaret's married name]. I distinctly feel them in your feet. There is not a particle of motion in your foot, but there is an unusual pulsation."

But the commission did not find that the rappings were supernatural; rather it suggested the noises might have been "produced in any portion [of her body] by some voluntary muscular action."

The Seybert Commission's findings were largely negative about spiritualist phenomena. The results outraged spiritualists; and some of their frustration might have been more than sour grapes. For one thing, out of eleven members on the commission there was only one spiritualist: Thomas Hazard, a close friend of Henry Seybert. Hazard had been designated by Seybert to determine the best means of testing mediums but he soon protested the techniques the commission members used to investigate spiritualism. However his complaints were ignored.

In May 1887, the Seybert Commission issued a "preliminary report" that was substantially unfavorable to the entire subject of "spiritualist phenomena." A final report was never released, and the commission ended its inquiry. The Commission's findings were damaging to spiritualism and psychical phenomena, especially in the eyes of many other scientists.

Several years later a commentary written by noted British skeptic Frank Podmore acknowledged that "spiritualists contend, and not without some justification, that the intentions of Mr. Seybert were never fairly carried out." That was typical of how psychical phenomena were often treated by the orthodox scientific community. In dismissing spiritualism as "humbug," a commonly used pejorative word in the nineteenth century, skeptics, scientists, and debunkers could be equally disingenuous.

Medical doctors were often among the most hostile to spiritualism, apparently fearing competition from mediums, some of whom employed spirit contact or clairvoyance to diagnose and treat illnesses.

In 1888, spiritualism suffered a far worse blow that sent it reeling when Margaret Fox, by then a woman in her mid-fifties, made a startling appearance at the Academy of Music in New York. She would send shock waves through the spiritualist movement that had been part of American culture—and controversy—for the past forty years. She had already written a letter in May to the *New York Herald* in which she "denounced spiritualism," and promised to expose it.

She kept her word with her public appearance at which she revealed the events that began when she and Kate were children in Hydesville. Margaret confessed to the audience that the spirit rappings had been "a complete fraud." Then she offered a demonstration of how she produced the noises by cracking her joints, especially the "the joint of her big toe."

The following day, the *New York Herald* carried Margaret's shocking admission: "That I have been mainly instrumental in perpetuating the fraud of spiritualism, you already know. It is the greatest sorrow of my life. I began with the deception when I was too young to know right from wrong."

In their coverage of the stunning turn of events, the *Herald* described the audience reaction to Margaret's public confession:

There was dead silence; everybody in the hall knew they were looking upon the woman who is principally responsible for spiritualism. She stood upon a little pine table with nothing on her feet but stockings. As she remained motionless, loud distinct rappings were heard, now in the flies, now behind the scenes, now in the gallery.

"It was Margaret who made the raps but, as before, it was the acoustical properties of the room that helped give the audience the illusion that the sounds were coming from different locations," author Georgess McHargue explained.

By now the Fox sisters were quarreling, and tensions were especially running high between Kate and Margaret on one side, and Leah on the other. Each sister blamed the other for her problems, and there were plenty of them. Margaret and Kate had become alcoholics, and both had serious financial problems verging on poverty. That may have been at the heart of their resentment of Leah.

Married three times, Leah had profited nicely from her career as a medium, at the expense of her sisters, they would maintain. There was also an accusation that Leah made to deny Kate custody of her two sons, by accusing her of being an "unfit mother." The charge was proven untrue, but it only fueled animosity between Kate and Leah.

Both of Kate's sons were said to have displayed "psychic powers" when they were young boys. Perhaps Leah had hoped to exploit them as working mediums, Kate thought, as she claimed she and Margaret were as children. They remained bitter that when they were young girls, their spirit circles and public appearances earned a tidy sum of money that Leah took for herself. The result of the family friction was that Margaret and Kate joined each other and "swore vengeance to ruin Leah," Nandor Fodor wrote. The story became even darker when Kate, possibly to smear Leah's reputation, supported Margaret's confession.

The reports of the Fox sisters' confessions were the news "antispiritualists" had long yearned for. Many of them were elated that both sisters claimed the rappings were their creation, not the work of the supernatural. It didn't take long for those opposed to spiritualism to grab the story. One of the first books about the confessions was *The Death-Blow to Spiritualism* in 1897, by Reuben Briggs Davenport. Skeptics loved the title that pretty well summed up what they'd long pressed for.

While the Fox sisters' admissions were certainly a blow to the credibility of spiritualism, they were too little too late to destroy a movement that had captivated much of the country for so long. Spiritualism and mediumship had not suffered a "death blow," to the frustration of its enemies.

But the convoluted story of the Fox sisters did not end with Margaret's stunning confession. The next surprise came a year later when, in November 1889, Margaret rescinded her confession. She explained that the financial pressures she faced were largely responsible for her disavowal of spiritualism. She also implied influence from certain groups who were hostile to the subject, possibly the churches, and she provided details in a signed written statement that was made public.

The obvious implication was that she and Kate would be paid to say that the spirit rappings were all a hoax. Now in her retraction, she said just the opposite. Some historians have suggested that the sisters had been promised a sum of money to announce that spiritualism was a hoax. However, they never saw the payments they expected, forcing them to return to mediumship to earn a meager living.

The combination of the confession and then its retraction produced public outrage, indignation, and confusion. But both Margaret and Kate were racked by poverty, alcoholism, loneliness, and a variety of serious physical and emotional problems, so the turmoil that surrounded them likely no longer mattered as much as it once might have. The publisher Isaac Funk, who knew the sisters, remarked at the time about Margaret that, "for five dollars she would have denied her mother, and would have sworn to anything."

Leah, on the other hand, lived well until the end of her life. She was the first to die, in 1890. Neither Margaret nor Kate attended her funeral. Although there has always been confusion about the dates of their births, Leah was believed to be about seventy-six years old.

Kate was the next to pass on in July 1892. She was probably no more than in her early fifties, if it was accurate that she was born in 1841. The confusion about their ages has never been satisfactorily settled.

Margaret, about a year-and-a-half older than Kate, spent her last days bedridden in a New York City tenement apartment, where she was tended by a woman physician named Dr. Mellen. The doctor was *not* a spiritualist, which makes her observations of Margaret on her death bed all the more curious.

Mrs. Mellen said that during Margaret's last hours of life in early 1893, there were sounds of loud raps in the room. The tiny apartment contained no hiding places; not even a closet. What's more, Margaret was paralyzed; she could move neither her arms nor legs. When the doctor asked about the noises, Margaret answered in a low and labored voice, "It was my friends watching over me." A short while later she died.

In 1904, more than a decade after the deaths of the Fox sisters, workmen renovating the old house in Hydesville where the spirit raps began found behind a wall in the cellar a human skeleton and nearby a peddler's "trunk" or tin box typical of the kind used in the early nineteenth century, and from which were sold "various trinkets, jewelry, and household necessities."

Were these the remains of the traveling peddler whose spirit gave its identity years earlier as the murder victim, Charles Rosna? Spiritualists considered the discovery to be evidence that the Fox sisters had been truthful. Skeptics, on the other hand, charged that the bones and trunk were planted there, a further indication, they said, of a hoax perpetrated by spiritualists.

Depending on your opinion, the sisters had either been the "original spirit rappers," or the "Rochester imposters."

In 1916, the Hydesville house was purchased and moved to Lily Dale, a small community in western New York where spiritualists had formed a gathering place and a headquarters. In 1955, the house "mysteriously" burned to the ground. It was rebuilt in 1968 as a tourist attraction. In Hydesville, on the spot where the original house stood, there is a marker that reads: BIRTHPLACE OF MODERN SPIRITUALISM 1848.

Often neglected in the story of the Fox sisters is the fact that once spiritualism became a huge movement in this country that attracted millions of adherents, all the way to the White House, its significance moved far beyond whether or not the sisters were genuine mediums.

If they were frauds, no one has explained how they so successfully perpetrated a hoax for so many years. Could their spirit rappings have been produced by trickery? Of course that was a possibility. But many questions remain unanswered so that no one can say with certainty what actually occurred. Perhaps the girls had demonstrated genuine spirit contact. It is also possible that they displayed psychic abilities such as telepathy, clairvoyance, and psychokinesis, by which they were able to manifest sounds, table movements, and other phenomena, using their own psychic energies, that had nothing to do with spirit communication.

Finally, from a historic perspective, looking back on what they accomplished, one has to be amazed that two young sisters from a tiny rural hamlet had caused a virtual seismic shift that captured the attention of millions of Americans for more than half a century.

Some sociologists, historians, and psychologists who have analyzed the reasons why spiritualism became so amazingly popular, claim "spiritualism as both a reflection and expression of the tensions inherent in nineteenth-century America," wrote Barbara Weisberg in 2004 in *Talking to the Dead*.

Spiritualism became a significant force that spurred science, psychology, and theology to think in new ways. While it challenged long-held notions and beliefs, it motivated millions to question the very nature of life and death. It also proved to be a valuable bereavement tool, especially following the Civil War. The movement the Fox sisters began grew to be much larger than them; confessions and recantations came too late to stop spiritualism and the surge of interest it sparked about the paranormal that continues to this day. The bottom line was that spiritualism represented *change*, a threat to many, but a new age for others.[8]

4

Spiritualism Spreading like Wildfire

They come and sit by my chair, they hover about my
  bed—
I am not always certain if they be alive or dead.
—ALFRED, LORD TENNYSON

From the inauspicious beginning of spiritualism in Hydesville, the movement spread quickly across the country, some would say at a gallop, until there were an estimated two million spiritualists in America by the early 1850s, and the movement showed no signs of slowing. In 1850, we were a nation of 23 million people; 3.2 million of them were black slaves, and slavery was the nation's most contentious domestic issue. We now had a population larger than that of Great Britain. Settlers were moving westward, in large numbers, all the way to California, which in 1850 joined the Union as a state. Immigrants from other countries had begun flooding into America as well, bringing with them elements of their own cultures and beliefs, spurring diversity. It was a time of both "expansion" and "social mobility," a number of writers and commentators observed.[1]

In 1848, when Maggie and Kate Fox first reported the spirit raps, the president of the United States was James Knox Polk. There's no evidence that he had any interest in spiritualism, but he did experience a premonition of his death in 1849. He died that June and was followed in office by Zachary Taylor, who'd become a hero during the Mexican War that ended in 1848. On a scorching day during a Fourth of July event in 1850, President Taylor became ill after eating a bowl of cherries and milk. He'd also had a foreboding that he would not survive. He lingered for several days and died on July 9, just as he'd predicted.

He was succeeded in office by Millard Fillmore, who ironically was from western New York—the same region that gave birth to the spiritualist movement.

The 1850s were a time of some of America's greatest literary figures, and most expressed curiosity—or disdain—about the growing spiritualist craze, but they did not reject supernatural or psychic events.

There was Ralph Waldo Emerson, a transcendentalist who believed that "immortality is a truth of the soul." Henry Wadsworth Longfellow wrote, "There is no death! What seems so is transition; / This life of mortal breath / Is but a suburb to the life elysian." Henry David Thoreau, also a transcendentalist, expressed interest in reincarnation. The poet William Cullen Bryant took part in séances. So did Nathaniel Hawthorne, who then rejected spiritualism, but created a spiritualist character for his 1852 novel, *The Blithedale Romance*. However, throughout his life he acknowledged that he'd witnessed apparitions. In one incident, Hawthorne, who went often to the Boston Athenaeum, always noticed an elderly minister there reading. One evening, as usual, Hawthorne observed the gentleman in his familiar chair. He was stunned to learn that the man had already died before he saw him. Hawthorne concluded that he'd seen the minister's apparition, which continued to appear for several more weeks.

A new novel about a great whale, published in 1851, was titled *Moby-Dick*. Its author, Herman Melville, was a believer in the afterlife. "Methinks that what they call my shadow here on earth is my true substance. . . . Methinks my body is but the lees of my better being," he wrote. Walt Whitman understood phrenology well enough to make literary allusions to it in his poetry. That same year, 1851, the great American novelist James Fenimore Cooper died; he'd attended séances with the Fox sisters. Later in the century, Henry James included spiritualists in his book *The Bostonians*. And the creator of Sherlock Holmes, Arthur Conan Doyle became deeply committed to the spiritualist movement.

The popular English poet Elizabeth Barrett Browning, drawn to spiritualism, joined in séances conducted by famed medium Daniel Dunglas

(D. D.) Home. However, her husband, poet Robert Browning despised Home and publicly mocked spiritualism as a fraud.

British novelist William Thackeray, whose works included the classic *Vanity Fair*, attended séances given by the Fox sisters and Home, but admitted his reaction to spiritualism was "mixed," at best.

In 1852, the best-selling author, Harriet Beecher Stowe published one of the most influential books of that or any other time: *Uncle Tom's Cabin*. It was responsible for coalescing considerable public opinion in the North against slavery. Stowe was seriously interested in the new spiritualist movement and attended séances, as did noted and outspoken abolitionist and newspaper publisher William Lloyd Garrison, whose other interests included mesmerism and phrenology.

The American poet Emily Dickinson considered the subject when she composed, "My life closed twice before its close; / It yet remains to see / If Immortality unveils / A third event to me."

Paranormal events did not occur only at séances as Louisa May Alcott discovered. Alcott, who would become the author of the classic *Little Women*, was just twenty-five years old in 1858 and lived in her family's home in Concord, Massachusetts. Despite the wave of interest in spiritualism, she remained uninvolved. But one did not need to be a spiritualist to have a psychic experience.

At the time her younger sister Beth, only twenty-three, was desperately ill with scarlet fever, and her condition was growing worse. Louisa and her mother remained at Beth's bedside as she grew increasingly "thin and emaciated." They knew their beloved Beth was dying. Louisa wrote the following in her diary on March 14, 1858:

My dear Beth died at three this morning, after two years of patient pain. Saturday, she slept, and at midnight became unconscious, quietly breathing her life away till three; then with one last look of the beautiful eyes, she was gone.

A curious thing happened, and I will tell it here, for Dr. G said it was a fact. A few moments after the last breath came, as Mother and I sat silently watching the shadow fall on the dear little face, I saw a light mist rise from the body and float up and vanish in the air. Mother's eyes followed mine, and when I said, "What did you see?" she described the same mist. Dr. G said it was the life departing visibly.[2]

Might Louisa and her mother have witnessed Beth's soul leaving her body? It seemed so. What is equally amazing is that Dr. G's answer made clear that he had seen this phenomenon on previous occasions. The Alcotts' experience also suggested that what they'd witnessed was more than a belief; it was a genuine paranormal or psychic event.

Here and abroad, scientists were experimenting with that most fascinating of energies: electricity and the workings of electromagnetism. The telegraph had already changed the nature of communication, and who dared doubt what other marvels were waiting to be discovered. Science and religion were not yet at serious odds, as would happen later in the nineteenth century.

One of the pioneers of photography, the Frenchman Louis Daguerre, died in 1851 in his sixty-second year. He would not live to see the controversy in the decades ahead about whether photography could capture the images of spirits, as it had of physical beings and places.

Also in 1851, New Yorkers had a new daily newspaper to read. It was called *The New York Times*, and it immediately took a strong antispiritualist stance. But if spiritualism caught your fancy, dozens of publications devoted to the new movement were readily available in towns and cities across the country.

One story about the paranormal that newspapers at the time could not ignore was the case of the poltergeist in the home of a New England minister.[3] Around 1850, the Reverend Eliakim Phelps, his wife, and their four children moved from Massachusetts to a house he purchased on Elm Street in Stratford, Connecticut.

Phelps, a Presbyterian minister and "mesmeric healer" had not been in the new home long when, inexplicably, strange and frightening poltergeist activity began. When the Phelps family returned from church one day they discovered furniture moved and objects thrown about the house. At first they thought vandals had broken in. But then to their horror more of their belongings hurtled through the air, including a pair of tongs and a shovel. Most chilling, however, was the discovery of small puppetlike figures made from scraps of cloth, and arranged as if they were praying. All but one of the effigies was female. There was also a description of one figure that looked like a "grotesque dwarf."

The *New Haven Journal* carried detailed accounts of the disturbances and subsequent investigations of the house but found no earthly explanation for events that occurred even in a locked room. "No visible power could have produced these manifestations," Reverend Phelps insisted.

Things grew worse when the Phelps children were "attacked in their beds" by the invisible force. Phelps said that one night he discovered strange writing on his desk, and later on the walls; much of it could not be deciphered. The reverend added that he'd witnessed the disturbances "hundreds and hundreds of times."

Most of the poltergeist activity occurred around Phelps's stepson, eleven-year-old Harry. Once, his bed was set afire. The famed medium Andrew Jackson Davis visited the house and conjectured that some form of energy or electricity was emanating from Harry. Activity in the house calmed when the boy was away from home; but the Phelps' poltergeist mystery was never solved, and the story made headlines around the country in the 1850s.

"Nothing quite like these manifestations has ever been recorded since in poltergeist cases," wrote author Rosemary Ellen Guiley. The Phelps case remains an example of a significant paranormal experience to emerge in the nineteenth century that had nothing to do with spiritualism. Nor could it be attributed to the trickery that many mediums would be accused of in the years to come, as the Fox sisters already had.

Around 1852, the terms *spiritualism* and *spiritualist* came into popular use. Before that no one was quite sure what to call the strange and inexplicable supernatural phenomena. Suddenly the Fox sisters were not the only mediums of note, although they were likely still the best known. Mediums, séances, and spirit circles could be found in most communities, large and small, throughout the country. New York City, for example, reported many hundreds of known mediums, and no less than forty thousand "serious believers" in spirit rapping. Even a small upstate town like Auburn, not far from where the Fox sisters grew up, had dozens of mediums by the 1850s. Throughout the country the number of mediums mushroomed, especially in the Northeast and New England. "In only a few years after the Hydesville rappings, it was estimated that more than 30,000 mediums were plying their trade," wrote Nancy Rubin Stuart in *The Reluctant Spiritualist* (2005).

Philadelphia claimed fifty to sixty private "spirit circles," and a large number of mediums as well. In Ohio there were two hundred spirit circles reported. In 1854, Illinois Senator James Shields presented to the United

States Congress a petition containing 15,000 signatures, calling on the federal government "to investigate communications from the dead." U.S. Senator N. P. Tallmadge and Ohio Congressman Joshua Giddings were among the politicians who were pro-spiritualist. If Margaret and Kate Fox created the spirit raps by trickery, they'd been very influential. By 1855, the New England Spiritualist Association estimated some two million believers in America.

The promise of communications with the spirit world had taken the country by storm, and was becoming even more popular in Great Britain.

In 1851, the young man destined to be the century's most famous medium, Daniel Dunglas (D. D.) Home, demonstrated one of his first séances in the Boston home of newspaper editor W. R. Hayden and his wife Maria, a medium whose ability mainly consisted of spirit raps. The next year, Mrs. Hayden became the first American medium to journey to England. Her accuracy was excellent, providing information for sitters that she could not possibly have known. As a result she became an influential figure in the early years of the spiritualist movement; when tested, she was deemed genuine. She later became a highly regarded medical doctor in Boston. Throughout the Great Age of Spiritualism there were many more women mediums than men. In a later chapter we'll explain the reasons that contributed to this fact.

Despite many well-known people attracted to spiritualism, by the early 1850s most major American newspapers railed against the craze. The *Boston Courier* thought it found a way to debunk the movement. It "offered five hundred dollars to any medium who could convince a committee of Harvard scientists that spirits communicated," explained R. Laurence Moore in his book *In Search of White Crows* (1977). Among the mediums willing to be tested were Kate and Leah Fox, and brothers Ira and William Henry Davenport, also from western New York State.

The Davenports would eventually achieve notoriety as mediums demonstrating spirit raps that they claimed they'd experienced in 1846, two years before the Fox sisters created the commotion in Hydesville.[4] Both boys were still in their teens in 1852 when they accepted the *Courier*'s challenge; five hundred dollars was a substantial amount at the time.

The Davenport brothers were tied tightly with "ropes drawn through holes bored in [a] cabinet and firmly knotted outside to make a network; the knots were tied with linen," according to the *Encyclopedia of Occultism and Parapsychology*. The reason for testing the brothers in this manner was because they'd become well known for being able to free themselves from a complicated series of knots. They claimed the spirit world communicated instructions to untie themselves. The Davenports made an entire public career in this manner.

During the *Boston Courier* test of the brothers a Harvard professor named Benjamin Peirce sat in a "cabinet" between the two. When Peirce went in, "an invisible hand shut the bolt and the din of musical instruments began. A phantom hand was thrust through a small, curtained opening near the top of the middle door of the wardrobe-like cabinet, and the professor felt it touch his head and face," explained the *Encyclopedia of Occultism and Parapsychology*.

When the demonstration was over, the Davenports were discovered to be untied. Then a rumor made the rounds that the ropes that bound the brothers were "twisted around Peirce's neck." The *Courier* immediately proclaimed the story "shamelessly false."

The Harvard committee never produced a final or conclusive report, and what little it said was not positive. But defending the Davenports was a Dr. Loomis, a professor at Georgetown Medical College. After studying the brothers he settled on the opinion that their abilities were the result of "some new unknown force."

Meanwhile, *The New York Times* established a position that has changed little in over 150 years of publication. On June 12, 1852, an editorial denounced spiritualism for "subversion of all respect and devotion to the only true faith." Throughout its history the *Times* has remained cautious and usually critical of the paranormal.

There was at least one newspaper supportive, or at least tolerant of spiritualism:[5] the *New York Tribune*, whose well-known publisher Horace Greeley welcomed the Fox sisters to his home when they visited the city in the summer of 1850. To many the *Tribune* was New York's "radical newspaper." But Greeley and his wife had reached out to spiritualism after the death of their son a year earlier.

In Washington, D.C., a newspaper called the *National Intelligencer* was so opposed to spiritualism that in April 1853, it branded it a "pestilence" and a product of "delusions." The paper accused spiritualism of being too close to, "if not actual atheism, and distracting the minds of the nervous, the feeble-witted, and the timid into actual insanity." The editors went so far as to demand laws to prohibit séances.

The popular magazine *Harper's Weekly* also strongly objected to spiritualism, suggesting that spirit circles, like "gambling dens and other places of ill-fame," should be shuttered.

But the several million American spiritualists had no lack of their own publications to choose from in answer to the angry anti-spiritualist screeds that appeared regularly in such periodicals as the *Catholic World*, *Christian Review*, *Christian World*, and *Church Review*, among others.[6] It's obvious from those few examples of titles that much of the antipathy toward spiritualism was based on religious grounds, and fear that the new movement posed a threat to Christianity and the churches.

For spiritualists there were literally, beginning in the 1850s and through the 1890s, hundreds of magazines, pamphlets, and newspapers devoted to their movement that came and went. Among the more successful publications were *Messenger of Light*, *The Christian Spiritualist*, *Banner of Light*, *The Spirit World*, *Spiritual Philosopher*, and perhaps the best known, the long-running *Spiritual Telegraph*, which began publishing in 1852. There were also many books published on the subject throughout the second half of the nineteenth century. By the early 1870s, annual sales of books about spiritualism totaled fifty thousand copies; and another fifty thousand pamphlets devoted to the subject were being sold yearly.

For both sides it was a lively time. There was even debate about whether spiritualism should be defined as a religion, as many of its adherents considered it. Some called it a "scientific religion"; others thought of it as a "quasi-religious" movement. But there were practical reasons for spiritualists to want their beliefs under the umbrella of religion. Many states were passing laws against "fortune-tellers and conjurers." It was wiser for spiritualists to claim protection as a religious denomination, than battle hostile governmental authorities eager to legislate spiritualism out of existence.

The growth of spiritualism had not gone unnoticed by its opponents. In Alabama, for example, a law was enacted that imposed a five-hundred-dollar fine on anyone who publicly demonstrated mediumship and other states followed, limiting or banning displays by mediums. Fortunately for Henry Gordon, New York City did not take so harsh a stand when he became one of the first American mediums to perform levitation, lifting off the ground in full view of audiences in 1852.[7]

But despite criticism and skepticism, the speed with which the interest in spiritualism grew across America was astonishing. Surprising to many who scoffed at the idea was the fact that it wasn't only the so-called superstitious or uneducated who were drawn to it. Increasingly, many educated, wealthy, and prominent people could be found at séances. Author R. Laurence Moore noted in *In Search of White Crows* that when a spiritualist society was founded in 1854 "its organizers [included] a former U.S. senator, four judges, two military officers, and several successful businessmen."

"Scarcely another cultural phenomenon affected as many people or stimulated as much interest as did spiritualism in the [decade] before the Civil War and, for that matter through the subsequent decades of the nineteenth century," Moore wrote.

Yet, nearly every recent traditional history book or biography about that period has chosen to ignore spiritualism entirely or brush it aside with a quick reference as if it had no significance, or was a short-lived fad or aberration. To the contrary, in its time, spiritualism became so popular that even many nonbelievers thought it might become "the religion of America." But spiritualism never assumed rigid or dogmatic strictures as most denominations did. It was accessible to everyone, and while that openness appealed to many, ironically, the lack of organization and coordination may have been among the movement's major weaknesses.

It quickly became apparent that the movement was riddled with much trickery and fraud. Still, people of all kinds sought mediums and séances for the promise of communication with an afterlife. However, there were those who remained incredulous that so many would believe such claims. The country was experiencing unprecedented growth and mobility, and spiritualism appeared to reflect the changes America was going through, in an age of religious and social agitation and excitement, coupled with new marvels in science and technology.

In 1859, barely a decade after the Fox sisters became public figures Charles Darwin published his *Origin of Species*.[8] The impact of his theory of evolution was stunning. "Accepting Darwin's theory meant replacing a perfect God in whose image you were deliberately, divinely created, with the anatomical results of natural selection and an ape for an ancestor."[9] "Into this, parapsychology—if its research proved strange phenomena to be real—threatened to redefine man's very nature, abilities, and purpose. For if, indeed, people did possess 'other abilities,' then the current concept of humankind, religion, perhaps even God, would have to be changed, or at the very least reexamined." Spiritualism became a starting point for many in their search for answers to some of the great mysteries about life and death.

For many bereaved people, spiritualism was a godsend. The early and mid-nineteenth century was a time when life expectancy was far shorter than today, and infant mortality rates were distressingly high: over 20 percent of babies born did not live to see their first birthday. It was not unusual for mothers to die during childbirth. Simply living to adulthood was an achievement, and many people did not live beyond their forties. Medical treatments were limited, often painful, even sometimes deadly.

Psychology had not yet been developed as a distinct field, and whether mediums realized it or not, they'd been cast into the role of grief counselors and therapists. Spirit contact spelled comfort, despite church condemnation, press hostility, and scientific ridicule; so attending séances was often more than merely "entertainment," as skeptics and debunkers cynically charged.

In the 1850s, "physical mediumship" became the most popular way of demonstrating communication from the spirit world, and many mediums put on quite a show. They seemingly made disembodied hands appear from nowhere in dark séance rooms. Sometimes the hands glowed or mysterious phosphorescent lights appeared. Strange noises might be heard. Some mediums produced spirit materializations. Musical instruments magically appeared, played a tune, and floated through the air; tables tipped, objects and furniture moved about, seemingly of their volition, even hurtling in the direction of those at the séance table.

In the first decade of America's Age of Spiritualism, physical manifestations, called "apports," were supposed to be evidence of contact with the departed. An apport was any object that a medium could materialize. They might be pieces of jewelry, vases, flowers, fruit, or even pets. One favorite apport was a dove—at one spirit circle in Boston, no less than eleven people confirmed that a white dove inexplicably materialized in a closed room. Often perfume was sprinkled on séance participants.

For believers, it was all wondrous work attributable to the spirit world.

To skeptics, séances were nothing but products of trickery and deception, the kind employed by stage magicians, not the souls of the departed. As séance participants and witnesses grew more sophisticated, many of the spirit materializations and apports were uncovered as fabrications perpetrated by unscrupulous mediums. But not every medium was exposed as a charlatan; sometimes their demonstrations of psychic ability were uncanny, even beyond the explanations of eagle-eyed debunkers.

One of the exceptions to the almost blanket accusation of apport fraud was Agnes Guppy-Volckman (1838–1917). Although she lived in London, her powers as a medium were also known in America. Often music would play, as if from thin air, and apports such as fruits and flowers would drop to the séance table. Other times, a dog, cat, or butterflies would materialize. At one séance, a small storm of feathers mysteriously drifted downward.

Debunkers made earnest efforts but were unable to determine how Mrs. Guppy-Volckman produced the phenomena. In 1869, when she was studied by an investigative committee one member noticed that the bottoms, or ends, of flower apports looked as if they'd been burned. When asked about it, she answered that electricity from the spirit world was responsible.

One last point about Mrs. Guppy-Volckman that set her apart from most other American and British mediums was that she could cause apports to materialize in lighted rooms.

Another British medium with a reputation in America was William Stainton Moses, also an ordained minister. He somehow was able to make a bell seemingly move by itself and ring as it went around the séance table. Among those who attended his sittings was Kate Fox.

How some of the apports were created is still subject to debate, but in the early years of spiritualism apports became important; supposedly proof of the spirit world at work.

Accusations of fraud followed physical mediums relentlessly. The fact was that when experiments were attempted under more or less controlled conditions, overwhelmingly they were uncovered as spurious. So many deceptive physical mediums were exposed that the credibility of all of them was called into question. In the latter years of the nineteenth century, far fewer mediums employed apports, until there were barely any.

One notable exception was the most famous medium of the nineteenth century, Daniel Dunglas (D. D.) Home, whose ability to levitate and produce a wide range of materializations was never exposed as fraudulent. In the next chapter we will detail his life and remarkable career, which baffled many, and is argued to this day.

From the pulpit to the political arena spiritualism was never free from debate.[10] Consider the story of John Worth Edmonds (1799–1874), a respected New York State Supreme Court judge who was forced from the bench because of controversy about his belief in spiritualism. Critics alleged that perhaps some of his judicial decisions were made with the help of spirit communications. He went on to become an influential figure in the early years of the spiritualist movement to which he devoted himself fully after resigning his judgeship.

One important concern raised by demonstrations of physical mediumship was exactly how much they elevated spirituality. Many people may have attended séances for contact with the Other Side. However, did a trumpet floating through the air in a darkened room, music inexplicably playing, bells ringing, a bird winging by, or even a levitating medium really add to one's spiritual growth? Or were the critics correct: was it just good theater? Was there anything to be learned otherwise? That criticism was leveled at the famed Davenport brothers. Even if their psychic powers were genuine, what inspired lessons could be gained from two young men bound in ropes who somehow became untied in a so-called "spirit cabinet"?

Even some of the most ardent spiritualists grew critical of the emphasis on showmanship. One of those was Andrew Jackson Davis, the respected medium and trance reader dubbed the "Poughkeepsie Seer." He eventually became so disenchanted with physical mediums that he broke with those who stubbornly defended them. Others critics warned ominously that physical manifestations of spirit phenomena encouraged contact with "lower level" or "evil spirits."

If the spirit world had any wisdom to impart, very little was communicated at most séances, critics charged. But if discarnate communication was genuine, the expectation that Grandpa, whose schooling had never gone beyond grade three on earth, would suddenly possess the wisdom of the ages now that he was on the Other Side was unrealistic. Time and time again, throughout the history of spirit communications, debunkers found fault with messages from departed loved ones that seemed rather trivial and mundane. Even when the message contained information known only to the recipient, it was rarely profound or revelatory. Spirit messages were more like letters or telegrams; often they were simply greetings or assurances to loved ones on earth.

In the early years of the spiritualist excitement, some mediums offered communications from famed historical figures that supposedly were now imparting worldly wisdom. One of the most popular of the spirits in that category was Benjamin Franklin. Hundreds of mediums claimed to have channeled him, but the messages were nearly always generalizations, or material already known. Isaac Post, who with his wife Amy had befriended the Fox sisters in Rochester, published a book in 1852 that purported to contain spirit communications from many of the late and great, such as George Washington and Thomas Jefferson.[11] However, his book revealed barely anything new. It disappointed readers and put into serious doubt the veracity of mediums who took this path, and the public quickly tired of it. Besides, more people preferred to hear from departed loved ones or to receive a materialized bouquet of flowers said to have come from their late mother's spirit handed to them by a medium.

In the 1850s, it was not unusual to be invited to "tea and table turning," or a demonstration of "table tipping."[12] Those who participated in this type of séance were asked to place their hands on the table and then wait until the table moved, tilted, or turned of its own volition. Not unlike spirit rapping, messages were tapped out in a code that corresponded to the alphabet. Séance participants would often communicate directly to the table by asking it questions that it answered through turns and tips.

Among those who demonstrated table tipping were the young Davenport brothers in Buffalo, New York. Ira was eleven years old and William was just nine in 1850 when they attempted it. Their father, a police official, swore he witnessed the table movements and accompanying knocks that tapped out spirit messages.

Although the process of table tipping dated back to ancient Rome, during the early years of spiritualism, it became enormously popular in America. Spiritualists explained it was the result of a form of universal psychic energy that was emitted from each and every object in the world. Mediums were said to be especially sensitive to this energy.

But table tipping was just as controversial as any other alleged psychic power. From their pulpits, many clergy railed against it as demonic; and a number of physicians warned of the danger to one's sanity from participating in such supernatural activity. Exactly what connection there was between table tipping and mental or emotional stability was never made clear.

In 1853, famed British scientist Michael Faraday rejected spiritualist explanations and announced his tests had produced the theory that table tipping and turnings were the result, not of spirits, but were caused by the séance participants through their own "unconscious muscular action." While many scientists agreed with Faraday, table tipping had its defenders who insisted that the movements were generated by spirit forces or some manner of psychic energy.

There was also a phenomenon known as "automatic writing," a type of mediumship that became hugely popular in the nineteenth century.[13] Simply explained, the medium's hand is controlled by a communicating spirit, so that what's written originates with the spirit, and the medium has no "conscious control" over what is being dictated or composed. Skeptics obviously disagreed, and some researchers concluded that automatic writing was the result of "subconscious activity" by the medium. What was curious about automatic writing is that sometimes, the style and content were unlike—and often beyond—the erudition of the medium.

From the 1850s until as recently as the 1970s, it was not unusual for some mediums to claim they were writing under spirit control, especially while in the trance state. In recent years, there have been fewer accounts of automatic writing. Today, mediums will sometimes jot down spirit messages received through clairaudience, but they rarely claim their hand is under any mysterious spirit control.

During the Great Age of Spiritualism, several mediums became especially recognized for automatic writing. Perhaps best known was the British spiritualist William Stainton Moses (1839–1892), an ordained minister who became a medium with a reputation in England and America.[14] He made the decision to pursue a career as a medium after he'd witnessed several séances and became convinced that spirit communication was genuine.

In addition to demonstrating various manifestations of physical mediumship, including apports, levitations, and so-called "psychic lights," Moses engaged in automatic writing, and eventually published his best-known examples in two popular books, *Spirit-Identity* (1879), and *Spirit Teachings* (1883). What helped Moses was that, unlike many other mediums, he had a sterling reputation for honesty and uprightness. Also, his automatic writing occurred when he was fully awake, not in trance.

Moses was also adept at "direct writing." By definition it was writing that was created independently by the spirit's hand, rather than by the medium, as in automatic writing. Of course, as did every other medium, he had his share of skeptics and detractors.

If séance participants wanted physical manifestations of spirit contact, so-called slate writing fit the bill. It became one of the favorite forms of psychical phenomena during the nineteenth century. The technique consisted of the medium and the subject seated opposite each other at a table small enough that each could hold a part or corner of a school slate. The slate was then held tightly against the bottom of the tabletop. Between the slate and the table a small piece of a "slate pencil" had been first placed for it to be used by the "spirit writer." If a short while later a scratching noise was audible, it presumably meant a spirit was writing something on the slate. When the process was completed, raps were heard, the slate was turned over and read; and there would be a message on it, supposedly written by spirits. It might be a communication specifically for the subject or something vague that could apply to virtually anyone.

Although slate writing was often criticized it remained popular through the nineteenth century. There was no question that it was a technique susceptible to fraud. Still there were an estimated two thousand "writing mediums" all over America who claimed they wrote down, under spirit control, messages communicated to them from the spirit world.

One American medium in particular became well known for slate writing: Henry Slade.[15] Following fifteen years of demonstrating in the United States, in 1876 he went to St. Petersburg, Russia, to be examined. Among those who observed him was Helena Petrovna Blavatsky, founder of the mystical Theosophical Society in 1875. She was impressed with Slade and proclaimed him to be genuine. She described his technique of employing "double slates, sometimes tied and sealed together, while they either lay upon the table in full view of all . . . or held in a . . . hand, without the medium touching it."

Then, at the peak of his fame, Slade became embroiled in allegations of fraud when debunkers found a previously written message on what was supposed to be a blank slate. In London, he faced criminal charges after similar deception was uncovered. He was found guilty, but the conviction was overturned on a technicality, and he wasted no time in departing from England.

In Philadelphia, Slade was tested by the Seybert Commission in 1885, which declared him a fraud. The accusations of trickery claimed that Slade prepared writings in advance on the slates, and the generalized messages offered no evidence that they were produced by spirit or psychic phenomena. By the end of the nineteenth century, slate writing had been largely discredited and was rarely seen again.

Another form of spirit communication became a lasting favorite.[16] In 1853, a French spiritualist named Planchette invented a device that was made from a piece of wood, shaped like a heart. On the bottom were three small wheels. Two of them held a pencil that was facing downward. The idea was for the medium to place his or her hand on the planchette, and the pencil would write automatically via spirit control through the psychic power of the medium. When the planchette became commercially available in America around 1868, thousands were sold. It was the forerunner of the immensely popular Ouija board. To what extent messages are derived from spirits or unconscious activity by the person holding the planchette is still debated today.

Direct voice phenomena like direct writing, was supposedly produced from spirits without intervention by the medium. One favorite test of debunkers was to have a medium fill her mouth with water while the discarnate entity spoke simultaneously. Assuming there were no confederates creating a second voice, that was one way to determine whether the medium had engaged in trickery by creating both voices through ventriloquism. In some cases, two distinct voices were heard, one presumed to come from a spirit, and the other from the medium. Several mediums confounded skeptics with "direct voice" phenomena, particularly inexplicable in an age before recordings.

One of the strangest of all the manifestations produced by nineteenth-century physical mediums was "ectoplasm."[17] The word comes from the Greek *ektos* and *plasma*, and translates to "exteriorized substance." Ectoplasm was "a mysterious vapor-like substance that, spiritualists claimed, streamed out of the body of an entranced medium," according to the *Encyclopedia of Occultism and Parapsychology*. It was a mainstay of many séances throughout the later nineteenth and early twentieth century.

Among the earliest references to ectoplasm those were from Swedish mystic Emanuel Swedenborg, who described "a kind of vapor" that exuded from his body when he first experienced visions. "Ectoplasm was used to form materializations, [and] usually said to be whitish and thready or vaporous," wrote Georgess McHargue in *Facts, Frauds, and Phantasms*.

There were countless witnesses to the peculiar substance emanating from mediums during séances. No one was certain what ectoplasm was composed of or what its function was. According to one spiritualist theory it may have been a physical manifestation of some kind of essential or life-giving energy that was then fully absorbed back into the medium's body. Mediums claimed that producing ectoplasm drained their own energy, supposedly placing them in such a sensitive state that no one was permitted to touch them or expose them to light. Obviously, those conditions made it difficult to examine ectoplasm. Not surprising, it became an easy target for debunkers and skeptics. In fact, some so-called ectoplasmic discharges proved to fabricated from soaked gauze or some other similar flimsy wet material. Many others were never explained, and remained a mystery. The fad eventually petered out.

Spirit materializations offered tangible and physical evidence supposedly from the spirit world. The best known "materialization medium" of the nineteenth century was Florence Cook (1856–1904). We'll tell much more about her life and career in a later chapter, but briefly, Cook, who was British, was known on both sides of the Atlantic for her ability to create "full materializations" of spirits in well-lighted rooms.

Another intriguing mediumistic display was something called "elongation."[18] Simply explained, some mediums were able to stretch their bodies, attributing the ability to the work of spirits. Actually, elongations dated back centuries to Hindu yogis; so skeptics questioned what that had to do with the spirit world. There was never a satisfactory explanation offered about what meaning elongations had in helping séance participants.

For a period of time so-called "cabinet materializations" held the attention of those who attended séances. Among the best known were the Davenport brothers we mentioned earlier. There were also the Eddy brothers from Chittenden, Vermont, in the years after the Civil War.

Much like our era of fads that come and go quickly, earlier generations of Americans also grew tired or bored with demonstrations of the same psychic phenomena. That is why many mediums found it necessary to progress from spirit rapping to table tipping and apports, and eventually to more elaborate demonstrations such as automatic writing, trance speaking, direct voice phenomena, levitations, and eventually spirit materializations. By the end of the 1850s, spiritualism was losing some of its appeal, and seemed to be—many hoped—on the wane. But national politics and war would soon intervene, and that would bring a renewed and even greater interest in the movement.

Most spiritualists had aligned themselves with the antislavery position from the beginning, as they had done with other social reform movements, such as women's rights. By the 1850s the nation was heading in an increasingly divisive and treacherous direction over the issue of slavery. It was an inexcusable institution, yet it had become entrenched in the Southern agrarian economy, while the North became increasingly industrialized.

Actually slavery had been a concern since the founding of the United States. "Nothing is more certainly written in the book of fate then that these people are to be free," Thomas Jefferson said about slavery.

"Hell" is how slaves described their own lives. In the North their allies were the increasingly influential abolitionists. In 1831, William Lloyd Garrison began publishing *The Liberator*, an antislavery newspaper, in Boston. Garrison, in addition to his interest in spiritualism, had an antislavery fervor that was nearly unequaled.

Then there was the amazing impact of Harriet Beecher Stowe's antislavery novel *Uncle Tom's Cabin*. It sold more than 300,000 copies in 1852, the year it was published, and another million and a half unauthorized copies were also in print. Its portrayal of the evils of slavery was so emotionally effective that it touched the hearts of millions in the North. Its power was more than Stowe, the "serious spiritualist," could ever have dreamed.

In October 1859, a militant abolitionist named John Brown and a band of followers staged a failed raid on the federal arsenal at Harper's Ferry, Virginia, hoping to foment antislavery sentiment. But Brown's attack backfired and he was hung in December. In the North he became a martyr for the abolitionist cause. Brown had prophesized that slavery would only be eradicated by bloodshed. Sadly, his prediction would soon be proven correct.

Several mediums also reported they'd had ominous visions of a terrible conflagration ahead. Increasingly, there was talk in the South of secession. The nation of some thirty million, nearly four million of them slaves, was in danger of dissolution. The South was intransigent; insisting its economy must have slavery to survive. In the North, the abolitionists were equally committed to ending the "evil institution." It appeared that no compromise could be reached on the question, and there were grave doubts that the Union could be preserved.

In November 1860, Abraham Lincoln was elected the sixteenth president of the United States, a victory that did not sit well in the South, although he'd pledged not to intervene in states where slavery already was in existence.[19] But there was such seething anger at Lincoln, viewed as antislavery, that South Carolina took the step all had feared. In the autumn of 1860, it became the first state to secede from the Union. Then other Southern states quickly followed. By February 1861, the Confederate States of America was created, and Jefferson Davis was named its president. In April 1861, the Confederate artillery fired on Fort Sumter, a federal fortress in Charleston harbor. The Civil War had begun.

"More than any other man in history, the foundation of his character was mystic," said the poet Walt Whitman about Abraham Lincoln. No one has ever explained with certainty what caused Lincoln to be our most psychic president, a fact largely ignored by traditional historians and Lincoln biographers. What is indisputable is that spiritualism, precognitive dreams, visions, premonitions, and clairvoyance played important roles in Lincoln's life and decisions.

Abraham Lincoln was born on February 12, 1809, in a one-room log cabin in Hardin County, Kentucky, where his father, Thomas Lincoln, worked as a farmer and carpenter. When he was seven years old, the family moved to Indiana. By then Abe was old enough to take on chores. One chore in particular, milling corn into meal, might well have been the event responsible for what some say was his sudden acquisition of psychic abilities while he was still an eight-year-old child. It was the result of a frightening accident that happened at a local mill some two miles from home. Anxious to complete the task and return before sundown, young Lincoln hurried the horse by striking her with a whip each time she circled. But the mare struck back with a kick that knocked Abe to the ground, where he hit his forehead and lay bleeding and unconscious until the miller discovered him and summoned his father, who hurried to the mill with his wagon and brought his son back to their house.

At first, the injury appeared so serious that Thomas Lincoln thought his son had been killed. Finally, after several hours during which he was unable to speak, Abraham appeared to recover. If there were lingering aftereffects or symptoms of brain damage, they were never reported. However, did the blow initiate psychic abilities? Some parapsychologists theorize that trauma to the head may cause a rerouting of neurological impulses in the brain, perhaps even creating new circuitry loops and awakening a dormant area in the brain where psychic abilities, and any accompanying emotional problems, manifest themselves. Whatever the root cause, Lincoln suffered from moderate to severe melancholia throughout the rest of his life.

In 1818, nine-year-old Abraham was at his mother Nancy's bedside when she died of "milk sickness." Abe was heartbroken and called her his "angel mother."

Thomas Lincoln remarried an attractive widow named Sarah Bush Johnston who had three young children of her own. For Abraham, she became a guardian angel in whom he found lifelong love, support, and encouragement. The affection was mutual, for she loved him as much. She also encouraged him to read and find a profession that would give him satisfaction. Her encouragement worked because, despite less than a year of formal schooling, young Abraham became a voracious reader.

By the time he was sixteen, he was six foot two inches tall and with his physical strength, became excellent at rail splitting. But father and son grew apart because Abraham had no desire to make a career of farming or rail splitting. Finally, in 1831, when he was twenty-two, he left home forever, yearning for more than he believed he could get by working his father's farm.

He traveled to New Orleans, where, for the first time in his life, he witnessed large numbers of newly arrived African slaves being brutally treated. The sight profoundly disturbed Lincoln, who'd been raised by strongly antislavery parents. For his entire life, that picture remained with him, as did his antislavery feelings.

He traveled back north and soon moved to the small village of New Salem, Illinois, where he lived for the next six years even while describing himself as a "piece of floating driftwood." There he worked as a clerk in a general store and later as the local postmaster.

After serving in the Black Hawk War, Lincoln returned to New Salem, ran his own general store, and worked as a surveyor. By now his lifelong belief in fatalism was firmly set, accepting the idea of predestination, that "events were ordained by immutable natural law." Although his parents were Baptists, Lincoln was never comfortable with evangelical belief. Freethinkers were more to his liking. When he found them, they'd gather at his general store to debate and ponder such things as the likelihood of miracles, and the reality of free will versus destiny. Lincoln also displayed an introspective side, sometimes becoming so quiet he appeared to be in trance, something not uncommon for individuals with a bent for the mystical and supernatural. He also developed a belief in dreams as well as "other signs and portents."

Lincoln ran for a seat in the Illinois State Legislature, studied law, and was admitted to the Illinois Bar. His prospects were rising. However, following a tragic love affair with a young New Salem woman named Ann Rutledge, who died of typhoid in August 1835, he fell into a deep and intractable depression. "Ann was the only woman he truly loved," said his law partner, William Herndon, who also claimed "her memory exerted a mystic, guiding influence throughout [Lincoln's] life."[20]

Lincoln seemed to recover from the shock of Ann's death as his stature in Illinois politics rose. In 1837, he moved to the larger and more prosperous community of Springfield to practice law. There he soon met and courted the pretty and socially prominent Mary Todd. She was the high-spirited daughter of the city's most successful banker and merchant. Although her family had owned slaves, she was antislavery. He, on the other hand, was the rough-hewn backwoodsman-turned-lawyer and an awkward-looking giant. But he proved gentle, courteous, an impeccably honest politician who had already caught the eye of the state's power brokers, and he quickly became Springfield's most successful new attorney.

Lincoln's relationship with Mary Todd grew and flourished, and the two became what today would be called the power couple of Springfield, despite the fact that Mary could be moody and hot-tempered. In 1842, notwithstanding Lincoln's trepidations about marriage and his year-and-a-half-long indecision about commitment, Lincoln and Mary Todd married and a year later, their first child, Robert, was born.

Arguments, differences, and Mary's explosive temper frequently marred the marriage. Today, Mary Todd would likely be diagnosed and treated for postpartum depression and bipolar personality disorder. But in the mid-nineteenth century, modern psychiatry was unknown. Her wild fluctuations in mood were attributed to her temperament; it was just the way she was; and people accepted it as her eccentricity.

Mary Todd was also eerily prescient and endowed with psychic gifts. However, she was emotionally needy, required constant attention, and could not tolerate being ignored, especially by her husband. But he also had to deal with his own depression, and their depressive personalities played off each other. At the same time he had a career to tend to in law and politics. Today we might call the Lincolns dysfunctional. However, that was an unknown term in their day, and the Lincolns remained two unhappy people, getting along as best they could.

Despite their blow-ups, they remained devoted to each other. No one questioned Lincoln's domestic difficulties, at least not publicly, for the sanctity of marriage was taken far more seriously in the mid-nineteenth century than today.

In 1846, the Lincolns' second son, Edward, was born; his birth drew the couple closer. But it wasn't long before they fell into the grips of depression and grief, when Eddie, not yet four, died of tuberculosis in February 1850. Their third son, William Wallace, called Willie, was born later that year in December. Then in 1853, a fourth son, Thomas, nicknamed Tad, was born.

As Lincoln's political stature grew in Illinois, he served one term in congress. Meanwhile, the country was sliding toward a constitutional crisis over the issues of states rights and the demands to abolish slavery. In 1850, the Fugitive Slave Act made it possible for vigilante groups to seize free blacks as runaway slaves with no due process of law. Then in 1854, the Kansas-Nebraska Act was passed. These were laws meant to preserve the Union not by interfering with slavery where it already existed, but by prohibiting its expansion. Many in the North who wanted slavery abolished even in the South were enraged, and that led to the creation of the Republican Party. Its compromise platform was that slavery would not be permitted in the new states and territories. The nation was bitterly divided, and already there were calls to arms.

Abraham Lincoln sadly predicted, "There is no peaceful extinction of slavery in prospect for us." To this day, no one can say with certainty whether his prognostication was prescient, born of political astuteness, or a combination of both. But Lincoln made clear his personal feelings about slavery: "No man is good enough to govern another man, without that other's consent."

Lincoln was considered a moderate in the presidential election. He'd carved out a position that he hoped would appeal to both North and South. With radical tensions running high on both sides, he had carefully chosen a fragile middle ground, and it worked: in November 1860, Lincoln was elected president.

It had been a difficult campaign, but the tall, gaunt, and "sorrowful" looking self-taught son of a farmer was now to be the new president of the United States. The strangely psychic Lincoln was still grieving over the death of his second son, Eddie, as he prepared to leave Springfield for the White House and the enormous task of "saving the Union" ahead.

But in early 1861, before his inauguration, Lincoln's psychic visions invaded his consciousness, when he experienced an unsettling premonition while still in Springfield.[21] He shared it with friends. "I was pretty well tired out and went home to rest," he said. "Opposite where I lay was a bureau with a swinging glass and looking in the mirror, I was astonished to see myself reflected, almost at full length, but with my face double. It had two separate and distinct images . . . I was more than a little bothered, perhaps startled, and I got up and looked in the glass. But the illusion vanished.

"On lying down again I saw it a second time, plainer if possible, than before. Then I noticed that one of the faces was paler, much paler than the other. I got up and the thing melted away. Later in the day, I told my wife about it, and a few days later I tried the experiment again, when, sure enough, the vision came.

"My wife thought it was a sign that I would be elected to a second term of office and that the paleness of one of the faces was an omen that I shall not live through the last term. . . ."

Four years later, as Lincoln began his second term, the foreboding vision recurred. "I have seen this evening what I saw on the evening of my confirmation. As I stood before a mirror I saw two images of myself: a bright one in front and one that was pallid, standing behind. It completely unnerved me. The bright one, I know is my past, and the pale one my coming life. I do not think I shall live to see the end of my second term. . . ."

But in 1861, his second term was still four years away, and his first presidential victory brought no celebrations in the Southern states, who fearing the effects of a Lincoln presidency, began to declare themselves for secession.

In his March inaugural address, Lincoln borrowed from the Bible when he said, without equivocation as he promised to preserve the Union, "A house divided against itself cannot stand." His words were put to the test only a month later when Fort Sumter was attacked, igniting the Civil War.

Throughout his career, especially in his leadership of the war, Lincoln was a fatalist, seeing himself as destiny's tool rather than someone who shaped destiny. "I have been controlled by some other power than my own will," he once said, reflecting on the degree to which his fate and fortunes depended not on his own actions, but were instead determined by some greater power. "I frequently see my way clear to a decision. I cannot recall one instance in which I have followed my own judgment, based upon such a decision, where the results were unsatisfactory; whereas in almost every instance where I have yielded to the views of others I have had occasions to regret it. I am satisfied that when the Almighty wants me to do or not do a particular thing, [He] finds a way of letting me know it. . . ."

Lincoln did not deny his psychic inclinations even though he did not publicly embrace them. However, he confided to friends that he was, indeed, a spiritual believer. As he once wrote to Joshua Speed, his friend from Springfield, "I always did have . . . a . . . strong tendency to mysticism." Nor was he alone given to psychic experiences. While president-elect, in January 1861, he traveled to Coles County, Illinois, to visit his beloved stepmother, Sarah. It was a moving experience for both, but when the time came to bid her farewell, she cried, fearful for his safety. Lincoln did his best to reassure her and to ease her fears: "No, no, Mama. Trust in the Lord and all will be well. We will see each other again." But it would be their last visit.

Years later she remembered, "I did not want Abe to run for president, did not want him elected, was afraid somehow or other . . . that something would happen [to] him . . . and that I should see him no more." Sarah Bush Lincoln outlived her stepson by four years.

From almost the time he was elected, there were threats to kidnap and murder him, but Lincoln, believing his life was in the hands of Providence, allowed few safeguards. On Inauguration Day, however, extra precautions were taken to shield him as he rode down Pennsylvania Avenue to be sworn in. Advisers convinced him that even though he believed his fate might be predetermined, a lucky shot from a crazed enemy would throw the country into chaos and change the course of the entire Union.

Shortly after his election in 1860,[22] the *Cleveland Plain Dealer* published an article based on comments from medium J. B. Conklin, who asserted Lincoln was a "sympathizer with spiritualism," because Conklin claimed he'd seen Lincoln anonymously at several of his New York séances. The newspaper's assertion that Lincoln was a spiritualist gained further credence from a report in the *Spiritualist Scientist* that the medium Mr. Conklin "was a guest at the Presidential Mansion." If the newspaper expected a denial from Lincoln, surely they were taken aback, for when shown the story, he answered, "The only falsehood in the statement is that the half of it has been told. This article does not begin to tell the wonderful things I have witnessed." It was one of the few times Lincoln would publicly state his belief in spiritualism, although he never denied it.

Most in the North expected the South would be quickly defeated, perhaps in a matter of months; after all, its population was more than double that of the Confederacy, and the nation's manufacturing and material centers were in the North. Author Charles Slack described the mood in the Union states as a "burst of optimism and euphoria."

However, with the prescience he often revealed, Lincoln strongly disagreed. He knew it would be a long and bitter fight. He also had knowledge about the limits of the North's preparedness in the opening months of the war that most were unaware of. Thus, Lincoln's pessimism was likely a combination of military facts and prescience.

While the burdens of the bitter and bloody war weighed heavily on the president, his personal world seemed to collapse in early 1862 when young Willie Lincoln was taken ill with "bilious fever," likely typhoid, caused by pollution in the White House water system. It was a devastating blow because Willie was the son whom the president had most doted on, especially after the death of Eddie. In fact, among the few pleasant diversions from the day-to-day pressures of the war were the times he spent with his sons, Willie and Tad, and their pets, a pony and two small goats.

Now Willie lay seriously ill, growing weaker by the day, and the Lincolns kept an anxious vigil at their son's bedside, too distraught to fully concentrate on anything else. Through agonizing days and nights, Mary Todd sat with her son for hours at a time, while the president broke away from often contentious cabinet meetings and war duties as often as he could to visit Willie's sickroom.

Then, on the afternoon of February 20, 1862, eleven-year-old Willie Lincoln passed from this world. Lincoln, choked with grief, told his secretary, John Nicolay, "Well Nicolay, my boy is gone. He is actually gone!" The president broke into tears. Mary Todd burst into hysterics and became inconsolable; she would never again set foot in the room where Willie died or in the East Room, where his body was embalmed. Nor could she summon the strength to attend her son's funeral in the White House on a dreary and stormy winter day. As the president gazed at the face of his dead son, he said, overwhelmed with emotion, "He was too good for this earth . . . but then we loved him so."

After Willie's passing, Lincoln sought comfort from the Almighty to a greater degree than he ever had before. He also pondered increasingly on the reality of life after death and believed that Willie's spirit was a presence close to him. "Did you ever find yourself talking with the dead?" the president asked his friend and treasury secretary Salmon P. Chase, who was at a loss for an answer. Lincoln told Chase, "Ever since Willie's death, I catch myself involuntarily talking to him, as if he were with me, and I feel he is."

On another occasion, Lincoln asked an aide, "Colonel, did you ever dream of a lost friend, and feel that you were holding sweet communion with that friend, and yet had a sad consciousness that it was not a reality? Just so I dream of my boy, Willie." Whether he realized it or not, that was no dream. The president had likely experienced what parapsychologists call an "after-death communication"; a visitation from a deceased loved one through the dream state. Its purpose was to bring a message of comfort from Willie to his father, a means of communicating that his spirit was still close by.

The president also found some solace in Shakespeare's *Macbeth* and *King Lear*. In *King John* he also read Constance's elegy for her dead son: "And, father cardinal, I have heard you say / That we shall see and know our friends in heaven: / If that be true, I shall see my boy again."

One night, several months after Willie died, fire erupted in the White House stables. Lincoln cried as he watched guards extinguish the fire, for in the blaze, Willie's pony had died. It was a sad irony and bitter post-script to Willie's death.

As desolate as Lincoln's life had become after his son's passing, it was even worse for his wife. Mary Todd at times became almost delusional in her grief and denial of the finality of death, so she turned to mediums and séances to communicate with her two deceased sons. She grasped for what-ever she could hold on to as she fell deeper into depression. She claimed she sometimes saw the apparitions of her sons standing by the foot of her bed at night. With every new medium Mary heard about, she held out the hope it would bring her into communication with Willie and Eddie as if to bring them back to life. Her husband became her only link to reality; she still fought with him when she thought he was paying too much at-tention to the war and not enough to their shared sorrow. For Lincoln, it was all he could do to keep his personal life from unraveling right before his eyes. As the War Between the States dragged on, he also had to deal with the war at home with his troubled wife.

Still, he maintained his belief in predestined events. "In the present civil war, it is quite possible that God's purpose is something different from the purpose of either party." Lincoln's thoughts overlapped reli-gious belief with the supernatural: "He permits [the war] for some wise purpose of His own, mysterious and unknown to us."

Mysticism remained an anchor for Lincoln because, like his belief in predestination, it offered hope that there was a greater intelligence behind the turmoil that seemed to beset him on every side. Many historians have attributed Lincoln's interest in mysticism and spiritualism entirely to his wife. While Mary certainly persuaded him to join her at séances after Willie's death, Lincoln wrote to his friend Joshua Speed expressing "his tendency to mysticism" in 1842, several years before the spiritualist craze swept America in 1848.

Although the president had made clear his belief in spiritualism, it is true that the driving force behind his visits to the séance table was Mrs. Lincoln, who sought consolation over the deaths of Willie and Eddie.

The Lincolns' first séance to communicate with Willie was conducted by the medium Mrs. Cranston Laurie, who practiced from her home in Georgetown.[22] Apparently, Mary Todd was so satisfied with the séance that she invited the Lauries to the White House or visited them at their home several times between 1862 and 1865. Shortly after their first sessions, Mrs. Laurie urged Nettie Colburn, a gifted twenty-year-old medium, to offer her services to the Lincolns. When the Lincolns agreed to meet her, spiritualist Thomas Foster introduced Nettie to Mary Todd, who then requested a sitting with the young woman. She "never charges for her séances," Mary Todd was told. "They were free."

Nettie's first sitting for Mary Todd was held at the Lauries' home, where, for an hour, she demonstrated her abilities while in trance.[23] The first lady was impressed: "This young lady must not leave Washington. I feel she must stay here, and Mr. Lincoln must hear what we have heard. It is all-important, and he must hear it." Mary Todd arranged for Nettie to work in the Agriculture Department. With her new salary-paying job, Nettie was able to accommodate the growing number of Washington society who sought her mediumistic gifts.

Before he became president, Lincoln made clear his belief, set forth in the Declaration of Independence, that all men were equal. However, he admitted that the Constitution restricted the idea of equality by counting each slave as three-fifths of a man. Lincoln conceded that he had no idea how to eliminate slavery, since the contentious issue was wrapped together with the question of states' rights. There was also Lincoln's campaign pledge not to interfere with slavery in the South, although abolitionists still pressed to rid the country of slavery entirely.

But as the war dragged on and the number of casualties mounted by 1862, public support began to teeter. Lincoln's thinking was undergoing a transformation: Would the nation support emancipation of the slaves? He began to consider an emancipation proclamation, an idea that sharply divided his advisors. The moral and political implications were immense, and the reactions predictable. Lincoln faced an enormous dilemma.

In September 1862, he wrote a draft of his proclamation, but then held back. He was waiting for a divine sign or portent, such as a Union victory, to help him back his momentous decision. Meanwhile he wrestled with the question of whether it was God's intention that the slaves be freed. But Lincoln said he had not received a sign to guide him. "The Almighty gives no audible answer to that question, and . . . the Bible gives none," he said. But, young Nettie Colburn had already set forth on a course that would ultimately intersect with the very choice Lincoln was struggling with himself to make.

In the 1850s, when she was in her teens, Nettie discovered she had mediumistic abilities when she induced spirit rappings. Despite her lack of political knowledge, she correctly predicted the winner of the presidential election in November 1856 would be James Buchanan, although her father was a staunch supporter of the opposing candidate, John C. Fremont.

With her father's approval and support, Nettie became a "spiritual lecturer" throughout New England towns and villages. When the Civil War erupted in 1861, despite Northern expectations of a quick victory, she predicted otherwise: "Our spirit friends . . . reply . . . it would continue four years, and require five practically to end it."

Nettie moved to Washington to be by the side of her youngest brother, who'd been wounded in the war and hospitalized. In a trance, Nettie said the spirits directed her to go to President Lincoln to seek aid for her brother, but she demurred, fearing she'd be thought an "escaped lunatic." However, in November 1862, a furlough was granted to her brother. Meanwhile, Nettie became friendly with a number of mediums who believed she was genuinely psychic.

One evening, after Nettie had demonstrated her abilities for Mary Todd at the Lauries' home, Mrs. Laurie was invited to the White House and asked to bring "Miss Nettie" along with her to meet the president. Nettie was frightened, approaching the event with the "natural trepidation of a young girl . . . about to meet some superior being . . . [I] was almost trembling [as] I entered . . . the . . . White House." Mary Todd ushered Nettie into the Blue Room, where they waited for the president to join them. President Lincoln soon arrived to meet Nettie and to greet his friends, the Lauries and their daughter, Mrs. Miller, a physical medium. Nettie was "led forward and introduced. He stood before me, tall and kindly, with a smile on his face. Dropping his hand upon my head, he said, 'So this is our little Nettie, is it, that we have heard so much about?' "

"Yes sir," Nettie smiled and answered.

The president led her to an ottoman at the foot of his chair, bade her to sit, and proceeded to question her about the details and practices of mediumship. Throughout, she said, "His manner . . . was genial and kind." A spirit circle was formed, and finally Lincoln asked her, "Well, how do you do it?"

Nettie was soon in a trance. "I lost all consciousness of my surroundings and passed under control," she would write years later. For the next hour, she offered spirit messages, which the president appeared to understand, and then turned to the subject of the forthcoming Emancipation Proclamation. From the spirit world, Nettie received and relayed a message for Lincoln "not to delay . . . [its] enforcement beyond the opening of the year [1863]." Her spirit control assured the president it would be "the crowning event of his administration and his life; and that while he was being counseled by strong parties to defer . . . [or] . . . delay action, he must in no way heed such counsel, but stand firm to his convictions and fearlessly perform the work and fulfill the mission for which he had been raised up by an overruling Providence." Those present in the room during the medium's trance state observed that "some strong masculine spirit force was giving speech to almost divine commands," rather than the voice of a young woman barely out of her teens. After Nettie's delivery of the message to Lincoln, one guest queried, "Mr. President, did you notice anything peculiar about the method of address?" Lincoln stood up "as if shaking off his spell," then glanced at a full-length portrait of Daniel Webster, which hung above the piano, and emphatically answered, "Yes, it is very singular, very!"

Former congressman Daniel Somes asked, "Mr. President would it be improper for me to inquire whether there has been any pressure brought to bear upon you to defer the enforcement of the proclamation?"

Lincoln replied, "It is taking all my nerve and strength to withstand such a pressure."

"When I regained consciousness," Nettie later wrote about the event, "I was standing in front of Mr. Lincoln, and he was sitting back in his chair, with his arms folded . . . looking intently at me." The group gathered around the room sat in "perfect silence." They watched the young girl and the melancholy president eye each other as if trying to figure out what hidden force was behind the message. Ultimately, Nettie's reading was summed up this way: "The Civil War will not end until the president issues an Emancipation Proclamation to set free the millions of slaves in the United States." She confirmed it was the spirit of Northern patriot, great orator, and politician Daniel Webster who communicated the emphatic message to her, a message Webster himself might have delivered because in life he "articulated a near-mystical devotion to the Union." Like Webster, Lincoln reflected the same devotion to the Union in his speeches.

When Nettie's channeling session was finished, the president turned to her, placed his hand upon her head, and said, "My child, you possess a very singular gift; but that it is of God, I have no doubt. I thank you for coming here tonight. It is more important than perhaps anyone present can understand. I must leave; but I hope I shall see you again." He shook Nettie's hand, bowed to the others present, and took his leave. Nettie remained for another hour, talking with Mary Todd and her friends, then returned to Georgetown.

Nettie's was not the only voice that had communicated messages to President Lincoln from the Other Side concerning the emancipation. Another paranormal influence brought to bear on the president to issue the proclamation came from U.S. Senator Thomas Richmond, who disclosed in his 1870 book, *God Dealing with Slavery*, letters that had been received psychically, which were then sent to the president, hoping to persuade him to issue the order. It took another few months of wavering before Lincoln issued the proclamation, but on January 1, 1863, it went into effect and changed the course of the Civil War.

Lincoln's stewardship of the country and his leadership of the Union to victory were arguably his greatest accomplishments as a statesman; history regards the Emancipation Proclamation as Lincoln's most significant political achievement. Not only did the proclamation make clear a moral purpose for pursing the war, it established the groundwork for the ongoing American civil rights movement a century later.

Still, Lincoln initially questioned whether the proclamation would succeed as a political and social document. Clearly, his doubts and anxiety seem to have been mitigated, in part, by his reliance on advice from the spirit world as communicated to him by Nettie. And, of course, once he resolved his hesitancy, Lincoln said, "I never, in my life, felt more certain that I was doing right, than I do in signing this paper."

The president had sought a divine portent to guide him morally along the right path. And the message from Daniel Webster's spirit may well have been the sign that convinced Lincoln to issue the proclamation. Many close friends and colleagues confirmed this, and years later, Mary

Todd acknowledged it herself. Finally, Nettie, who wrote that she had looked directly into Lincoln's face when she awakened from her trance state after delivering Daniel Webster's message, believed with all her heart that the president was influenced by her séance.

On another occasion, in December 1862, Philadelphia railroad magnate Colonel Chase witnessed the Lauries' younger daughter, who possessed mediumistic abilities, induce a trance, walk up to President Lincoln, and say, "A congress of wise spirits hold the welfare of [the] nation in their keeping. You, sir, have been called to . . . serve a great and mighty purpose . . . Thou art the man. Issue a proclamation of emancipation giving a freedom to the slaves and from that hour victory will crown the Union Army and humanity will be served." Chase later told a newspaper reporter, "We listened spellbound to her burning words, and when she ended there was not a dry eye in the room." The young girl claimed to be controlled by the Roman philosopher Seneca. Chase described the spirit address as an "inspiration. It was one of the most powerful pleas for human rights I have ever heard." The president said, "I am deeply impressed."

When Chase was asked by the incredulous reporter, "Do you contend that the Emancipation Proclamation was issued as result of communication with the world of the spirits?" Chase answered, "There is not the least doubt that the communications turned the scales and was the pivot upon which one of the most important events in American history revolved." From the time of Miss Laurie's trance reading, Union forces won more than two-dozen battles, precisely as the young girl predicted.

Lincoln's interest in the paranormal and spiritual had only been whetted by the events preceding his announcement of the Emancipation Proclamation. They continued through 1863, an especially active period of White House séances and the assemblage of spirit circles. On February 5, there was another séance at the Laurie home, requested by Mary Todd for herself and several friends. At the last minute, the president decided to attend. Nettie thought Lincoln "appeared tired and haggard," more so than only several weeks earlier. "Well, Miss Nettie, do you think you have anything to say to me tonight?" the president asked. "Suppose we see what they will have to tell us."

Nettie's psychic communiqués were translated to her through entities called "spirit controls," one of which was known as "old Dr. Bamford." He was Lincoln's particular favorite. Once the spirit took hold of Nettie and her waking personality was transformed into the medium for the stentorian Dr. Bamford, it announced its message in prophetic tones, denouncing the current state of the army and military strategy and demanding that the president take action. "The army [is] totally demoralized," began the spirit control's lament. "Regiments are stacking arms, refusing to obey orders to do duty; threatening a general retreat." Then "a vivid picture was drawn of the terrible state of affairs." The others present were surprised, but not the president.

"You seem to understand the situation," he said. "Can you point out the remedy?"

"Yes, if you have the courage to use it," the spirit control answered.

Lincoln smiled and replied, "Try me."

Dr. Bamford proceeded. "It is one of the simplest. The remedy lies with yourself. Go in person to the front, taking with you your wife and children, leaving behind your official dignity and all manner of display. Resist the importunities of officials to accompany you. Avoid the officers and seek the tents of the private soldiers. Inquire into their grievances. Show yourself to be what you are, the Father of your People! Make them feel that you are interested in their sufferings . . . the many trials which beset them . . . whereby both their courage and numbers have been depleted."

"It shall be done," Lincoln answered unhesitatingly.

"It will do all that is required," Dr. Bamford continued. "It will unite them to you in bands of steel. And now, if you would prevent a serious, if not fatal, disaster to your cause, let the news [be] disseminated throughout the camp of the Army of the Potomac. Have it scattered and broadcast that you are on the eve of visiting the front. . . . This will stop insubordination and hold the soldiers in check . . ."

"If that will do any good, it is easily done," the president said.

In the ensuing conversation, the spirit control told the president he would be reelected, particularly on the wings of a Union victory in the war. After the séance, Lincoln, while confirming the gravity of the army's situation, asked those present not to speak about it. Lincoln took seriously the urging of Nettie's spirit control that he personally visit the Union troops. The day after the séance, newspaper headlines proclaimed: THE PRESIDENT IS ABOUT TO VISIT THE ARMY OF THE POTOMAC.

At the battle line, "the ovation tendered him showed the spontaneous uprising of a people to receive a beloved ruler . . . he was literally borne on the shoulders of soldiers through the camp, and everywhere the 'boys in blue' rallied around him . . . and [he left] a united and devoted army behind him when he returned to Washington." Nettie wrote, "The wisdom of [the president's] action told the result." The soldiers saw Lincoln as a "man . . . in all his simplicity," not the "president," and with him he carried "a personal influence which would be felt throughout the camp."

Lincoln realized that although he might be a spiritual believer in the privacy of the family quarters of the White House, he could not let the population at-large think that matters of national policy and war strategy were discussed with advisors from an ethereal world on the Other Side. In particular, he wanted no one to know that he'd received advice from the ghost of Daniel Webster. Nettie, too, was frequently cautioned not to discuss her psychic sessions with reporters because the presidential séances were strictly a private matter. It was nearly thirty years later that she wrote a book about her experiences and disclosed some of the private and sensitive information she shared with Lincoln.

In April 1863, the president paid another visit to the world of the paranormal when he observed the abilities of the medium Charles Schockle at a White House demonstration, which included spirit rappings and levitations.[24] Also present that evening were several friends and two Lincoln cabinet officials, Secretary of War Edwin Stanton and Secretary of the Navy Gideon Welles. The audience watched tables move, a portrait of Henry Clay shift back and forth, and two candelabra that were gifts to John Adams lift themselves almost to the ceiling. The president also heard loud rappings under his feet, which, Schockle explained, came from the spirit of an Indian who wished to make his presence known. Following more rappings, a message from the spirit of Henry Knox, Lincoln's first secretary of war, was delivered to the medium through a demonstration of mechanical writing. Knox advised the president to "use every means to subdue; make a bold front and fight the enemy."

The president asked Schockle, "I should like to ask General Knox if it is within the scope of his ability to tell when this rebellion will be put down."

Schockle answered, "Washington, Lafayette, Franklin, Napoleon . . . and myself have had frequent consultations on this point. This is something which our spiritual eyes cannot detect . . . Franklin sees the end approaching. Other spirits have conflicting opinions."

"Opinions differ among the spirits as well as among humans," Lincoln remarked, perhaps as much to the spirit of General Henry Knox as to his living White House guests. "They don't seem to understand running the machines among the celestials much better than we do. Their talk and advice sound much like the talk of my cabinet." The president seemed clearly disappointed in the medium's evasive answer, but there was little he could do to elicit a consensus from the assembled spirits.

Next came a series of loud rappings, which Schockle was able to decipher through an alphabetical code. Room lights dimmed and "a supernatural picture, on a large mirror . . . was witnessed," of the Confederate steamer *Alabama* being chased by another large vessel, then floating idly with no sign of life on board. The picture seemed to answer Lincoln's question about how best to capture the *Alabama*, which had devastated Union shipping on both sides of the Atlantic and had sunk the USS *Hatteras* off the coast of Texas. When the séance ended, the president told Schockle the supernatural pictures persuaded him they were of a "heavenly nature."

In fact, the CSS *Alabama* was chased across the Atlantic and into French territorial waters by the American steam sloop-of-war USS *Kearsarge* where a furious firefight ensued between the two vessels. The *Alabama* sank off France on June 11, 1864. The wreck was only located in 1988.

As the war progressed, there was no lack of mediums claiming contact with Lincoln. J. B. Conklin told of receiving a telepathic message from Edward D. Baker, a longtime friend of the president, who had been killed in battle. According to Conklin, Baker's message two months after his death was, "Gone elsewhere. Elsewhere is everywhere." Other mediums introduced to the president included Charles Foster, Charles J. Colchester, Lucy Hamilton, and Charles Redmond. Redmond once warned Lincoln of enemy danger as he traveled from Philadelphia to Washington, which, the medium claimed, saved the president's life. At a Colchester séance, Mary Todd, while holding hands with others gathered around the table in a darkened room, heard tapping sounds and noises she believed were from Willie in the spirit world. Colchester, however, was of dubious reputation and ability and was subsequently exposed as a fraud after it was discovered that he, not spirits, produced the rapping sounds.

On one occasion, the president was part of the audience when the Lauries' daughter, Belle Miller, played a piano that began to vibrate intensely, levitated, then lurched and shifted across the floor toward Nettie Colburn.[25] Those present in the fully lit room searched for an explanation by examining every part of the grand piano, but found no evidence of chicanery or deception. Someone suggested, "Let's sit on the piano and see if the spirit force can still raise it." Lincoln, along with three others, quickly seated himself on the large instrument. The combined weight of four full-sized men planted firmly atop the concert grand should have made it impossible for the piano to raise itself from the floor. However, moments later, Nettie said she felt a huge burst of energy jolt through her body and asked Mrs. Miller to play the piano once more. Again, the instrument levitated with all four upon it, and those gathered watched in awe as the piano sat suspended in midair, then finally returned to the floor. Sworn statements given by witnesses attested to the veracity of the experience.

In May, Nettie was again asked to visit Mary Todd.[26] This time, the Confederates were winning the Battle of Chancellorsville and the president was distraught over the communiqués received from the front. "Oh, Miss Nettie, such dreadful news. They are fighting at the front. Such terrible slaughter. All our generals are killed and our army is in full retreat. Such is the latest news," said a distressed Mary Todd. "Oh, I am glad you have come. Will you sit . . . and see if we can get anything from 'beyond'?" Nettie complied and instantly her spirit control, this one named Pinkie, took over and "assured Mrs. Lincoln that her alarm was groundless." Nettie predicted there "would be better news by nightfall, and the next day would bring more cheerful results." The messages calmed Mary Todd somewhat. Lincoln, looking anxious and careworn, later entered the room, and Mary Todd immediately shared what the medium said. Nettie repeated the spirit control's communication that the news would soon brighten—which it ultimately did—and the assurances seemed to boost the president's mood.

In early 1864, several private séances were held for the Lincolns, usually at one P.M. when the president took his lunch.[27] One day, Lincoln himself summoned Nettie to the White House and cautioned her *this* séance was in strictest confidence. She was ushered into a room where two military officers were seated. Nettie induced a trance and when she was again conscious of her surroundings, an hour later, she was standing at a long table "upon which was a large map of the Southern states." She was holding a pencil. While the two military men quickly stepped back and stared at her, the president continued to study the map. Not certain what occurred or what her spirit control had said, Nettie was able to catch several remarks from those assembled around the table. "It is astonishing, how every line she has drawn conforms to the plan agreed upon," she heard the president say.

"Yes, it is very astonishing," the older of the two military officers agreed.

Former Congressman Daniel Somes joined the others in the room. "Well, was everything satisfactory?" he asked.

"Perfectly," answered Lincoln. "Miss Nettie does not seem to require eyes to do anything."

Apparently, Nettie had traced lines upon the map and, although she never learned the purpose, concluded that what she had drawn was of the utmost importance. "Those . . . were not days of indulgence or idle curiosity in any direction, nor was Mr. Lincoln a man to waste his time in giving exhibitions in occult for the amusement of his friends," she later wrote.

Still, Somes cautioned the president that there were those who would say, "You did not see what you in reality *did* see." To which the president gave no response.

Later that same evening when Nettie called on the president to thank him and say good-bye before she returned home, the president took both her hands in his and asked, "When you return next year you will come and see us again, won't you?"

"Yes, I will return if you are here," Nettie answered. This time, Lincoln's forlorn expression made clear that he understood the significance of her reply. "Do your spirit friends warn me, too? Colchester has been telling me that for months." Nettie could only tell him that the spirits she had contacted warned her of danger hanging over the president's life.

Almost a year later, prior to Lincoln's second inauguration in March 1865, Nettie again repeated the ominous message that the spirits "reaffirm the shadow they have spoken of still hangs over you."

"Yes, I know," the president answered impatiently. "I have letters from all over the country from your kind of people—mediums, I mean—

warning me [of] some dreadful plot against my life. But I don't think the knife is made, or the bullet run, that will reach it. Besides nobody wants to harm me."

"Therein lies your danger, Mr. Lincoln, your overconfidence in your fellow men," Nettie answered.

"Well, Miss Nettie, I shall live till my work is done, and no earthly power can prevent it. And then it doesn't matter so that I am ready, and that I ever mean to be," the president replied. And that was the last time Nettie saw Lincoln alive. "Never again would we meet his welcome smile," she wrote.

How much of an adherent was Lincoln to the new spiritualist movement that had swept across nineteenth-century America?[28] The evidence indeed suggests that he was a strong believer because of his relationships with several mediums during his presidency, and he never disavowed the movement publicly. Nettie wrote, "He would have connected himself with it, especially in peculiarly dangerous times, while the fate of the nation was in peril. A man does not usually follow or obey dictation in which he has no faith, and which does not contain information of active present value *to him*." In his times of greatest anxiety, particularly as he wrestled with the issuance of the Emancipation Proclamation, he drew upon spiritual guidance to strengthen his resolve that he had already made the morally right decision.

But Nettie also made clear that despite the president's openness and interest, "Mrs. Lincoln was more enthusiastic regarding the subject than her husband, and openly and avowedly professed herself connected with the new religion." Had the president "declared an open belief in [spiritualism], he would have been pronounced insane and probably incarcerated," Nettie concluded.

Throughout his life, Lincoln took his dreams very seriously, many of which were psychic and frequently required that he interpret their meaning.[29] One night, in June 1863, in a particularly disturbing dream, Lincoln saw his son Tad with a pistol he'd given the boy, "big enough to snap caps, but no cartridges or powder." At the time, Mary Todd and Tad were on a shopping trip in Philadelphia, but the apparent dream warning so concerned the president that he hurriedly telegraphed his wife at the hotel where she stayed, "Think you had better put Tad's pistol away safely. I had an ugly dream about him."

In 1864, while Mary Todd worried that "poor Mr. Lincoln is looking so brokenhearted, so completely worn-out," another of his strange dreams shook her. While the Lincolns were away from the nation's capital, the president dreamed the White House was on fire, motivating Mary Todd to send two telegrams to Washington to be certain all was safe in the Executive Mansion.

Were the president's dreams born of anxiety or clairvoyant to the point of having had premonitions whose outcomes were altered by intervention? We know that Lincoln believed himself to be clairvoyant. For example, one telling comment by Lincoln revealed his dependence on precognitive abilities. Predicting the unfavorable outcome of one Union loss in battle, he admitted, "I believe I feel trouble in the air before it comes." Even among those who dismissed Lincoln's psychic ability as "superstition," there was unanimity of opinion that "he was a very sensitive man," noted his Springfield law partner, William Herndon.

In 1864, Lincoln was elected to a second term. While the population in the North cheered, the South and their sympathizers in the Northern states seethed. Lincoln knew that winning the war was not enough, and in his second inaugural address on March 4, 1865, he vowed to bring the nation back together: "With malice toward none; with charity for all; with firmness in the right, as God gives us to see the right, let us strive on to finish the work we are in; to bind up the nation's wounds." He saw himself as a divine instrument, carrying out a Providential intent to heal what had been torn apart. He'd once told his friend Ward Hill Lamon that he was certain "the star under which he was born was at once brilliant and malignant; the horoscope was cast, fixed, irreversible."

Now, in his second term, there were more concerns for Lincoln's safety as the number of threats increased. He once showed a newspaper editor visiting the White House a cubicle in his desk that contained more than eighty threatening letters: "I know I am in danger, but I am not going to worry over threats like these." Lincoln knew that his wartime policies had made him lots of enemies, some of whom still fervently believed the military outcome of the war could be reversed politically were Lincoln to be removed from office. Lincoln also believed that a determined assassin would find a way to get him no matter what the level of protection. Ever the fatalist, the president ordered the most threatening letters to be discarded: "No vigilance would keep them out . . . a conspiracy to assassinate, if such there were, could easily obtain a pass to see me for any one or more of its instruments." He even told friends he could see images in his dreams that were portents of a violent end to his life. But he believed that if fate had meted out for him a violent end, then it would be a destiny he could not escape.

Some feel the strongest evidence of Lincoln's psychic ability was his precognitive dreams, some of which were painfully obvious, while others required interpretation.[30] One particularly significant recurring dream occurred to Lincoln prior to almost every major Union triumph over Confederate forces, including the victories at Antietam, Gettysburg, and Vicksburg. In April 1865, the dream reoccurred. "I had a warning dream again last night," Lincoln told colleagues and family. "It related to water. I seemed to be in a singular and indescribable vessel that was moving with great rapidity toward a dark and indefinite shore. I have always had this dream preceding every great event of the war. Victory has not always followed this dream . . . I think the dream must apply to General Sherman who is campaigning in Virginia, for there is no other great event that I know of which is apt to happen." When General Ulysses Grant expressed skepticism in such prophetic dreams, the president insisted his dream surely must be interpreted as good news. "I think it must be from Sherman."

On April 9, 1865, Confederate General Robert E. Lee surrendered to General Grant at Appomattox Court House, Virginia. The long and costly Civil War that claimed 600,000 lives was finally over, and the celebrations throughout the North quickly began. However, that same month, the president experienced an unusually vivid dream, as dream premonitions nearly always are, which he described to his wife and closest friends in great detail.

"I retired very late," the president said. "I had not been long in bed when I fell into a dream. There seemed to be a deathlike stillness about me. Then I heard subdued sobs, as if a large number of people were weeping. I thought I left my bed and wandered downstairs. I went from room to room in the White House. No living person was in sight. But the same mournful sounds of distress met me as I passed along. It was in all the rooms, every object was familiar to me, but where were all the people who were grieving as if their hearts would break? I was puzzled and alarmed. What could be the meaning of all this?

"Determined to find the cause of a state of things so mysterious and so shocking, I kept on until I arrived in the East Room, which I entered. Before me was a catafalque, on which there was a form, wrapped in funeral vestments. Around it were soldiers who were stationed as guards. There was a throng of people, some gazing, mourning upon the corpse, whose face was covered, others weeping pitifully. 'Who is dead in the White House?' I demanded of one of the soldiers. 'The president!' was the answer. 'He was killed by an assassin!' Then came a loud burst of grief from the crowd, which woke me from my dream. I slept no more that night; and although it was only a dream, I have been strangely annoyed by it ever since."

Mary Todd thought the dream "horrid," and regretted having been told. The president reassured her, "Well, it is only a dream, Mary." Yet for Mary Todd, who had endured the deaths of her two sons and who had seen firsthand proof that premonitions and predictions did come true, her husband's sorrowful dream filled her with dread no matter how he tried to minimize it. Forces from her darker side engulfed her and for the next few days after her husband's report of his dream, she sought constant reassurances from him that everything would be all right. But she believed none of them, fearing the worst was about to happen. Days later, those fears came true.

Lincoln seemed to have brushed aside the memories of his nightmare days earlier and with the war over, he sought respite from the arduous task of rebuilding the South that lay ahead. He agreed to attend a play with his wife at Ford's Theatre on the evening of Good Friday, April 14, 1865, to see if he could lift her spirits as well. She'd fallen into one of her moods as a result of her husband's report of his nightmare, and Lincoln thought attending the popular comedy *Our American Cousin*, starring the actress Laura Keene, might bring her a little levity. And since the invitation had been made by the theater manager himself and had so pleased the usually dour Mary Todd, the president acquiesced. At least that was what he had told friends. But why, despite dream warnings of danger, threats to his life, and the advice of friends, would Lincoln tempt fate?

The president's former law partner, William Herndon, remembered being told often by Lincoln, "I am sure I shall meet with some terrible end." Mary Todd said her husband's "only philosophy was, what is to be, will be, and no prayers of ours can reverse the decree." Herndon recalled, "He always contended that he was doomed to a sad fate." It is characteristic of premonitions that those who experience them often cannot tell exactly when they will come true. Possibly, as Herndon said, the president, "felt the nearness of the awful hour." And that was why, perhaps, the president put himself into the hands of fate that Good Friday and allowed his destiny to play itself out.

Having promised, in the face of his own dire premonitions and nightmares to attend Ford's Theatre, the president invited the victorious General Grant and his wife to accompany the first family as they celebrated the end of the war.[31] The two couples, Lincoln promised, would share the same box at Ford's, to the delight of the audience that night. The Grants, however, declined the invitation saying they had to return to their home in New Jersey, which was only partially true.

Actually there were other explanations for why the Grants did not attend the theater with the Lincolns. First was the intense dislike the two wives had for each other, which caused Julia Grant to flatly refuse to be in Mary Todd's company. But there was a second and more ominous reason: That Friday morning Mrs. Grant awoke with a strong sense of uneasiness and impending danger. Troubled by a vague premonition that something was amiss, Mrs. Grant was unable to shake the feeling that either a tragic accident or terrible disaster was about to overtake her husband if they attended the theater with the Lincolns. Concerned for his personal safety, she demanded they leave Washington immediately. At first General Grant protested against his wife's pleadings, but so insistent was she that Grant eventually yielded to her. Mrs. Grant's premonition had become too strong a force for her husband to resist. So the general made his apologies to the president and would leave Washington before evening.

Friday, April 14, began with breakfast, which Lincoln shared with his eldest son, Robert.[32] There followed meetings with government officials, his cabinet, the victorious General Grant, and various friends. At the cabinet meeting, the premonitions were on Lincoln's mind: "Gentlemen, something extraordinary is going to happen, and that soon." Then he described his recurring water dream: "I am on a great, broad, rolling river, and I am in a boat . . . and I drift . . . and I drift." Those present thought him unusually distracted and morose. Nonetheless, later in the afternoon, the president and Mary Todd enjoyed a carriage ride.

Lincoln confided to W. H. Crook, his bodyguard, that he'd dreamed for three consecutive nights that he would be assassinated. "Crook, do you know, I believe there are men who would want to take my life. And I have no doubt that they will do it. It would be impossible to prevent it." Crook pleaded with the president not to attend Ford's Theatre that evening. But it was to no avail. Uncharacteristically, as if sensing impending tragedy, he said to Crook, "Good-bye" rather than "Good night," his usual farewell.

The president and his party arrived at the theater at 9:20 P.M. and as they ascended to the "state box" reserved for them, the large audience "rose and cheered enthusiastically." At the same time, however, in what can only be called another unfortunate twist of fate, the police officer assigned to protect the president left his post outside the box. And so, John Wilkes Booth, the actor and Southern sympathizer who so vehemently hated Lincoln he planned to kill him with his own hand, gained ready access to the theater and lurked nearby. Undetected, he hid in the shadows outside the theater box, where he waited for his chance to carry out "the last and greatest tragedy of the war," as Herndon so aptly said.

Meanwhile, in the White House, at about the same time as the curtain was rising at Ford's, the Lincolns' dog, as animals sometimes do before catastrophic events, psychically sensed something terrible about to happen and became frantic. The usually quiet and gentle pet inexplicably started barking uncontrollably, and began running around the family quarters in a frenzy looking for its master, the president. No one could calm the dog that then began to wail as if its own life were in danger.

With the police officer absent from his guard post, John Wilkes Booth was free to wait outside the box until the sound of laughter and applause filled the theater. Even Mary Todd, always on the lookout for foul play, had lowered her guard, and was engrossed in watching the performance. Now Booth, seeing his chance, stealthily sneaked into the president's box and moved up behind the president, who was seated in a rocking chair, smiling, laughing, and winking at Mary Todd seated to his right. To their right were Miss Clara Harris and Major Henry R. Rathbone, invited when General and Mrs. Grant declined to attend. Booth was as silent as a shadow inside the president's box as he quickly pulled out a tiny derringer and pointed it directly at the back of Lincoln's head. Without announcing his presence, Booth immediately fired a single round that penetrated Lincoln's skull, mortally wounding him. It was nearly 10:15 P.M.

The shot startled Mary Todd, who began screaming. However, it all happened so quickly that the audience, completely unaware of what occurred, thought it part of the play. Then, with Mary Todd shrieking, "They have shot the president!" the audience turned in their seats to see Major Rathbone struggling with the assassin until Booth pulled out his knife and stabbed him repeatedly. Still, Rathbone held on, hoping he could prevent Booth from escaping until help came, but he was too weakened from the wounds and loss of blood. Booth, now desperate to get away, pushed Rathbone aside and leaped out of the presidential box, catching his spur in the folds of an American flag that draped the box as he fell to the stage below. Hobbled and in pain from the sprained ankle he received in the fall and waving his knife as if to strike at phantom spirits around him, the demented actor shouted to the audience, *"Sic semper tyrannis!"* ("Ever thus to tyrants!") as he "quickly limped across the stage" and escaped behind the proscenium. Meanwhile, as the president's life's blood ebbed away, pandemonium broke out in the theater.

The unconscious president was carried to a house across the street as onlookers hoped that the doctor, who had already been summoned, might be able to stanch the flow of blood and remove the tiny bullet. But it was already too late. The wound had been fatal. Although he struggled through the night, stubbornly rallying even as his life signs faltered, at 7:22 on the morning of April 15, Abraham Lincoln stopped breathing, his heart failed, and he passed over from this world to the next. Secretary of War Edwin Stanton uttered the memorable words, "Now he belongs to the ages." And a pall fell over the entire country.

General Ulysses and Mrs. Grant heard the terrible news that stunned the nation when they arrived in Philadelphia: President Lincoln had been assassinated. Julia's seemingly groundless prediction of a disaster had been completely validated. By heeding her foreboding Mrs. Grant likely saved her husband's life. When John Wilkes Booth's papers were later found, Grant was discovered to be one of the intended assassination targets. Grant went on to be elected president in 1868.

Just as he'd seen in his dream premonition, within a day after his death, Lincoln's casket was positioned on a platform in the White House East Room, protected by soldiers. Then after lying in state for crowds of mourners, a special train took his body home to Springfield, Illinois, for burial. Along the route of the sorrowful journey as the train slowly made its way through town and cities were grieving citizens who tearfully paid their final respects to the Great Emancipator. Even the train tracks them- selves, observers wrote, seemed silenced by the overwhelming sadness of Lincoln's sudden passing. The president's death was, Herndon said, "an indescribable shock," which plunged the nation into deep and unprece- dented grief.

While the nation mourned in the days following the assassination and funeral, the police pursued Booth and his fellow conspirators. Booth, trapped in a Virginia barn, was shot to death eleven days after his crime. His confederates were captured and ultimately tried and convicted. Three of them were hanged. As it turned out, the plot to assassinate Lincoln was more elaborate than it had first seemed, targeting other members of his administration and cabinet, and General Grant as well. It was a true assassination plot aimed at overthrowing the leader who had prosecuted the War Between the States, emancipated the slaves, and ultimately de- feated the Confederacy. It was certainly not borne out of the delusions of a lone gunman, and to the extent that Vice President Andrew Johnson was unable to pursue Reconstruction, the plot succeeded. For the next one hundred years, until Hubert Humphrey's first Civil Rights plank in the Democratic Party platform in the 1948 election, the South seemed to have gained politically what it lost on the battlefield: its own version of apartheid.

Mary Todd Lincoln has been a misunderstood and sometimes unfairly maligned figure in American history.[33] Most of the later biographies of her life, if they refer at all to her interest in spiritualism, regard it as a re- flection of her emotional problems or eccentricity, giving it scant atten- tion beyond that. At the same time, her husband's interest is ignored almost entirely.

But there is a more sympathetic view that deserves mention. Like Jane Pierce, her predecessor in office, Mrs. Lincoln experienced the untimely deaths of two of her young children, Eddie and Willie. By the end of the Civil War, notwithstanding whatever personality disorder she may have suffered, she was also a bereaved mother and a disconsolate widow. While the divided country was reeling from the war's devastation, Mary—and the nation—suffered another staggering loss when President Lincoln was assassinated. Still, her faith in her ability to make contact with the spirit world remained largely intact, and she pursued her spiritualistic endeavors throughout the rest of her life. In 1869, she wrote to a friend, "I am not *either* a spiritualist, but I sincerely believe our loved ones, who have only 'gone before' are permitted to watch over those who were dearer to them than life."

Just as she'd been desperate to hear from Willie at séances, so, too, did she ache for a message from her departed husband, a sign to skeptics that she'd become "unhinged." In fact, people believed that Mary Lincoln had lost her mind when, in reality, she'd retreated into herself as a refuge against the loneliness and bereavement she felt. Her grief would soon become exacerbated once again as a result of another personal tragedy in 1871 when Tad, who'd been his mother's nearly constant companion since his father's murder, fell ill with tuberculosis and died at the age of eighteen.

"Ill luck presided over my birth and has been a faithful attendant ever since," Mary said bitterly. And again she found sanctuary in her long-held beliefs when she took up residence for a time in a "spiritualist commune" to develop her ability to see spirit faces and to converse with Mr. Lincoln in the beyond. Mary later traveled to Boston, where, using an alias to prevent detection, she attended a séance, reported contact with her husband's spirit, and said she felt his hands on her shoulders. She also participated in one of spiritualism's more questionable practices: spirit photography.

In the 1870s, photography was still quite primitive, and few were sufficiently expert about taking pictures to recognize a fraud.[34] Many other people, however, believed that if a camera could photograph a person, it could also capture the image of a ghost, an apparition, or a spirit. So it was that spirit photography became a popular fascination both in the United States and in Europe during the latter half of the nineteenth century. The concept was quite simple: the spirit photographer claimed he could take a picture—then known as a daguerreotype—of a live subject, and when the plate was developed, the apparition of a deceased loved one would appear behind the subject. Typically the spirit appeared ethereal or dreamlike so that it projected an otherworldly quality on the developed print.

Mrs. Lincoln yearned for her husband to be manifest in such a photo, and so under the assumed name "Mrs. Tundall," she visited William Mumler, the best-known spirit photographer of the time. From 1861 on,

Mumler had pursued a lively and profitable business producing daguerreotypes that showed shadowy likenesses of deceased loved ones poised behind his customers. Wearing her widow's black, Mary Lincoln sat, her hands folded, her round face older, more tired, and heavier than only a few years earlier, while Mumler slid the photo plates into his camera and asked her to stay motionless so that he could expose the picture he was taking of her.

When the daguerreotype was developed, Mrs. Lincoln was not disappointed because behind she could make out the nearly transparent image of Abraham Lincoln's face meant to seem heavenly, with his hand on his wife's shoulder. He was bathed in cloudlike fog and his body appeared as a white form. Many suspected an obvious double exposure, although Mumler had supporters who vouched for his honesty. Mrs. Lincoln was certain Mumler had not recognized her and that the picture was genuine. The spirit photograph of Mary Lincoln, with her husband's ghostly presence hovering over, became Mumler's most famous.

Mrs. Lincoln's last years were spent in misery and depression. She died in Springfield, Illinois, on July 16, 1882, at the age of sixty-three. When she was laid to rest, she wore her wedding band with the inscription that read: *LOVE IS ETERNAL.*

At the end of the Civil War, interest in spiritualism, which had ebbed, increased again among the bereaved who'd lost loved ones in the fighting and yearned to hear from them. Nearly every family in the North and South had been touched by the unwelcome presence of death and was wrapped in grief. The scale of the carnage was almost unimaginable: the war had left more than 600,000 men and boys dead, and nearly another million wounded. As a result, many turned to mediums in the hope of hearing from their departed sons, husbands, brothers, and friends. Physical mediums proliferated, and so did mental or speaking mediums who brought forth spirit messages. One in particular did more to attract interest in spiritualism during the latter half of the nineteenth century than any other. His name was Daniel Dunglas (D. D.) Home, and he was perhaps the greatest medium of the Great Age of Spiritualism.

5

Home and the Power of Levitation

A Remarkable Demonstration

We were touched by the invisible.

—ELIZABETH BARRETT BROWNING,
poet, commenting on a Daniel Dunglas
(D. D.) Home séance, 1855[1]

The mid-nineteenth century was not a celebrity-driven era comparable to our own time. Few people achieved the star status we've grown accustomed to in our age of mass media. One notable exception was Daniel Dunglas (D. D.) Home (pronounced "Hume"), who became the most famous and enigmatic physical medium of his time. In his day, no one was better known or more successful, even as skeptics and debunkers continually attacked spiritualism, and the exposure of fraudulent mediums became so common, it threatened the entire movement.

But even recent obdurate skeptics, such as Gordon Stein, conceded that Home was a "superstar," who is "still recognized as the finest physical medium of the nineteenth century," a time when spiritualism was profoundly important, and "the desire to contact dead loved ones was very strong."[2]

Born near Edinburgh, Scotland, on March 20, 1833, as an infant, Home was adopted by an aunt, Mary Cook, who had no children of her own, and brought him to the United States when he was nine to be raised in Connecticut. Much about his ancestry remains a mystery, and exactly why he was given to his aunt has never been satisfactorily explained. Described as sickly and possessing a tendency toward consumption, he was not expected to survive childhood. Too frail and high-strung to engage in strenuous physical activity, he turned instead to nature and reading, and developed a love of both; later he also became a talented musician at the piano.

His aunt noticed that even when Daniel was a baby, his cradle rocked strangely from side to side, as if someone—or something—was moving it. He may also have experienced visions as young as age four, but his aunt had dismissed them as childish imagination or dreams.

The first paranormal experience he could recall occurred when he was about thirteen. Home had become friendly with a fifteen-year-old boy named Edwin, and together, they'd walk in the woods and read the Bible. The two boys had made a pact that whoever died first would appear to the other. Edwin moved with his family to Troy, in Upstate New York, and there he died a few years later. One evening, Home saw a "vision" of his friend's face bathed in light, at about the same moment Edwin succumbed, although obviously, at that time, about 1846, since they were many miles apart there would have been no other way for Home to immediately know of his friend's death, other than psychically. It wasn't until several days later that Daniel received a letter informing him about Edwin's passing.

When Home's mother moved to America, she lived only about a dozen miles from her son. She was also psychic and had the ability of "second sight," or clairvoyance, possibly inherited from her family. In fact, she accurately predicted her own death down to the exact day, through a precognitive dream she had. Daniel, too, experienced a vision that precisely foretold his mother's passing.

In his teens, Home's range of paranormal abilities expanded. It was around the same time the Fox sisters made news around the country with reports of spirit raps in Hydesville, New York, so Daniel surely knew of the story and the resulting commotion. By 1850, he also began experiencing spirit rappings, just as the Fox girls had. But the mysterious noises badly upset and alarmed his Aunt Mary. A deeply religious and fearful woman, she decided the raps were of some evil origin, and jumped to the conclusion that her nephew was demonically possessed. She wasted no time in summoning three ministers to pray for him and to perform an exorcism. However, that only seemed to intensify the spirit noises.

Now certain he was possessed, Home's aunt angrily ordered Daniel— and "his spirits"—from her house. He was about seventeen (some sources say he was closer to twenty at the time) and completely on his own. Fortunately, there were a sufficient number of people curious about his paranormal gifts, and he was invited to reside with them. For the next several years, he lived with people who were pleased to have a medium under their roof. In fact, for virtually his entire life, Home was provided for by what he called "kind friends"; likely they were people drawn to his abilities as a medium, rather than for any reasons of altruism. No matter, Home's mediumship allowed him to enter an elite circle of influential and wealthy people that otherwise would never have been open to him; and it was a lifestyle he reveled in. Ironically, the same psychic powers for which he was evicted from home ultimately saved him. Although he made it a practice not to charge for his séances, he was never reluctant to accept gifts—even expensive ones—from the grateful.

As a young man, Home demonstrated a variety of psychic abilities. At his séances, he was able to make various objects and items, even furniture, move about of their volition. Tables "tipped" and sometimes even hovered in the air. Ornaments and containers seemed to dance around the séance parlor. Musical instruments played, and bells rang themselves. Glowing "spirit hands" materialized and floated by, but if physical contact was made by any of the séance participants, the "hands" often faded or disappeared.

Once he became known, by his own admission, he never again during his career knew peace or privacy. He was constantly in demand by thousands for his psychic abilities. Home always kept a distance from other mediums, however, wanting nothing to do with them, and not wishing to be considered part of the herd of deceptive and dishonest physical mediums who were increasingly being exposed as frauds.

In 1852, when he was only nineteen, Home did pay a visit to one of the early and best-known young mediums, Henry Gordon, in Springfield, Massachusetts. Home always maintained that he'd simply attended one of Gordon's séances, but in later years, skeptics claimed otherwise, saying that Home spent considerable time with Gordon, and learned much from him, possibly even levitations. By then, Gordon had already successfully demonstrated his ability to rise from the ground and seemingly float on air. Had Gordon—not the spirits—taught D. D. Home at least some of what he knew? It was one of many accusations that no one could ever answer with certainty.

Other physical mediums of the time attempted to create similar effects and materializations, but no one could demonstrate them with the skill and alacrity of Home. A Home séance, at the very least, was marvelous theater—both entertaining and intriguing. If it gave evidence of the spirit world or some supernatural ability, that made it all the more extraordinary. Therein lay the controversy that surrounded the charming, tall, and slender young man with wavy brownish-auburn hair, full moustache, and penetrating blue-gray eyes. He was bright and well mannered, but many found him to be "vain and affected." Some described his looks as "striking." He could be moody, given to bouts of depression, and often nervous, a trait he'd had since childhood, but he also had a keen memory and strong powers of observation.

Was he performing his amazing feats by employing a magician's skills? Or was he genuinely in contact with the spirit dimension that was responsible for the remarkable manifestations? The first scientist to study Home's abilities was the respected New York theology professor George Bush. Noted individuals also observed him, including the famed poet and journalist William Cullen Bryant. Some people were so impressed by what they'd witnessed, that Home was credited as one reason why many converted to spiritualism, including several scientists and the jurist John Worth Edmonds.

Home was so confident of his abilities that he encouraged séance participants to stop him at any time to search for any concealed devices, the kinds used by stage magicians. But no one ever discovered him engaged in any chicanery; many were stumped when they were sure they had determined how the psychic effects were created, only to be proven wrong.

Tables lifted off the ground, spirit hands that appeared then vanished, and musical instruments played on their own. Yet, of the many Home demonstrations, the one that still provokes the most wonder—and debate—was his ability to levitate. Was it a paranormal phenomenon or a clever illusion? Historically, levitations have been associated with the holy of various faiths: Catholic saints, Hindu fakirs, and a handful of mystics. Otherwise, levitating was the domain of theatrical magicians who performed for the entertainment of audiences.

Home initially demonstrated his power to rise and float in the air in 1852, at the residence of a Connecticut industrialist named Ward Cheney. At that séance, music was also heard playing, although no instruments were present. Remember, that was at a time long before recording devices. How Home achieved the effect—whether by trickery or supernatural means—is still argued today. Home's levitation at Cheney's house was reported in the *Hartford Times*:

> Suddenly and without any expectation on the part of the company, Mr. Home was taken up in the air. I had hold of his hand at the time, and I felt his feet—they were lifted a foot from the floor. He palpitated from head to foot with the contending emotions of joy and fear which choked his utterance. Again and again he was taken from the floor, and the third time he was carried to the ceiling of the apartment with which his hands and feet came in gentle contact. I felt the distance from the soles of his boots to the floor, and it was nearly three feet. Others touched his feet to satisfy themselves.

No medium during that era would come close to D. D. Home for the frequency of levitations or the number of witnesses to them. Home and his supporters, of course, claimed his gifts were entirely supernatural, evidence of his extraordinary paranormal abilities. He could not only levitate himself, but he also sometimes caused séance participants to rise and float around the room. At one sitting, a woman felt her hand being inexplicably raised, and nothing she did would bring her arm down. Suddenly, as stunned witnesses watched, the woman was lifted from her seat to dangle in mid-air for a few seconds, and then mysteriously was placed back in her chair.

Those determined to debunk him simply dismissed his levitations as trickery. Others were convinced his demonstrations were the result of genuine spirit contact. Skeptic or believer, no one could doubt that Home's abilities—whatever their origin—were fascinating and far beyond what other mediums displayed. His levitations were usually performed in dimly lit or darkened rooms; but most times—unlike many other mediums of that era—séances were held in fully lighted settings.

In the spring of 1855, he traveled to England. His second wife later wrote that he needed a respite because of his poor health and because of the energy he exerted by giving too many séances. He arrived in April, looking pallid, feeling physically ill and depressed, but he settled comfortably in London where his reputation as a famed medium preceded him. Why with pulmonary problems and a bad cough, he'd chosen London with its then dreadful air quality from fog and smokestacks is an unanswered question. As he had in America, Home resided with those who invited him to be their guest, and in return, he displayed his powers as a medium. In England, as in the United States, his audiences included many distinguished figures, including Sir David Brewster (1781–1868), a well-known British scientist and inventor of the kaleidoscope, who described himself as "deeply impressed" by his observations of Home at a London séance.[3]

Home wrote to friends in America describing the séance that Brewster attended, and detailing how those present could not determine any "natural means" by which he could have manifested the phenomena they saw. That letter found its way into the American press, and then appeared in British newspapers. The paranormal and controversy, forever joined, this time surfaced to Brewster's chagrin. Sir Brewster, whose reputation was earned as a researcher of the "polarization of light," apparently was shaken when he read about his attendance at Home's séances. Brewster wasted no time in writing to the London *Daily Advertiser*, adamantly insisting that he did *not* believe in spiritualism, and that any demonstration by a medium claiming contact with the spirit world was the work of a charlatan or imposter. Brewster ended his letter by stating, "I saw enough to satisfy myself that they could all be produced by human hands and feet."

The abrupt change in Brewster's position was likely spurred by his fear of peer pressure, and what it might do to his standing in the traditional scientific community that largely disdained spiritualism. But the controversy did not end there. Edward William Cox, an attorney and recognized psychic investigator and a strong supporter of Home, carefully scrutinized spiritualist phenomena, cognizant of the trickery often employed by spurious mediums. Cox, who had attended the same séance as Brewster, also wrote to the *Advertiser*, and took strong issue with Brewster's public conclusions about Home's abilities. Cox chided Brewster for acknowledging Home's psychic gifts in private, then denouncing them in the press.

The dispute continued, and Brewster retorted, "Rather than believe that spirits made the noise, I will conjecture that the raps were produced by Mr. Home's toes, and rather than believe that spirits raised the table, I will conjecture that it was done by the agency of Mr. Home's feet, which were always below it."

But others present at that same séance pointed out that at the time of Home's demonstrations, Brewster did not express doubt "of their genuineness."

Brewster answered that he'd not been permitted to search beneath the table where Home sat for any evidence of machinery or trickery.

Another witness to the séance came forward: T. A. Trollope, a noted author, who also defended the medium and took issue with Brewster. A man named Benjamin Coleman joined the fray when he published an account critical of Brewster for his change of mind. So the battle of words continued.

Years later, Cox wrote that a Lord Brougham told him that he'd been "satisfied at the time that it was no trick, and that some unknown power was in action." Cox said that when he asked Sir Brewster his opinion of Home, Brewster answered by quoting Shakespeare: "There are more things in heaven and earth, Horatio, than are dreamt of in your philosophy."

Home was not pleased by Brewster's about-face, and in 1863, when the medium wrote *Incidents in My Life,* he criticized Brewster for taking credit for the work of others. Brewster threatened to sue for libel, but never did.

The last word in the debate did not come until 1869 when Sir Brewster's daughter published her late father's papers—he had died the year before. In Brewster's documents and letters were his own writings about the Home experience. They left no doubt about Brewster's positive reaction the first time he witnessed the medium's abilities. Quoted in *D. D. Home: His Life and Mission,* by Mrs. D. D. Home,[4] it read, in part:

Last of all, I went with Lord Brougham to a séance of the new spirit rapper, Mr. Home, a lad of [about] twenty. We four sat down at a moderately sized table, the structure of which we were invited to examine. In a short time the table shuttered, and a tremulous motion ran up all our arms; at our bidding these motions ceased and returned. The most unaccountable rappings were produced in various parts of the table; and the table actually rose from the ground when no hand was upon it. A larger table was produced and exhibited similar movement. A small hand-bell was then laid down with its mouth on the carpet: and, after lying for some time, it actually rang when nothing touched it. The bell was then placed on the other side, still upon the carpet, and it came over to me and placed itself in

my hand. It did the same to Lord Brougham. These were the principal experiments. We could give no explanation of them and could not conjecture how they could be produced by any kind of mechanism.

Posthumously, Sir Brewster's credibility suffered a blow as a result
of the Home controversy. But that would not be Home's only public
confrontation about his powers as a medium.

Despite or because of his poor health, he conveyed a feeling of sensitivity that many people, especially Victorian-era women, found appealing, wrote author Georgess McHargue. It's known that Home had
tuberculosis or, as it was then called, "consumption." But his demeanor
also raised questions about his sexuality and may have caused suspicion
or criticism of him.

When the young medium arrived in England, among the first to attend
his séances were the well-known poets Robert Browning and his wife
Elizabeth Barrett Browning.[5] At one sitting, Home produced—seemingly
from the "unseen world"—a wreath of flowers, held by a "spirit hand"
that set the garland on Elizabeth's head.

She wrote to her sister about her experiences: "We were touched by
the invisible, heard . . . music and raps, saw the table moved, and had
sight of hands . . ." But she made clear that discussing spiritualism was
off-limits in the Browning household. While Elizabeth was open to spiritualism, and enthusiastic about Home, her husband's attitude was quite
the opposite. He took a nearly instant dislike to Home, although the reasons were never clear. It's possible that Browning became envious when
Home's spirits suggested that Elizabeth was a better poet than her husband. More likely is that Robert Browning might have reacted more
against Home's alleged homosexuality than to any questions about his
mediumistic gifts. He may also have been jealous of the attention Home
paid to Elizabeth, a delicate-looking young woman with dark hair, huge
captivating eyes, and pale complexion. She also was in poor health, but
the letters Browning wrote her are some of the most beautiful and touching expressions of love in the English language. For whatever the reason,
Robert's animosity toward Home was so intense he did not want the
medium visiting the Browning residence, and ordered him from the house,
"or I'll fling you down the stairs!" he barked. Browning also told his wife

that he would "shoot the scoundrel" should he and Home meet again. All Elizabeth could do was apologize to Home for her husband's behavior.

Browning's hostility was no secret, so when he published a long and rambling parody titled "Mr. Sludge, 'The Medium,' " it was clear the object of his ridicule was D. D. Home. Browning painted Home in the most unflattering of terms: loathsome, dishonest, and a show-off. Browning's poem included the following lines:

> *Now don't sir! Don't expose me! Just this once!*
> *This was the first and only time, I swear.*
> *Look at me—see, I kneel—the only time,*
> *I swear I ever cheated . . . yes, by the soul!*
> *Of Her who hears (your sainted mother, sir!)*
> *All, except this last accident, was truth.*
> *You've heard what I confess; I don't unsay*
> *A single word: I cheated when I could,*
> *Rapped with toe-joints, see sham hands at work,*
> *Wrote down names weak in sympathetic ink,*
> *Rubbed odic lights with ends of phosphor-match,*
> *And all the rest.*

Despite the poem's implication that Browning uncovered fraud on Home's part, that simply was not true. One perceptive aspect of the bitter and sarcastic poem, which goes on for many more stanzas, was Browning's understanding of the psychology or mind-set of those who attended séances: people wanted to believe they were communicating with the dead. Skeptics have long pointed to this "need to believe" on the part of those who consult mediums. Browning actually had substantial knowledge of the occult and a family tradition of mystical subjects. Whatever caused his resentment, it was clearly a personal attack aimed at Home. Had Browning wished to attack spiritualism, he could have lashed out at any of countless mediums, but he targeted only one: D. D. Home. Three years later, Browning was still complaining. When the American author Nathaniel Hawthorne, no fan of spiritualism, visited Browning in London, Hawthorne asked Browning to ease off on criticizing Home. Even if he agreed, Hawthorne was bored listening to the tirades.

The poem did not help Home's reputation, but it did less damage than it might have because in Browning's obvious rage, he had written a poem far too long and dreary—some two thousand lines—and difficult to read and decipher. Home's career as a medium survived Browning—and "Mr. Sludge."

Another literary foe was famed author Charles Dickens. Although he'd written one of the most popular of all ghost stories, *A Christmas Carol*, Dickens branded the medium an "imposter," and he flatly refused to attend any Home séances, an attitude that irritated Elizabeth Barrett Browning. "Dickens is so fond of ghost stories, so long as they are impossible," she said.

From London, Home went next to Italy in the autumn of 1855. In England he'd dealt with criticisms about his paranormal abilities and gossip about his personal life. In Italy, he faced other problems. Home was walking in the city of Florence when someone stabbed him several times with a dagger. Fortunately, he was not seriously injured. Although the attacker was never found, some speculated that the assault might have been related to rumors among the "superstitious" that he practiced sorcery because he "raised the dead," and among local peasants, necromancy was a sin.

Soon after, Home announced that he would lose his powers as a medium for a year. The strange prediction had come to him psychically, he said, but the lapse may have been a result of his poor physical health. In any event, for the next year Home remained in virtual seclusion, and neither gave séances nor did he receive any spirit communications. About that depressing time, his wife later wrote, "Clouds darkened the natural sunshine of his spirit; a veil had suddenly dropped between him and the world beyond, and all counsel and comfort from it was withdrawn."

While he waited for his abilities to return, Home converted to Catholicism, and even considered joining a monastery. He was "warmly received" by Pope Pius IX. But he soon had a change of mind and left Rome.

Why his abilities abruptly stopped was not clear, but they reemerged by early 1857 when Home was in Paris. With his psychic powers restored and his reputation once more intact, Home was called before Emperor Napoleon III and the Empress Eugenie. There are no written records of Home's sessions for the royal couple, but apparently they were pleased, for he conducted several séances for them. At one of the sittings, it was reported that psychokinetic energy caused the room to shake, while tables lifted themselves from the floor.

The emperor was an amateur magician, and watched the medium closely for signs of deception, but found none. For the empress, Home demonstrated telepathy by answering her "unspoken thoughts." She "was said to have been convinced she held the hand of her dead father in hers, declaring she would know it anywhere because of a scar or deformity on one of the fingers," wrote Georgess McHargue.[6]

Following his séances in France, Home returned briefly to the United States, but soon departed again for Europe. His reputation as a medium was now known far and wide; he'd become internationally famous. The next year he was on his way to Russia, where he demonstrated his abilities for Czar Alexander II. During his stay there, in 1858, Home married a wealthy and attractive young woman, Alexandrina de Kroll, who belonged to the Russian aristocracy. Thanks to the marriage, Home achieved considerable affluence, and expensive gifts from the czar. When his son was born, the czar bestowed jewelry on the renowned medium and his wife. One of the witnesses at Home's wedding was the noted literary figure Alexandre Dumas, who'd written *The Three Musketeers*. Several of Dumas's stories about spirit phenomena were inspired by Home's psychic powers, although Dumas showed no personal interest in spiritualism.

Home remained away from the United States from 1859 to 1862. In England and on the European continent he continued to conduct successful séances and demonstrations for the wealthy and famous. Among those who attended Home's sittings was Alexis Tolstoy, poet and cousin of the famed writer Leo Tolstoy.

Alexis Tolstoy shared his experience about Home: "What would have, above all, convinced me, were I a skeptic, are the hands I have felt which were placed in mine and melted when I tried to retain them. A cold wind passed around the circle very distinctly, and perfumes were wafted to us," he wrote to his wife.[7]

Robert Chambers was a nineteenth-century British writer and publisher. He'd been an outspoken skeptic of spiritualism, but became a convert largely due to his encounters with Home. Reportedly, he received messages from both his departed father and daughter. But because Chambers feared his new pro-spiritualist thinking might hurt his professional standing, he insisted on anonymity. In 1859, he'd written *Testimony: Its Posture in the Scientific World* in which he discussed the need for "scientific evidence" of psychic phenomena. Then in 1863 he wrote the "anonymous preface" for Home's successful book, *Incidents in My Life*. Among spiritualists, Chambers' switch from skeptic to believer was no secret, and proved a boost to Home's status.

Around that same time, while in France, Home predicted that President Abraham Lincoln would be assassinated. In 1862, Home's wife Alexandrina died and without her wealth to depend on, his economic situation changed for the worse, and his income plunged. Her family contested his rights to any inheritance. It would be nearly another decade before the case was resolved in his favor. Meanwhile, he was no longer welcome in Italy because of the allegation that he was a "sorcerer." Nor had the papacy forgiven his broken promise to enter a monastery. In 1864, the Italian government ordered Home to leave Rome. But he protested and was allowed to remain to study sculpture, if he would not engage in any spiritualist practices or séances. It was a short-lived agreement; he seemed to have no control over the spontaneous paranormal manifestations, and this time he had to depart from Rome, by order of the papacy.

He returned to the United States where he gave a series of well-received "dramatic readings." But Home was unable or unwilling to remain in any one place for very long. One writer accurately described him as a nineteenth-century version of a "globetrotter." In fact he never had a permanent residence.

In 1866, he again went to London where he resumed his sittings. Among the noted figures who attended was William Makepeace Thackery, author of *Vanity Fair*, who'd visit Home séances as often as he could both in London and America. Thackery was bitterly criticized by some for engaging in spiritualism, especially after a popular periodical he edited, *Cornhill Magazine*, published an article in August 1860 favorable to Home. Actually, Thackery was not a spiritualist. He'd simply commissioned a writer to describe what he'd witnessed regarding Home. Another author who took a similar noncommittal position was Edward Bulwer-Lytton, who wrote *The Last Days of Pompeii*. Although a student of the "mystical and occult," and curious about Home, he never accepted spiritualism.

Home had other commitments to meet; he was also in demand by royalty in Germany and Holland. But Home's health was not up to the rigors of enduring such a busy schedule. Fortunately, a number of his friends came together to form an organization, called the Spiritual Atheneum. Home was named the "residential secretary," which provided an income and did not require strenuous work on his part. He also continued to give private readings, but did not accept fees.

Between 1867 and 1869, Home became the focus of several séances that have intrigued psychical researchers, skeptics, and believers in America and Europe ever since. Home's frequent levitations expended a great deal of his energy, especially difficult considering his frail health; nonetheless, he continued them. One demonstration in particular has been incessantly studied, analyzed, and debated since it occurred in December 1868: the Ashley Place Levitation. It has been described as "the most famous case in the history of levitation." Author Georgess McHargue wrote the "Ashley Place levitation stands as one of the great landmarks among spiritualist phenomena."

In the West, the ancient phenomenon of levitation was largely kept within the bounds of religion. Defying gravity was attributed to a handful of saints of the Catholic Church. During the witch hysteria of medieval times, it was considered evidence of "possession." But, in the Great Age of Spiritualism during the nineteenth century, levitation was presumed to be of psychic origin, and attributed to the work of spirits.

At the Ashley Place levitation with Home were two young men well known among British society: Lord Lindsay and Lord Adare, the latter a close friend of Home. Also present was Adare's cousin, Captain Charles Wynne. As they watched, "Home floated out of a third story window and came in through the window of another room," the *Encyclopedia of Occultism and Parapsychology* wrote about the startling event.

Each of the witnesses later recounted what occurred. This was Lord Adare's version, as quoted in *D. D. Home: His Life and Mission*, written years later by the second Mrs. D. D. Home:

"Wynne and I went over to Ashley House after dinner. There we found Home and the Master of Lindsay. Home proposed a sitting. We accordingly sat round a table in the small room. There was no light in the room, but the light from the window was sufficient for us to distinguish each other and to see the different articles of furniture. Home went into a trance . . .

"Home then said to us, 'Do not be afraid, and on no account leave your places,' and he went out into the passage. Lindsay suddenly said, 'Oh, good heavens! I know what he is going to do; it is too fearful.'

"Adare: 'What is it?'

"Lindsay: 'I cannot tell you; it is too horrible. Adah [the spirit of a deceased American actress] says I must tell you. He is going out of the window in the other room, and coming in at this window.'

"We heard Home go into the next room, heard the window thrown up, and presently Home appeared standing upright outside our window. He opened the window and walked in quite coolly. 'Ah,' he said, 'you were good this time,' referring to our having sat still and not wished to prevent him. 'Adare, shut the window in the next room.' "

Lord Lindsay shared his experience in a letter he wrote in 1871 to the newspaper, *The Spiritualist*:

I was sitting with Mr. Home and Lord Adare and a cousin of his. During the sitting Mr. Home went into a trance, and in that state was carried out of the window in the room next to where we were, and was brought in at our window. The distance between the windows was about seven feet six inches, and there was not the slightest foothold between them, nor was there more than a twelve-inch projection to each window, which served as a ledge to put flowers on. We heard the window in the next room lifted up, and almost immediately after we saw Home floating in the air outside our window. The moon was shining full into the room; my back was to the light, and I saw the shadow on the wall of the window-sill and Home's feet about six inches above it. He remained in this position for a few seconds, then raised the window and glided into the room feet foremost and sat down.

In 1869, Lord Lindsay spoke before the London Dialectical Society about his experience with Home:

I saw the levitations in Victoria Street, when Home floated out of the window; he first went into a trance and walked about uneasily; then he went into the hall, while he was away, I heard a voice whisper in my ear, 'He will go out of one window and in at another.' I was alarmed and shocked at the idea of so dangerous an experiment. I told the company what I heard, and we waited for Home's return. Shortly after he entered the room, I heard the window go up, but I could not see it, for I sat with my back to it. I, however, saw his shadow on the opposite wall; he went out of the window in a horizontal position, and I saw him outside the other window [that in the next room] floating in the air. It was eighty-five feet from the ground. There was no balcony along the windows, merely a string course an inch and a half wide; each window had a small plant stand, but there was no connection between them.

What might explain Home's levitations? The longest-held belief is that they were caused by some mystical or supernatural power. Some scientists have experimented with levitation, describing their explorations into what's known as "electro-gravities," the "science of antigravity effects." Other parapsychologists have suggested levitation may be the result of psychokinetic or telekinetic energy. Yet another theory offered is that levitation can be induced by "hypnotic suggestion." Eastern mystics and yogis who've demonstrated levitations for centuries have been credited with using "special breathing techniques"; one in particular is known as "pranayama breathing." Still other levitation theories range from "possession" to "states of exaltation."

Just as there have been various suppositions that attempt to clarify levitation, there have been many efforts to demystify D. D. Home's ability. How he was seemingly able to suspend himself in mid-air has been a source of unceasing debate and controversy. There are no less than a hundred separate incidents of levitation attributed to Home, yet not one theory satisfactorily explains all the demonstrations in which he rose off the ground while bewildered witnesses observed him.

Home's abilities attracted attention wherever he went, and the press never failed to report on his exhibitions here and abroad.[8] Some of the explanations offered about Home were nothing short of bizarre. One suggested that he used a small "trained monkey" that shook hands and performed other acts to fool séance participants. There was the exotic theory that the medium slept with many cats whose electricity would charge his body so he could create psychic effects. There were rumors that witnesses were hypnotized. Some speculated that those who participated were chloroformed. And, even in an age long before special-effects wizardry, others maintained that Home somehow created illusions with a device of that era known as a "magic lantern," an early version of a slide projector.

Of course, there was that old standby skeptics love: Home's demonstrations and readings were made possible by the use of confederates; some helped with "trick" illusions, others secretly gathered information about séance participants. There was no end to people's imaginative assertions where Home's psychic gifts were concerned.

It raised a problem for the paranormal that still exists. When skeptics attack a psychic ability or paranormal experience, but cannot find evidence of fraud or deception, often their explanation is stranger or more far-fetched than any psychic power. Thus, in Home's time, it made more sense to some that a "trained monkey" assisted him than the possibility of a telekinetic force moving an object or table.

As we pointed out earlier, the Age of Spiritualism was marked by a high incidence of fraud and deception. But Home stood apart from other physical mediums in that regard. Yet when friends attempted to arrange for him to meet the respected scientist Michael Faraday so that Home's abilities could be examined, Faraday proved to be less than open-minded.[9] His answer for how tables and other objects were able to move by themselves was based on his theory of "involuntary muscular action" on the part of Home or séance participants. Faraday deemed spiritualism so absurd and beyond reason that he would not agree to see Home unless the medium publicly disclaimed the phenomena as Faraday had; thus no séance was ever arranged between the two.

Home's life took a strange turn when he met a prosperous, elderly English widow named Jane Lyon, who offered to adopt him, although he was already an adult. She apparently liked him so much she offered him permanent financial security if she could legally take him as her own, and if Home would agree to take her name. He approved and became Mr. Home-Lyon. As she promised, Jane Lyon placed sixty thousand pounds in his bank account, and also prepared a will that would maintain his wealth. But the story didn't end there.

Mrs. Lyon later had a change of mind and brought a lawsuit against Home to regain her money. Why then had she originally offered him a small fortune? Lyon claimed she'd been under the influence of her late husband's spirit who communicated to her through none other than D. D. Home. Critics seized on the incident as evidence that Home "had taken advantage of a wealthy widow." But supporters maintained that the medium was the actual victim of a manipulative and unbalanced woman who wanted him to bring her into the inner circle of the upper crust of society. Lyon later turned her attention to another medium.

During the time the lawsuit was being heard, someone tried to murder Home with a stiletto, a short dagger with a thick blade. He was able to throw off his attacker, but was stabbed in the hand during the struggle. The assault made good copy for the press. The *New York World* reported that Home had been killed, while other newspapers created stories worthy of today's supermarket tabloids. One story claimed that Mrs. Lyon had an artificial hand that Home said he could bring back to life.

Between 1867 and 1869, Home reportedly gave about eighty séances, a number suggested by Lord Adare in a book he published in 1869, *Experiences in Spiritualism with D. D. Home*. That same year, the London Dialectical Society arranged for a committee to examine spiritualism. The group's members included several hard-nosed skeptics; one was an atheist. When Home was tested at four separate séances, the results were less than what was expected. There was some evidence of spirit raps and table tipping. However, Home's energy was sapped by his continuing and chronic struggle with tuberculosis; he was simply too weak to summon the energy he once possessed. The committee's conclusion was that little had occurred, but the group's members acknowledged that Home had been open and willing to be studied every step of the way.

That would not be the last probe of Home's abilities. In 1871, he became the subject of an examination by the highly respected British scientist Sir William Crookes (1832–1916).[10] The eminent physicist's accomplishments had included research and inventions in chemistry and electrical engineering. His reputation was such that when he investigated psychic powers, like it or not, other scientists had little choice but to sit up and pay attention. He apparently first became curious about spiritualism following the death of his brother in 1867, and he'd witnessed other mediums before beginning his tests of Home.

When Crookes made his intentions public, and it was reported in the press that one of the greatest scientists of the century would investigate "spiritualist phenomena," skeptics and debunkers were thrilled since Crookes had announced in the past that he hoped to "drive the worthless residuum of spiritualism hence to the unknown limbo of magic and necromancy." It was a statement that encouraged the so-called rational thinkers and skeptics far and wide, on both sides of Atlantic. But, alas, those poised for victory over spiritualism were premature in their celebrations, for Sir Crookes would surprise them.

Crookes invited members of the Royal Society to take part in his testing, but they declined. However, he brought four others with him to act as witnesses during his examination of Home. Crookes, as he'd promised, conducted many tests using whatever was the best instrumentation available in the mid-nineteenth century. For example, he employed weights and balances, among other devices, to "measure" any differences in the heaviness of items or articles held by the medium. It was a means to test table tipping and levitation.

In another test, Crookes, to examine so-called "spirit music," placed an accordion *he'd* chosen in a wire cage, so there was no way Home could handle or manipulate it. Soon the accordion began moving around, and then as the instrument "contracted and expanded," it played music, although no one present had caused it.

Following his lengthy and detailed testing of Home, Crookes came to a startling conclusion—that is, to skeptics who fervently wanted the spiritualist movement squelched. He became certain that spiritualism was, in fact, due to some kind of "unknown force." It was, he said, comparable to gravity or electricity, and believed it could be measured. When Crookes's report was published, not surprisingly, it provoked a huge debate, notably among his fellow scientists. It's an attitude that still often greets openminded scientists who claim evidence of the paranormal, to the frustration of their more traditional and conservative colleagues. Crookes, the highly respected scientist, found himself the target of angry criticism, although not many dared to openly accuse him of any deception. Most of his colleagues accepted Crookes's good faith although some questioned the instruments he used to measure Home's psychic abilities.

But there were detractors, who, while trying not to impune Crookes's stellar reputation as a scientist, cautiously suggested that professionals who examine psychic phenomena are as suggestible as anyone else to deception by a fraudulent medium. No matter how honest the scientist or researcher was, he also could be duped. In other words, even brilliant scientists somehow became engulfed in some inexplicable fog once they entered the séance room, at least according to those whose minds were made up before they examined the phenomena.

We have no way to know, of course, what the precise test conditions under which Home was observed were, but there are statements from Crookes that shed some light on what transpired. He wrote that his "experiments [were] numerous." He also admitted having "an imperfect knowledge of the conditions which favor or oppose the manifestations of this force . . . Mr. Home . . . is subject to unaccountable ebbs and flows of the force, it has seldom happened that a result obtained on one occasion could be subsequently confirmed or tested with apparatus specifically contrived for this purpose." Simply put, Crookes recognized that it was difficult to create test conditions that would insure "repeatability," something scientists have long criticized about testing psychic or paranormal events. The criticism is valid—to a point—and something we'll explore more fully in a later chapter.

Whatever the shortcomings of Home's tests were, they carried weight with both the scientific community and the public. However, in June 1871, when Crookes handed his report about Home to the Royal Society, it was rejected. The reason? Crookes had failed to debunk spiritualism. His study first became public a month later when it was published in the *Quarterly Journal of Science*. The report gave the public a glimpse of what was witnessed during Home's séance, held at the physicist's residence. According to Crookes, the room was well lighted, and among the manifestations he emphasized was the accordion that played music on its own. Crookes summed up his observations of Home this way:

> Of all the persons endowed with a powerful development of this psychic force . . . Mr. Daniel Dunglas Home is the most remarkable, and it is mainly owing to the many opportunities I have had of carrying on my investigation in his presence that I am enabled to affirm so conclusively the existence of this force.

Crookes continued his investigations of mediumship in the following years, notably testing the young British medium Florence Cook. Home's important séances and sittings ended soon after he submitted to Crookes's tests.

Crookes regarded the accordion test as significant. Some theorized that perhaps some form of electromagnetic energy was responsible and was emitted from Home in a way not understood. Many would regard this as a form of psychic or supernatural energy. However, if the electromagnetic theory had any validity, then scientists were not dealing with anything supernatural. Rather, this was an energy that was natural, and Home was one of the rare individuals whose body had an abnormally large amount.

Unfortunately, many scientists then—as now—expended more time dismissing and disparaging the paranormal, rather than seeking reasonable scientific theories to explain how it might occur. Perhaps Home had some anomalous or rare telekinetic ability that was psychic in nature, but did not concern spirit contact? What explained the medium's gifts for clairvoyance and mental telepathy? From where did that information come?

In 1872, Home wrote a sequel to his 1863 autobiography, *Incidents in My Life*. Later in the 1870s, he wrote another book, *Lights and Shadows of Spiritualism*, in which he revealed some of the tricks other mediums employed. About the only medium he'd remained friendly with was one of the famed Fox sisters, Kate Fox Jenckens, who went to London in 1872, where the two renowned mediums together conducted a séance. After 1873, Home stopped completely and never gave another séance.

Home was deeply resented by many other mediums, partly because he was a harsh critic of deceptive practices, and also took strong issue with those who held séances only in darkened rooms. Surprisingly, he did not trust "public mediums," unless he'd witnessed them personally; what he didn't see, he didn't believe. Angry mediums protested that he did not understand the way they worked. Others were, no doubt, jealous of Home. From his writings and comments, one comes away with the idea that he thought only one medium was entirely genuine: himself. However, when Home was asked about Kate Fox and the allegations that she'd created the spirit raps by cracking the joints of her toes, he just laughed, as if the proposition was too ludicrous to answer. Crookes also maintained it was not possible for cracking toes to create the loud spirit raps that had been produced by the Fox sisters.

In October 1871, Home remarried, and his new wife, Julie de Gloumeline, like the first, was a wealthy, attractive, upper-class Russian woman. They'd met in St. Petersburg, Russia, where he was conducting séances. She may have been concerned about her standing in fashionable society for once they were married she preferred that Home not offer séances. After his death though, she obviously wanted his memory kept alive, and wrote a biography of her husband titled *D. D. Home: His Life and Mission*, published in 1888.

By 1876, Home's health had noticeably worsened because of his tuberculosis, forcing him into virtual retirement, but thanks to his marriage, money was no longer a concern. By then he had little if any contact with his former circle of friends. His long struggle with tuberculosis had debilitated him, yet he'd made it clear that he had no fear of death. Perhaps he knew what awaited him in the afterlife. He lived quietly for another ten years, patiently cared for by his wife, and died in Paris on June 21, 1886, at the age of fifty-three. Because he always viewed his work in the context of Christianity, his epitaph is not surprising. It was taken from St. Paul in I Corinthians and reads: "To another discerning of spirits."

But Home's death did not end the curiosity and controversy that encompassed him in life. Although he was never publicly detected committing any fraud or deception, no one could say with certainty how he produced some of the most amazing manifestations of physical mediumship ever witnessed.

One of the most determined skeptics to emerge in the latter part of the nineteenth century was Frank Podmore (1856–1910).[11] Although he was British, his opinions were well known in America, as well. He was unyielding in his position that all spiritualist phenomena were fraudulent, the result of trickery or delusion. He criticized Sir Crookes for the latter's positive conclusions about Home. Podmore branded Home as "an accomplished conjurer and psychological manipulator," wrote Georgess McHargue. He discredited the levitations as illusions caused by Home's opening and closing of windows so that witnesses *thought* that Home had floated in and out of rooms. But for all of his tireless efforts to debunk the medium, neither Podmore nor anyone else ever did. Podmore finally had to admit that "Home was never publicly exposed as an imposter; there is no evidence of any weight that he was even privately detected of trickery." Those were strong words in Home's favor from an influential and relentless skeptic who never made a similar statement about any other physical medium of the nineteenth century. No one could deny Home's vanity, but all who knew him agreed that he was an honest man.

Podmore never gave up discrediting Home, however, and in 1903, a letter that was dated 1855 somehow came into his possession. The writer alleged he once saw a "spirit hand" extended from Home's own arm. It was a specious allegation at best, but Podmore used it to accuse Home of being a "conjurer" whose demonstrations were the result of "trickery." But even that did not answer the many puzzles about Home, and Podmore had to admit, "We don't quite see how some of the things were done and we leave the subject [Home] with an almost painful sense of bewilderment."

Years after Home's death, debunkers were secure in hindsight that somehow Home had employed deception, even if they could not explain his feats, and even though no one had ever discovered any chicanery on Home's part. Every skeptic and debunker had some explanation for Home's abilities, ranging from secret magnets to hidden wires, even mechanisms in his musical instruments, similar to music boxes, that were responsible for the mysterious melodies at séances.

America's most famous illusionist and escapologist, Harry Houdini, no stranger to vanity and self-promotion, could not resist trying to debunk D. D. Home, or at least brag that he could. By the early twentieth century, Houdini was waging a virtual one-man war against spiritualism, mediums, and psychics. Houdini, the great debunker, made a note in his diary on May 6, 1920, that he'd "offered to do the D. D. Home levitation stunt at the same place that Home did it in 1868." But Houdini's assistant thought the feat was too dangerous and adamantly declined to help the magician. The result was that Houdini never performed or duplicated Home's famed 1868 levitation. Note that Houdini admitted he required an accomplice; Home never had an assistant during his levitations, however they were accomplished.

Home was quite accessible to being studied and tested during his career. He'd demonstrated nearly every form of physical mediumship there was. He was excellent at calling attention to himself, and the publicity he generated, if nothing else, kept the lively debate about spiritualism in the news both in America and in Europe.

Could the man called the "greatest physical medium of the nineteenth century" have engaged in clever trickery and deception? Of course he could have. But, for example, when debunkers who were not present at his levitations dismissed them as "illusions," they took issue with the many witnesses who insisted they knew what they saw. There is also the unanswered question about how certain effects, such as floating through the air horizontally, could have been so readily achieved. How was furniture able to move, seemingly of its own energy? Since Home often conducted séances in lighted rooms, wouldn't at least some witnesses have detected fraud?

Virtually every other nineteenth-century medium, at one time or another, was accused of some deception, according to the debunkers. Of course, many skeptics attended séances with only one goal: to uncover fraud. Why then were neither skeptics nor scientists unable to detect any chicanery on Home's part? Of course, what is to be said about those scientists who refused to even observe D. D. Home and other mediums? Perhaps they feared ridicule—or worse, the inability to explain by the known laws of science, how the paranormal events were occurring. Then, as now, acknowledging that any psychic phenomena was genuine would have meant redefining science, religion, and the very nature of life and death. It was more convenient to ignore or discredit a medium than to rewrite long-held scientific and theological dogma.

Home left many unanswered and frustrating questions for future generations to ponder. Was he in contact with the spirit world? Might his paranormal abilities have been manifestations of some form of psychokinetic or telekinetic energy, the kind often reported in poltergeist cases? Perhaps they were beyond his control. Theories and speculations can go on indefinitely. But the choices come down to two possibilities: Daniel Dunglas Home was a unique and remarkable individual who actually possessed the powers attributed to him; or he was one of the most cunning and ingenious frauds in all of history. The final question that cannot be answered is, Will we ever discover which he was?

6 Women at the Séance Table

The only question left to settle, now, is: Are women persons?

—SUSAN B. ANTHONY, Women's rights advocate

Mary Fenn Love paid a high price to end an unhappy nine-year marriage to a man named Samuel Love. In order to obtain a divorce, she had to leave New York for another state where the law was less strict. The divorce was granted, but Mary had to relinquish custody of her children. Such was the law in the 1850s against any woman who dared divorce her husband. She later met the medium and seer Andrew Jackson Davis, a widower at the time, and they married in 1855. "She spent the next decade trying to regain custody of her children," wrote author Ann Braude in *Radical Spirits*. Mary Fenn Davis, a spiritualist, spoke harshly about the yoke that marriage placed on women. Thirty years later, Davis left her for a younger woman.

By the mid-nineteenth century, it had been a "man's world" for so long that no one could remember life being any other way.[1] American society was all very neatly structured: men went to work; they were the breadwinners, the leaders and decision makers; they made and enforced the laws. They could even be tyrants to their wives, and many were. It was not illegal for a man to beat his wife or child. Women were meant to remain home, obediently, and duty-bound to tend the household and raise the children. If a woman chose or was forced to work it was generally in the poorest paying occupations. With the exception of teachers, head-mistresses, midwives, and a handful of writers and poets, opportunities for women were few. If they needed employment to support themselves and family members, it was for wages well below what men earned, and in jobs such as servant, domestic, mill worker, seamstress, or laundress. As America became more industrialized, many young women toiled for as long as sixteen hours a day in factories for pathetically little money, often as meager as three dollars a week. Prostitution was common in every city. When families moved west, wives also performed heavy and tiring farm labor.

The legal rights of women were severely limited, if they existed at all. Once they married, rich or poor, women were essentially the property of their husbands. Their most important function was procreation. It was not unusual for desperately poor girls and young women who became pregnant to abandon or kill their babies. There were no social service programs, as we know them today, and help was scant, while girls and women dwelling in wretched poverty and squalor was not uncommon.

When a woman married she had no property rights, and if she worked, her salary went to her husband. Seeking a divorce meant disgrace and forfeiting custody of her children, but she could not withhold sex from her husband. Women could not serve on juries or give testimony in court. Universities, medical, and law schools barred their admission. Even upon death she had no legal rights to distribute her personal belongings as she saw fit. To seek redress was nearly impossible. Suffrage, the right of women to vote, was a long way off. But not everyone was content with this restrictive social structure. Many women chafed at the inequality and the inherent unfairness of the system; and were depressed, angry, and frustrated by its constraints and inequities. Some became physically and emotionally ill. Yet by mid-century, little progress had been made to improve the status of American women.

Then, in 1848, two important and separate events occurred in western New York that would ultimately bring about drastic change to the social landscape of the country. In March of that year, the two young Fox sisters reported spirit rappings in their Hydesville home, and the spiritualist movement was born. Across the country interest in communicating with the dead moved with such astonishing speed that many were caught off guard. Mediums and séances seemed to pop up virtually overnight in nearly every town and city, and attracted several million adherents all the way to the White House. The other important event was a push for women's rights.

Elizabeth Cady Stanton and Lucretia Mott

Not far from Rochester, where Katie and Margaret Fox only a few months later, during the summer of 1848, had moved with their astounding spirit raps, a landmark gathering took place in the small and picturesque village of Seneca Falls, New York. It was a conference about women's rights organized by two firebrands—a positive or negative reference, depending which side you were on. Elizabeth Cady Stanton and Lucretia Mott were great leaders—or outrageous agitators. They'd organized the Seneca Falls Convention to deliberate women's equality, and press for "social, civil, and religious rights."

Stanton, a native of upstate New York, and a spiritualist, said she'd heard spirit raps. Mott was a Quaker from Philadelphia. While Quakers were numerous in Pennsylvania, dating back to William Penn, there were far fewer in western New York, but they were deeply committed to social causes, and considered to be among the "liberal religions," which also included Unitarians and Universalists. For example, in Rochester, the Quaker community numbered perhaps six hundred, but was in the forefront of the abolitionist movement in that region, tending the Underground Railroad to help escaped slaves flee. Many Quakers also became deeply involved in both the spiritualist movement and the cause of women's rights.

Spiritualists, by their own definition, opposed Christian orthodoxy and churches that preached centuries-old dogma, such as Calvinism.[2] Spiritualism's emphasis was on personal responsibility and the right of the individual to find God and salvation in his or her own way. "Spiritualists saw themselves as champions not only of liberal religion but of liberal politics and social conventions, as well," wrote author Mary Farrell Bednarowski. Therefore, it was not surprising that spiritualism embraced the women's movement, as well as other later reform efforts for temperance, prisons, and labor. Spiritualists represented "rebellion against death and rebellion against authority," wrote Ann Braude.[3] They saw the need for women to move beyond their traditional roles. In fact, "Spiritualism became a major—if not *the* major—vehicle for the spread of women's rights ideas in mid-century America," Braude explained.

Women could not be ordained as clergy in Christian churches; in fact, many churches banned them from even publicly addressing congregations. The ban stemmed from a biblical prohibition against women "preaching in public," first stated by St. Paul in the New Testament. In contrast, within the spiritualist movement, males and females had equal standing. What's more, many women mediums became well known. As the ones who brought messages from the dead, women assumed leadership roles; while Americans who maintained traditional beliefs were appalled by both spiritualists and feminists. Although there were many male mediums throughout the nineteenth century, the popular perception held that mediumship was the domain of women.

"Perhaps the most startling discovery was the extent to which spiritualism and the inception of women's rights were intertwined," wrote Barbara Goldsmith in her book *Other Powers*.

While most men ignored or scoffed at foolish talk about women assuming positions of power, influence, and affluence through hard work or schooling, by mid-century there was an angry undercurrent that would grow into the women's rights movement, stirred by strong and determined leaders such as Susan B. Anthony (1820–1906), Elizabeth Cady Stanton (1815–1902), and several others. Men reacted by defending the status quo: women were the "fairer sex," and at the same time were considered fragile beings that needed to be protected and sheltered.

Spiritualism's contribution to women's emancipation was significant. The Fox sisters and their spirit raps came along at the right time, and punctured the insular male-only mentality that was taken for granted in American society. Despite there being men mediums, once the spiritualist movement became identified with women and girls, it was a perception that remained intact for generations, well into the twentieth century. For many females, spiritualism opened a door to career opportunities that were virtually unprecedented. The world of spirits had literally placed women at the head of séance tables.

The reception women mediums received, however, was mixed at best. Primarily, the chief opposition came from religion, not science—at least not yet. The noted jurist Oliver Wendell Holmes called the Fox sisters the "Nemesis of the pulpit." The press was largely antagonistic toward spiritualism, and many newspapers took note of the association between mediumship and femininity. Author R. Laurence Moore quoted a newspaper article from the 1850s that labeled male mediums as "addled-headed feminine men." Eventually, when studies were conducted, it was found that by the end of the nineteenth century as many as eighty percent of mediums were female.

Americans in their religious beliefs had come far from the days when women associated with the supernatural were tortured and executed, as happened in Salem in 1692. Spiritualists had fought hard to distance themselves from the occult, with its medieval stereotypes of witches and evil spells, among other superstitions. By the mid-1800s, spiritualists regarded their principles as a "scientific religion." But there were still fundamentalist ministers who attempted to convince Christians that spiritualism was the "work of the devil," and some went farther, branding mediums as "witches." Most Americans had moved beyond such Calvinist doctrine, so the "fire and brimstone" preached by evangelical ministers found only a limited reception, especially in the North, and was criticized by both spiritualists and leaders of liberal religions. The Roman Catholic Church took no chances concerning spiritualism: it forbade Catholics from consulting mediums or attending séances.

Spiritualism had become a force to reckon with, and was a concern to many established Christian denominations. It also posed a threat of a social and political nature. Here was a movement that was upsetting the very foundation of church and society. Spiritualism's close cooperation with the new women's rights crusade created a two-fold problem. Both radical movements had the potential to weaken Christian conformity while, at the same time, challenge the traditional—and servile—role of women. Spiritualists were strong advocates for a woman's right to vote as a means of "political empowerment."

Who exactly were the mediums, those women who sat at the head of the séance table, and the others who traveled the country as "trance speakers"—and why had they chosen to do so?

For one thing, mediumship was a career that afforded females a degree of independence that in the Victorian era was rare. It also gave women a measure of attention and importance that few other occupations offered in the nineteenth century. Curiously, few girls and women saw mediumship as a way of earning a large amount of money. Actually, for most male and female mediums who charged for séances, the compensation was modest. If asked, most replied that they felt a "calling" to bring communications from the spirit world. For many, that may well have been true, for very few achieved wealth. Some claimed they had not even wanted to demonstrate their abilities in public, but that spirits insisted they do.

The fact that some requested a fee for séances became controversial. There were critics who lashed out that mediums who'd been given a "spiritual gift" had no right to accept money. After all, they'd not attended school or had any formal training. Spiritualists countered that mediums had expenses, as did everyone, and therefore had every right to a fee. As far as not requiring an education to conduct séances, mediums reminded critics they provided a skill or ability relatively few had, and asking to be paid was not unreasonable for a service that helped many, especially the bereaved.

That raised another question from skeptics: If a medium charged a price for attending a séance, was the client certain he or she had chosen a genuine medium? The movement was rife with fraud, and how many people had been conned into paying for bogus séances? For legitimate mediums it was a serious concern, and they understood the difficult task of building a reputation for honesty if they wanted people to pay, especially when there was competition from many charlatans.

Some did not request remuneration at all.[4] Nettie Colburn, Mrs. Lincoln's favorite medium, who helped the president and Mary Todd Lincoln cope with the death of their son Willie from typhus, never charged for sittings. She had to earn a living working in a government office by day, while conducting séances in the evenings in the White House. It was also Nettie Colburn who invoked the spirit of Daniel Webster when President Lincoln was in doubt over signing the Emancipation Proclamation.

The most famous medium of the nineteenth century, Daniel Dunglas (D. D.) Home, did not receive money for séances. However, he made it a lifelong practice to accept "gifts," some of them quite expensive, from clients, most of whom were wealthy.

The Fox sisters, on the other hand, nearly always asked for a fee for their séances and public demonstrations. But Katherine and Margaretta Fox both died in poverty, apparently exploited by their elder sister, Leah, who enjoyed a comfortable living from her mediumship.

The average woman medium earned between 400 and 600 dollars annually, modest even in the economy of the mid-nineteenth century. However, most of the females who became professional mediums were from poor or unassuming backgrounds, and it's doubtful they could have earned any more in another line of work. No one has a precise figure of how many female mediums there were in America during the nineteenth century. However, to say there were several thousand would not be an exaggeration.

Spiritualist publications, such as *The Banner of Light*, advertised mediums and the fees they charged: a private sitting in a medium's home was generally one dollar. A séance conducted at a client's residence could cost as much as five dollars. The same periodicals often carried letters from women mediums who complained about poor compensation and the difficulty of the work; but still, most maintained their commitment to spiritualism.

If female mediums felt something positive about what they were doing, that was not an opinion shared by everyone. Skeptics and critics found nothing commendable about the so-called "feminine" personality required to be a medium. The "stereotype of nineteenth century womanhood" considered that she was "more spiritual, sensitive, and passive than the male," wrote author Mary Farrell Bednarowski. "In fact, the typical female medium fits this description perfectly."

To critics at that time, women mediums "represented above all else the corruption of femininity," R. Laurence Moore observed.[5] But both friends and foes of spiritualism agreed that women had the characteristics that best qualified them to be mediums.

Many agreed that a woman's enhanced sensitivity and spirituality, as well as her intuitive nature, passivity, and tendency toward "nervousness" were all qualities that a good medium required. She was also believed to be more virtuous than men, and more willing to sacrifice herself for others, even if it meant suffering, bearing pain, or foregoing her own happiness. In fact, these were the same qualities that women were thought to employ as wife and mother. Stereotypical masculine traits such as strength, willpower, and logical thinking were supposedly not seen in mediums, according to the Victorian view. A man with an aggressive, intense, or forceful personality or intellect—all considered male characteristics—would not make a good medium. If you wanted "expert" opinions about these qualities, phrenologists who'd studied such matters supported the idea that females were better suited for mediumship than men. The shape and size of a female medium's cranium indicated the necessary character and mental faculties for this type of work, according to phrenology, then a popular—though later discredited—"science" taken quite seriously by many.

Although Victorian-era generalizations and stereotypes may jolt or offend modern sensibilities, in their time they were accepted by nearly all women and men with little question.[6] But women mediums applied a positive spin to the labels critics assigned them. Yes, many women acknowledged, they were willing to "sacrifice for the spiritual benefit of others," as Moore explained. Female mediums saw their "sacrifice" as an indication of how important their work was.

Women and girls who were spiritualist mediums not only attained a certain distinction, they also achieved unique entry into the male-controlled world. Where else in nineteenth-century America could a young woman, like Nettie Colburn or Kate Fox, dare offer advice to the president of the United States? Was there any other place but at a séance where a female could express her opinions, especially to men—some of them important figures in business, law, literature, science, politics, and myriad other occupations that were otherwise closed to women? What's more, men actually listened to what they were told, a rarity in a society where the woman's voice was largely ignored. Female mediums found the freedom to say things in public that would be unthinkable in any other situation. Spiritualist séances and lectures were, in fact, among the few venues women even had to speak in public.

A medium could claim immunity from anything disagreeable or erroneous she said because she'd given spirit messages while in a trance state. Therefore, if a male sitter was displeased, it was not the medium's fault. Remember, she was just a passive conduit who merely repeated what the spirits had imparted to her. A man couldn't blame the medium. After all, she did not control the spirits. It was the other way around; the spirits controlled her.

While many women mediums conducted séances in private homes or settings, some girls and women broke another social barrier by appearing in public before audiences who paid to hear them. These mediums were called "trance speakers," and some became quite well known.

A Victorian-era taboo deemed public speaking to audiences inappropriate for girls and women, but trance speakers defied that prohibition. They earned a slightly better income than those who gave private séances, and trance speaking fascinated audiences. Typically, there was a one-dollar admission fee per person. However, when mediums traveled, they were responsible for their own expenses, which diminished their income. Traveling was not easy or comfortable in the nineteenth century, especially for women, so those who toured as trance speakers required stamina, in addition to the energy they needed for their demonstrations; it was not a glamorous life. Audience size and reaction varied from town to town. Meanwhile, wherever female mediums went, fundamentalist clergy attacked them for doing the work of the devil or evil spirits, while secular critics branded the whole business as chicanery.[7]

Emma Hardinge and Cora Richmond

Two of the best-known trance speakers during the nineteenth century were Emma Hardinge and Cora Richmond.[8] Richmond (1840–1923) has been described as America's "most famous spiritualist speaker." If the story of her birth is true, she was destined for a life dedicated to "psychical awareness." For Richmond was born with a "veil" or membrane over her face, considered a foreshadowing of her life's work. She was also born into a family with spiritualist leanings. When she was eleven she was permitted to live in a spiritualist community called Hopedale, founded by a Universalist minister named Adin Ballou who became one of spiritualism's earliest advocates and writers.

By the age of sixteen, Richmond had become a popular public speaker, and traveled around the country giving inspirational lectures while she was in trance. The subjects she spoke about were often chosen by scientists and addressed by her with remarkable eloquence. It was assumed that she and other trance speakers would not know the answers unless they had spirit help. She settled in Baltimore for many years, and then moved to England in 1873. There she gave an astounding three thousand trance lectures, winning many compliments.

When Richmond returned to the United States, she moved to Chicago where she became one of spiritualism's most important leaders. In 1892, she conducted funeral services for the Lincolns' former medium Nettie

Colburn Maynard. A year later she helped found the National Spiritualist Association of Churches, still in existence, with headquarters now in Casadaga, the well-known spiritualist community in Florida. Richmond continued her trance speaking, and those who heard her said she offered fascinating revelations about the spirit world. She claimed that the federal government's Joint Congressional Committee on Reconstruction requested her advice from the spirit world on questions facing the nation following the Civil War. She was also a highly regarded healer; and unlike many other women mediums, Richmond maintained control of the money she earned.

Emma Hardinge was born in London's East End in 1823. By age eleven, she was working as a music teacher, and her theatrical talents brought her to the United States in 1856. Once here she met a medium named Ada Hoyt; that experience resulted in her converting to spiritualism, and she began the task of fostering her own "psychic powers." Hardinge demonstrated her abilities, which included mediumship, automatic writing, prophecy, and psychometry, before the Society for the Diffusion of Spiritual Knowledge, the first spiritualist organization in America, founded in New York in 1854. Its members included a number of prominent people including Judge John Worth Edmonds and former Wisconsin governor N. P. Tallmadge.[9] The latter was an early convert to spiritualism, and sat for a séance with the Fox sisters in the 1850s.

One technique employed in the early years of spiritualism was to select a committee from the audience attending a medium's demonstration, and have its members ask the medium to speak spontaneously on a subject selected by the committee. Hardinge was considered quite adept in these situations. In one well-documented case, she provided remarkably accurate details of a steamer that sank at sea. The information, which she could not have obtained any other way but psychically, came to her from the spirit of a crew member who'd drowned in the disaster.

Hardinge's greatest success was as a highly effective spokesperson for spiritualism, and she praised mesmerism and "its kindred phenomenon of clairvoyance." She spoke passionately for the movement, and traveled widely to promote it. She was also a successful editor and author on the subject. Hardinge wrote that "the spirits claimed [their] method of communion was organized by scientific minds in the spirit spheres," and that the spirits "referred to the [Fox] house at Hydesville as one peculiarly suited to their purpose from the fact of it being charged with the aura requisite to make a battery for the working of the telegraph, also to the Fox family as being similarly endowed." The suggestion that spirit communication was somehow related to or caused by electricity remained a common theory among nineteenth-century spiritualists.

In 1875, Hardinge-Britten (her married name) was one of the founders of the Theosophical Society in New York, with Madame Helena Petrovna Blavatsky. Her influence on spiritualism was considered so important that after her death in 1899, an institute and library were named for her in Manchester, England. Throughout her career, Hardinge-Britten earned a better living than most mediums, while her husband successfully managed her business affairs.

Trance medium Samantha Mettler used her income to help support her family when her husband's business fell into bankruptcy. But others were badly exploited; taken advantage of by fathers and husbands. When that occurred, there was little if any sympathy from the community.

Occasionally female mediums caught the attention of a wealthy patron who provided her with a respectable income. During the nineteenth century there were a number of successful and affluent men who could afford a medium exclusively to hold their own private séances. Cornelius J. Vanderbilt, Henry Seybert, David Underhill, and Horace Day were among the rich and powerful who employed mediums this way. Even a woman who was a fraud might find herself lucky enough to cash in. In New York during the 1880s, such largess fell to an infamous and spurious medium named Madame Debar, when a wealthy attorney provided her with an elegant home, reported *The New York Times*.

Another understandable lure for women who became mediums was the attention they received. Whether it was criticism or praise, here was a way to gain notoriety that virtually no other occupation brought. For a young woman who'd had an unhappy or lonely childhood, as plenty did, mediumship became an escape and at the same time it attracted public notice. For some, any attention was better than none.

It was not unusual to find children working as professional mediums. It was a fact that audiences liked attractive young female mediums; and rarely would the public see a girl or woman speak on stage. You'll recall how young the Fox sisters were when they began their public careers.

Children were considered less likely to engage in "trickery or deception than an adult," the spiritualist newspaper *Banner of Light* noted in what was typical nineteenth-century thinking. Who could be more innocent than eleven-year-old trance medium Laura Ellis? Others were slightly older and many "child mediums" traveled around the country during the 1850s when trance speaking reached its peak of popularity. If something a child medium said seemed dishonest, as with adults, there was a ready excuse: blame it on the spirits that controlled her. "Innocence, ignorance, and youth were the best qualifications for female trance speakers," Ann Braud wrote.

"Woman does not need to cultivate her intellect in order to perceive spiritual truths," said trance speaker Elizabeth Doten (1829–1913), who became one of the best-known woman trance speakers of her day.[10] She was immensely popular for offering inspirational advice and wisdom that she said came to her from spirits, and she often gave public recitations of improvised poetry. Doten once claimed she'd received spirit communications from Edgar Allan Poe. While in trance she composed a poem that was said to be remarkably similar to Poe's style and use of language. In 1885, when Doten was in her mid-fifties, she ceased mediumship and public lectures, saying she could no longer discern between messages that were from her mind, and those that came to her from the spirit world.

Among the better known "lady trance mediums," in addition to Cora Hatch Richmond, Emma Hardinge, and Elizabeth Doten, were Emily Beebe, Emma Jay, Sarah Horton, and Melvina Townsend—names now all but lost to history.

Females could not have been as "fragile and passive" as their male critics charged in the nineteenth century. Consider the distances trance mediums traveled on poorly paved and rutted roads, in every kind of weather, by horse and wagon, stagecoach, boat, and train. Jennie Leys journeyed the coast of California from San Francisco to Los Angeles, with many speaking stops in between; trance medium K. Graves traversed the Midwest even in bitter cold weather; and Mrs. C. M. Stowe tirelessly went from place to place, covering hundreds of miles, to demonstrate her powers. There were others, including the very popular Laura Cuppy, Addie Ballou, Charlotte Wilbour, and too many more to name them all.

Laura de Force Gordon

Laura de Force Gordon (1838–1907) was both a trance speaker and suffragist.[11] She had a gift for speaking spontaneously on any subject given her by audience members, even specific areas of the sciences which presumably she knew little if anything about in her waking state. A native of Pennsylvania, who traveled through the northeast as a trance speaker, Gordon and her husband eventually moved to California where she continued to publicly advocate for suffrage. Elizabeth Lowe Watson was a medium and suffragist, as well as a friend of Susan B. Anthony.[12] When Anthony was an elderly woman, after a long career fighting for women's rights, she wrote Watson, curious about what awaited her in the afterlife. When Anthony died in 1906, Watson wrote:

> *She is not dead but more alive*
> *Than in her fairest earthly days.*

Achsa Sprague [13]

It was not unusual for mediums—male and female—to discover their psychic abilities in childhood. Others who began their careers later in life had struggled with bad marriages, abusive relationships with men; some had been abandoned, or were ill and spiritualism had given them the strength to go on with life.

By 1853, when she was twenty-five, Achsa Sprague had been an invalid for five years, stricken with a painful and disabling disease that affected her joints and left her bedridden in a dimly lighted room. A schoolteacher by the age of twelve, she was now permanently confined to home in Plymouth Notch, Vermont, with no hope of ever recovering. Achsa, a pretty young woman with long dark hair and intense eyes, faced a bleak future. Most frustrating was the fact that her crippling illness made Achsa wholly dependent upon her mother, and what she missed most was her independence. Traditional medical treatments, such as were available at the time, had failed and Achsa had begun to think about other ways of healing.

When spiritualism swept across America she was open-minded to its possibilities. She found she had the ability to communicate with spirits and after several months began to heal herself. By late in 1853, Achsa received sufficient help from the spirit world through her self-taught mediumship that she actually began to recover from her long and debilitating illness. In her diary and journal, Achsa noted that mediumship had changed her life from invalid to trance speaker; and she always credited her "spirit guides" for her healing.

Achsa wrote in her diary in 1849: "Once more I am unable to walk or do anything else." She described herself as "miserable both in mind and body." At another point she wrote, "I do not begin to improve any yet and fear I shant. . . ."

She also detailed her frustrating experiences with doctors and "magnetizers," an early term for mesmerists or hypnotists. She wrote: " 'Tis a hard life to live." Other entries read: "I have looked with gloomy eyes into the dark mysterious future. . . ." "I am slowly but surely giving up all of being much better. . . ." "What hope is there for me but in Death. And what will Death bring?"

After her miraculous healing in 1854, her tone changed: "I had a beautiful walk last evening by moonlight," she wrote in her journal.

Whether her illness had made her more suggestible to becoming a medium is open to debate; but many mediums claimed they'd been seriously ill prior to the development of their psychic abilities. There has long been speculation that head injuries, fevers, and trauma, among other afflictions, preceded mediumistic powers, and therefore there might a connection between certain maladies and emerging psychic ability.

Because of the state of medical science in the nineteenth century, precise names of some diseases were unknown or not yet identified; therefore, we cannot be certain what condition Achsa suffered from before her miraculous healing. However, the symptoms described by her at the time suggest she may have had a form of tuberculosis, rheumatoid arthritis, or an autoimmune disease such as lupus, which typically attacks young women, but was too poorly understood to diagnose or treat in that era. How spirits might help the healing process remains a medical mystery. Achsa's explanation was that spirits had released her from the "chains of disease," not exactly a scientific interpretation, but surely one she believed.

Achsa was moved to write a poem about her ordeal, mediumship, and recovery, titled "The Angel's Visit." A portion read:

A young girl in a darkened room,
Chained by disease,—a living tomb!

In another verse, she wrote:

> *And stronger grew her form each day,*
> *All pain and languor swept away,*

Still later in the poem, Achsa said:

> *When loved ones, called away from earth,*
> *Awake in heaven to purer birth,*
> *But that they come in love,*
> *To point the weary heart above,*
> *To light with hope each weary eye,*
> *And teach the soul it cannot die.*

Once she was healed and had regained her strength Achsa left home in Vermont in 1854 and became a deeply dedicated spiritualist trance lecturer who traveled the country and spoke about her experiences. She embraced mediumship with the fervor of a religious calling, and as a result of her dedication, rejected all suitors and marriage proposals. An unusually independent young woman for the times she lived in, Achsa became very popular, earned a reputation for her sincerity, and was one of the women most in demand as a speaker in the entire country—a rare distinction. She constantly had requests for speaking engagements, more than she could physically keep up with, and her personal story and praise for spiritualism motivated others.

Well thought of within the spiritualist community, she nonetheless faced the same scorn from critics and skeptics that greeted other independent women, especially mediums. Achsa continued as a successful trance lecturer until a recurrence of her illness resulted in her death in 1862 when she was only thirty-four. Remarkably, her diary and journal still exists and is held at the Vermont Historical Society. It provides a rare glimpse into the life and work of one of the most inspiring trance speakers of the mid-nineteenth century.

It was not uncommon for mediums to claim spirits had helped them overcome illness, similar to Achsa Sprague's experience. Rachel Baker was a trance speaker who said she was cured of a serious ailment with the aid of spirits. Another was a medium named Amanda Jones who thanked "spirit guides" for helping her triumph over sickness.

Some young women turned to spiritualism because they'd experienced personal loss, and one of the most useful purposes a medium could have was to comfort the bereaved. In 1857, Annie Denton Cridge lost her first-born baby who was only several months old. Grief stricken, she began to see and sense spirits after the infant's death, and became a professional medium. She and her husband later moved from Ohio to California, where she died in 1874. Following her death, Cridge's surviving son and daughter, both spiritualists, claimed they were in contact with their departed mother.

Nettie Colburn

Nettie Colburn was one medium with startling influence during her career, as you'll recall from earlier in the book. Nettie was only twenty when she conducted White House séances for President and Mrs. Lincoln. Many years later she wrote a book about her life and work titled *Was Abraham Lincoln a Spiritualist?* Nettie Colburn Maynard (her married name) marveled when she thought back on her White House experiences. She described herself as "an unlettered girl" who'd gone on "to become the honored guest of the Ruler of Our Great Nation, during the most memorable events in its history."

There were witnesses to the séances Nettie conducted who later recalled that when she went into trance, a "masculine spirit force" communicated through her. The men present listened carefully to what the "masculine spirit" had to say. Had she not been a medium, there is no chance whatsoever that she would have had the attention of high government and military officials, the first lady, and President Lincoln. Nettie derived huge satisfaction from her experiences as a medium, no matter what other obstacles and criticisms she faced.

Many conservative and matronly women of "respectable" social standing were horrified that young girls were professional mediums. Some suggested that mediumship was an actual disease or illness; that the girls were out of touch with reality, or worse, that *male* spirits took them over! Ralph Waldo Emerson didn't go that far, but he labeled spiritualism "trite," and often disparaged it.

Spiritualists were divided about Christianity and the divinity of Jesus Christ, but the majority regarded their beliefs from a Christian perspective. Although some of their scientific critics were atheists, most women mediums viewed the spirit world in a religious context, even if fundamentalists condemned them and spiritualism's view of the afterlife that did not include a place called "hell."

The more skilled female mediums were able to channel a number of spirits, both male and female. Those who became "medical mediums" were women who applied their powers towards helping patients by turning to the "laws of nature"; often with mild herbal concoctions to effect healings. Typically, while she was in trance, the medium offered a diagnosis through her clairvoyant ability; then with the advice of spirit guides prescribed remedies for whatever ailment the patient suffered.

Medical mediums increased in popularity throughout the nineteenth century. Risky treatments provided by traditional physicians ranged from dangerous mercury in medications, to powerful and highly addictive opium, as well as an array of ineffective cures and worthless pills. Right or wrong, it's no wonder that many considered medical mediums as an alternative to orthodox or so-called established medicine. Obviously, traditional doctors despised and attacked medical mediums and other unconventional healers. But from the point of view of spiritualism, mediums had helped the bereaved to emotionally and spiritually cope with loss. Now some found they could also treat physical ailments.

Medical Mediums

One of the more accomplished medical mediums was Mrs. J. H. Conant of Boston (1831–1875), who said her "spirit control" was an elderly Boston doctor, and while in trance she felt as if she was "outside her body." She once saved her own life after a doctor gave her an overdose of morphine. In trance she "prescribed herself" the correct medication to return to health. For seventeen years, until her death, Conant was engaged by the spiritualist newspaper the *Banner of Light* to conduct séances for the public at no charge. Then a transcript of each séance appeared weekly in the *Banner*.

Lottie Fowler (1836–1899) was a clairvoyant with the ability to medically diagnose. She visited England to work with royal physicians when the Prince of Wales was critically ill, and immediately, she psychically predicted he would recuperate.

Controversy was always at hand. There were many matrimonial problems during the nineteenth century, not unlike today. However, because a
divorced woman was often stigmatized, and her options to leave were
few, there was less divorce, but many unhappy and unfulfilled marriages,
as well as outrageous amounts of wife and child abuse, alcoholic husbands, and others who deserted their families. In fact, many women who
became mediums understood these problems in others, for they'd come
from similar backgrounds, although it should be added that a number of
women mediums managed successful marriages.

In cases where women mediums psychically discovered that their female clients had serious marital problems, or were in danger because of
physical or sexual abuse, and with no laws to protect them, the spirit world
often advised that "wives divorce their husbands." Not surprisingly, outraged critics charged that female mediumship was encouraging "immoral
behavior." For spiritualists and mediums, divorce seemed a reasonable response to misery or abuse. For the more conservative, the dissolution of a
marriage by a woman was not considered an option, and spiritualist advice
to the contrary posed a grave threat to family stability.

"Purity was the one trait of Victorian womanhood that did not seem at
all necessary to the practice of good mediumship," R. Laurence Moore
wrote. Women mediums were nonconformists, and symbolized defiance
of nineteenth century values, many complained. Female trance speakers
often traveled alone, and there's no question that some found themselves
in circumstances that permitted promiscuity. Surely, some women mediums engaged in activity that defied rigid Victorian sexual mores. The
strict morality of that era did not encourage sexual relations—except for
procreation by married couples. Public discussions of sex were taboo;
often the subject was also avoided in private. Obviously, some mediums and
spiritualists ignored propriety, but so did many nonspiritualists. Nonetheless, the issue gave the enemies of spiritualism and woman's rights another
line of attack.

The traditionalists particularly accused spiritualists of supporting
"free love," which, in Victorian times, meant "promiscuity and infi-
delity," Ann Braude explained. Thus spiritualists posed a threat to the
"sacred institution" of marriage and shocked religious opponents. Actually, most spiritualists were not in favor of free love; but the two were
connected in the public mind. The heart of the debate stemmed from the

fact that many women spiritualists criticized "marriage as the root of women's oppression," Braude wrote.

Spiritualists did not oppose unions between women and men. What they vehemently criticized was the unfairness of marriage and laws that deprived women of equal rights, kept them subservient, and often amounted to their subjugation and virtual tyranny by men. Further, spiritualists argued, women were frequently forced to marry because of the lack of economic opportunities, and then have children—whether they wanted to or not. The answer was not to abolish marriage, but to improve the laws that governed it.

Attitudes toward mediumship changed after the Civil War, even as many who'd lost loved ones in the brutal conflict sought contact with the deceased, as a result of the staggering death toll. Following the war, mediums faced new demands from the public "to perform miracles at every séance," Barbara Weisberg wrote in *Talking to the Dead*. What had happened was that Katie Fox materialized a spirit, and that "set a standard," Weisberg explained. Now other mediums felt they were under pressure to emulate Fox, and when they found they could not, they resorted to fraud.

By the 1870s, mediums stepped up showmanship during séances to better hold public attention. During the decade, many mediums resorted to spectacular displays of supposed spirit manifestations that some observed were more theatrical than spiritual. Fantastic displays of flying objects, birds, and musical instruments, glowing spirit hands, spirit music, table tipping, and spirit materializations became séance staples. As the dazzling and dramatic became a part of more séances, spiritualism's credibility was increasingly challenged. The press and clergy were as hostile as ever; and some scientists had joined skeptics in their efforts to debunk the entire movement. With the exposure of many physical mediums as frauds, and their array of electrifying effects debunked as tricks, spiritualism was barraged with criticism. As a result, becoming a medium no longer held the appeal for girls and women it had been before the war when it played a significant role in the growth of the woman's rights movement.

During the 1860s, travel by many American female mediums to England increased. Interest in spiritualism there had grown into its own strong movement. Although Maria Hayden of Boston was the first American medium to visit England in the early 1850s, it's likely some who went later were motivated by the international success of the medium D. D. Home who spent considerable time in England in the 1860s.

The 1870s were a time when American spiritualism was marked by several problems and scandals that threatened the movement. Two new movements emerged, Theosophy and Christian Science, both of which drew members away from spiritualism, diminishing its influence. Three highly independent women were largely responsible for the turmoil, and they became well known in America during the decade: Victoria Woodhull, Helena Petrovna Blavatsky, and Mary Baker Eddy. Each of them confronted or contradicted spiritualism with new systems of thinking.

Victoria Woodhull[14]

If the word "controversial" seems overused, when applied to Victoria Woodhull it may be understatement. As the contentious "free love" debate continued, Woodhull was at the center of the uproar when she became one of its most outspoken and militant advocates. She wore many hats during her long and tumultuous life: "spiritualist, feminist, and social reformer," her biographers noted. Born Victoria Claflin in Homer, Ohio, in September 1838, her career began, along with her younger sister Tennessee (1846–1923), when as young children they gave séances and performed as fortune-tellers in a traveling medicine show. At the age of sixteen, Victoria married a physician named Canning Woodhull, but they divorced in 1864, and she later married two more times. She would always maintain that she was a spiritualist, but also realized that identifying with spiritualism was a way for her to call attention to herself, especially in the woman's rights movement.

In 1868, Victoria and Tennessee moved from small town life in the Midwest to bustling New York City, where business and industry were growing rapidly in the post–Civil War years, and even millionaires were being made: Gould, Morgan, Belmont, and Vanderbilt. Through a series of fortunate circumstances that put the sisters in the right place at the right time, they met Cornelius Vanderbilt, shipping magnate, famed financier, and the richest man in America. He had a genuine interest in spiritualism, and an eye for attractive women. Victoria Woodhull was beautiful.

Once, when someone asked him for business advice, Vanderbilt confidently answered, "Do as I do, consult the spirits!" It might have been a reference to Woodhull's stock advice that she received from the spirits of deceased bankers and moneymen. The sisters became known as the "lady brokers" when Vanderbilt helped them establish a stock brokerage office, an extremely rare opportunity for a woman in that era. Victoria and Tennessee did well financially and realized a sizable profit.

With the money they earned, the sisters began publishing a periodical in 1870 called *Woodhull and Claflin's Weekly*. The thrust of it was to cast attention on topics of particular interest to feminists, such as equal rights, suffrage, and that hot button issue: free love. By the next year, 1871, Woodhull—and her political positions—had become sufficiently well known that she appeared before the House Judiciary Committee to speak on behalf of woman's rights. In doing so, she became the first woman to ever testify before a congressional committee, a recognized voice in the fight for woman's suffrage.

In 1872, Victoria Woodhull entered the history books for a daring move that certainly caught the attention of politicians, the press, and the public. She became the first woman in American history to run for president of the United States. She also was the first spiritualist to seek the highest office in the land. When she was nominated as the Equal Rights Party candidate, she knew she had no chance whatsoever of winning the election. Technically, she could not have assumed the presidency anyway because of her age. She was thirty-four in 1872, and the legal minimum age to be president was thirty-five. Woodhull was one year too young.

But none of that mattered, for her goal was to call attention to women's rights—and to herself. She then made a further stir when she and her sister attempted to vote, something women could not legally do. In her run for the presidency, she garnered the support of *some* in the woman's rights and spiritualist movements. But her radical positions and advocacy of free love alienated even many women. Meanwhile, with her as the example, traditional Christian clergy accused every one of America's estimated four million—or more—spiritualists of supporting free love. Although it was a false charge, it inflamed passions. Few regarded Woodhull's candidacy seriously; but the press was more than happy to publicize her effort—it sold newspapers. Incidentally, the winner of the 1872 presidential election was Ulysses S. Grant, who went on to a second term in office.

Woodhull's stance on free love and other social issues was so controversial that it actually caused rifts in both the spiritualist and women's rights movements, even as she held the presidency of the American Association of Spiritualists, where she also caused divisiveness for much the same reason. Many mediums felt that the entire spiritualist movement would be labeled "radical" because of Woodhull's extreme positions. But others disagreed, feeling spiritualism and her positions should be separated. The answer came when the spiritualist group Woodhull headed attracted fewer and fewer people, while other similar organizations drew much larger numbers.

Meanwhile, the sisters were still publishing their magazine and in 1872 they printed a bombshell, worthy of the tabloids that would follow in the years ahead. *Woodhull and Claflin's Weekly* carried a shocking story that claimed one of the country's most famed ministers, the Reverend Henry Ward Beecher, was having an adulterous affair with a parishioner, Mrs. Elizabeth Tilton. The result of the allegations was a full-blown scandal, and an embarrassing trial for Beecher on adultery charges, although he was ultimately exonerated. Woodhull may have published the accusations as revenge for the Beecher family's opposition to her free love position that she dropped and backed away from after the Beecher-Tilton scandal.

In 1877, the embattled sisters moved to England where they continued their work for woman's rights, and Woodhull, married to a successful London banker, devoted much of her time to various charities until her death in 1927.

Looking back on her contribution to spiritualism, it appears that Woodhull used the movement to further her radical women's rights agenda. But following the Civil War more people had grown interested in mediums contacting their dead loved ones than in spiritualists pontificating on reform movements. Before the war there was abolitionist fervor to end slavery, but nothing after the war seemed as emotional or compelling. Now a bereaved parent, for example, was more immediately concerned with hearing from her departed child than listening to endless speeches about social injustice.

Woodhull's radical positions—especially about free love—caused serious and irreparable rifts between her and others in both the spiritualist and woman's rights movements. Even such bold feminist leaders as Susan B. Anthony, who once welcomed Woodhull, later distanced herself. When Anthony and Elizabeth Cady Stanton wrote the definitive history of the early women's rights movement, Woodhull's contributions were reduced to one brief mention. Her name was virtually exorcised, and largely forgotten in the years ahead.

Helena Petrovna Blavatsky

There is no simple or uncomplicated way to describe Madame Helena Petrovna Blavatsky; nor is there any way to dismiss her importance as "one of the most influential occult thinkers of the nineteenth century," as the *Encyclopedia of Occultism and Parapsychology* described her.[15] Noted for founding the Theosophical movement, Blavatsky was multifaceted: "occultist, author, guru, mystic, and charlatan," biographers have variously described her. Although she developed Theosophy during the Great Age of Spiritualism, its ideas differed in many ways from those of the spiritualist movement. She is especially important for having introduced Eastern philosophy to vast numbers of people in the West.

Blavatsky was born in Russia in 1831, to a family related to minor royalty, a child with a vivid mind's eye, especially for the supernatural. She was only a young girl when she first claimed she saw "phantasms" that sent her screaming in fright around her family's home. By the time she was in her teens Blavatsky was fiercely independent, hot-tempered, and strong-willed. Because she was so difficult to control, her family was thrilled to marry her off to a much older Russian general when she was only seventeen. But the marriage lasted only a few months when the impulsive Helena ran off. She went first to Constantinople; then traveled all over the world, supporting herself with a variety of jobs. In France in the late 1850s, she claimed she first witnessed the famed medium D. D. Home, an experience that impressed her to convert to spiritualism. While there she began a short-lived psychic organization, but gave it up when she was accused of committing fraud.

In addition to her unpredictable behavior, Blavatsky had a propensity to embellish, exaggerate, and sometimes downright lie, so there's no way to know exactly where she was or what she did before coming to the United States. In her words, she'd been a "wanderer." Despite charges of fraud that would always dog her, Blavatsky also displayed genuine psychic abilities. She was a skilled medium.

When she made her voyage as an immigrant to the United States in 1873, it's doubtful anyone could have guessed her eventual influence.

She'd traveled there in steerage as millions of poor immigrants to the United States had—and would—to seek a better life. But Blavatsky's dreams were loftier than most when she took her first look at New York City. As other newly arrived immigrants, she found a job in one of the notorious sweatshops where garments were made; and a place to live in a tenement in the city's teeming Lower East Side. But she was not fated to remain in these impoverished circumstances for long. Her deep desire to learn about the unexplained and mysterious coupled with her strong determination could not be contained. She would later say that she felt some "strange sustaining power around her," perhaps an allusion to a guiding spirit or guardian angel for her life soon took enough strange twists and turns to convince her she had a particular destiny to fulfill.

There was something hypnotic about her penetrating, deep sky-blue eyes. They were, in fact, her only outstanding physical feature. Otherwise, Helena Petrovna Blavatsky was an unexceptional looking and overweight middle-aged woman with a round face and frizzy brown hair. She dressed carelessly in worn clothing, typically accompanied by a shawl on her head or shoulders. She cursed like a sailor, chain-smoked, used drugs, and her temper remained fearsome. She wasn't exactly a picture of Victorian femininity, so what attracted people to her? Blavatsky's powerful and "intense" personality was capable of captivating and influencing people, and perhaps those magnetic eyes drew many to her.

In October 1874, there were rumors of strange supernatural events occurring at a house in the tiny community of Chittenden, Vermont. Two brothers, William and Horatio Eddy, both farmers and mediums, claimed a range of psychic manifestations, from spirit raps to spirit materializations.[16] William was in his early forties, and Horatio in his early thirties. The talk about the Eddy brothers reached all the way to New York, and soon newspapers were sending reporters to Vermont to delve into the story. One of those assigned was a correspondent for the New York *Daily Graphic*, forty-two-year-old Henry Olcott, who traveled to the Eddy farm although he knew virtually nothing about spiritualism or any other form of psychic phenomena.

Olcott discovered that the two brothers had been badly mistreated when they were boys by their abusive father who'd tried to beat the psychic powers out of them; that is, until he discovered he could make money from his sons' abilities. Then he sent them to work as mediums.

Both William and Horatio were left with permanent physical scars from the maltreatment their father inflicted.

Olcott spent more than two months probing the Eddy brothers, and witnessed firsthand some four hundred apparitions or spirit materializations emerge from their "spirit cabinet." He said the spirits varied in size, gender, and race, and gathered enough material to write fifteen articles reporting what he saw, convinced the manifestations were genuine. The next year, his newspaper stories were compiled as a book, *People From the Other World*. Skeptics, of course, dismissed the Eddy stories as chicanery, but not Olcott.

Then, who should appear at the Eddy farm to witness the phenomena for herself? None other than Madame Blavatsky; and there in a small Vermont hamlet she met the erudite-looking, full-bearded Henry Olcott. Blavatsky watched the Eddy brothers' demonstrations. She proclaimed her life was devoted to spiritualism, and then brought forth her own impressive array of spirit materializations—"a Russian soldier, a Kurd, an Islamic scholar, and several Indian gurus"—that dwarfed anything the Eddy brothers produced. Olcott was plainly in awe, and became an ardent student of Blavatsky. He had no doubt he'd seen authentic spirit phenomena.

In 1875, with the help of her new friend Henry Olcott and a young attorney named William Q. Judge, also a student of the occult, Blavatsky was about to make a name for herself when she founded the Theosophical Society. "Theosophy is a complex of philosophical and religious ideas centering on an attempt to gain access to the spiritual reality beyond material existence," is how *The World Almanac Book of the Strange* described Blavatsky's ideas. Her teachings also embraced Buddhism and the lofty goal of creating a "universal brotherhood of man." Theosophy offered the study and knowledge of the "ancient religions," an examination of the "laws of nature," and the advancement of the "positive powers" that are "latent" in each of us.

Blavatsky also took issue with Charles Darwin's theory of evolution. "Man had not descended from apes but from spirit beings," she insisted. In his fascinating book, *Madame Blavatsky's Baboon*, author Peter Washington explained how "As a reminder, she kept a stuffed baboon in her parlor dressed in a wing collar, tail-coat, and spectacles, and holding a copy of [Darwin's book] *The Origin of Species* in its hand."

Olcott was named president of the new theosophical movement to which he was deeply devoted and that he tirelessly promoted, and he proved to be perfect for Blavatsky's intents. While Olcott held her in the highest esteem, she did not regard him with the same respect. Privately, as she came to know him better, she considered Olcott a "blockhead," a "baby," and a "conceited windbag."

Blavatsky laid out the goals of the Theosophical Society in a weighty, and some said, cumbersome book titled *Isis Unveiled*, published in 1877. She claimed that it had been "dictated to her by the Masters of Wisdom via astral light and spirit guides." Critics savaged the book, calling it everything from "plagiarized poppycock" to a "heap of rubbish." While it was true that her 1,200-page tome contained a confused mixture of tenets and teachings comprised of Buddhism, Hinduism, Taoism, Kabbalah, Pythagoras, as well as Blavatsky's own ideas, the underlying principles she espoused were positive and appealed to many.

As Theosophy became widely known, it also attracted notice from the Society for Psychical Research (SPR) in London. At the time, the Theosophical Society had its headquarters in India and in 1884, the SPR sent Richard Hodgson there to examine the movement. The results of the visit almost destroyed Theosophy. Hodgson concluded it was entirely a fraud.

In fact, Blavatsky's extraordinary supernatural displays were revealed as trickery when two friends acting as accomplices confessed to helping her create some of the psychic manifestations by deception. One example was written messages from "invisible spirit masters" that mysteriously materialized, but were found to be planted.

Based on Hodgson's investigation, the SPR issued its conclusion:

For our part we regard [Blavatsky] neither as the mouthpiece of hidden seers nor as a mere vulgar adventuress; we think that she has achieved a title to permanent remembrance as one of the most accomplished and interesting imposters in history.[17]

When the SPR report was made public in 1885, it brought critics out of the woodwork and created such a commotion between Theosophy's followers and detractors that even Henry Olcott was shaken, and although his integrity was never in doubt, he banned Blavatsky from the

Theosophical Society's headquarters in India despite their years of close friendship. Another critic was the famed medium D. D. Home, who also accused her of fraud.

Amazingly, Blavatsky survived the barrage of criticism and accusations of chicanery. She continued writing, and in 1888, *The Secret Doctrine* was published in two volumes, and supposedly was written by her in an altered or "supernormal" state. Then in 1889, she wrote *The Voice of the Silence*, followed by a third volume of *The Secret Doctrine*, published posthumously.

In her last years she had the good fortune to attract to Theosophy a British social reformer named Annie Besant, who would become Blavatsky's successor. Besant strongly defended Theosophy against the SPR's damning conclusions.

But even her critics had to acknowledge that Blavatsky had genuine psychic ability, notwithstanding her propensity for fraud. Like so many other mediums, she apparently felt the need or pressure to embellish or fabricate supernatural phenomena, and combine or mingle them with her real psychic powers, such as clairvoyance and telekinetic ability, for greater effect on witnesses. She also had "unusual hypnotic powers," Henry Olcott said.

Nothing the SPR reported had any impact on her prestige in India, where she was considered pro-Hindu and touted Indian culture. That was at a time when many Indians desired "home rule," and there was much anti-British sentiment.

Blavatsky was a complicated and eccentric individual, both intelligent and cunning. She definitely engaged in fraud at times, but she also had an incredible grasp of philosophical and religious concepts. At its peak, Theosophy attracted one hundred thousand members. Today, its adherents number approximately thirty to thirty-five thousand.

During her last several years, Blavatsky was seriously ill and suffered from obesity from a lifetime of neglecting herself. Fortunately, Annie Besant invited Blavatsky to live in her London home, where she passed on in May 1891.

Putting aside questions of alleged fraud, Blavatsky's influence on Western culture and thinking was significant. Without doubt, Theosophy was helped by the fact that it was developed at a time when there was a national interest and consciousness about spiritualism, although spiritualists were careful not to be defined as "occult." On the other hand, Theosophy was an "important source for the spread of occult beliefs."

Blavatsky and later Theosophists said they "revived an ancient mystical tradition" that was a major part of Indian history. Theosophy also encouraged the English translations of significant Hindu sacred writings. Both Blavatsky and Olcott had studied Eastern beliefs, learning from Hindu and Buddhist teachers and gurus, and both claimed they'd communicated with those spirits known as "masters," meaning those who'd achieved "higher states of perfection."

"The Theosophical Society was probably the most important agent in introducing Eastern thought to large Western audiences, and it helped break down Western attitudes of condescension toward non-Western cultures. It also played a significant role in stimulating Hindu and Buddhist revivals in Asia," explained *The World Almanac of the Strange*, and it influenced the later writings of some important literary figures including the Irish poet William Butler Yeats.

Finally, as an example of the complexity—and cynicism—of Madame Blavatsky, consider the following quotes attributed to her: "It's all in the glamour. People think they see what they don't." She once admitted to a friend, "What is one to do, when in order to rule men, it is necessary to deceive them? For almost invariably the more simple, the more silly, and the more gross the phenomenon, the more likely it is to succeed."

Mary Baker Eddy and Christian Science

"The mind as the key to health," explains succinctly the underlying principle of Christian Science founded in the 1870s by Mary Baker Eddy, who distanced her movement from mediums and séances. "She was a sworn enemy of spiritualism," Barbara Weisberg wrote.

"Perhaps the most serious challenge to mediumship came from the new religious movement Christian Science," wrote Ann Braude. Eddy insisted she was neither a spiritualist nor a medium.

Born Mary Ann Morse Baker in the tiny farming community of Bow, New Hampshire, in 1821, she was the youngest of six children. For generations, her family attended the Congregational Church, but Mary had difficulty accepting the harsh Calvinist doctrine of "predestination" the church preached. She was a frail child with a recurring health problem poorly understood in the early nineteenth century by traditional medicine.

She suffered from what were then known as "spells," and when they occurred she fell into convulsions or seizures. Sometimes, she'd lapse into unconsciousness, numb and unable to move. Other times, violent body spasms caused her to shriek and cry in severe pain. The family tried their best to find treatment; however, nothing proved successful, despite efforts by a number of doctors.

Homoeopathy had become a favorite method of treating disease in the early nineteenth century. It consisted of administering minute doses of drugs to the patient that in a healthy person would produce symptoms of the disease. Mary was treated by homoeopathic doctors, but to no avail.

Little was understood about her ailment; diagnosis and treatments then were crude at best. Each time she was gripped by a "spell," her terrified parents, fearing she would die as a result, hurriedly sent for their family physician, Dr. Ladd, who was somehow always able to bring Mary out of her frightening episodes. He was unusually perceptive and forward thinking for that era. His diagnosis was that Mary's illness was "hysterical" in nature. In other words, it had an emotional basis, an idea not then well understood by medical science. Her convulsions usually occurred when she was under "great mental stress" or experiencing a crisis. Dr. Ladd thought that Mary might be helped by mesmerism or hypnosis, highly regarded in the early nineteenth century; and he was correct: hypnotism or the power of suggestion did help to partially control her "spells." Unfortunately, the debilitating spasms would be a lifelong condition for Mary Baker.

Not far from where the Bakers lived was a Shaker community, and Mary grew curious about the sect, especially their belief that God was "both masculine and feminine." When they prayed it was to "Our Father and Mother which are in Heaven." Their leader was Ann Lee, called "Mother Ann," who claimed she had the "gift of healing."

When Mary was twenty-two she married, but her husband died unexpectedly the next year from fever, leaving her a young widow with an infant son. Not surprisingly, she suffered from worsening bouts of paralyzing seizures no doubt caused by extreme stress. Morphine was given to ease her pain, but it "made her crazy," observed a friend.

Right after the Fox sisters and their spirit rappings became a virtual national obsession, Mary was exposed to spiritualism, as were millions of other Americans. For a short while she dabbled in both hypnotism and spiritualism, and even attended séances. But she apparently never developed psychic powers, such as clairvoyance or mediumship; however she found she was highly suggestible to mesmeric trances.

She remarried in 1853, and for a time her health problems eased. While her husband was serving in the Civil War, Mary again suffered her crippling hysterical spells, and sought help at a "water cure sanitorium." Then she was told of a "mental healer" in Portland, Maine, Phineas Parkhurst Quimby, who was able to cure even severe pain, with no medicines or surgery. "The patient's own faith" healed them, suggesting that the "curative process was wholly a mental one," Quimby explained.

Who was Phineas Quimby? By trade he'd been a New England clockmaker when he became interested in mesmerism and applied its principles to develop a healing technique based on "suggestibility." By about this time, the 1860s, the terms *mesmerism* and *hypnosis* were being used interchangeably when referring to the "power of suggestion."

After testing subjects, Quimby realized suggestion worked on patients. "At last I found out that the mind was something that could be changed. I called it spiritual matter, because I found it could be condensed into a solid and receive a name called 'tumor,'" and by the same power under a different direction it might be dissolved and made to disappear," he wrote. Quimby was not a doctor or a medium, and his healings did not appear to be related to spiritualism.

He concluded, "the stand I now take; that the cure is not in the medicine, but in the confidence of the doctor or medium." In other words, he realized that his influence by itself was enough to heal an ill person, and that a patient's mental attitude and emotions were important to curing them. "Diseases and their cures" resulted from "suggestion," he was certain.

Quimby opened a successful healing practice in Portland, and Mary Baker Patterson, then her married name, became a patient in 1862. (We know her better by the surname of her third husband, Ada Eddy.) She was already past forty, thin, slightly built, and frail after years of suffering. Her disease had affected her spine and caused agonizing pain, weakness, and depression. Quimby was a kindly looking man with short-cropped white hair and beard; his manner was sympathetic, and he healed her pain, at least for a time.

Impressed with Quimby's results, she was motivated to develop her own system of healing that she called Christian Science. It was very similar to his approach, except Mrs. Eddy placed her healings within the context of Christianity; Quimby had not done that.

Like Quimby she believed "illness and health are illusions; there is no physical world, therefore there is no disease, and no need for medical intervention." She concluded that if a person changed their perception, they would be restored to health. Christian Science's teachings required its believers to cast aside most traditional ideas about medicine.

One day in 1866, Eddy fell on ice, was badly hurt, and not able to move at all for three days. During that time she read the Bible, and learned about healing. "God is all," she realized, and she was instantly cured. That encouraged her to think further; and she began to jot down her ideas. That same year, Quimby died; he had been a "mentor" to her; she his student. Then in 1875, she wrote what would be the "textbook" for Christian Science, *Science and Health*. By the next year, she was training students to become Christian Science healers.

What was the relationship between Christian Science and spiritualism? Eddy made it clear in her book that her movement did not accept mediumship although she understood spiritualism and said she was sympathetic to the bereaved who sought its help. But, she emphasized, Christian Science and spiritualism were *not* the same, and in her book she clearly detailed what the differences were.

Most people, however, presumed she was a medium because her healings were accomplished without surgical tools or medicines. Therefore, many took for granted that she had the help of spirits, although she repeatedly insisted that was not true.

There was a certain irony in her rejection of mediumship, since most who were open to her healings and philosophy were those who also accepted spiritualism. If the confusion frustrated her, some was of her own doing, for when she first advertised for students she did so in the major spiritualist magazine, *Banner of Light*. Following are the exact words of an 1868 ad she placed in the *Banner*:

Any person desiring to learn how to heal the sick can receive of the undersigned instruction that will enable them to commence healing on a principle of science with a success far beyond any of the present modes. No medicine, electricity, physiology or hygiene required for unparalleled success in the most difficult cases.

The advertisement gave her name and address in Massachusetts. The fact that the ad was in the *Banner* suggested that she understood its readership was the audience she needed to reach. But by being in a major spiritualist periodical, Eddy obviously gave the impression that somehow she was connected to spiritualism and mediumship. Still she insisted Christian Science and spiritualism were *not* related, although it seems certain that some of her ideas had their basis in spiritualism.

Eddy dissuaded her students from it; and she did not accept the idea of spirit communication. Spirit contact was possible, she said, but did not require the intervention of a medium; Eddy suggested that a person could access spirits directly. Her one spirit was God; "all that He created was good"; and He was within each of us. Another significant difference pointed out by author Ann Braude was that "spiritualists emphasized personal spiritual knowledge; Christian Science emphasized doctrinal uniformity." In other words, spiritualists were individualistic; Christian Scientists were not. Mary Baker Eddy held tightly to the reins of her movement, and she was very much in charge. Spiritualism, on the other hand, was barely organized.

Yet, in some ways the two movements were similar. Both were meant to heal; neither believed in death. Both offered hope and rejected disease; and both Christian Science and spiritualism opposed religious and medical inflexibility. As one example, both movements encouraged women to become practitioners. By contrast, traditional churches and the medical establishment did not welcome women as clergy or physicians.

In 1879, Mary Baker Eddy founded the Church of Christ, Scientist and in 1881, a college of metaphysics in Boston. Two years later, as her movement grew, she began publishing the *Journal of Christian Science*. Throughout the 1880s, there was further expansion, although some of her former students began teaching their own versions of Christian Science, albeit under new and different names, a situation that greatly disturbed her.

In the 1890s, Eddy faced a contentious legal battle when a lawsuit accused her of plagiarizing Quimby's work. Ultimately, the suit was decided in her favor, but there was no question that her ideas of Christian Science had started with Quimby's practices, although she later dismissed them as largely "mesmerism." In 1892, she officially formed the First Church of Christ, Scientist in Boston. The Christian Science movement had become nationwide by the time of her death in 1910.

It may seem that the 1870s were a breakthrough for women with the recognition Woodhull, Blavatsky, and Mary Baker Eddy received. The fact is, that despite their individual achievements, none of the three actually contributed very much to advance women's rights, unlike the spiritualist movement that had long promoted suffrage and reform efforts. Eddy was not concerned with advocating anything but Christian Science, although she had a "significant impact on American religious life," noted author Robert C. Fuller, who added, the role of Christian Science "in introducing Americans to metaphysical spirituality has been enormous." Christian Science became one of the largest churches founded in America, and at its peak it had some 100,000 members. The newspaper the *Christian Science Monitor*, begun by her in 1908, still publishes today.

Curiously, from the 1860s through the 1880s, American society was advancing in science and technology, even as new spiritual and religious movements were still developing. It seems we were attempting to move forward both mechanically and metaphysically. It may seem unusual that as medical progress was made in the era of Louis Pasteur's theory of germs as the cause of infection, and Joseph Lister's discovery of antiseptic surgery, many still sought "mental healing" and spirit contact. It was also a time that saw incredible inventions such as the telephone, phonograph, and the first electric lights. Yet trance speakers remained popular, and many women mediums still used their public visibility to make a case for suffrage; the spiritualist movement and suffrage would remain close to each other through the end of the nineteenth century, despite critics like novelist Henry James who wrote that both movements promoted "immorality."

It was also during the 1870s and beyond that spiritualist summer camps and retreats, such as the one that would later be called Lily Dale in western New York, became gathering places for many.

Mary Baker Eddy was hardly the only one who disliked physical mediumship. By the 1870s, although spiritualism was still in vogue, many people questioned the sensationalism that had become a staple of séances, such as spirit materializations and oozing ectoplasm.

The most famous, if dubious, "materialization medium" in the latter part of the nineteenth century was Florence Cook, whose fully materialized spirit control "Katie King" made news in America, even though Cook was in England.

There were also Mr. and Mrs. Nelson Holmes, well-known materialization mediums from Philadelphia during the 1870s. They were well regarded until they were accused of using a confederate to create a false materialization of a spirit who was also named "Katie King." The press was only too happy to expose their alleged chicanery. But at a later séance, under tightly controlled conditions, they produced spirit materializations in front of twenty witnesses. What about the accomplice's confession? It turned out she was the Holmes' landlady, who was discredited when it was revealed that she'd attempted to blackmail the couple. Apparently, the Holmes saw their integrity restored.

The era produced some colorful and long forgotten characters; far too many to name, but a few provide an example of American spiritualism in the nineteenth century.

There were materialization mediums everywhere. Among the better known were Mary Murphy-Lydy, Carrie Sawyer, and Etta Roberts in Massachusetts. A woman named Elizabeth Comptom was found to be a "powerful medium." Katherine Tingley was a successful medium who later switched over to Theosophy from spiritualism. There was Laura Edmonds, whose father, a noted judge, was forced from the bench because it was alleged spirits were advising his judicial decisions. Mary Hollis-Billings, from Indiana, was a materialization medium in the 1870s; she could produce thirty or forty spirits in just one sitting. What made them especially entertaining was that they could sing along with those attending the séance. Let's not forget Mary Hardy, the Boston medium from whom the "first paraffin casts of spirit hands" were found in the mid 1870s.

By the 1880s, there was another resurgence of interest in spiritualism, and a new form of mediumship developed. Its practitioners were called "mental mediums," and the best-known American in that category was Mrs. Leonora Piper who began her career in 1884. Mental mediums communicated messages from the departed to their loved ones on earth, but without spirit materializations or other physical phenomena, as there had been in earlier years. Mental and physical mediums were *not* the same. American psychologist William James exhaustively tested Mrs. Piper's mediumship with surprising results—more about that in the next chapter.

Meanwhile, some scientists had organized to examine spiritualism's claims. The Society for Psychical Research (SPR) in England was founded in1882; three years later the American Society for Psychical Research

(ASPR) was begun. They had sharp-eyed investigators, and the result was that many physical mediums were found to be fraudulent. A materialization medium named Mrs. Williams became a "spirit" when she put on "flesh colored tights" in her darkened spirit cabinet. Some had accomplices. Others produced "spirits" from crude cardboard cut outs and even puppets.

The spiritualist movement was not helped when the Fox sisters confessed in 1888 that they'd created spirit raps by cracking their toe and knee joints; and then recanted the confessions. But it was not the "death blow" to spiritualism that its enemies gleefully predicted.

In fact, by the turn of the century some mediums continued to make names for themselves, including Gladys Osborne Leonard, known as the British Mrs. Piper; Eusapia Palladino, a temperamental Italian medium; Mina Crandon in Boston, and many others whose names may not be well remembered, although they certainly attracted attention in their own time.

Don't think bogus mediums didn't keep up with technology a hundred or more years ago. The Bangs sisters in Chicago created "spirit portraits" in the 1890s. Then they got the bright idea in 1896, to have four men hold a typewriter in the air while a spirit hand typed. Their trick was later discovered and Lizzie and May Bangs were exposed as charlatans.

It is important to remember that despite skeptics, debunkers, and revisionist historians, not all mediums cheated or engaged in fraud and deception. There were—and are—genuine mediums and psychics, and spiritualism played a large part in the lives of many.

The Great Age of Spiritualism was running out of steam, sputtering, but not quite gone. Even the long-running spiritualist newspaper, *Banner of Light*, founded in 1857, had stopped publishing before 1910. At its peak in the mid-nineteenth century, the number of American spiritualists were estimated at anywhere from 2.5 million to 11 million. Now the numbers had dwindled.

The last hurrah, so to speak, came at the end of World War I. Many bereaved families sought contact with their men and boys lost in the Great War, especially England that counted 700,000 dead soldiers.

Spiritualism had fought for women's rights and opposed church orthodoxy, but as the nineteenth century drew to a close, it was no longer part of social reform efforts.

Spiritualism had changed the way many thought about the nature of life and death. When people sought mediums at the end of World War I, it was not for theatrical demonstrations of physical phenomena, exposés, or political screeds. The reason was much more simple and touching: the grieving simply wanted to know what happened to their loved ones after they left this earth; and they sought a message from the deceased. It all came down to comfort: the assurance that there is no death, only a transition to the spirit world, and the promise that someday they—all of us— would be reunited with the departed. Women had taken their place at the séance table, and in the process opened many doors—here and hereafter.

7

From Séance to Science

If you wish to upset the law that all crows are black,
you must not seek to show that no crows are; it is
enough if you prove one single crow to be white.

—WILLIAM JAMES, *What Psychical Research Has
Accomplished* (1897)[1]

How could nineteenth-century thinkers prove the existence of the paranormal? Where was the science? Where was the evidence? What constituted evidence? These were only some of the questions that scientists and spiritualists, believers and skeptics, advocates and debunkers struggled with as the nineteenth-century Age of Spiritualism rolled toward the early twentieth century's age of social sciences.

The Great Unknowing
There is a story about a schoolteacher a century or more ago who tore page nineteen out of the arithmetic book of every child in her class. When a visiting friend noticed the one missing page in each book, she asked what had happened to them. The teacher explained she'd quietly removed that particular page from every book because it contained a question she could not answer. "I didn't want any of my students to think there is something I do not know," the teacher admitted.

The apocryphal story is not unlike the circumstances scientists found themselves in when spiritualism captured America's attention. When many learned men could not explain mediumship and other psychical phenomena within the limits of their training or expertise, it was easier to debunk or dismiss the entire movement than wrestle with what it was and how it worked.

That's unfortunately where the relationship between traditional science and the paranormal has more or less remained throughout the history of America. Those courageous and open-minded individuals who dared to go beyond prescribed limits to examine or test psychical claims often paid a heavy price when colleagues scorned them and even called their reputations into question.

From practically the first reports of spirit rappings in Hydesville in 1848, the people who openly doubted the Fox sisters' claims of communication from the spirit world included those who held a skeptical or so-called rational view about the supernatural. Many men of science were hopeful that anything in the realm of occult or psychical phenomena had long ago been relegated to some dark corner of the human experience for all time and forgotten.

Those who thought that way could not have been more mistaken. Once millions of Americans were captivated by spiritualism, it was folly to suppose they were not thinking about what awaited them after death; the suggestion that we on Earth could contact the spirit world held the promise of life everlasting; immortality. What's more, many ordinary people did not especially care what scientists thought. Scientists would claim they were acting in the public's behalf. However, it often seemed they were acting in their own self-interest. Grief-stricken people were more concerned with hearing from a departed loved one than being hammered by scientific or psychological explanations about why there was no afterlife.

Some insisted that such questions were not the responsibility of scientists, that supernatural or miraculous claims belonged in the domain of religious belief or faith, not within science, that "orderly branch of knowledge involving systematized observations and experimentation." Psychic phenomena were elusive, and the question of testing for an invisible spirit world seemed to many to be specious or even impossible.

When the Fox sisters initially claimed they'd heard spirit raps, few were even sure what to call the strange occurrences. The paranormal has always been mired in the confusion of terminology. Were these events occult? Supernatural? Psychical? Demonic? Electromagnetic? If a scientist wasn't even certain what to call the unseen phenomena, where and how did he begin to test its existence? No one had arrived at a generally accepted definition of the inexplicable force that came to be known as "psychic."

The spirit world was not very cooperative with those earthly beings investigating it. Psychical phenomena did not seem to conform to any established scientific protocols. When many mediums and psychics were exposed as frauds and charlatans it became a convenient excuse for skeptics and orthodox scientists to discredit all of them. But what if there were no signs of chicanery? What was to be done with evidence of genuine psychic phenomena and legitimate mediums? How were they to be explained? Too often, doubting scientists and psychologists found the easiest way out was to conclude that all psychic events were fraudulent. It was a disingenuous approach. The press was also quick to jump on any allegation of fraud, but was rarely moved to pronounce a psychical event to be genuine.

In fairness, doctors, scientists, and psychologists of the nineteenth century had little of the knowledge, experience, or technology to test the paranormal even had they sincerely wanted to. In fact, the irony was that spiritualism "played a significant, though usually unwitting, role in the development of American psychology," wrote author and historian R. Laurence Moore. Prior to the appearance of Sigmund Freud's concepts, spiritualism was already paving the way for theories of the subconscious and unconscious mind. Phrenology, long ago discredited, actually helped in the evolution of American psychiatry.

But neurology, psychiatry, chemistry, physics, and other disciplines were not as well understood in the nineteenth century. For example, theories to explain mediumship ranged from branding it as blatant fraud, to involuntary muscle action, to physical disease or insanity. One notion was that mediums experienced hallucinations or delusions that could be blamed on "excessive excitement of the nervous system," Moore said. "Nervous system disorders" were often an explanation for mediumistic or psychical experiences. Spiritualists frequently contended that contact with the afterlife was something electromagnetic. Electricity was the wonder of the nineteenth century because it was clearly present, could be proven, and had been tested as far back as Ben Franklin and his kite in the eighteenth century. In addition, the electric telegraph connected the

United States from New York to California during the nineteenth century, so the analogy that defined mediumship as the "spiritual telegraph was quickly adopted."

When finally in the early 1850s, the movement became popularly known as "spiritualism," few scientists showed interest at first, while the cynical dismissed it as "humbug," the nineteenth-century's term for "hokum," "drivel," "quackery," and downright garbage. It was pure fluff; the stuff "dreams are made of."

Eliab W. Capron was a reporter and a zealot devoted to social causes who lived in Auburn, not far from Rochester, New York, where Katie and Margaret Fox went right after the commotion they'd caused in Hydesville. Capron quickly made his way to the sisters in 1848 to witness the spirit raps and to report on them. Although not a scientist, he performed one of the first experiments with the girls, a simple test he'd designed.

In a foreshadowing of the kinds of tests performed over the last twenty years by groups such as the Society for Scientific Exploration, Capron placed several small shells in his clenched fist and held them behind his back so neither sister could see them. Then he asked the spirit to make the number of raps equal to the number of shells he was holding. The spirit raps answered correctly.

Next, Capron grabbed a handful of shells but purposely avoided counting them, so even he did not know how many he held. He asked the spirit to produce the number of raps equal to the amount of tiny shells in his closed fist. Again, the spirit raps produced an accurate reply. That presumably ruled out telepathy on the part of the Fox sisters. In 1855, Capron went on to write one of the first important books on the new phenomena, *Modern Spiritualism*, and based on his experiences, he continued to support spiritualism and the Fox sisters.

But not everyone agreed with Capron's conclusion that the spirit raps might be genuine. "Exposures from time to time, were common," wrote R. G. Pressing.[2] In February 1851, for the first time, the public heard the theory that the raps were produced by the Fox sisters' "snapping of the knee joints" when three medical professors from the University of Buffalo—Doctors Austin Flint, Charles A. Lee, and C. B. Coventry—published that conclusion in the *Buffalo Commercial Advertiser* after they'd visited the girls and observed them. Not long after came the added supposition that Katie and Margaret had also cracked their toe joints to create the spirit noises. The Buffalo professors found that not everyone agreed with them. In fact, the growing number of spiritualists in America either ignored or criticized the doctors, mocking their theory of "toe-ology." Obviously, skeptics happily embraced the "joint snapping" explanation.

A second investigation supported the doctors' conclusion. Then, in April 1851, Mrs. Norman Culver, an in-law of the girls' brother David, published an "alleged confession" supposedly from Katie. Mrs. Culver had sworn to get to the bottom of the spirit raps controversy, with no intention of taking a neutral or objective stance. She made it perfectly clear that she wanted to "bury" the girls and the growing spiritualist movement.

But Mrs. Culver tripped herself up in the admission she attributed to Katie. According to Culver's allegation, when another committee tested the sisters in Rochester, they held Margaret's ankles so she could not move either her legs or toes. But the raps were still heard, allegedly made by the Fox family's Dutch servant girl hiding in the cellar who created the knockings when she heard those upstairs calling for spirit answers. So the raps sounded as if they were coming from beneath the floor, at least according to Mrs. Culver.

Culver hadn't bothered to check her facts before claiming this was a genuine confession. For one thing, the Rochester investigations were held in committee members' homes or in a public hall. Neither Margaret nor Katie had any servants, Dutch or any other kind. Finally, Margaret was the only one there to be tested. Katie was not present—she was living in Auburn at the time—so she could not have acted as an accomplice, or even witnessed the events.

Culver also contended that Katie admitted to her "other tricks" the girls used, including learning to read facial and body language of spirit circle participants for clues, and distracting witnesses to make them think the raps were coming from elsewhere in a room.

It turned out that Mrs. Culver had not acted alone in her campaign to discredit Margaret and Katie. She'd been lured into making the sworn statement by one of the Fox sisters' most bitterly hostile detractors, C. Chauncey Burr, a lawyer, Universalist minister, mesmerist, and self-proclaimed opponent of spiritualism. Another enemy of the sisters was a mesmerist and phrenologist named Stanley Grimes who'd hypnotized Andrew Jackson Davis before the latter gained fame as a medium and seer. Grimes accused the girls of every imaginable trick and deception he could think of from "ventriloquism to mechanical devices to collusion," wrote Barbara Weisberg in *Talking to the Dead*.

It was bound to happen: As the girls became better known, the number of foes and detractors increased in proportion to their fame. The revelations by Mrs. Culver resulted in many in the press dubbing the Fox sisters, the "Rochester imposters." The only one that steadfastly came to their defense was *New York Tribune* editor Horace Greeley.

After the attack by Culver, Eliab Capron answered her every accusation against Katie and Margaret. But that would not be the last word. Skeptics found out that some of the testing on Margaret had been conducted at the Rochester home of Isaac and Amy Post, the Quakers who'd befriended the girls. Guess what? The Posts had a servant girl fascinated by the spirit communications. What's more, she was Dutch.

Of course, even if all this were true, it did not explain how the spirit raps responded to the questioners' thoughts, knew the number of shells Capron held, or provided information to sitters that could not have been known, except psychically. Was it really possible for two young girls to perpetrate a fraud that was "tested thousands of times?"

"Investigations into the reality of the phenomena were always numerous," R. G. Pressing wrote.[3] "Test after test was applied. The skeptics faced two problems, to explain the production of the rappings, and the intelligence [that] answered the questions in many cases mentally asked. The second problem was seldom tackled, the first often and with very great ardor."

As the Fox sisters became more famous, not only were the straight-out detractors after them, but, as if in direct response to the debunkers, there began a genuine investigation among scientists as well as interested lay people in the phenomena surrounding the paranormal, albeit an ad hoc movement. When scientists during the early years of the spiritualist movement wanted to investigate the claims of mediums and psychics they often functioned independently. There was little coordination among those interested in paranormal research; there would not be a permanent American organization dedicated to psychical investigations until 1885, and that was three years after the British created the Society for Psychical Research. The British were first, and ahead of Americans, in their examination of mediumship, survival of death, and other psychical phenomena including crisis apparitions, deathbed visions, hauntings, clairvoyance, telepathy, premonitions, and telekinetic experiences.

One example of a mid-nineteenth-century American scientist motivated to research psychical phenomena on his own was William Denton (1823–1883), a Boston geology professor. His goal was to investigate psychometry, an ability named by another American scientist, Joseph Rhodes Buchanan, in 1842.

Psychometry was a power that many mediums, psychics, and clairvoyants have to hold an inanimate object or article—such as jewelry or a watch—that belonged to a subject, and from that psychically describe the subject's circumstances or emotional state. Often, holding an article that was the property of a person who died gives a medium "psychic impressions" about that individual. Denton performed a number of experiments and concluded psychometry was genuine. However, without a serious research organization to report such findings, the opportunity to evaluate, publish, and share test outcomes was sadly wanting.

At mid-century, interest in spiritualism by traditional American science was often erratic or haphazard. Perhaps many scientists did not consider the subject worthy of serious attention. In those relatively rare instances where a man of science came forward to examine a psychic claim, he was expected to debunk or dismiss it. William B. Carpenter, a noted British physiologist during the nineteenth century, observed the growing spiritualist fascination in America and England with disgust. He called it an "epidemic delusion," similar to the witchcraft hysteria that had racked Europe and New England in past centuries. Some early physicians believed mediumship and a propensity toward spiritualistic experiences was an illness that required treatment and which needed to be cured.

Robert Hare (1781–1858) was a respected chemistry professor at the University of Pennsylvania, who became one of the few early American scientists with the courage to support spiritualism, a position that made him an exception among his colleagues.[4] But that's not the way his story began. In 1853, Hare was one of the first scientists to publicly criticize and attack spiritualism's credibility. He said he wrote about spiritualism as "an act of duty to his fellow creatures to bring whatever influence he possessed to stem the tide of popular madness which, in defiance of reason and science, was fast setting in favor of the gross delusion called spiritualism."

Hare was seventy-two when he undertook his probe of spiritualism and expected to discredit it scientifically. He created his own testing devices; one of them was designed to measure minute changes in the weight of a glass of water in a metal cage. Could a medium influence the balance of the glass without touching it? Hare's test subject was the medium Henry Gordon, and to the professor's surprise Gordon found substantial changes in weight. The eminent British scientist Sir William Crookes later tested the famed medium D. D. Home similarly.

Another instrument was a wheel or "disc" with the alphabet printed on it to spell out messages. The disc was placed so it could not be seen by the medium. Hare discovered that Gordon could affect the letters by some unknown manner to spell out messages that had specific meaning for people witnessing the test. Hare's original purpose was to confirm that spiritualism was a fraud, but to the contrary, he concluded that there was "some rational being" of an unknown nature that caused the spirit communications. What is so fascinating about this experiment is that it was repeated, in another format, over 125 years later with very similar results.

Hare said he had taken "the greatest possible precaution and precision." But now he arrived at an entirely different explanation. He'd shown that a "power and intelligence other than that of those present was at work." No longer a critic, he instead became a proponent of spiritualism. His colleagues in the scientific community roundly criticized him; some of the verbal attacks were quite vicious. At Harvard University the reaction to Hare's findings was equally hostile. The faculty passed a formal motion strongly condemning Hare's "insane adherence as a giant humbug." (Nineteenth-century skeptics seemed to love that word when they disagreed with a pro-spiritualist result.) In much the same way, during the 1990s, Harvard professor John Mack was vilified by colleagues both at Harvard and at Harvard Medical School when he dared to examine "alien abductions" as real or perceived events and not simply as a form of sleep paralysis, as his colleagues had argued.

In 1854, the American Association for the Advancement of Science (AAAS) refused to even listen when Hare attempted to speak to its members about spiritualism; they literally shouted him down. He responded to the animosity by resigning from the association.

Hare also experimented with several other mediums including one named A. D. Ruggles who, in trance, spoke several foreign languages he did not know in his normal state. Hare again examined Henry Gordon when the latter demonstrated levitation in 1852, one of America's first mediums to demonstrate this facility, and concluded that Gordon's powers were evidence of some inexplicable psychic force.

Before his death in 1858, at the age of seventy-seven, Hare became a medium. His skeptical colleagues had a ready explanation: The poor man had gone senile.

From the 1850s on, there were many advances in science and technology, even as the Great Age of Spiritualism continued to grow. To some it may seem that science and spiritualism could not be further apart, each functioning in a separate world. But that was not necessarily so; they had to meet at some point.

"During the mid-nineteenth century no force in nature was more intriguing to the popular mind than electricity," wrote R. Laurence Moore. The marvel of electricity, notably dating from the successful introduction of Morse's telegraph in 1844, just four years before the first spirit raps at Hydesville, joined science and spiritualism in the minds of those who believed spirit contact was of an electrical nature. Many considered spiritualism a "scientific religion," and the comparison to electricity was obvious in the then-popular term, *spiritual telegraph*, a reference to spirit communications. Further, both spirit contact and electricity were invisible forms of energy.

One theory was that "souls vibrated with a mysterious electric charge that could be detected by mediums," wrote Linda Simon in *Dark Light* (2004).[5] But just as some feared mesmerists might control them—as Edgar Allan Poe wrote about in several frightening stories[6]—so also did many fear that electricity or electrical energy might run wildly amok. That thought may have fostered a comparison in some minds to the ancient fear of spirit possession, being taken over or inhabited by negative spirits beyond one's control. It all came down to the human need to master our lives and environment, wary of unseen forces such as hypnotic and electrical phenomena.

In 1853, Michael Faraday, one of England's most respected scientists, turned his attention to spiritualism. Faraday was both a physicist and chemist who became widely known for his experiments with electromagnetism and for inventing the first electric generator in 1831. He was deeply religious; he and his wife belonged to a sect known as the Sandemanians, but he had no personal desire to become a spiritualist. His interest was motivated by annoyance that psychical researchers were not testing spiritualist claims with what he considered the correct scientific approach. So, Faraday conducted his own experiments. In the early 1850s, that meant probing spirit raps and table-tippings, the best-known psychic manifestations at the time.

After Faraday observed many demonstrations of table-tippings he drew his conclusion about what was causing them. His theory was that, as Georgess McHargue wrote, "the unconscious expectations of the sitters, which expressed themselves in muscular pressure" was responsible. Faraday designed an apparatus to measure even the minutest movement at the séance table. He found that those motions were sufficient to make a small lightweight table move. Skeptics often point to the same theory to explain why a planchette—the pointer—moves from letter to letter on a Ouija board. Of course, most spiritualists disagreed with Faraday's thinking, maintaining that people's hands attracted "spiritual energy" and the messages came from discarnate entities or spirits.

Faraday's conclusion may be an explanation for a limited part of spiritualist or psychical occurrences, especially telekinetic activity. But it left unanswered many other questions about spiritualism, including how accurate messages were given by mediums, and did not explain other phenomena, ranging from levitations to spirit materializations, clairvoyance, telepathy, and hauntings.

When Faraday had the opportunity to meet and test the world-famous medium D. D. Home, the noted scientist refused, and so he and Home never came face to face. It is only speculation, but how much more interesting and scientifically revealing it might have been if Faraday had agreed to test Home.

No story is more bizarre in the history of American spiritualism's collision with science than the escapades of John Murray Spear (1804–1887), which is saying a lot.[7] He had been renowned in Boston as a Universalist minister and social reformer, especially in the effort to improve prisons; then he became interested in spiritualism, and converted to it in 1851. He wasted no time developing his own psychic abilities.

In 1854, Spear announced that a group of spirits calling themselves the "Association of Electricizers" told him to build what they called a "New

Motor" that would be a source of inexhaustible and "self-generated power" utilizing the "magnetic life" found in nature. The machine would behave as a "living organism," not unlike the human body. R. Laurence Moore described it as "a spirit designed perpetual motion machine."

According to the instructions from the spirit world, Spear and his followers constructed the strange apparatus near Lynn, Massachusetts. It was made of copper and zinc, and cost about two thousand dollars. Spear and the others genuinely believed there was evidence of "life in the machine."

Spear's construction received wide press attention; and when the public learned about his "new life force" many were not pleased. In fact, some compared it to a Frankenstein's monster. In Mary Shelley's 1818 classic, a being is created from the body parts of others but it has no soul. The monster, denied love, becomes evil, and eventually turns on its inventor, Dr. Frankenstein, killing him. The story raised questions about the ethics of science and technology, and what its limits should be, still a troubling societal dilemma.

In this case, the public need not have been concerned; Spear's contraption did not work. He blamed it on the vagaries of the spirit world, and would not surrender. The "New Motor" was moved from Lynn to Randolph, New York, in the western part of the state; supposedly a location with a higher elevation where the machine was expected to function as it was intended. But one night, a mob of angry and fearful townspeople destroyed it, contending it was "blasphemous." Following this, Spear wisely abandoned his misguided venture, but spiritualist publications were sympathetic. In one of the era's most important books, *Modern American Spiritualism*,[8] Emma Hardinge-Britten complimented Spear's patience, sincerity, and unswerving belief in the "spiritual origin for the various missions he undertook."

In the many years since Spear attempted to produce a new source of power, others have professed finding a new "motor force in nature." The best known were Nikola Tesla, John Worrell Keely, and Wilhelm Reich, whose controversial 1940s theory of "cosmic orgone energy" drove him to build a device to gather the orgone energy.

Despite all of the interest mainstream science expended upon spiritualism, true scientific investigation of spiritualism and other psychical phenomena remained largely a scattered effort in America until late in the nineteenth century. Many continued to be baffled about the nature of what they were examining, while there were on-going debates about whether everything from spirit raps to physical phenomena—tipping tables, flying trumpets, and spirits materializing—were even possible.

There also remained valid concern about exactly what instruments could investigate something as amorphous as spirit phenomena. What could you build? What would you measure? There were very legitimate questions some asked about the possibility of clairvoyance, premonitions, and telepathy, as to whether they were actually psychical or "supernormal" in nature, an energy yet to be discovered, which did not originate from discarnate entities, who had a nonphysical existence. Of course, that kind of talk raised the ire of most spiritualists, for it called into doubt their hard and fast belief that all psychic experiences were somehow caused by the spirit world, just as many religious fundamentalists attributed all things to God.

The issue of testing was critical, however. In a century fascinated with electricity, modern machinery, and theories about invisible forms of energy, measurement became a goal in itself. It was no surprise that legitimate science wanted to measure the abilities of spiritualists in a way that guaranteed a nonbiased result. And it wasn't as if professional mediums objected to being tested: many in the movement actually urged scientists to examine physical and spiritual phenomena. However, the nineteenth and early twentieth centuries were a time when there were scarcely any organized academic studies of the paranormal, and the handful of university investigations always came to the same conclusion: there was no scientific evidence of psychical phenomena. And even though there was no conclusive scientific evidence that spiritual phenomena weren't real, the prevailing rationalist opinion was that you had to prove it to be so, for it to be accepted as so.

Some cynics suggested that professors had made up their minds to oppose the paranormal before they examined it, regardless of what was presented. In other words, was the answer in before the questions were asked so as to make the resulting testing completely biased? Whatever the explanation, the paranormal was rarely welcomed in the hallowed halls of American academia.

Yet there were academics who pushed for investigating the spiritual world, among them famed British physicist Sir William Crookes (1832–1919), who was one of the first scientists in England or America to advocate the scientific investigation of psychic phenomena. Although later he would veer dangerously close to scandal, his investigation began with, most people believe, the most honest of intentions. His interest in spiritualism was spurred by the death of his younger brother in 1867. After that he consulted several mediums, and when Henry Slade, the American medium best known for slate writing, visited London, Crookes announced that he would personally probe spiritualism, claiming he had "no preconceived notions" about it. But he also noted that "scientific methods" were the best way of ferreting out the truth "to drive the worthless residuum of spiritualism hence into the unknown limbo of magic and necromancy." Sir Crookes would prove spiritualism to be a fraud—once and for all.

In 1871, Crookes embarked on his inquiry when he studied famed medium D. D. Home. For his scientific colleagues at the Royal Society there was only one acceptable conclusion, that the medium was a fraud. In fact, no member of the Society would participate with Crookes, so he undertook the task on his own, accompanied by several assistants acting as witnesses.

Crookes arranged for Home to demonstrate his physical mediumship in a fully lighted room in the scientist's own residence where Home caused an accordion and then himself to levitate, while Crookes carefully measured changes in their weights with apparatus he'd devised specifically for the tests.

After Home had been tested, Crookes wrote in the July 1871 issue of the *Quarterly Journal of Science*, "Of all the persons with a powerful development of this Psychic Force . . . Mr. Daniel Dunglas Home is the most remarkable, and it is mainly owing to the many opportunities I have had of carrying on my investigation in his presence that I am enabled to affirm so conclusively the existence of this force."

As expected, most scientists were highly critical of Crookes, concluding that somehow he'd been deceived by Home. Crookes withstood the criticism, insisting his scientific examination was correct. When he investigated the psychic abilities of the Fox sisters, his support of them was also met by disbelief from his colleagues.

And what would the history of the paranormal be without the whisper of at least one romantic scandal? The story involved Crookes and an attractive young medium named Florence Cook (1856–1904) who claimed to produce spirit materializations. Their relationship would be his most contentious foray into spiritualism; and would become a celebrated and lustful chapter in nineteenth-century paranormal history.

By the 1860s and '70s, there was an addition to the furnishings in many séance rooms in America and England: the spirit cabinet. So-called "materialization mediums," such as Florence Cook, claimed they could manifest actual spirit forms that could be seen, but the phenomenon was only able be produced by them while they were in a closed cabinet. Obviously, skeptics and critics pointed out that observers had no way to determine what trickery might be employed within the cabinet. But the mediums were ready with a clever defense: they insisted it was only possible to manifest the materializations in this way, since the "spirit energy" necessary would only accumulate in an enclosure, and the medium required intense "concentration" to gather the energy and convert it into a visible spirit entity.

Sitters were always cautioned never to touch the medium or the materialized spirit. Apparently it was dangerous, for it might cause the mysterious substance known as ectoplasm that the spirit was composed of to suddenly be absorbed back into the medium's body.

By the 1870s, full materializations became the specialty of one medium in particular, Florence Cook. It had not taken her long to become one of the most noted mediums in the annals of spiritualism; she is still cited in the investigation of the paranormal. In fact, during her career, her materializations became a religious analogy; often compared to the Resurrection of Jesus. She was only fifteen and quite pretty when she began her career, although many suspected she was older than she claimed.

Table tipping, clairvoyance, and clairaudience were among her early "gifts." Later she gave spirit messages while in trance. By the mid-1870s, Cook had attracted scientific interest and soon became the subject of psychic investigations, and the inevitable arguments about whether she was genuine or a fraud.

It was around this time that Cook manifested a "spirit control" named "Katie King," who'd materialized so that her face was visible from the spirit cabinet. Had Cook performed an obvious trick, or was this a genuine spirit manifestation?

All, of course, noticed the difference in attire from Florence's long, dark full dress with sizable sleeves, to that of the spirit materialization—Katie King—who peeked out from the cabinet. Some thought she resembled

Florence Cook, except that Katie had a quantity of white cloth draped over her head. When she emerged from the cabinet, séance participants saw the young and pretty spirit dressed in a white gown, barefoot, and in short sleeves, a rather revealing costume for Victorian times, and not at all the way Cook dressed.

Spiritualists considered Cook's materializations a marvelous spirit phenomenon. Skeptics were certain the alleged materialization was actually a thinly disguised Florence Cook. But many wondered how Cook, who was tied in the cabinet with cords knotted around her, could release herself in only moments to become Katie, then tie herself again as she'd been before. One observer, a British minister, after witnessing Cook's cabinet materialization, remarked, "Spiritual or material, it was clever." In other words, even if you didn't believe you'd seen a genuine spirit take a physical form, the event was entertaining.

The Katie King materialization made Florence Cook a famous young woman on both sides of the Atlantic; spiritualists boasted this was absolute physical proof that there was no such thing as "death," for Katie King had materialized from the spirit world.

It wasn't long before Cook caught the attention of the distinguished British physicist, Sir William Crookes. He'd decided that Katie King would be the subject of his next scientific investigation of the paranormal; her good looks evidently an enticement. His examination of Florence/Katie got underway in late 1873. By early 1874, Crookes arrived at the conclusion that the only way to prove Cook and Katie were not the same person would be to witness them both at once. Crookes said he'd heard Florence weeping and sighing from within the closed cabinet, while Katie was elsewhere in the room at that moment. That was sufficient evidence to satisfy him that Florence Cook's psychic abilities were authentic.

Crookes next organized several séances to serve as experiments of Cook's abilities. To best control the testing he chose his own home and arranged two rooms for the demonstration. One room served as the spirit cabinet, where Cook would be sequestered, the door locked and the lights turned out; while in the adjoining lighted room a group of witnesses waited.

Then Cook proceeded to produce her spirit materialization. The surprised observers watched as Katie King appeared, giving Crookes and the others the opportunity to take more than forty photographs of her, only a few of which have survived.

When Crookes was permitted to open the curtain that separated the two rooms, he looked in and saw Cook, in trance, reclining on a couch. Meanwhile, Katie was in the other room with the witnesses.

On other occasions Crookes and several eyewitnesses went into the room that served as the spirit cabinet, and saw both Florence and Katie as two separate and distinct beings.

After this Crookes was even more confident that Cook and King were not the same person, and he studied them carefully, looking for physical differences between the two. Crookes was observant enough to notice that Florence had a raised sore or "blister" on her neck, as well as pierced ears, but Katie had neither.

Could one of England's most respected scientists have been taken in by an elaborate deception? Critics have pointed out that when Crookes tested D. D. Home in 1870, he'd applied much stricter controls then when he examined Cook/King. One skeptical explanation was that perhaps the person Crookes observed on the couch was a dummy figure arranged to look like her silhouette, but not actually Florence Cook.

What about the surviving photographs taken of Cook and King? In no one photograph do they appear together, and the poor quality of the handful of pictures obscures any detail that would help identify either one with certainty.

One of Crookes's assistants was a man named Edward Cox, then one of Britain's better-known psychical researchers as well as an attorney. He'd also helped Crookes's testing of Home, and was supportive after he witnessed his levitations and other psychical abilities. Cox had a sharp eye for detail, and knew the chicanery that mediums were capable of. Also, he was skeptical about the existence of spirit phenomena even though he believed it was possible that some inexplicable "forces" existed, "having both power and intelligence, but imperceptible to our senses."

His opinion of Florence Cook was largely negative, implying that she was fraudulent. To prove it, Cox designed a simple test that would conclusively prove if Cook and King were one in the same—or two separate beings: one human; the other a spirit.

Cox suggested that a dab of indelible India ink be placed on Florence Cook's forehead. Then if the alleged entity, Katie, emerged with ink on her forehead obviously Florence was pretending to be the spirit. Strangely, Crookes never proceeded with Cox's suggestion, and the simple India ink test was never done.

But each time the Florence Cook story seemed to reach a tentative conclusion—pro or con—some strange twist or turn would occur to further confuse matters and change minds. For example, in 1874, Crookes and a man who was Florence's benefactor were permitted entry into the spirit cabinet where they saw and touched two separate beings. That apparently put to rest the accusation that Florence was pretending to be Katie. But the next question was, if Katie were an independent being, was she a spirit materialization—or another person?

When Cox examined Cook and King he realized that both were "solid flesh," both breathed, and even showed beads of perspiration. He thought it highly improbable that a spirit entity would manifest such clearly human functions. Cox expressed his doubts about spirit materializations in a letter to D. D. Home:

> I am satisfied that a large amount of fraud has been and still is practiced. The great field for fraud has been offered by the production and presentation of alleged spirit forms. The lesson to be learned from all this is, that no phenomena should be accepted as genuine that are not produced under strict test conditions. Investigators should be satisfied with no evidence short of the very best that the circumstances will permit.

Was it possible that Florence Cook had a confederate disguised as Katie King, so the two figures could be seen together? Many historians—and every skeptic—have reached that conclusion. One likely suspect was Cook's close friend, Mary Showers, also a medium, who was only in her teens by the mid-1870s; that would explain why some thought Katie appeared to be younger than Florence.

But, as they used to say, the sixty-four-dollar question was how someone as astute as Sir William Crookes, an eminent scientist who invented the radiometer and discovered the element thallium, could be so easily duped by so obvious a ruse? Also, why was he willing to risk his well-earned reputation to engage in a spiritualist hoax, by insisting Katie King was a materialized spirit? Could he actually have believed that to be the truth? It seems unlikely.

Some years later, a British researcher claimed there was substantial documentation that Crookes and Cook had an extramarital love affair. That would explain Crookes's willingness to accept the existence of Katie, sans rigorous testing. At the time they met around 1874, Crookes was in his early forties and married with a large family; Cook was eighteen. His infatuation with the pretty young woman likely clouded his judgment and objectivity; pronouncing Cook genuine assured him easy access to her affections.

Having a scientist of Crookes's reputation declare her legitimate served Florence well, even if it meant a romantic liaison. They were hardly the first—or last—couple in the world to manipulate each other for sexual reasons. His virtual endorsement of her materializations must have been a huge relief for her. Still, by May 1874, Cook had grown worried, and rather then take further chances of exposure, she suddenly and unexpectedly proclaimed Katie's spirit visits to "dear Florrie" were over.

Those present at that last séance said later that it had been a moving good-bye. Some cried, and Katie offered "locks of her hair" as a parting keepsake, a remembrance of her. Katie's last words were to compliment Sir William and ask that he look after Florence's best interests. Their affair did not last much longer; without Katie, she no longer needed Crookes. Soon after, wealthy spiritualist Charles Blackburn stopped Cook's financial support; and Crookes returned to his work as a physicist.

If there had been any public revelation of his liaison with Florence, Crookes would have been plunged into a major scandal that would have titillated the public; and likely, in combination with the exposure of Cook's fraud, have badly damaged or destroyed both their careers.

Some years later, in the early 1890s, two of her former lovers separately claimed she'd confessed that the Katie King saga had been a hoax. One of those men, in turn, reported it to the Society of Psychical Research, another disappointing chapter for the spiritualist movement in England and America. Whatever the truth about her life and career as a materialization medium, Florence Cook died in London, in virtual poverty, in 1904; she'd barely reached the age of fifty.

In 1883, when one of Philadelphia's wealthiest men, Henry Seybert, died, he bequeathed sixty thousand dollars to the University of Pennsylvania specifically to create a "chair in philosophy," with the proviso that the university name a committee solely for the study of spiritualism. How pleased school officials were with Seybert's caveat we can't be certain, but they complied with the terms of the bequest and chose a commission of noted and learned men, supposedly representing pro and anti-spiritualist positions. In fact, the committee chairman, Dr. Horace H. Furman was initially inclined to favor spiritualism. However, he soon changed his mind; whether it was because the commission uncovered fraud or Furman had been pressured to alter his opinion is open to speculation. When the Seybert Commission finally issued its only report in 1887, it was negative and hardly went farther than revealing the trickery of deceptive physical mediums.

Approaching the Fin de Siècle

The last decades of the nineteenth century were a hectic time for America; the country was expanding and experiencing major societal changes. The period was marked by a flood of immigrants; growing and increasingly crowded cities. In the early 1880s, New York City's population was 1.2 million; twenty years later it had soared to almost four million; mechanization had spurred new factories and mills were humming around the country, benefiting from cheap labor and consumers eager for new products. Science, inventions, and medical discoveries had profoundly transformed thinking and attitudes about life, and the power of technology appeared to dwarf even religion, a concern for many who feared that a purely mechanistic view of America might emerge. Psychology and sociology were emerging as new branches of learning, and those also disputed traditional religious beliefs, especially among academics and intellectuals, author Robert C. Fuller noted, adding, "belief in miracles or supernatural intervention seemed the stuff of ancient folklore."

Science Catches Up with Spiritualism

Between 1876 and 1900, the world saw a burst of amazing inventions and discoveries: the telephone, the marvel of electric lights, the science of fingerprinting, the Kodak "box camera," a rabies vaccine, improvements in surgery, advances against diabetes, the automobile, motion pictures, wireless telegraphy, the discovery of radioactivity and radium, the first airship, the Zeppelin, and many others; although not everyone was comfortable with the rapid pace of technology. By 1904, when Tesla's alternating current turned the Chicago World's Fair into the City of Light, most people who had grown up after the Civil War had begun to think that the new technology of the twentieth century was more phenomenal than the spiritualism of the previous century.

At the same time, however, thanks to several poets and writers, more Americans began to explore esoteric thinking and mysticism as a path to new spiritual truths and experiences. Walt Whitman, for example, had encouraged readers to contemplate Eastern beliefs in such popular works as *Leaves of Grass* and *Passage to India* that "calls for the imaginative leap by the soul to a symbolic India, with spiritual achievements to match those of wondrous technology," wrote James E. Miller, a Whitman historian. But the sense of religious curiosity threatened the more conservative and orthodox Christian denominations, which were ever wary of new philosophies.

Meanwhile, the battle over Darwin's highly contentious and controversial theory of evolution as an explanation for the origin of species had become a metaphor for the collision between science and religion in America. Virtually every important scientist in the country eventually embraced evolution, a contradiction to Christianity's certitude in the literal word of the Bible that "In the beginning God created the universe" in only six days. Anti-Darwin cartoons typically showed the bearded scientist's head on a monkey's body.

Spiritualism experienced a renewed interest during the 1880s, but a decade later and through the early twentieth century, the movement was clearly on the wane in America, although it remained longer in England because World War I brought a desperate need to comfort many of the hundreds of thousands who'd lost sons and husbands in the Great War.

By the turn of the century what became clear was that fraudulent physical mediums had run their course. And as Americans were living longer and healthier lives, there was less thought of imminent death. However, in our increasingly mechanized society, many felt psychic phenomena needed to be explained scientifically and rationally. Spiritualism had tried to define itself as a "scientific religion," but that was difficult to establish. On the other hand, by seeking the protection of "religion," spiritualists also hoped to avoid stepped up efforts by law enforcement around the country to crack down on so-called "fortune-tellers"; the movement had proven woefully incapable of controlling or expelling the frauds in its midst.

What was obviously needed if science was to seriously and systematically investigate spiritualism and other psychic claims was an organization of objective researchers dedicated to seeking the truth, whatever that might prove to be, since there had never been a cohesiveness to the movement, or a single authoritative voice to represent it.

Toward that goal, psychical research took a giant leap forward from the séance room to a scientific setting in 1882 when a group of insightful British men—most of them educated at Cambridge University—formed a new organization and named it the Society for Psychical Research, or SPR as it came to be called. It made its purpose clear from the very start: "to examine without prejudice or prepossession and in a scientific spirit those faculties of man, real or supposed, which appear to be inexplicable on any generally recognized hypothesis."

Why this landmark in the history of the paranormal occurred first in England, not America was perhaps because Great Britain was a much older and longer established society and, some suggested, "better organized" by the nineteenth century. It had its own thriving spiritualist movement, with many mediums and spiritualist publications. America was larger and more diverse, still growing, and moving west; and the American psyche also had a streak of independence that some Europeans regarded as "unruly." Many British scientists and thinkers, whether pro- or anti-spiritualist, seemed less intimidated about approaching the subject than their American counterparts.

One day, toward the end of 1881, a respected physicist from Dublin, Professor William Barrett, on a visit to London was invited to the home of journalist and spiritualist Edmond Dawson Rogers. The two men soon were engaged in lively conversation about spiritualism when Rogers suggested that a society be formed specifically to encourage the brightest scientists in England to investigate psychical phenomena. Barrett, who long had an interest in mesmerism and spiritualism, ran with the idea.

There had been earlier attempts to create such organizations in England and America, but they were all short-lived. Barrett took the idea to his friend Frederic W. H. Myers, and then to Edmund Gurney; but neither was very optimistic about such a society proving successful. Myers was an educator in Cambridge with a curiosity about what evidence there was for a spirit world. Gurney, a scholar, had interest in telepathy and hypnotism.

However, they agreed that if Professor Henry Sidgwick would accept the presidency, they'd support the new effort.[9] He said yes. Sidgwick was a well-regarded philosopher at Cambridge with a reputation for being highly "skeptical and critical." His remarks are as relevant today as they were when he became the SPR's first president in 1882. He regarded the state of psychic phenomena as "scandalous," wondering why "so many competent witnesses [that] declared their belief in [the phenomena], and so many others should be so profoundly interested in [them], and yet the educated world, as a body, should still be simply in an attitude of incredulity."

On February 20, 1882, the Society for Psychical Research was "formally constituted" with Sidgwick at the helm. Including him, a nineteen-member council was named: thirteen of them were spiritualists, six—including Sidgwick—were not. One spiritualist chosen was Mrs. George Boole, an author. Several months later, displeased that she was the only female appointee to the council, Boole resigned. It would be nearly twenty more years before another woman—Sidgwick's wife—was named. How ironic and imprudent given that women so dominated the spiritualist movement.

Despite what many later thought, the SPR was not founded by only "scholars and scientists," the group was comprised of a variety of occupations, including a schoolmaster, an accountant, a businessman, a lawyer, and a hotel keeper, and they'd all had religious upbringings.

From the start the SPR was successful, where previous groups had failed. Some historians have suggested that one reason was the ages of the founding officers and members. Most were in their twenties and thirties at the time—the "oldest" was Sidgwick, at forty-three. Their youth endowed them with "zest, imagination, and drive," wrote historian Fraser Nicol who added that from its outset the SPR maintained "very high standards of scholarship" in its journal, and its members took their investigations and research very seriously.

Under Sidgwick's leadership, SPR members were divided into committees, each to investigate a particular phenomenon, including thought-reading [telepathy], hauntings, physical mediumship, spontaneous experiences, and mesmerism; and each group was charged with issuing reports of their findings. Sidgwick named those he considered best qualified to examine specific topics: Barrett researched dowsing; Gurney studied phantasms of the living; Mrs. Sidgwick was responsible for the

Census of Hallucinations, which was a study of apparitions; and Richard Hodgson, trained in law, and with a fierce dedication to exposing frauds, investigated Theosophy. Other SPR members examined deathbed visions, clairvoyance, and the statistical probabilities of chance.

Close attention was paid to a phenomenon known as the "crisis apparition," in which an individual witnesses an apparition of someone they know at the same time that person, although at a distance, has suffered a crisis, such as injury, serious illness, or even death.

The SPR received a surprisingly large number of responses from people who'd experienced crisis apparitions, and the researchers attempted to confirm and authenticate thousands of such incidents, a Herculean task. When the SPR made its findings public in 1886, it likely disappointed many spiritualists, for the conclusion was that crisis apparitions were not spirits, but rather hallucinations projected telepathically from the individual in crisis to the person who sees or hears the "apparition."

The scholar Edmund Gurney, an original SPR committee member who was not a spiritualist, wrote a highly regarded book, *Phantasms of the Living*, that carefully examined cases of crisis apparitions.[10] Gurney collaborated with F. W. H. Myers and Frank Podmore, the "British opponent of spiritualism," a skeptic who considered most phenomena fraudulent. The book has been called "the first classic of modern psychical research."

The SPR's approach to its study of crisis apparitions remains a model for parapsychologists engaged in similar research today. *Phantasms of the Living* is still a valid tool and huge—at 1,300 pages—although some dispute the conclusion that crisis apparitions are hallucinations, and instead suggest the apparition may be the spirit of the person in crisis. Whatever the explanation for crisis apparitions, they still occur—too many to be ignored—and science is no closer to an explanation today than it was back in 1886, when Gurney wrote *Phantasms*.

The committees and investigators worked so diligently that within just several years after the SPR was founded they were producing well over five hundred pages annually; a remarkable amount of research. The SPR quickly earned a reputation for being "notoriously tough in its investigations," said parapsychologist Richard Broughton. One of the first to be examined was Madame Blavatsky's mystical Theosophy movement and her physical phenomena that impressed many, which she often described as "miracles." The investigation by Richard Hodgson resulted in a scathing SPR report that unequivocally labeled Blavatsky a fraud, and seriously damaged her credibility and Theosophy in England and America. The Hodgson report was itself later criticized by some for being too hasty in its conclusions.

Another SPR investigation targeted the well-known Italian medium Eusapia Palladino (1854–1918). Born into a peasant family, she was orphaned as a child and raised by friends. She first heard spirit raps at a young age, and at her first séance, while still a girl, she demonstrated table tipping. She said initially her powers frightened her. Nevertheless, she later produced spirit raps, breezes, lights, materializations, and levitations. Throughout her entire career she depended on a spirit control named "John King," who'd supposedly been a pirate in life.

Despite her rather ill-mannered behavior and disagreeable temperament, the illiterate and carelessly dressed Palladino caught the attention of an Italian scientist named Ercole Chiaia. He wrote to a respected Italian psychiatrist named Cesare Lombroso who eventually observed her at a séance where a bell dangled in the air, then fell to a table, only to move on its own to a bed—a distance of about six feet. That feat was all the convincing Dr. Lombroso needed to persuade him that Palladino was genuine. Once accounts of her abilities were published in a medical journal, other scientists came forward.

She conducted séances that were witnessed by such preeminent scientists as the French physiologist Charles Richet. By 1894, she came to the SPR's attention, and demonstrated her psychic powers for several of its leading members, who concluded that what they saw was "genuine physical phenomena." As a result, she was written about favorably in the *SPR Journal*.[11]

But one SPR investigator, Richard Hodgson, was more cautious and critical of the testing procedures, which he claimed gave Palladino room for chicanery. As a result, in 1895, she went to Cambridge to be tested. That's when Hodgson caught her engaging in deception. Other SPR members then discounted every demonstration by Palladino they'd ever seen and praised.

Palladino was no stranger to accusations of fraud, and she did not deny the charge. Her answer was simply that when she became tired, her psychic powers weakened, and rather than disappoint her sitters, she'd engage in whatever trickery she thought would go undetected, explained

Joseph Rinn in *Sixty Years of Psychical Research*.[12] The SPR was notoriously hard on physical mediums, and quick to dismiss or expose them, and that answer was no excuse where researchers were concerned.

But in 1908, the SPR returned to examine Palladino. By then Hodgson had died, and the investigations of her were conducted by a committee of three; one of them was Hereward Carrington. The group, impressed by her abilities, published its conclusions in the *SPR Journal* in November 1909.

Carrington arranged for Palladino to appear in New York, where she arrived in November 1909 and remained until June 1910. In all, she gave thirty-one séances. Carrington oversaw twenty-seven of them to prevent her from cheating. When she was in a controlled situation, her physical mediumship was impressive. However, Carrington was not present at the last four séances, and that's when Palladino resorted to trickery. Two private detectives were present for just that reason and she was quickly exposed. Her acts of fraud received major press attention and irrevocably damaged her reputation in America, although it left her unscathed in Europe.

On May 10, 1910, a *New York Times* editorial carried the headline: A FAMOUS MEDIUM EXPOSED. It read in part: "The *Times* presents to its readers this morning the news and the first critical account by Professor Dickenson S. Miller, one of the committee of American professors who brought her to this country for investigation, of the methods by which the 'spiritualistic medium Eusapia Palladino' has for the past twenty years successfully duped the public and the leading scientists of Europe.

"In the séances held in this city [New York] recently, this greatest spiritualistic imposter in history was unmasked."

Her supporters rallied to her defense, explaining that as she grew older her powers grew weaker. They may have been correct, for it was generally acknowledged that Mrs. Palladino possessed genuine psychokinetic (PK) powers. By the time she died in 1918, she'd "been one of the best studied mediums in history," wrote Rosemary Ellen Guiley.

Eventually, PK research moved from the séance room to the scientific laboratory, a change that Mrs. Palladino did not live to see. If she'd been tested properly, under strictly controlled conditions, in a laboratory setting, might scientists have gained more knowledge about psychokinetic ability?

"The impact of PK on our everyday world may be more pervasive than we realize. Through PK, our consciousness may directly affect the constitution of our reality on a quantum level," Guiley concluded.

Another famed physical medium tested by the SPR in its early years was William Eglinton (1858–1933). Apports seemed to "appear from nowhere," phantoms "moved about," and he "levitated to the ceiling," wrote historian Fraser Nicol. Eglinton's most accomplished skill was slate writing, which he began demonstrating in 1884. He once gave a séance attended by British Prime Minister William Gladstone who was "so impressed" he joined the SPR. The well-known English naturalist Alfred Russel Wallace was also satisfied that Eglinton was genuine.

The SPR managed to gather many accounts from those who'd attended Eglinton's sittings, but the organization disliked slate writing, and once again it was Richard Hodgson to the rescue. He watched Eglinton carefully then concluded there was trickery afoot. Eglinton, he said, had employed "distraction," among other deceptions. On that basis, the SPR declared that Eglinton's abilities amounted to "clever conjuring." Others were much less skeptical; many spoke on Eglinton's behalf, and spiritualists bristled at Hodgson's criticism. Eglinton's response was to provide dozens of testimonials in the British spiritualist publication, *Light*. After giving thousands of sittings, and receiving only a handful of accusations of fraud, Eglinton threw in the slate, so to speak—gave up mediumship and became a successful journalist.

His story raises the question about how so many people could claim he was genuine if he was not? Could they all have been deceived? Or, had the SPR, for all its good intentions and diligence, depended too heavily on the word of one investigator, Richard Hodgson?

In 1885, three years after the start of the SPR, William Barrett encouraged the beginning of a similar organization here; and the American Society for Psychical Research (ASPR) was founded in Boston by several scientifically minded researchers. The long overdue idea quickly gained the support and interest of famed philosopher and psychologist William James. His investigation of the mental medium Leonora Piper and his conclusions pose one of the most significant chapters in America's paranormal history.

What was needed was exactly what James offered: a respected scientist with intellect and integrity who was unafraid to wade into the frequently turbulent waters of psychical research. James looked every bit the intense scholar he was: with his spectacles, neatly trimmed beard and mustache, and nattily dressed in suit and bow tie; he earned a reputation as "one of the most influential U.S. thinkers of his generation, a seminal figure in philosophy, as well as in early psychology, [and] was perhaps the most remarkable pioneer ever to explore the wilderness of psychic research," wrote the editors of *Into the Unknown*.

James was born in New York City in 1842, to a most unusual family that motivated intellectual curiosity. His father read Swedenborg, and one of his four siblings was Henry James, who became a popular novelist. By the time William was three years old, he'd already traveled to Europe, and eventually learned to speak several foreign languages.

A brilliant man, accomplished in both philosophy and psychology, James also earned a degree from the Harvard Medical School, joined its faculty by the time he was thirty, and taught there for many years.

Early in his career he went through a period of depression and anxiety following the death of a dear friend; then he encountered what he believed was a hallucination of a former patient he'd once observed in an asylum. James wrote, "After this the universe changed for me altogether." He spent much of his life in a quest for a "personal spiritual philosophy," Robert C. Fuller explained.

James became especially drawn to the paranormal after learning of a New Hampshire woman's dream vision that proved so accurate she was able to locate the body of a drowned girl. Once his inquisitiveness about psychical research was awakened, he became one of its most preeminent voices. Among his most notable achievements was his study of Leonora Piper's mediumship. He was also interested in reuniting science and religion; and hoped to extend science so it would embrace the relationship between "mind, body and spirit." This concept, lost as medicine became increasingly specialized in the twentieth century, has been rediscovered in the holistic health movement of recent decades.

James regarded traditional, Bible-based religious beliefs as "absurd," but recognized the useful role they play in people's lives, Fuller noted, adding that James eventually arrived at the conclusion that "the core of genuine spirituality is an inner, mystical experience." Many of James's ideas and his philosophy are part of current "New Age" thought, notably his belief that religious dogma was not necessarily the same as spirituality; an outlook embraced today by millions of Americans. James's search for a personal spiritual perspective that began with his interest in psychic phenomena later developed into his careful investigations of the trance medium Leonora Piper.

Piper, born in Nashua, New Hampshire, in 1859, had her first paranormal experience as a child when she psychically knew her aunt had died. By 1881, she was a pleasant-looking, dark-haired young woman married to a shop assistant, and was living in Boston. One day, she went into a brief trance state following a visit to a blind doctor who clairvoyantly diagnosed and healed patients. The next time Piper went to the same physician, she again fell into a trance during which she gave a highly accurate spirit message to a well-known local judge: it was from his deceased son. That incident propelled her to popularity, and many clamored for readings with her. Piper said she was both disarmed and disturbed by the unexpected attention. As a result, she declined most requests for readings, or sittings as they were then called.

For reasons never fully explained, she did agree to a sitting for an anonymous woman who was, in fact, the mother-in-law of William James. Later, James's wife also visited Mrs. Piper. When both his wife and her mother told him about their astonishing experiences with Piper, James was curious to observe her in person, hopefully to explain her powers as a "mental medium."

He approached Piper skeptically, but after seeing and hearing her for himself, James was greatly surprised and impressed with her abilities. As a result, he continued his sittings with her, and asked if she'd be amenable to stringent testing. She agreed and James undertook a lengthy and valuable investigation of Piper's séances that would last eighteen months, during which time he supervised nearly every aspect of her readings; his purpose was to eliminate any possibility of collusion or fraud on her part. His observations convinced him that Mrs. Piper had no advance knowledge of her subjects for whom the readings were highly accurate; her only help seemed to come from her "spirit guides," one of whom was named Dr. Phinuit. James's tests were also able to rule out mind reading—telepathy—on Piper's part. She was psychically strongest on the first names of subjects, personalities, and health problems of both sitters and the departed.

Unlike physical mediums, Piper did not engage in extravagant theatrical displays of flying objects, flowing ectoplasm, knockings, rappings, table tiltings, automatic writing, or alleged spirit materializations. On rare occasions she would inexplicably produce the sweet scent of flowers; otherwise her ability as a mental medium consisted only of her providing accurate messages from the deceased to their families and friends. Never during her career did Mrs. Piper demonstrate physical phenomena.

By 1890, James was ready to report his experiences with Piper in the *SPR Journal*. A portion read:

> Taking everything that I know of Mrs. Piper into account, the result is to make me feel as absolutely certain as I am of any personal fact in the world that she knows things in her trances which she cannot possibly have heard in her waking state, and that the definite philosophy of her trances is yet to be found.

James was certain that Piper possessed genuine psychic ability, and although he was unable to determine its source, he remained doubtful about spirits as an explanation, and questioned whether some other form of psychic or supernormal phenomenon was responsible.

In his often quoted statement that appears in the opening of this chapter, James said: "If you wish to upset the law that all crows are black . . . it is enough to prove that one crow is white. My white crow is Mrs. Piper."

Because of time and work considerations James regretted that he was unable to continue supervising Piper's séances to the extent he'd wanted. As a consequence, he contacted SPR members in England about her. The outcome was that Richard Hodgson, one of the hardest working and most dedicated SPR investigators, came to the United States, took up residence in Boston, and proceeded with Piper's testing "under permanent engagement to the SPR," for which she was paid an annual stipend for her exclusivity to the organization. The arrangement gave the SPR unprecedented access to test her powers as a medium.

Hodgson had earned a reputation as a sharp-eyed psychical investigator. Remember, his dogged persistence had already helped expose as frauds such well-known mediums as Madame Blavatsky and Eusapia Palladino.

In his work with Mrs. Piper, Hodgson took every possible caution to prevent her from obtaining any information prior to her sittings. He would not allow her to read newspapers on days of séances and even had a detective follow her. Only Hodgson knew the identities of her subjects or sitters; Piper was never given their names. Sometimes she gave readings for people who were chosen by Hodgson at the last minute.

After a sufficient number of tests had been conducted, Hodgson, William James, Sir Oliver Lodge, and others conferred about the possibility of deception on Mrs. Piper's part, but the group concluded that was not possible. James wrote up Hodgson's conclusions, and neither man believed Piper had resorted to any fraud or trickery, especially considering the "close observation, as to most of the conditions of her life," James noted in 1898. Later he added that he would be willing to wager money that Mrs. Piper was honest.

But Hodgson was not yet through when he announced that he wanted even stricter controls for testing Piper. He hit upon the idea of inviting her to England, an unfamiliar country where she'd be among people she did not know. Mrs. Piper agreed, and her first visit to England was made in November 1889. F. W. H. Myers met her upon arrival, and she resided at Myers's Cambridge home. It was more than hospitality that prompted the invitation; by having Piper as his guest, Myers was able to observe her every coming and going. He chose sitters for her séances at random, and their identities were completely unknown to her. During her visit to England, from November 1889 until February 1890, Piper gave eighty-eight sittings. Any place she went was carefully supervised, as was anyone she spoke to, and anything she read. While some may have bristled at such intense scrutiny and reins on their activities, Piper remained remarkably patient and cooperative.

After being tested in England, as if she was some laboratory mouse running through a maze, and with astounding results, Piper returned to America, and once again the responsibility for testing her fell to Richard Hodgson. This situation was nothing like the exposure of Blavatsky and Palladino: Piper had become the SPR's prize, a woman with genuine psychical ability whom the researchers were able to observe and test exclusively—even obsessively.

Virtually everyone who scrutinized Piper came away with the same conclusion: she had some manner of "supernormal" power or ability; but there was disagreement on exactly what it was. The so-called "spirit hypothesis" was unpalatable to many scientific men, who opted instead for such theories as telepathy, clairvoyance, hallucinations, some unknown energy—anything but spirits. Hodgson was firmly in that camp; he did not believe that spirits could communicate with those in the physical world.

Psychical and spirit phenomena have always been easy to dismiss—until an individual has his or her first encounter with it, then suddenly their perspective changes. What was thought impossible—such as a spirit contacts, apparitions, premonitions, among many other experiences—becomes an inexplicable reality, an event that reaches far beyond one's imagination. That's exactly what happened to the SPR's skeptical Richard Hodgson.

Hodgson, an intensely private man, rarely spoke of his own life or shared his feelings with Mrs. Piper, despite spending countless hours observing her sittings. One day when he was the subject of a reading, Piper told Hodgson that the spirit of a young woman was communicating a message she wanted him to know. The spirit psychically identified herself to Piper, then told the medium that she had recently passed away. Hodgson stiffened as he instantly recognized to whom Piper was referring.

Years earlier, during his youth in his native Australia, Hodgson fell in love with a young woman he very much wanted to marry. However, her parents refused to give their permission because of differences in the couple's religions. Hodgson was deeply disappointed, moved to England, but never married. Nor did he ever again see or speak to his former love.

This was the young woman whose spirit was now conveying the news of her recent death. Hodgson was both shaken and moved by the message, but had no way to confirm or deny it; he simply did not know what had become of her. He realized that meant Piper's communication was not based on telepathy, and further, Mrs. Piper could not have known about this deeply personal and painful part of his life long ago.

Hodgson made it his business to prove or disprove Piper's message by contacting those in Australia who would know his beloved's fate. It was exactly as Piper said: the woman had died not long ago. Notwithstanding his personal sadness, he was greatly taken with Piper's accuracy.

That sitting with Piper had a profound effect on Hodgson who had for so long rejected the "spirit hypothesis" to explain mediumship. In 1897, he wrote in the *SPR Journal* that he now had no doubt he'd experienced genuine spirit communication. That statement was quite an acknowledgment from an obdurate skeptic and no-nonsense psychical researcher quick to expose fraud wherever he found it. After fifteen years of investigating Mrs. Piper he finally—if reluctantly—accepted the spirit theory following his sitting with her. He issued a second statement on the matter and planned a third report, but died suddenly of heart failure in 1905, at the age of fifty. At the time Hodgson was the secretary for the ASPR and an important presence in the organization. What's more, this once uncompromising critic, not long before his death developed his own mediumistic abilities.

There is a postscript to the story of Richard Hodgson following his untimely death: his spirit allegedly communicated messages to several people, including an SPR colleague, James Hyslop, and a British medium named Mrs. Holland. Finally, on a less speculative question, the significance of Hodgson's many years of study and testing of Mrs. Piper cannot be overstated for its value to scientific research of the paranormal. He'd spent more time examining her than anyone else.

Hodgson also trained Columbia University's philosophy professor James Hyslop to become one of the best psychical researchers ever in American history, and one of the first to link psychic phenomena with psychology. After Hodgson's death the baton was passed to Hyslop to continue the investigation of Piper's psychical ability. He had also been quite skeptical of mediumship until he met Mrs. Piper in 1888, after employing every possible caution in testing her. Hyslop would require at least a dozen sittings with Piper to persuade him that he'd observed genuine mediumship. Her sessions with him changed his mind after he received many messages from his late father, brother, and several uncles whose personalities came through the medium.

Once convinced, he was confident enough to write in the *SPR Journal*, "I give my adhesion to the theory that there is a future life and persistence of personal identity." This was a strong affirmation from a man who'd approached the Piper tests very skeptically, and would not have hesitated for even a moment if he thought there was any reason to declare her a fraud.

When the dynamic Hodgson died in 1905, it left a terrible void in the ASPR, and a year later the organization was disbanded. But Hyslop soon reactivated it and became the ASPR's principal researcher of Piper's abilities. He became a strong advocate for "survival of death," and made that position crystal clear in his book *Life After Death*, published in 1918. "I regard the existence of discarnate spirits as scientifically proved and I no longer refer to the skeptic as having any right to speak on the subject." His sittings with Mrs. Piper "convinced [him] of survival," he said.

By 1906, several of the original SPR leadership and brain trust had died, including Hodgson, Edmund Gurney, and F. W. H. Myers. There were "cross-correspondence" experiments conducted to determine if the trio of spirits could—or would—communicate from the afterlife. The results seemed to indicate that several mediums participating in the tests each received a part of a spirit message from them that had to be deciphered and pieced together to make an entire message. Although the conclusion seemed to suggest the accuracy of the communications were beyond chance, some researchers were not absolutely certain.

In 1906, a year after Hodgson's death, Piper made another trip to England for more testing. Her third visit there was during the autumn of 1909. Then in 1915, while in a trance state, she predicted that Sir Oliver Lodge's son Raymond would die. She proved to be accurate.

Her first sitting for Sir Oliver Lodge (1851–1940), respected British physicist and SPR member, produced many accurate details about the personal lives of several of Lodge's deceased relatives, including a young child the Lodges lost. In later sittings, Lodge was given more names of departed family members, as well as spirit communications about his entire family.

In 1890, Lodge published a report about his sittings with Piper attesting to her accuracy, stating that she could not have had prior knowledge about his relatives, and that there was no evidence of fraud or trickery. He concluded by writing, "no conceivable deception on the part of Mrs. Piper can explain the facts." It was indeed high praise from one of England's most renowned scientists whose research included radio waves and electrons, and "theories of matter and ether." In 1894, he correctly surmised that radio signals emanated from the sun—it would be another half-century before the signals were discovered and identified. More than a decade later he began to ponder by what means science and religion could be brought together; and it resulted in his thinking about the conceivability of communications with the deceased.

Lodge's initial interest in psychic phenomena had been telepathy, or thought-transference, but his pursuit of evidence for survival became intense after his youngest son Raymond was tragically killed in action on September 14, 1915, during World War I.

After Raymond's death, Lodge visited several mediums in addition to Mrs. Piper, including England's well-regarded Gladys Osborne Leonard, and became convinced he'd made genuine spirit contact with his son. In 1916, Lodge wrote about these experiences in a book titled, *Raymond: of Life and Death*, which received much public acclaim. It was a compilation of Raymond's spirit communications; many were spelled out in the famed book. Lodge "found massive, incontrovertible hard evidence in the material including the most intimate details of his son's life and family history," wrote author John G. Fuller.[13] He also explained that *Raymond* was more than a result of his grief over his son's death, and reiterated that he was "absolutely convinced of demonstrated survival."

Through Mrs. Leonard, Raymond gave the message, "Tell father I have met some of his friends here." When Lodge asked for specific names, Raymond referred to the spirit of Frederick Myers, among others.

Meanwhile, Leonora Piper continued to be tested through most of the 1920s. By then she was in her late sixties, and Dr. Gardner Murphy (1895–1979), respected American psychical researcher and psychologist with the SPR and later the ASPR, was in charge of examining her. Mrs. Piper died in 1950 at the age of ninety-one.

Piper's contributions to psychical research were enormous. She was the only medium to be so extensively and exhaustively tested; and her efforts provided an immense amount of research for both the SPR and ASPR. She said she was never certain how to explain her psychic gifts, and wasn't sure whether she was receiving spirit communications or if her ability could be explained by some form of mental telepathy.

The large number of documented eyewitness accounts, evidence from the many tests Piper had undergone, and published reports by researchers and scientists provided an unequaled and unique legacy in the nineteenth- and early-twentieth-century history of mediumship.

"The founding of the SPR fundamentally changed the nature of psychical research," parapsychologist Richard Broughton wrote.[14] "In short, psychical research was becoming a science, with disciplined experimental methods and standardized methods of description, established by some of the finest minds of the day," he explained.

While the SPR thrived, in part due to the donations of several upper middle class members, its American counterpart was not as fortunate; and its early history was considerably more turbulent, a state the paranormal was nearly always in. Given the controversial nature of psychical research, financial and scientific support was lacking in the United States. The ASPR could not sustain itself as an independent entity, so ASPR research was undertaken by the SPR beginning in 1889.

Richard Hodgson carried out ASPR investigations until his death in 1905, but without him the teetering society disbanded the next year. After its dissolution, Professor Hyslop absorbed it into his own organization, the American Institute for Scientific Research.

Following Hyslop's death in 1920, the ASPR once again became self-sufficient, and Dr. Walter Franklin Prince conducted its research. But it wouldn't be smooth sailing for him, either. Just a few years later, he became embroiled in one of the most controversial—there's that word again—episodes in America's paranormal history. It concerned a Boston medium named Mina Crandon, known professionally as "Margery." We'll explain more about her and the confrontation she had with famed illusionist Harry Houdini in the next chapter, but suffice to say that the ASPR's board believed Crandon to be genuine, while Prince was certain she was fraudulent. She'd even had favorable articles in *Scientific American*, and when the magazine's assistant editor was named to a research position with the ASPR, it was an affront Prince could not tolerate. Outraged by this turn of events, he resigned from the ASPR, and with several other equally disgruntled members, they formed the Boston Society for Psychical Research.

Finally, in 1941, the internal dissension was resolved, and the Boston SPR and the ASPR united. The new president was George Hyslop, whose father James had been one of the SPR's distinguished early pioneers. The younger Hyslop immediately went to work to raise the group's research standards that had fallen during the organization's political tumult.

Dr. Gardner Murphy led the ASPR for the next twenty years; he was both a commanding and influential presence. The nature of science had changed and grown immeasurably during his tenure, and Gardner pressed for parapsychologists to engage in more laboratory research, as the famed Dr. J. B. Rhine had done with ESP during the 1930s at Duke University.[15] In 1962, Dr. Karlis Osis joined the ASPR as its research director, and remained with the organization until his death in 1997. He'd once worked with Rhine at Duke, and was especially interested in extra-sensory perception (ESP), psychokinesis (PK), and deathbed visions. (Rhine is discussed later on in this chapter.)

Another respected researcher long associated with the ASPR was Dr. Gertrude Schmeidler, a psychologist and professor who engaged her students in ESP experiments. Her theory was that those "who believed in ESP scored better as subjects in ESP tests than those who did not," explained the *Encyclopedia of Occultism and Parapsychology*.

With credit to the ASPR's tenacity, through all its ups and downs, its *Journal and Proceedings*, first published in 1907 has continued without interruption since then, for many years edited by Rhea White (1931–2007), a respected parapsychologist.

In recent years, the ASPR, long based in New York, has merged psychical research with other scientific disciplines, an approach potentially beneficial to a greater understanding of the nature of parapsychology and its applications to human behavior.

While the SPR and ASPR were working through their problems and politics, one of the more curious incidents in America's paranormal history occurred, and it involved one of the most famous Americans who ever lived: Thomas Edison (1847–1931).

In 1920, Edison, this country's greatest inventor, surprised many when he gave an interview to *Scientific American* magazine about, of all things, communication with the dead. Born in Ohio to parents who accepted spiritualism, Edison was "contradictory . . . about spiritual and metaphysical matters," wrote author Linda Simon.[16]

He held the Swedish mystic Emanuel Swedenborg in high esteem, and kept his books in his personal library. Despite Edison's tireless work on "practical" inventions, "he thought it possible to sustain beliefs in the inexplicable," such as the "immortality of the soul," Simon explained. Yet Edison said he was unable to "conceive of such a thing as a spirit, and also denounced mediums as "mysterious" [and] "weird." But he kept a collection of SPR journals, although he was leery about spiritualism. He once filled out an application to join Madame Blavatsky's Theosophical Society, but then changed his mind and declined her invitation for them to meet. However, one of his assistants, Bert Reese (1851–1926), was a clairvoyant, and Edison participated with Reese in psychic experiments.

While Edison's thinking about psychical phenomena and the question of survival zigzagged, he'd become a great celebrity for his many inventions, especially the electric light in 1879. The press dubbed him the "Wizard of Menlo Park," the story made news around the world, and the incandescent electric lightbulb was deemed a "wonder." During his lifetime, he patented 1,300 inventions—an incredible number.

But he raised more then a few eyebrows when he told *Scientific American* that, "if personality exists after what we call death, it's reasonable to conclude that those who leave this earth would like to communicate with those they have left here." Edison's idea was to invent a device to communicate with the dead. He explained, "There has always been a certain amount of life on this world and there will always be the same amount. You cannot create life, you cannot multiply life."

The magazine quoted the great inventor as saying he "does not believe in the present theories of life and death. Long ago he turned his back on the various old and accepted theories because he felt they were fundamentally wrong."

Edison continued, "Now follow me carefully. I don't claim that our personalities pass on to another existence or sphere. I don't claim anything because I don't know anything. For that matter, no human being knows. But I do claim that it is possible to construct an apparatus which will be so delicate that if there are personalities in another existence or sphere who wish to get in touch with us this apparatus will at least give them a better opportunity than the crude methods now purported to be the only means. Why should personalities in another existence waste their time working a little triangular piece of wood over a board with certain lettering on it?" (Edison was referring to the Ouija board, then a popular form of parlor entertainment.)

The public response to the article was considerably more enthusiastic than that of those with strong vested interests in the status quo, specifically certain scientists and church leaders. To rationalize Edison's idea away, critics noted that he was already seventy-three, and perhaps death was on his mind or he was on the verge of senility. Many mistakenly believed this was Edison's first foray into psychical phenomena; of course it was not. In his last years, he worked on developing his machine to communicate with the afterlife. However, the device was not yet completed when Edison died in 1931, in Menlo Park, New Jersey, at the age of eighty-four.

The postscript to the story is that after the famed inventor's death, all of his notes and plans for the apparatus mysteriously vanished. It's not much of a stretch to surmise that his papers were purposely destroyed to prevent the possibility that some future researcher would complete the machine. Might Edison have actually hit on some electrical or other means to contact the dead?

Several decades later, ironically, some contemporary scientists and engineers would pick up on Edison's idea when they undertook the search for an electronic means to make contact with the departed that became known as electronic voice phenomena, or EVP.

Upton Sinclair (1878–1968) distinguished himself as one of a group of American authors dubbed the "muckrakers," whose writings emphasized social reform at the beginning of the twentieth century when neglect for public health and safety was scandalous. Of the eighty books Sinclair wrote, his most famous was *The Jungle*, a 1906 novel that exposed the filthy conditions in Chicago stockyards and led to the U.S. Pure Food and Drugs Act.

The erudite and socially conscious Sinclair later turned to a study of telepathy and other psychic phenomena, and in 1930 wrote about his experiences in *Mental Radio: Does It Work, and How?*[17]

His research developed as a result of a series of tests with his wife, Mary, who'd demonstrated her abilities as a psychic or "sensitive" following the deaths of some close friends. Actually, for a time, Sinclair was rather perturbed by his wife's powers since she used them, while awake or dreaming, to know his comings and goings.

Sinclair came up with the idea that he would test Mary. He drew whatever he thought of, and then placed the folded drawings, typically about six, on his wife's stomach one by one, each in an envelope. This was always done in a darkened room. Her task was to describe what her husband had drawn. Often, Mary would know what the second drawing was before she'd even concluded her description of the first.

After he'd considered his wife's psychic gifts, Sinclair wrote:

We have something more than telepathy, for no human mind knows what drawings she has taken from that envelope. No human mind but her own even knows that she is trying an experiment. Either there is some superhuman mind or else there is something that comes from the drawings, some way of seeing other than the way we know and use all the time.

The Sinclair tests attracted the attention of many psychical researchers. *Mental Radio* was published in 1930, and its introduction was by William McDougall, a respected parapsychologist and psychology professor who became president of the ASPR in 1921, and participated in several investigations of the paranormal, including the contentious examination of the Boston medium, Mina Crandon.

There is a fascinating footnote about *Mental Radio*: when the book was published in Germany, the introduction was written by a German physicist and winner of the 1921 Nobel Prize. His name was Albert Einstein.

Following the decline of the spiritualist movement in the early twentieth century, organized scientific interest in the paranormal slowed, until very little important research was being conducted. Frustration and disappointment discouraged many scientists from further testing. Following the deaths of most the original SPR and ASPR founders who'd dedicated themselves to psychical research, the next generation of their members was hampered by the extensive revelations of fraud that had plagued so much of the movement.

The World of the Unseen Probed by Science

Spiritualism was also forced off the stage in the early twentieth century by the development of new measurements of the unseen worlds in the realms of psychology and physics, soft science and hard science. By the late 1920s, the world of the unseen—inhabited only by visions of spirits and the rappings of invisible beings—had become the subject of real scientific scrutiny. We could see neither the atom nor the subconscious, but both medical and physical science took us there.

In the science of Sigmund Freud, dreams and the messages they bore were not passageways to the world of the paranormal but into the individual's unconscious mind, where entire dramas played themselves out. For Einstein, they were atomic particles, which themselves looked like submicroscopic solar systems. For physicists Max Planck and Werner Heisenberg, they were "particles or waves" that exerted strong and weak forces on all mass in the universe. And that's not all. For the Cubist artists, Einstein's and Heisenberg's theories of physics became expressed as the vision of all points of reality at the same time. Forms were turned inside out, and the passage of time could be expressed on a single canvas. In music, Alban Berg and his contemporaries exploded classical exposition into atonality, and the growth of jazz in America created a popular music fervor that remains to this day. Such was the new world of the unseen that overtook the spiritualists, psychics, and mediums.

Spiritualism would never again reach the fever pitch that followed the Hydesville rappings. Its golden age had lasted more than a half-century and at its peak there were nearly eleven million spiritualists in the country, according to some estimates. Physical mediums and séances gave way to lower-key, less-flamboyant practitioners, the best of whom applied their gifts to communicate psychically with the deceased and bring messages of hope and comfort to loved ones on earth.

In its prime, spiritualism attracted many of society's elite and those at the highest levels of industry and government. Did the spirit world indeed help shape some of their important decisions and even change the course of American history?

J. B. Rhine

When a young psychology instructor named Joseph Banks Rhine joined the faculty of Duke University in Durham, North Carolina, in 1927 he was destined to elevate parapsychology by placing it in a scientifically controlled and academic setting.

In taking the path he did, J. B. Rhine, as he was always called, showed courage and vision, and through his long and distinguished career, he moved psychical research in the twentieth century to a new point where both defenders and detractors agreed he was one of the most important figures and "pioneers of parapsychology" in America, and arguably "the best known name in parapsychology," wrote Richard Broughton.

Born in a small western Pennsylvania town in 1895, Rhine went on to earn a Ph.D. in biology by 1925. Five years later he married a childhood friend, Louisa Weckesser, who would share his life and work; she also became a highly regarded parapsychologist. Early in their careers, the Rhines agreed that for them, researching psychical phenomena was more intriguing, and they left teaching biology to others. Their epiphany, so to speak, came in 1922 when they attended a lecture on spiritualism given by Sir Arthur Conan Doyle.

Rhine's interest was further peaked when he participated in psychical research conducted at Harvard University by Dr. Walter Franklin Prince, who'd been president of the ASPR. While in Boston, the Rhines attended a sitting with the well-known medium Mina Crandon or "Margery," but they were dissatisfied and concluded she was fraudulent. Doyle, an ardent spiritualist, disagreed when the Rhines exposed Margery. Rhine also was critical of the ASPR for supporting her as a genuine medium. He reached the conclusion that "experimental science" was the best way for psychical research to advance, and he named the field of study parapsychology.

Rhine had the good fortune to have the support of Dr. William Mc-Dougall, chairman of Duke's psychology department and a parapsychology pioneer; thus the young instructor was able to plan an entire project that would test psychical abilities by utilizing "statistical validation." This was a significant advance by science; subjecting psychical phenomena to strict experimental conditions.

Although Rhine's first attempt was to examine mediumship, he soon found it as frustrating as other scientists before him. The search for evidence of survival was so difficult. It proved impossible to measure or quantify it in a laboratory setting. Rhine agreed it was valuable to investigate the question of life after death, however, he had to begin somewhere, and it was simply a matter of practicality that motivated him to test more manageable phenomena. "The first objective and obvious starting point was telepathy," Dr. Louisa Rhine announced. They also planned to test clairvoyance, and Rhine gave those two abilities a new name, extrasensory perception, or ESP as it came to be popularly known. Later, he added to his studies psychokinesis, or PK, the mind's ability to move objects "at a distance."

With the cooperation of McDougall, Rhine set in motion plans to create the Parapsychology Institute at Duke University. He developed the idea to test for ESP by using what he called Zener cards, named for a Duke colleague, Karl Zener, a perception expert, who designed them specifically for Rhine's experiments. Could a "sender" communicate or transmit an image on the cards to a "receiver"? Each card contained one of five shapes: circle, cross, square, star, or wavy lines; and a deck contained five of each card, for a total of twenty-five cards per deck.

By the summer of 1930, the Rhines were officially engaged in the experimental psychic research that would occupy their entire lives and careers. Rhine's means of testing psychical phenomena was best described as "the application of mathematical probability theory to massive accumulation of data; and an experimental design for gathering such data, based on card-guessing," explained author Laile Bartlett.[18] By this procedure, the Rhines hoped to determine if psychic phenomena was genuine. They chose Duke students as subjects, and maintained strict test conditions.

The Zener card experiments came down to the question of whether there were individuals sufficiently psychic to identify the symbols on the cards without seeing them. Those results could then be analyzed to determine whether they represented "chance alone," or "better than chance," and if the test conclusions were "statistically significant."

Parapsychologist and author Richard Broughton gave an example in his book about one of the "many students" Rhine tested with the Zener cards. His name was A. J. Linzmayer and his test results were constant; always "better than chance." Out of 1,500 guesses, 300 correct were considered "chance." But Linzmayer was "correct 404 out 1,500." The next year, Rhine found another student, Hubert Pearce, who also tested above chance.

Encouraged by the results, Rhine felt he'd "demonstrated the existence of psychic phenomena," Broughton explained; and Rhine proceeded to show that ESP conformed to behaviors similar to other "psychological phenomena." For example, Rhine noted that those who tested better than chance displayed less ESP ability when they were fatigued or administered certain drugs. Rhine was optimistic that other scientists would come around to his way of thinking, once they saw that ESP observed definite laws of nature.

Meanwhile, he continued to study more students who displayed psychic abilities above the statistical probabilities of chance; and he also tested the variations between telepathy and clairvoyance, and whether distance had any effect on a participant's ability. For example, Hubert Pearce demonstrated clairvoyance correctly 558 out of 1,850 times. Chance would have been 370. Therefore, the statistical odds or probability of chance was 22 billion to 1, Rhine explained in a published report.

In 1934, Rhine published a paper titled "Extra-Sensory Perception," considered by many psychic researchers to be a milestone in the history of the paranormal. While most parapsychologists reacted positively and realized Rhine's efforts were significant, skeptics, of course, criticized Rhine's test conditions and likely no amount of evidence would have changed their minds, since their single purpose was to debunk the paranormal.

Some criticized his methods of compiling statistics; others flatly stated that his work had no value. There were also those who questioned whether subjects might have been able to read through the backs of cards, and thus see the shapes on them. That was one of the most disingenuous of the accusations, since Rhine had taken every possible caution to prevent such "sensory cues." The fact was that one could not read through the back of a Zener card to know what design was on the front of it; further, in many tests the subjects were not permitted to glimpse even the backs of the ESP cards. Rhine ignored his detractors and continued his experiments.

In 1934, Rhine tested the telepathic and clairvoyant abilities of the noted Irish medium, Mrs. Eileen Garrett, when she visited the United States. She had already earned an "international reputation among psychical research societies," Rhine noted.

Garrett once participated in a long-distance telepathy experiment from California where she was, to a doctor in Iceland. She psychically described exactly what the subject, 4,000 miles away, was doing at a particular moment. She was astoundingly accurate, down to even small details.

That event impressed Rhine deeply. His tests of Mrs. Garrett dealt with her telepathic and clairvoyant abilities; although she was best known for mediumship there was no controlled way to test that ability. Rhine considered that "telepathy and clairvoyance are basically rooted in the same process," and the results of testing Garrett left Rhine with no doubt that she had "significant telepathic powers," as well as clairvoyant ability; although Rhine remarked that she disliked being tested with ESP cards. Eileen Garrett later settled in the United States and was recognized as one of the most accomplished—and genuine—mediums of the twentieth century.

Many other psychic researchers were motivated to follow Rhine's experimental protocols; and when they also reported finding statistically significant results, he felt his findings were confirmed. He next worked diligently to expand his studies to include psychokinesis and precognition, the knowledge of events before they occur.

There was no way he could have kept his work private, nor did he necessarily want to. By the mid-1930s, even as the country remained in the grip of the Great Depression, the media took note of Rhine's ESP tests, and soon there were stories and articles in some of America's most popular magazines: *Reader's Digest, Harper's, Time,* and *Scientific American*.

The year 1937 was busy and productive for the hard-working Rhines.

The *Journal of Parapsychology* began publishing, under the imprint of Duke University Press; it told its readers it was "devoted primarily to the original publication of experimental results and other research findings in extrasensory perception and psychokinesis." For many years the *Journal*'s editor was Louisa Rhine. Later that same year, J. B. received the benefits that mass-media attention can bestow. Network radio programs talked about his ESP research; there were more national magazine articles; and "ESP cards" were being sold so Americans could test their own psychic abilities right in their own homes, an inexpensive way for friends and families to spend an evening.

That same year, Rhine wrote a new book about his experiments at Duke, titled *New Frontiers of the Mind*. In it, he explained his goal was to "find out whether or not the recognized senses are the only channels through which the mind can perceive," and he described his ESP tests in detail. The book sold very well, and now as the hectic year 1937 drew to a close, J. B. Rhine had become nationally known and the clever term he coined, "extra-sensory perception," or ESP, as it was commonly called, was familiar to millions of Americans in every part of the country.

But there was a downside: as Rhine became better known, criticism of him and his wife increased precipitously, and some was surprisingly malicious; particularly hostile were psychologists. In 1938, the American Psychological Association held a debate devoted to Rhine's Duke tests. At least one well-regarded psychologist, Gardner Murphy, was on Rhine's side. He'd had his share of battles and was certainly up to the task of defending Rhine's research. Together, Murphy and Rhine were forceful and articulate; they presented a good argument for parapsychology. Later, Murphy became ASPR president.

Overall, however, most psychologists of that era remained antagonistic to Rhine and the paranormal. The reason wasn't very complicated: many psychologists were concerned with stubbornly protecting their own theories and careers. If Rhine and other parapsychologists were correct about ESP and could prove it genuine, traditional assumptions about the limits and capacities of the human mind and behavior would have to be reconfigured. It was the same old story; it was easier to dismiss Rhine and others like him than face the threat of new paranormal theories. It apparently dawned on few in that era that psychology and psychic phenomena could be integrated, so one could benefit from the other.

Meanwhile, Rhine diligently continued his research, and in 1940 published another book to answer critics. This one was titled *Extra-Sensory Perception After Sixty Years*. The "sixty" was a reference to the approximate number of years of psychical research since the founding of the SPR in 1882. Rhine's book was successful in convincing many traditional psychologists that there was a place in the sciences for psychical research, even if one did not allow that ESP was genuine.

"After weighing all the criticisms we have been able to get . . . I have come to feel as much security in the general soundness of the research as is good for an investigator in science to have," Rhine concluded.

Parapsychology owes a tremendous debt to the Rhines. By the sheer force of their remarkable determination and dedication they opened the door for psychic researchers to be accepted as "a legitimate scientific activity," Broughton wrote. The Rhines were also role models for others in the scientific and academic communities engaged in examining ESP and other psychical phenomena.

They continued their work through the 1930s, and resumed it following World War II with more students at the Duke Parapsychology Laboratory. Eventually some of those students, inspired by their experiences with J. B. Rhine, moved on to develop their own programs elsewhere.

Rhine's reputation and prestige remained intact until his death in 1980. Dr. Louisa Rhine died in 1983. His greatest disappointment may have been not living to see parapsychology readily accepted by orthodox science once genuine experimental evidence was presented.

In 1951, the acclaimed medium Eileen Garrett was the force behind the beginning of the Parapsychology Foundation in New York City. The organization has concentrated on both research and education, published journals, and a library devoted to psychical matters.

Then, in 1957, the Parapsychological Association was founded to further the subject as a scientific discipline. In 1969, a significant step for the paranormal occurred when the American Association for the Advancement of Science finally received the Parapsychological Association for membership after declining its bid three previous times.

The Psychical Research Foundation was founded in 1960, in Durham, North Carolina, and among its most noted examinations were poltergeist phenomena and out-of-body experiences. Interest in the paranormal mushroomed from the 1960s on, with the definition broadening to include past lives research, dream telepathy, psychic healing, near-death experiences, remote viewing, and a renewed interest in mediums; as well as the "New Age" fascination with angels, alternative health remedies, magic, and Eastern philosophies and practices. There was also the covert side to the paranormal that emerged following World War II, when the government and military secretly appropriated psychic research for national defense, intelligence, and espionage during the Cold War.

New theories of physics, advances in neurology, brain scanning devices, and computer analysis all play an important part in a more mature and open-minded attitude by an increasingly large number of scientists, physicians, and psychologists who've entered into the elusive and puzzling world of parapsychology that still hovers somewhere between science and spirituality, uncertain if it belongs with either or both.

8

A Magician Among the Spirits

I am a skeptic . . .

—HARRY HOUDINI,
world-famous escape artist

It's not that I believe in spiritualism, but that I *know*.

—SIR ARTHUR CONAN DOYLE,
author and spiritualist

As the Great Age of Spiritualism hobbled uneasily into the twentieth century, it had survived a gauntlet of criticism, derision, and more accusations of fraud than could be counted. Yet it survived, albeit under a cloud of increasing suspicion. For those who held steadfastly to their belief in communicating with an afterlife, there seemed to be an unshakable faith, although the number of ardent spiritualists had dwindled. The decline in interest and investigations of mediumship was not entirely the fault of skeptics, rationalists, and debunkers. The spiritualist movement could partially blame itself for the exposure of numerous physical mediums in the country by tolerating the chicanery in its midst.

But the skeptical were once again premature in pronouncing the end of spiritualism as a nineteenth-century aberration that was finally laid to rest, as dead as naysayers believed people and pets were when they gasped their last breath of life on earth. Debunkers paid little attention and consideration to those mediums who defied explanation; in other words, the ones who demonstrated what appeared to be genuine psychic powers, such as Mrs. Piper, Gladys Leonard, D. D. Home, and others.

The Age of Spiritualism did not exit center stage quietly. One last explosion of anger and emotion was destined to occur. It would be a public feud between two of the world's most famous men of mystery: Harry Houdini (1874–1926), the celebrated illusionist and escapologist, and Sir Arthur Conan Doyle (1859–1930), author and creator of the world's best known fictional detective, Sherlock Holmes. The two were larger-than-life-celebrities, whose accomplishments few could argue with, and whose beliefs about spiritualism would prove vastly different.

Even their physical appearances were at odds: Doyle was a large man, tall, with a distinctive full mustache. He liked and trusted people and was gregarious by nature. Houdini was smaller in stature with intense eyes and thick wavy hair. He was a tireless performer, always in the spotlight, driven and excitable. They'd first met in London in 1920, when Houdini was on tour. Both men were strongly opinionated and uncompromising, yet the unlikely friendship grew.

They remained friends until their collision over the question of whether spiritualism was genuine. Houdini would emerge as the first important psychic debunker in America, the ultimate skeptic. Doyle became one of spiritualism's most fanatical but naïve defenders. Their conflict over the nature of the existence of the spiritual realm exemplified the nineteenth-century debate: Was the spirit world possible? This was an argument that broke out on practically the first day of the Hydesville raps. The debate raged in newspapers, parlor rooms, across dinner tables, and before the hearths at private clubs. It raged among scholars, lay people, and among the bereaved. But nothing matched the intemperance of Houdini and Doyle's verbal and written battles over the existence of the supernatural.

Harry Houdini

Born in Budapest, Hungary, Houdini's birth name was Erik Weisz, which was later changed to Ehrich Weiss. He was still an infant when his parents migrated to America in 1874, and settled in Appleton, Wisconsin, where his father served as a rabbi. As a youth he developed two life-long preoccupations: a love of magic and an obsessive devotion to his mother. At seventeen, he gave himself the name "Houdini," after a famed nineteenth-century French magician, Robert-Houdin. He was just twenty when he married; his wife Beatrice, whom he called Bess, became his stage partner and soon they were appearing in vaudeville.

His career took off when he devised his escape acts, and they earned him wide publicity. It appeared no restraints could hold him, and he freed himself—seemingly by magic—from shackles, ropes, and anything with which he could be bound. He constantly pushed his taut body to its physical limits, especially in his famed Chinese Water Torture, and the time he dangled from a skyscraper, while in a straitjacket, as the crowds on the street below watched him twist and turn to set himself free. The media of that era—silent film, newspapers—loved him, and he felt the same way about them. He toured tirelessly, and his reputation grew until he was the world's most famous escape artist and magician.

What would later become the catalyst for his battle of words with Sir Arthur Conan Doyle was the death in 1913 of Houdini's beloved mother, Cecilia Weiss. Houdini was on stage performing one night when he glanced over and caught sight of her. What he did not know was that only a short time before, she had passed from this life to the next. After his show, when Houdini was given the news that his mother had died, he was devastated. Those who knew him well were aware of his extreme emotional closeness and devotion to her. With the trauma of her death, and the void it left in his life, Houdini was so grief-stricken he was nearly inconsolable, and whenever he was in New York he spent hours at a time at her gravesite. His fixation became the search for a means to communicate with her spirit. For years, he earnestly tried to find a genuine medium to facilitate contact with his departed mother; but he became increasingly frustrated after repeated failures to receive an accurate message. And he was left bereft and disconsolate.

Sir Arthur Conan Doyle

Doyle was born in Edinburgh in 1859, to an Irish Catholic family. He received a Jesuit education and then graduated from Edinburgh University with a medical degree in 1881. Doyle became a physician specializing in diseases of the eye, and he turned to writing to earn extra income. He'd always been affable and a gifted storyteller. Now he put his words on paper, and found fame and fortune as a novelist, mainly thanks to his creation of the great detective, the master of deductive logic and forensic science, Sherlock Holmes.

The first of the Holmes stories, *A Study in Scarlet*, was published in 1887, and Doyle partially modeled the fictional detective after Dr. Joseph Bell, a respected Scottish surgeon and one of his favorite professors at the

University of Edinburgh. Doyle was particularly intrigued by Bell's use of deductive reasoning to diagnose patients.

Sherlock Holmes applied that same deductive reasoning to solve the most complex crimes, the process of elimination, he said. He always sought small and subtle clues that were less obvious, and he was meticulous in his investigations, and displayed extremely keen powers of observation. He and his sometimes bewildered but devoted associate Dr. Watson became enormously popular with readers. The characters, plots, and other details Doyle crafted seemed so realistic that for the first time in literary history, readers forgot the stories were fiction, and that Holmes and Watson were invented. The crime-solving pair soon overshadowed their creator.

Doyle never liked Holmes very much, and he regarded the mysteries to be less important than the historical fiction he'd written. Obviously, millions of readers disagreed, and there was quite a hue and cry when he killed off Sherlock Holmes—who'd become the most famous fictional detective the literary world had ever known—after writing more than fifty Holmes stories.

Why did Doyle abandon a potentially successful medical career, and then the wealth and fame the Holmes books brought him, in favor of his conversion to spiritualism in 1916? That's a mystery worthy of a Sherlock Holmes story.

Doyle may have become interested in spiritualism after attending a séance at a patient's home, where he observed such physical phenomena as table tipping. Like Houdini, he'd also suffered personal loss: Doyle's son Kingsley was killed in battle during World War I, and a brother-in-law had also died. At first, he was both skeptical and disparaging of mediumship but then he became curious enough to read many books about the subject.

He was also impressed that famed scientists such as Sir William Crookes and Alfred Russel Wallace had taken spirit contact seriously. That moved the study of spiritualism into an entirely different class as far as Doyle was concerned; this was not just a foolish indulgence of the ignorant and superstitious. "When I regarded Spiritualism as a vulgar delusion of the uneducated, I could afford to look down upon it; but when it was endorsed by Crookes, whom I knew to be the most rising British chemist, [and] by Wallace, who was the rival of Darwin . . . I could not afford to dismiss it." If learned men of science found something worthwhile about the paranormal to investigate, that was sufficient for Doyle.

Doyle was annoyed, however, when he discovered that Charles Darwin, among other scientists, had written off spiritualism without bothering to investigate it. "I was bound to admit that however great they were in their science, their action in this respect was most unscientific . . . while the action of those who studied the phenomena and tried to find out the laws that governed them was following the true path which has given all human advance and knowledge."

But it would take the carnage and suffering of World War I to give Doyle pause to rethink questions about the meaning of life and death— and what might await us after we depart this physical plane.

> In the presence of an agonized world, hearing every day of the deaths of the flower of our race . . . I seemed suddenly to see that this subject with which I had so long dallied was not merely a study of force outside the rules of science, but that it was something tremendous, a breaking down of the walls between two worlds, a direct undeniable message from beyond, a call of hope and of guidance to the human race at the time of its deepest affliction. . . .

Doyle's sorrow for the millions of casualties was genuine, and following the end of the Great War in 1918, he was deeply troubled by the sense of collective bereavement that England and countries on the European continent were suffering. The British Empire alone lost more than 900,000 men and boys. The loss of so many lives in battle deeply disturbed him on a humanitarian level. His motives were not self-serving, but he'd converted to spiritualism at a time when it was losing credibility as a movement. He raised many skeptics' eyebrows when he publicly announced his conversion in the British spiritualist publication *Light*.

Although he'd been raised a Roman Catholic and believed in God, Doyle had discarded many rituals and dogmas of the Church. But when he found his calling in spiritualism he became one of its most outspoken crusaders whose sole purpose was to proselytize on its behalf; and he remained dedicated to this mission for the rest of his life. In fact, he felt spiritualism represented a more rational and reasoned way of looking at traditional religion rather than merely accepting church tenets as a matter of "blind faith" and obedience. "Spiritualism is a religion for those who find themselves outside all religions; while on the contrary it greatly strengthens the faith of those who already possess religious beliefs," Doyle said.

Houdini and Doyle had talked about the subject and knew they strongly disagreed, especially as Houdini grew increasingly discouraged about ever contacting his mother's spirit. Doyle, on the other hand, accepted nearly every paranormal or spiritualist claim. He was gullible, naïve, overly credulous, and displayed none of the critical thinking and precision that Sherlock Holmes gave to every investigation. How was it possible that the creator of a character so logical and exacting could in real life be so easily deceived?

Doyle, ever the optimist, felt with time and patience Houdini would see the light, so to speak, and come around to share his spiritualist beliefs. There is a long-held assumption that Houdini did not believe in God, an afterlife, or the ability to communicate with the dead. Skeptics are proud to boast that Houdini was America's premier psychic debunker, and that he exposed every medium in the world as a fraud. That simply is not true. Houdini made it clear in a book he wrote in 1924, *A Magician Among the Spirits*, that he began his quest for spirit contact because he thought it was possible. It was only after repeated disappointment with inept or fraudulent mediums that he turned ferociously against all of them. If he had heard what he believed was a genuine message from his late mother, his behavior and attitude toward the question of spirit contact might have been entirely different. Instead the last years of his life were spent in a wild public rant against all mediums that was as extreme as Doyle's naïvety in the other direction.

The breaking point between Houdini and Doyle occurred in 1922, and sparked the beginning of a feud that spilled over into a debate that went to the very core of spiritualism. Doyle had persuaded Houdini to sit with Lady Doyle, who'd fancied herself a medium with the ability to discern spirit communications through automatic writing. At the séance, Lady Doyle claimed she'd received messages from Cecilia Weiss, Houdini's mother. But when Houdini heard the messages from Lady Doyle, purported to be from Weiss's spirit, he was mortified. The communication contained all manner of Christian allusions about the nature of the afterlife. Houdini exploded in rage and screamed, "She's Jewish, you imbecile, as am I!" Houdini was certain that Lady Doyle's mediumship was nothing but a fraud, and that she pieced together contrived messages to deceive unsuspecting subjects. Also, Mrs. Weiss spoke only broken English in life because her native languages were Hungarian and Yiddish, yet when her spirit allegedly came through Lady Doyle, her English was perfect. Houdini found that to be a troubling inconsistency.

Houdini unleashed a volley of insults at Lady Doyle, who remained at her séance table, pale and shaken. Then the furious magician turned his rage toward Arthur Conan Doyle, screaming that the entire spiritualist movement was based on trickery. As he continued his tirade, he made it clear that, in his opinion, there was no truth whatsoever to mediumship.

Houdini's explosion caught the Doyles off guard. But soon Sir Arthur, infuriated at Houdini's outburst and lack of civility, regained his composure, rose to his feet, his hands clenched into fists. An incensed Doyle struck back with his own verbal barrage. Both men became so angry that Doyle bordered on incoherence, and Houdini was flushed from the confrontation. There was no way to undo what had been said, and the clash ended the friendship forever.

A few months later, the two self-absorbed and opinionated celebrities became embroiled in a bitter public feud that made news across America and England as it escalated. They even argued about whether Abraham Lincoln was a spiritualist. Lincoln had been a lifelong hero to the magician and Houdini was furious to think that the "great Abraham Lincoln" was a spiritualist, when "such is not the case," Houdini raged. Doyle's answer to his former friend was that Lincoln *was* "a convinced spiritualist."

Houdini had not forgotten that at the heart of his anger and frustration was his inability to hear from his mother; he'd tried for nine years. Once he became convinced his efforts were futile, he turned with a vengeance against the entire spiritualist movement. He had a new calling in life: to prove all mediums were frauds—whether or not he had evidence to back up his accusations.

Houdini's animus against Lady Doyle grew into a virtual one-man war against mediumship and attracted much public attention. He'd always been brilliant at promoting himself as a magician, and he was just as effective in garnering publicity for exposing deceptive mediums, a task he seemed to relish. But he wasn't exactly an objective or impartial investigator. His wrath now made that impossible. When he attacked *every* medium, in his bitterness he swung too far and wide with too little investigation.

Doyle's gullibility was as unfortunate as Houdini's blind opposition. Doyle could not bring himself to acknowledge frauds any more than Houdini would allow for the possibility of genuine psychic powers.

The two men had boxed themselves into extreme positions that served neither one of them. Yet while both were misguided, they were also on the right track. Houdini had performed a real service in exposing charlatans; and though Doyle's open-mindedness toward psychic phenomena was admirable, he was apparently unable or unwilling to discern obvious deception. To Doyle, anything and everything about the paranormal was genuine, no matter how far-fetched, such as his belief in fairies. For Houdini, all of spiritualism was fraudulent.

To make matters worse, Houdini grew even more incensed when Doyle publicly insisted that the magician's "remarkable feats of escape" were a result of psychic or supernatural powers. That was an affront to Houdini almost beyond words. "They're tricks! Illusions. My tricks are just that, tricks," he insisted.

Meanwhile, Houdini stepped up his anti-spiritualist campaign until it became a virtual obsession. And his anger escalated until he proved he was also capable of deception if it served his larger cause: eradicating spiritualism, and every medium with it.

In 1924, the highly regarded *Scientific American* magazine offered a cash prize for anyone who could demonstrate mediumship to its satisfaction. After strict tests were conducted, the cash prize was about to be awarded to Boston medium Mina Crandon, known professionally as "Margery." Houdini was furious at this turn of events; upset that science had not proven Mrs. Crandon was a fraud.

Houdini was able to re-create many of Margery's physical phenomena by employing various props to devise the illusion that spirits were responsible for such activity as table tipping. However, he was unable to discredit her mediumship, some of which was in the form of direct voice communications from her late brother Walter.

So Houdini vowed that he would do it himself by any means possible and that, he said, meant testing Crandon personally. Refusing to acknowledge that Crandon might be genuine, the exasperated magician ordered his assistant to hide a folding ruler close to her where it would be discovered. That led the others who tested Crandon to conclude that she cheated by using the ruler to surreptitiously move objects. Both Houdini and Crandon denied any responsibility for the hidden ruler, but the accusation of wrong-doing fell on Crandon. The investigators never thought to doubt Houdini. Their conclusion was to accept his word; so they decided against Crandon and denied her the magazine's prize. It seemed to the *Scientific American* committee that Houdini had exposed another charlatan.

Many years later, long after Houdini had passed on, his assistant during the Crandon examination made a startling confession: it was actually Houdini who had planted the ruler when he could find no other way to debunk Crandon. Despite the oft-repeated myth that Houdini exposed every medium he ever tested, that simply is not true. As the facts in the Crandon incident showed, Harry Houdini, master illusionist, was perfectly willing to commit a little chicanery of his own if it would serve his purpose to expose a medium as a cheat. And if there was no evidence, Houdini could manufacture it.

The famed magician did not stop with Mrs. Crandon. His fury against spiritualism seemed never-ending. This had become Houdini's personal vendetta, and it did not matter how he caught mediums in his dragnet, as long as he won, and could proclaim that all of spiritualism was trickery, a "swindle," and those who believed in it "poor misguided souls."

Through all of this, Doyle's faith was unwavering. "Spiritualism is the greatest revelation the world has ever known," he confidently proclaimed. In 1922, and again in 1923, he had embarked on tours of America to lecture on behalf of his spiritualist beliefs. The events were hugely successful wherever he spoke.

Meanwhile, Houdini had further plans to decimate spiritualism. His incessant hounding of mediums took him to the nation's capital, where he complained that the District of Columbia had no law against fortune-tellers. Houdini contended this made Washington, D.C., a haven for countless numbers of deceitful mediums. In fact, it was alleged that some of the mediums practicing in Washington had given séances and sittings for very influential people. Some of their clients were congressmen, senators, and other high level officials. Houdini had sounded the alarm: What if spirit communications influenced legislative, executive, or judicial decisions? For Houdini, this was a disaster of near-cataclysmic proportions. And it got worse.

First Lady Florence Harding visited mediums during her husband's scandal-scarred presidency (1921–1923). Houdini claimed that he'd heard "on rather good authority that they did hold séances in the White House." Equally appalling to the magician were the "persistent rumors" that First Lady Grace Coolidge also consulted mediums during the time she resided in the White House (1923–1929). Houdini was almost apoplectic about the situation, for this was a de facto acceptance of spiritualism at the highest levels of government. He wasted no time calling for federal legislation to ban mediums, psychics, and other occult practitioners, and he asked President Coolidge to order an investigation. But the president never replied to Houdini's demands for a law banning the practice of mediumship.

However, the egotistical illusionist was in no mood to surrender to spirit forces or their allies in Congress. Houdini convinced a New York congressman he knew to introduce legislation to prohibit fortune-telling in the District of Columbia. The proposed law called for a 250-dollar fine, six months in jail, or both for anyone convicted of passing themselves off as a "professional medium offering services to the public."

In February 1926, the bill was the subject of a House committee hearing and Houdini was there to strongly urge its passage. Also on hand were literally hundreds of outraged mediums and other psychic practitioners. When the legislation did not pass, Houdini put his best spin on his failed effort by insisting he'd "performed a public service by exposing fraudulent mediums who preyed on the vulnerable, gullible, and bereaved."

In 1924, he wrote *A Magician Among the Spirits* in which he continued his ceaseless debunking. In the book, Houdini made his purpose clear: to discredit all of spiritualism as a "fake" based on what he claimed was thirty years of "exploring the history of spiritualism and its practice . . ."

He acknowledged the great wave of interest in spiritualism following World War I, saying "I was impressed by the eagerness of grief-stricken parents for the solace of a word from the boy who had passed on. . . ." But Houdini made no effort to find anything positive to say about spiritualism or his adversary, Sir Arthur Conan Doyle. In fact, he quoted a psychopathologist who claimed there was a "danger of insanity resulting from strong belief in spiritualism by neurotics."

The magician offered his assessment of Doyle and the renowned scientist Sir Oliver Lodge by dismissing the spiritualist interests of both. "I do not consider either . . . to be safe judges, whose opinion should be accepted on this difficult and important subject."

About scientists who had shown interest in studying spiritualism, Houdini was not impressed. "The fact they are *scientists* does not endow them with an especial gift for detecting the particular sort of fraud used by mediums, nor does it bar them from being deceived, especially when they are fortified in their belief by grief. . . ."

Houdini maintained a substantial library of books about "psychic phenomena, spiritualism, magic, demonology, evil spirits, some of the material going back as far as 1489." Yet, he said, "nothing has impressed me as being genuine." Houdini admitted that "some of the things I read seemed mystifying . . ." but he doubted that inexplicable supernatural phenomena could be "reproduced . . . under *test conditions*, and before expert mystifiers and open minded committees."

Houdini, of course, had every right to his opinions, but he was no longer open minded about spiritualism, although he readily used the phrase. It was all a "trick" or perhaps "hallucination of the senses," he suggested. "But up to the present time everything that I have investigated has been the result of deluded brains or those which were too actively and intensely willing to believe." He concluded that spiritualism was a "monstrous fiction."

In 1926, Sir Arthur Conan Doyle was at a séance when he received a disturbing message: "Houdini is doomed, doomed, doomed!" Doyle realized it would be useless to warn Houdini, who would only disparage him. The situation left Doyle in the frustrating position of waiting for the spirit prophecy to come true. It did on Halloween 1926, when, after an accidental punch to his stomach that severely injured the muscles of his solar plexus, Houdini died of peritonitis at the age of fifty-two.

Doyle was possibly the only one who could have warned his former friend to be cautious, because the blow that claimed Houdini's life might have been avoided—or could it have? Was the medium's prediction alterable if Doyle had cautioned Houdini in advance of the unexpected punch from a visiting student? Or had the medium psychically seen in the future an immutable event that would be Houdini's fate, regardless of any warning to the magician?

Doyle had no choice but to remain silent in the face of a prediction that he feared would come to pass. There was an irony in Houdini's position against spiritualism that would no doubt have resulted in him ignoring an admonition that might have saved his life.

Houdini has long been cited as America's first and most important psychic debunker. But later skeptics and debunkers, some of them magicians, often conveniently neglected to quote Houdini accurately. In *A Magician Among the Spirits*, he wrote, "I believe in a Hereafter and no greater blessing could be bestowed upon me than the opportunity, once again, to speak to my Sainted Mother who awaits me with open arms to press me to her heart in welcome, just as she did when I entered this mundane sphere."

The famed escapologist made it crystal clear that he had no doubt about the existence of an afterlife. There is no ambiguity in his statement. Unfortunately, he never met a medium that satisfied him. What if he had? Would he have still waged his crusade against spiritualism?

Houdini acknowledged that he'd studied the occult and paranormal for "thirty years," and had an extensive private library about psychic phenomena and the supernatural. Why then did he wait until after his mother died to launch his attack on fraudulent mediums? There were plenty of charlatans he could have exposed from the first time he stepped on stage to hold audiences spellbound with his escape tricks from locked containers, coffins, water tanks, straitjackets, handcuffs, jail cells, and so on. One of the first routines he and his wife Bess performed years earlier was a mind reading act that depended on a series of secret signals and code words between them. He knew how to pretend to be a fortune-teller. Couldn't he have exposed the chicanery of fraudulent physical and materialization mediums long before he did?

The night of his mother's death, when Houdini glanced to his side and saw her momentarily, he must have known enough about the paranormal to later realize he'd witnessed a crisis apparition, an experience he accepted as genuine. He even admitted that he always felt her spirit was close to him.

When he wrote that people who seek contact with spirits of departed loved ones have "deluded brains for being willing to believe," he apparently forgot he was one of them; for his first inclination was to seek a message from his late mother.

In his book, Houdini denounced the nineteenth-century medium Daniel Dunglas Home's famed levitation in which he floated out of one window and glided back through another. Houdini claimed Home's exploits were accomplished by trickery, and he could reproduce them. In fact, Houdini boasted that, "every one of [Home's] feats can be duplicated by modern conjurers under the same conditions." However, Houdini never did replicate Home's levitation, however it was achieved.

Houdini was an emotional man with a gargantuan ego, and the idea that someone claimed psychic powers, as D. D. Home had, no doubt irked Houdini unless he could perform as well or preferably better. Houdini the magician never met Home, who died in 1886, when Houdini, known then by his given name, Ehrich Weiss, was just a boy of twelve.

For a time, in the early years of the twentieth century, Houdini and his wife lived in a comfortable brownstone in upper Manhattan. Two houses away lived the William Cohen family. Cohen was an ardent fan of Houdini and marveled when he saw him on stage. Many years later he recalled having seen Houdini come and go, often hurriedly, to and from his home when he was in New York. Cohen, out of respect, always addressed him as Mr. Weiss when they exchanged greetings, but beyond that, there was barely any conversation. When Cohen's young children dared to politely approach Houdini, the most they could hope for was a slight nod or faint smile. Cohen remembered his famous neighbor as reserved, vain, aloof, and an individual of few words, quite the opposite of the brash showman the public saw on stage, or the vociferous and angry psychic debunker.

Sir Arthur Conan Doyle, for his part, never lost faith in spiritual and supernatural phenomena. The famed British scientist Sir Oliver Lodge described Doyle's persistence in seeking converts to spiritualism as "missionary." Doyle deeply needed to "believe," and he pressed forward with evangelical zeal. Sometimes the path he took strayed so far that he found others were reluctant to join him.

That's what happened when Doyle acknowledged his long-held fascination about fairies. In 1917, he'd accepted as "proof" that fairies were genuine, "crude photographs of young girls staring at what were obviously pictures of fairies cut out from books and placed on branches and lawns," we wrote in an earlier book, *We Don't Die*.[2] When one looks at those photographs today, it is difficult to fathom that Doyle—or anyone—could have been fooled by them. The fairies in the pictures appear to be tiny female beings, wearing gowns with "transparent" wings, each playing the "double pipe," an instrument long associated with elves and fairies.

When Doyle wrote *The Coming of the Fairies* in 1922, he included the dubious photos in the book. The pictures had been taken by sixteen-year-old Elsie Wright and her younger cousin, both from Cottingley, West Yorkshire. When questioned, the girls described the color scheme of the fairies: their bodies were white with "pale green, pink, and pale purple" wings. The incident became an embarrassment for Doyle, when nearly everyone who saw the photographs concluded they were fraudulent, and he finally conceded that he might have been the victim of deception. Many years after Doyle's death, the girls confessed the pictures were a hoax.

Why had the cousins fabricated the photos? They said it was their way of getting even with adults who reprimanded them for claiming they played with the tiny beings. The two insisted that when they were children, they had indeed witnessed fairies in the wooded glen near their homes, but no one at the time believed them.

"[Doyle] could not bring himself to see this case as a minor drama of two lonely children translating their daydreams and their parents' beliefs into a substitute for reality by means of doctored or staged photographs," wrote Sherman Yellen in the *International Journal of Parapsychology*.

It is almost impossible to accept that the man responsible for creating the very demanding character of Sherlock Holmes could be so gullible. However, Doyle had earned a reputation for never closely examining evidence for paranormal or supernatural phenomena, such as when he defended spirit photography against criticism by a psychic researcher named Harry Price. Doyle's credulity eventually became an embarrassment to many other spiritualists, despite his sincerity and enthusiasm.

The heated arguments between Doyle and Houdini continued until the magician's death in 1926. Four years later, in 1930, Arthur Conan Doyle died, ending the great debate between the two. But even that was not the last word on the question of contact with the afterlife. Houdini, true to his style as the consummate showman, managed to keep the debate alive *after* his passing.

As noted, early in his stage career, during the 1890s, Houdini and his wife performed an act in which he played the part of a medium or fortune-teller. In the process of creating staged séances, the couple employed a code between them, containing both alphabetical and numerical symbols. Much later, Houdini used that code to leave his wife Bess a secret message that he promised to communicate to her after his death—if he found spirit communication was attainable. After all, Houdini had made a long career as a famed escape artist; if anyone could break through from the Other Side, it would be Houdini.

It may sound contradictory given that Houdini's last years were devoted to derailing spiritualism, but he maintained a glimmer of hope that contact with the afterlife was possible. Only Mrs. Houdini knew what the message was: "a ten-word code that could be further distilled to a two-word message: ROSABELLE BELIEVE." It was a phrase that dated back to their mind-reading act, and an affectionate name Houdini had for his wife.

By the 1920s the interest in the spiritualist movement had fallen dramatically. However there remained a strong curiosity about spirit communications, and for that reason Ouija boards were selling briskly. There were still mediums to be found; one of them was a young man named Arthur Augustus Ford (1897–1971). He was born in Florida, raised in a Southern Baptist family, and was later ordained a minister. While serving in World War I he began experiencing psychic visions and voices. His first clairvoyant incident was about his brother George, on the very day that George was stricken with a serious illness that claimed his life not long after.

By 1924, Ford began communication with a spirit guide named "Fletcher," who had been a friend killed during the war. Then in 1927, just a year after Houdini's unexpected death, Ford made his first public appearance at a lecture about spiritualism given by Sir Arthur Conan Doyle. Ford's powers apparently impressed many, and he was on his way to a career as a medium, with encouragement from Doyle.

In 1928, Ford claimed that he'd received a "secret message" from the spirit of Cecilia Weiss, Houdini's mother, that Bess Houdini would understand. Mrs. Houdini conceded the message was accurate. She had attended several séances following her husband's death, hoping for a message from him; however she never received their well-concealed code words. Meanwhile, Ford continued with "a series of sittings" during which he received messages claiming to be from Houdini. "Every session after the first was attended by an editor of *Scientific American*—where the entire case was ultimately published—and taken down by a stenographer," Ford explained.

Then in January 1929, many readers were surprised when *The New York Times* reported that Mrs. Houdini had at last acknowledged that she'd received the secret message from her late husband. The startling event occurred during a private reading with the medium Arthur Ford, and Beatrice Houdini confirmed it to the world. She said that the communication from Ford was "the correct message prearranged between Mr. Houdini and myself," and newspapers carried her words around the globe. One report claimed that upon hearing the message, Mrs. Houdini fainted.

"Beatrice Houdini testified, when the long sequence was completed, that the message was the one she and her deceased husband had agreed upon, and that it had been transmitted in their private code. Fletcher and I found ourselves world-famous overnight. We were praised in the press of two continents—and denounced by skeptics from coast to coast," Ford later wrote.[3]

That seemed to make it official: the famous Houdini code was broken. But how had Ford accomplished it? About that the debate has never ended. If the story about Houdini and Ford ceased at that point, the acceptance of mediumship in America might have taken quite a different turn. But if the history of the paranormal has taught us anything, it's that when one mystery is resolved, it opens the door to another puzzle, then another, and another. . . .

So the controversy continued. If Ford received his information from Houdini's spirit, as he claimed, it would have to be regarded as one of the most extraordinary psychic breakthroughs in history. But for some reason that has never been made clear, Mrs. Houdini later retracted her confirmation of the message, although she'd signed a sworn statement attesting to its accuracy. Even though she originally said the communication—"Rosabelle Believe"—was correct, her retraction raised new doubts about if and how Ford obtained it. Had it genuinely come from the spirit world—or was there a more earthly explanation? Why had Beatrice Houdini absolutely confirmed the message from her husband, only to later deny it?

How Ford broke the Houdini code depends on which of several versions one believes. Skeptics and debunkers were certain that Ford somehow cheated or had advanced knowledge; they would make no allowance for the possibility of an actual spirit or psychic message.

One account, offered by a long-time associate and friend of Houdini, Joseph Rinn, was that Mrs. Houdini unintentionally disclosed the coded message while she was ill and delirious. According to Rinn, psychics and mediums got wind of the message and circulated it among themselves, and one of those who'd learned it in advance of the famed séance was none other than the medium Arthur Ford.

A tabloid newspaper claimed it tricked Ford into confessing that he'd known the message *before* the séance. A variation of that story was that Mrs. Houdini, who later had an accidental fall, revealed the secret message, possibly to a nurse who, in turn, forwarded it Ford, perhaps hoping she'd receive money for the information. Another newspaper, the *New York Graphic*, also denied Ford was accurate, alleging that he and a reporter had fabricated the entire episode.

The debunkers' stories were convoluted and based on a series of coincidences that stretched credulity. While spiritualists were elated, skeptics were desperate. They had to concoct some version of events to fit the conclusion that Ford was a charlatan and virtually any theory that discredited the medium would suffice. It would have been less frustrating to some of the detractors if the explanation had been that Arthur Ford disguised himself as a spider, climbed a wall into Mrs. Houdini's home, and heard her giving the coded message while she talked in her sleep.

Ford received a great deal of attention for the séance, followed by Mrs. Houdini's confirmation, and then her retraction. He followed the torrent of publicity and the reactions, and when he wrote his autobiography, offered a very different version of events. Ford claimed that the tabloid fabricated his "confession," and even had someone impersonate him.

Most convincingly, Ford suggested that pressure was brought to bear on Beatrice Houdini by those vehemently opposed to spiritualism; and it had plenty of enemies. The Old Testament condemned mediums and Christianity had forever carried that prohibition forward. At the other end of the spectrum, atheists wanted no evidence that would affirm the existence of an afterlife, while scientists were at a complete loss to explain the nature of spirit communications.

In order to debunk Arthur Ford, it was much easier to pressure Mrs. Houdini into retracting the affirmation of her husband's message than to disturb long-accepted dogmas of church and science, and the deeply entrenched and vested interests of those who abhorred spiritualism. One rumor spiritualists circulated was that Beatrice Houdini had been paid a substantial sum of money to discredit Ford's communication. In fact, she later denounced his séance, and there were rumors that she was to make a motion picture debunking mediumship, although that never came to fruition.

In the frenzy of allegations and denials, Ford's accuracy was nearly forgotten, and with constant reminders from debunkers, the public became understandably confused, not certain whom to believe. For several more years Mrs. Houdini held séances on Halloween, but never heard from her husband's spirit. Eventually, her retraction prevailed, although evidence strongly suggests that Ford gave her the message she'd sought. Beatrice Houdini died in 1943, without ever again speaking about the séance. She reportedly told friends she had no wish to communicate back from the hereafter.

For the public the question came down to whom they gave credence: the tabloid press and Houdini's cronies or Arthur Ford. Might Ford have cheated? Of course he could have. Is it possible Ford was genuinely psychic? The answer is yes. But the two sides remained bitterly polarized; so the controversy was not resolved, and likely never will be. One can imagine the spirit of Harry Houdini who in life loved publicity smiling with satisfaction at the uproar about him that continued long after he departed this world for the next.

In 1931, Ford was in a near-fatal automobile accident. The excruciating pain from his injuries was treated with morphine, which left him addicted. This was followed by years of alcoholism. Nonetheless, the Houdini séance propelled Ford to worldwide recognition, enabling him to become one of the twentieth century's best-known mediums. He again made front-page news in 1967, with a televised séance for Episcopal Bishop James Pike to communicate with his deceased son who'd committed suicide.

Of what value to the paranormal was the dispute between Harry Houdini and Sir Arthur Conan Doyle? Behind the commotion and theatrics of the two famed figures were some serious and important lessons. For one thing, their long-running debate kept the subject of spiritualism in the media and on the public's mind. Their feud arguably increased awareness and consciousness about questions of life after death. Ironically, their diametrically opposing stances probably created one of the few episodes in the history of the paranormal that allowed the public to hear both sides of the controversy by two individuals who claimed to have studied the subject carefully and were more than happy to share their opinions with anyone who'd listen.

On the other hand, "Doyle's contribution to [psychic research] is mainly a negative one. He stands out as a warning of how one's personal views can create an atmosphere in which the serious examination of psychic phenomena becomes impossible," concluded writer Sherman Yellen.

Houdini's interminable crusade against spiritualism uncovered trickery, but allowed no room to investigate those genuinely inexplicable events we call psychic or supernatural. He alleged that all mediums were charlatans, as he did with D. D. Home, the Davenport brothers, and Mina Crandon, among many others, but often provided no evidence beyond his word. Doyle increasingly acted on faith, and less on reason, an equally frustrating and unproductive position. Neither Doyle nor Houdini served to advance an understanding of the paranormal in general, or life after death specifically. The answers that eluded both men lay somewhere between the extremes, and neither of them were qualified by virtue of training or temperament to rationally or open-mindedly examine the subject.

With the passing of Houdini and Sir Arthur Conan Doyle[4] came the natural end to the feud. But the legends of Houdini still survive, right alongside the literary legend of Conan Doyle and his timeless detective, Sherlock Holmes. Their feud, the basis of which was discovering the truth behind claims of the paranormal—life after death and the immortality of the human spirit—still lingers on, however, even as the twenty-first century opens up new possibilities for discovery.

What will the science of the twenty-first century tell us about the promise of the Age of Spiritualism that ushered in the twentieth century? Do the physics of Max Planck and Werner Heisenberg explain today's Law of Attraction? Will the proponents of string theory and the multiverse be able to demonstrate that what we call spirits and ghosts are actually manifestations of energy from another dimension? And if that's so, can we cross the barriers of dimensions as easily as we step on and off the subway?

One thing we can be sure about is that even as we think about this, someone is hunting for the answer.

Introduction: What Is New Age?

1. W. H. McNeill, *The Rise of the West* (New York: Mentor, 1963), 20.

2. Zecharia Sitchin, *The 12th Planet* (Rochester, Vermont: Bear & Company, 1976), 15.

3. McNeill, *The Rise of the West*, 19.

4. Alan F. Alford, *Gods of the New Millennium* (Southampton, United Kingdom, 1998). Alford is a leading authority on ancient mythology and the origin of ancient and modern religions. He has written several books on his "quest for the truth of human existence," he noted in his Web site; and explained he was influenced by the theories of the controversial authors Erich von Daniken and Zecharia Sitchin.

5. Alan and Sally Landsburg, *In Search of Ancient Mysteries* (New York: Bantam Books, 1974), 87.

6. Jim Marrs, *Rule by Secrecy* (New York: HarperCollins, 2000), 378.

7. Ibid, 11.

8. Ibid, 13.

9. Ibid, 11.

10. McNeill, *The Rise of the West*, chapters I, II, III, VIII. Other details of Sumerian civilization compiled from the books of Zecharia Sitchin; and author (Martin) interviews with the Howard Metz, a recognized researcher and historian on the subject of ancient civilizations. Note that Sumerian and several later civilizations are strangely similar.

11. "Anunnaki." Sitchin discusses the "Anunnaki" throughout his book, especially the question of the Anunnaki as the "rank and file gods who had been involved in the settlement of Earth": 292–297; 321–322; 349; 353–354, 368, among many other references.

12. "first landing of the Nefilim": Sitchin, *The 12th Planet*, 229.

13. "the sons of the gods": Ibid, 364.

14. Since the 1980s, and as recently as 2004, there have been reports of scientists seeking a tenth planet. It is within human nature to explore the unknown, pushing our knowledge further. Since the 1960s, scientific exploration has taken us to outer space. There is precedent for this human desire to explore; consider, as examples, the European explorers who braved the unknown to discover the "New World," including Christopher Columbus and Henry Hudson, among many others. Later, there was the expedition Lewis and Clark made westward across America. Our curiosity about outer space includes questions about whether other planets might exist, and beyond that, whether

they could sustain life. Perhaps we will eventually answer the nagging question that has led many scientists in their search for extraterrestrial intelligence and "interplanetary travel." Sitchin discusses this point in his book *The 12th Planet*, 229–232. The *Holman Bible Dictionary* also refers to this question.

15. Ibid, 105–106. Marduk was the "lord god of Babylon": McNeill, 73.

16. The great Sumerian civilization was remarkably advanced. Its achievements ranged from metal-making and the first use of the wheel for carts and chariots to the discovery of copper and bronze, according to H. E. L. Mellresh, author of *The Sumerians* (New York: Crowell, 1965). There were also accomplishments in the arts and architecture, including the construction of tall temples, known as ziggurats. The most famous ziggurat was the Tower of Babel, according to Susan Pollock, author of *Ancient Mesopotamia* (Cambridge University, 1999). Among the "firsts" credited to the Sumerians included the first school, bicameral congress, historian, library, poetry, aquarium, cuneiform writing, and biblical parallels, wrote author Samuel Noah Kramer in *History Begins at Sumer* (Philadelphia: University of Pennsylvania Press, 1981). Conventional books about ancient Sumeria and Mesopotamia nearly always omit references to Zecharia Sitchin's theories of "extraterrestrial involvement" in Earth's origins.

17. *Reader's Digest: Into the Unknown*, (Pleasantville, NY: Reader's Digest Association, 1981), 13. Traditional books about early civilizations typically ignore or criticize as superstition the important role astrology and other forms of divination played in Sumer, Babylonia, and Egypt.

18. For the section about ancient Egypt we employed a number of sources, including *Reader's Digest: Into the Unknown*; several Sitchin books; *Pyramid Power* and *Pyramid Prophecies*, both by Max Toth; *Encyclopedia of Occultism and Parapsychology* by Lewis Spence; *The Curse of the Pharaohs* by Philipp Vandenberg; *In Search of Ancient Mysteries* by Alan and Sally Landsburg; *Ancient Mesopotamia* by Susan Pollock; *The Atlas of Mysterious Places* by Jennifer Westwood, ed. (New York: Weidenfeld & Nicolson, 1987); author interviews with author Max Toth, and pyramidologist Howard Metz.

19. Landsburg, *In Search of Ancient Mysteries*, 87.

20. *Encyclopedia of Occultism and Parapsychology*, Volume 1 (Detroit: Gale Research, 1996), 391–394.

21. *Into the Unknown*, 15, 18, and 19.

22. Joel Martin and Patricia Romanowski, *We Don't Die* (New York: Putnam, 1988), 266.

23. *Into the Unknown*, 18.

24. Robert A. F. Thurman (translator) *The Tibetan Book of the Dead* (New York: Bantam, 1994); *We Don't Die*, 266.

25. Ibid. Also, author interviews with Hindu spiritual teacher, author, and poet Sri Chinmoy.

26. *Egyptian Mummies*, Encyclopedia Smithsonian Web site: http://www.si.edu/ Encyclopedia_SI/nmnh/mummies.htm; *Death in Ancient Egypt*: Oriental Institute Re-

search Archives: http://oi.uchicago.edu/OI/DEPT/RA/ABZU/DEATH_SITES .HTML; Max Toth and Greg Nielsen, *Pyramid Power* (New York: Warner/Destiny, 1974), 142–144, 154–156, 171–174, 194–196.

27. *Encyclopedia of Occultism and Parapsychology*, 392.

28. Ibid.

29. Ibid, 1338–1340; Philipp Vandenberg, *The Curse of the Pharaohs*.

30. Max Toth, *Pyramid Prophecies* (Rochester, VT: Destiny Books, 1979). Author interviews with Toth.

31. Toth, *Pyramid Power*, 147–167.

32. Ibid, 1, 5, 133–146, 163, 165.

33. Landsburg, *In Search of Ancient Mysteries*, 99.

34. Author interviews with Howard Metz.

35. Landsburg, *In Search of Ancient Mysteries*, 108.

36. Michael Perry, *Psychic Studies: A Christian's View* (Northamptonshire, Great Britain: The Aquarian Press, 1984), 30.

37. Amplified Bible: Leviticus 19:31. There might be slight variations in wording depending on which version of the Bible one uses. However, the meaning of the chapter and verse is the same.

38. *Reader's Digest: Into the Unknown*, 155.

39. Amplified Bible: Matthew 2:16.

40. Herbert B. Greenhouse, *The Book of Psychic Knowledge* (New York: Taplinger, 1973).

41. Josef F. Blumrich, *The Spaceships of Ezekiel* (New York: Bantam Books, 1974).

42. The reference to Cayce's ability to "diagnose clairvoyantly" was drawn from several sources including a private tour of the A.R.E., the Edgar Cayce Foundation in Virginia Beach, and the book, *There Is a River: the Story of Edgar Cayce* by Thomas Sugrue (New York: Holt, Rinehart & Winston, 1942), who noted that "Cayce practiced medical clairvoyance for forty-three years. He left stenographic reports of 30,000 of these diagnoses to the Association for Research and Enlightenment." He also left hundreds of case reports and patients' affidavits.

43. Ignatius Donnelly, *Atlantis: The Antediluvian World* (New York: Harper's, 1882). The book has been in print ever since.

44. *Edgar Cayce on Atlantis* (New York: Paperback Library, 1968).

45. Charles Pellegrino, *Unearthing Atlantis: An Archaeological Odyssey* (New York: Random House, 1991). Also, interview with author.

46. *Encyclopedia of Occultism and Parapsychology*, 93.

47. Ibid; 1103–1105.

48. Bob O'Gorman and Mary Faulkner, *The Complete Idiot's Guide to Understanding Catholicism* (New York: Alpha, 2006).

49. Richard Woods, *The Occult Revolution* (New York: Herder and Herder, 1971), 19.

50. *Into the Unknown*, p. 155.

51. Joel Martin and Patricia Romanowski, *We Don't Die: George Anderson's Conversations with the Other Side* (New York: G. P. Putnam's Sons, 1988).

52. *Into the Unknown*, 78–86.

53. *We Don't Die*, 269–271.

54. Barbara W. Tuchman, *A Distant Mirror: The Calamitous 14th Century* (New York: Alfred A. Knopf, 1978).

55. Kurt Seligmann, *The History of Magic and the Occult* (New York: Harmony Books, 1975).

56. Richard Woods, *The Occult Revolution*, 102–111. *Encyclopedia of Occultism and Parapsychology*, 1409–1413.

57. Mary Gordon, *Joan of Arc* (New York: Viking, 2000).

58. Woodeene Koenig-Bricker, *365 Saints* (New York: HarperCollins, 1995).

59. D. Scott Rogo, *Miracles: A Parascientific Inquiry into Wondrous Phenomena* (New York: Dial Press, 1982). Also, author interview with Rogo at the time *Miracles* was published.

60. Translations about Joan of Arc from French to English for this book by Jacques LeVaillant.

61. *Encyclopedia of Occultism and Parapsychology*, 807–808.

62. *Reader's Digest: Into the Unknown*, 78–87.

63. Ibid, 130–131.

64. Henry C. Roberts, *The Complete Prophecies of Nostradamus* (Oyster Bay, NY: Nostradamus Company, 1982, revised edition. Originally published in 1947), 17. *Encyclopedia of Occultism and Parapsychology*, 938. Erika Cheetham, *The Man Who Saw Tomorrow: The Prophecies of Nostradamus* (New York: Berkley, 1981; first published in 1973), 32–33.

65. Woods, *The Occult Revolution*, 76; *Encyclopedia of Occultism and Parapsychology*, 312–315.

66. Michael Perry, *Psychic Studies: A Christian's View*.

67. Bruce Chilton, *Rabbi Jesus: An Intimate Biography* (New York: Image Books, 2002), 175; Woods, *The Occult Revolution*, 35–37.

68. Marrs, *Rule by Secrecy*, 355–360; *Encyclopedia of Occultism and Parapsychology*, 697–698. Note that there are several spellings: Kabbalah, Kabala, Cabala, Cabbalah.

69. Georgess McHargue, *Facts, Frauds, and Phantasms* (Garden City, NY: Doubleday, 1972), 10.

70. *Into the Unknown*, 289.

71. *Pope Benedict XIV*. Britannica Concise Encyclopedia. http://www.answers.com/topic/pope-benedict-xiv

72. Rogo, *Miracles*; Michael Walsh, ed. *Butler's Lives of the Saints* (San Francisco: Harper & Row, 1985). Note that Butler's book was first published in England in 1756–1759. There have been a number of revised editions since of this well-known book; Carolyn Trickey-Bapty, *Martyrs and Miracles* (Owing Mills, MD: Halo Press, 1996).

73. This paragraph is based on interviews with and writings of Sri Chinmoy, who was for many years a Hindu teacher and writer.

74. This paragraph and the reference to Rogo's book *Miracles* explain the phenomenon. However, it is noteworthy to mention that during Joel Martin's many years of paranormal research, he had personally known a Franciscan priest, the late Father John Papallo (1943–1989), who mysteriously manifested bleeding hands or stigmata, shortly before his untimely death in an automobile accident.

75. Rogo, *Miracles*. In addition to bilocation attributed to saints and other religious figures, the phenomenon is also familiar to secular parapsychologists, and sometimes known as the "double" or appearing in two different places at the same time. One of the best-known researchers on this subject was the late Robert Monroe, who taught and wrote about out-of-body experiences.

76. John McCaffery, *Tales of Padre Pio: The Friar of San Giovanni* (New York: Image Books, 1981). "Padre Pio was an Italian Capuchin monk born in 1887," McCaffery wrote. For a half century, Pio lived in an Italian monastery. Until his death in 1968, Pio demonstrated remarkable gifts that religious people consider miracles. However, others less inclined to Catholicism have described Pio as an individual with amazing psychic abilities. Among them were out-of-body travel, bilocation, stigmata, and healings. He also possessed ESP abilities that included telepathy, clairvoyance, and precognition— although those were not terms used by the Church. What distinguished Padre Pio were the large number of witnesses to his gifts, and the fact that he lived well into the twentieth century, and not in the far distant past, as did medieval saints, whose accomplishments time has blurred. Now designated a saint of the Church, he will be known to future generations as St. Pio. During the course of research, Joel Martin interviewed several people who personally met Padre Pio and testified to his spiritual or paranormal abilities.

77. For more details about this inexplicable phenomenon, there is an excellent book, *The Incorruptibles* by Joan Carroll Cruz (Rockford, IL: Tan Books & Publishers, 1977) devoted entirely to the subject.

78. The "odor of sanctity" has been reported for centuries. However, there is a secular version that many people tell of when they lose loved ones; it is typically reported as sensing an aroma associated with the departed individual. Perfume and tobacco are two of the most common scents. Such experiences are now known as "after-death communications." It will be discussed in a later chapter. As well, there are several books devoted entirely to the subject of after-death communications.

79. There are many books and online sites about religious apparitions, divine images, and weeping icons. The debate about them will probably never be resolved, as author Martin Ebon stated, "One man's miracle is another's superstition."

80. Rogo, *Miracles*; Francis M. Johnston, *The Wonder of Guadalupe* (Rockford, IL: TAN Books, 1981); *Encyclopedia of Occultism and Parapsychology*, 1996.

81. Thomas Goldstein, *Dawn of Modern Science* (Boston: Houghton Mifflin Company, 1980).

82. Ibid.

83. Gleick, *Isaac Newton* (New York: HarperCollins, 2003).

84. Chadwick Hansen, *Witchcraft at Salem* (New York: George Braziller, 1969), 8–9.

85. Stuart Hampshire, *The Age of Reason: The Seventeenth Century Philosophers* (Boston: Houghton Mifflin, 1957), 11–18; Goldstein, *Dawn of Modern Science*; Pietro Redondi, *Galileo Heretic* (Princeton University Press, 1987).

86. Emanuel Swedenborg, *Heaven and Hell* (London: 1758; first English translation published in U.S., 1852. Edition used, 1979); *Encyclopedia of Occultism and Parapsychology*, 1269–1271; *Into the Unknown*, 186.

Chapter 1: *Colonial America: The Devil in Salem*

1. Kimberly's story is based entirely on interviews with her about her personal and psychic experiences.

2. The details in this chapter about the "Salem witch hysteria" of 1692 are based on a compilation of books, online materials, and visits by author [Joel Martin] to Boston and Salem, Massachusetts. There was also an interview conducted by Martin with Roxanne Salch Kaplan, a direct descendant of a seventeenth-century woman accused of practicing witchcraft and tried under Connecticut law.

3. The books used included: Chadwick Hansen, *Witchcraft in Salem* (New York: George Braziller, 1969); Alice Dickinson, *The Salem Witchcraft Delusion: 1692* (New York: Franklin Watts, 1974); Raymond Buckland, *Buckland's Complete Book of Witchcraft* (St. Paul, MN: Llewellyn, 1986); Marion Starkey, *The Devil in Massachusetts* (New York: Anchor Books, 1949); Marion Starkey, *The Visionary Girls: Witchcraft in Salem Village* (Boston: Little, Brown, 1973); Jakob Sprenger and Heinrich Kramer, *Malleus Maleficarum* (Hammer of Witches), 1486, Montague Summers, translator and ed. (Reprinted by Dover, 1971); Deodat Lawson, *A Brief and True Narrative* (Boston: Benjamin Harris, printer, 1692). Lawson had been the minister in Salem between 1684 and 1688. His ten-page pamphlet was his observations of the Salem Witchcraft outbreak in 1692; *Salem Witch Trials of 1692* (Salem Witch Museum Education); Linda Caporael, *Ergotism: The Satan Loosed in Salem?* (Science, Volume 192, April 1976); *The Salem Witch Trials, 1692* (Eyewitness to History.com); *Salem Witch Trials* (wikipedia.org); *Into the Unknown*, 78–87; *Encyclopedia of Occultism and Parapsychology*, biographies of Increase Mather and Cotton Mather, 831–832, story of Malleus Maleficarum, 807–808, story of Sarah Good, 534, story of Rebecca Nurse, 939; Cotton Mather, *Memorable Provinces, Relating to Witchcraft and Possessions* (Boston, 1689).

———, *The Wonders of the Invisible World* (Boston: Benjamin Harris, 1693); H. W. Brands, *The First American: The Life and Times of Benjamin Franklin* (New York: Doubleday, 2000).

Chapter 2: *Whig, Tory, and Spiritualist*

1. There is general agreement among historians and parapsychologists that 1760 to 1848 was a time of very little activity concerning spiritualism. Jon Butler, author of several books about religion in early America called the period the "Dark Ages of American Spiritualism." Butler's titles include *Religion in Colonial America* (New York: Oxford University Press, 1999) and *New World Faiths: Religion in Colonial America* (New York: Oxford, 2008).

2. Rosemary Ellen Guiley, *The Encyclopedia of Ghosts and Spirits* (New York: Facts on File, 1992).

3. Sir David Brewster (1781–1868) insisted, "Sir Isaac Newton was not a believer in the doctrine of alchemy." Although Brewster was a respected Scottish physicist, and Newton's biographer, historical records confirm that Newton did indeed experiment with alchemy, astrology, and studied biblical prophecy. Brewster's statement represents his own deep skepticism and dislike of occult subjects, and he strongly spoke and wrote against spiritualism in the nineteenth century. Brewster's field of expertise was optical science, but his comments purposely misstated Newton's interest in mystical and occult subjects.

4. Gilbert Osofsky, *Harlem: The Making of a Ghetto: Negro New York 1890–1930.*

5. Statistics, to the extent they were maintained in colonial America, paint a picture of the population and the racial breakdown in the colonies. Many of the figures we have used in this book are taken from *Timetables of History* by Bernard Grun (New York: Simon & Schuster, 1975), an excellent reference book, as well as from data in early periodicals and almanacs.

6. Lawrence Levine, *Black Culture and Black Consciousness: Afro-American Folk Thought From Slavery to Freedom* (New York: Oxford University Press, 1977).

7. Ibid.

8. H. W. Brands, *The First American: The Life and Times of Benjamin Franklin* (New York: Doubleday, 2000).

9. As a young man, Franklin wrote his own epitaph, suggesting a belief in reincarnation. Herbert B. Greenhouse, *The Book of Psychic Knowledge* (New York: Taplinger, 1973); also, Brands, *The First American*, 657.

10. Brands, *The First American*, 657–658.

11. Ibid, 113; J. Hugo Tatsch, *Freemasonry in the Thirteen Colonies* (New York: Macoy, 1929).

12. Author visit to Ephrata Cloister in Ephrata, Pennsylvania, provided opportunity for interviews with staff, and written materials, including *Ephrata Cloister: An Introduction* (pamphlet).

13. Brands, *The First American*, 631–633; Robert C. Fuller, *Mesmerism and the Cure of Souls* (Philadelphia: University of Pennsylvania Press, 1982); Walter Isaacson, "Benjamin Franklin's Enlightenment Deism," *Skeptical Inquirer* (magazine), April 2004, 63–67.

14. Tatsch, *Freemasonry in the Thirteen Colonies*.

15. Ibid.

16. Brands, *The First American*, 2, 465–6.

17. Fay was a French historian and author of *Revolution and Freemasonry—1680–1800* (Boston: Little, Brown, 1935).

18. Paul A. Fisher, *Behind the Lodge Door* (Rockford, IL: TAN Books, 1988), 42.

19. Ibid., 207.

20. The discussion of the images on the U.S. dollar bill was based on an interview with Vladimir Rus, Ph.D., a respected educator and Latin translator who provided us with the English translations and meaning of the symbols.

21. Interview with Max Toth, author of *Pyramid Prophecies*. Toth is also a Freemason. W. Kirk MacNulty, *Freemasonry: A Journey Through Ritual and Symbol* (New York: Thames and Hudson, 1991).

22. From interview with Dr. Vladimir Rus.

23. Tatsch, *Freemasonry in the Thirteen Colonies*, 71.

24. Old Testament Book of Genesis 49:13–33 includes the blessing by Jacob of his son Joseph (Amplified Bible).

25. This section about the new nation, numerology, and Kabbalistic references is drawn largely from the research of Max Toth. Also see MacNulty, *Freemasonry*, and Fisher, *Behind the Lodge Door*.

26. Fisher, *Behind the Lodge Door*, 9–13; John Sutherland Bonnell, *Presidential Profiles: Religion in the Lives of American Presidents* (Philadelphia: Westminster Press, 1971).

27. Joel Martin and William J. Birnes, *The Haunting of the Presidents* (New York: Signet Books, 2003), 139–141.

28. Ibid, 16–32; Sylvan Muldoon, *Psychic Experiences of Famous People* (Chicago: The Aries Press, 1947), 49–53; "Presidential Prophecies" TV documentary, History Channel, 2005. Included segment on Washington's angelic vision at Valley Forge.

    Author (Martin) researched the story at The David Library of the American Revolution, Washington Crossing, Pennsylvania. The David Library has a large collection of documents from the American Revolutionary era. Martin also interviewed a librarian there familiar with the story.

    Note: there is some historic confusion about Washington's writings to other officials of the young American nation. Recent books offer differing interpretations of his letters to and from others at the time (1777). What there is no argument about, were the dreadful conditions at Valley Forge during the winter of 1777–78. Letters and journal entries written by those who were there tell of poorly clothed and hungry American troops. When Washington wrote to Thomas Nelson he complained about his troop's condition.

    For their book, *The Haunting of the Presidents*, Martin and Birnes extensively researched historical discrepancies. For example, H. W. Brands noted in his writing about Valley Forge in *The First American* that the winter was "mild" by eighteenth century standards. We would, today, be more likely to describe the winter of 1777–78 as very cold, especially without proper winter clothing. (See Brands, 572–573.)

Also well worth reading is the best seller by Joseph J. Ellis, *His Excellency George Washington* (New York: Alfred A. Knopf, 2004). About Valley Forge, Ellis agrees conditions were miserable: "Men naked in the snow," 112. How much hardship George Washington personally experienced is a matter of debate. Not surprisingly, there is also debate about the angelic vision that virtually every traditional biography about Washington ignores.

29. Washington did not keep diaries during the war years, 1775–1780. Many letters Washington wrote to his wife, Martha, she destroyed before her death in 1802; only a couple of years after her husband died in December 1799. Ellis, *His Excellency George Washington*, 116.

30. Muldoon, *Psychic Experiences of Famous People*, 91–98.

31. Martin and Birnes, *The Haunting of the Presidents*, 43–47; Jean Anderson, *The Haunting of America* (Boston: Houghton Mifflin, 1973); Dennis William Hauck, *The National Directory of Haunted Places* (Sacramento, CA: Athanor Press, 1994).

32. Martin and Birnes, *The Haunting of the Presidents*, 109–118; Hauck, *The National Directory*, 325–326. Jean Anderson, *The Haunting of America*; Joan Bingham and Dolores Riccio, *More Haunted Houses* (New York: Pocket Books, 1991); Daniel Cohen, *Encyclopedia of Ghosts* (New York: Dorset Press, 1984); Nancy Roberts, *America's Most Haunted Places* (Orangeburg, SC: Sandlapper, 1987); Susy Smith, *Prominent American Ghosts* (Cleveland: World Publishing, 1969). Also, author (Martin) interview with Smith; Rosemary Ellen Guiley, *Encyclopedia of Ghosts and Spirits* (New York: Checkmark Books, 1992).

33. Pope Benedict XIV. Britannica Concise Encyclopedia. http://www.answers.com/topic/pope-benedict-xiv; R. Haynes, *Philosopher King: The Humanist Pope Benedict XIV* (London: Weidenfield & Nicolson, 1970); *Encyclopedia of Occultism and Parapsychology*; Kenneth L. Woodward, *Making Saints: How the Catholic Church Determines Who Becomes a Saint* (New York: Touchstone, 1990).

34. Robert C. Fuller, *Mesmerism and the American Cure of Souls* (Philadelphia: University of Pennsylvania Press, 1982); James R. Lewis, *Encyclopedia of Afterlife Beliefs and Phenomena* (Detroit: Gale Research, 1994), 234–235; *Encyclopedia of Occultism and Parapsychology*, 854–856; Brands, *The First American*, 630–632; *Into the Unknown*, 132, 291, 299.

35. Poe captured the public fascination in a short story titled "Mesmeric Revelation." It was first published in *Columbian Magazine* in August 1844.

36. Ralph Waldo Emerson (1803–1882) was one of America's best-known philosophers and writers in the nineteenth century. He was also a successful essayist, poet, and lecturer. Emerson was a leader of the Transcendental movement, a liberal religious philosophy. He was also a Unitarian minister in the Boston area whose contemporaries included such

liberal thinkers, reformers, and literary figures as Henry David Thoreau, Henry Wadsworth Longfellow, Louisa May Alcott, and Nathaniel Hawthorne. A quote from "Essays," written by Emerson in 1844, sums up his attitude toward religion: "If I should go out of church whenever I hear a false sentiment, I could never stay there five minutes. But why come out? The street is as false as the church." About God, Emerson said, "God builds his temple in the heart on the ruins of churches and religions."

37. Mrs. W. B. Hayden was one of America's first successful trance mediums. By 1852, she was also known in England. She convinced many people that when she was induced into a trance state, she was able to communicate with the spirits of the departed. Her husband was a newspaper editor in Boston. Her manner was somewhat low-key and her name has largely been lost to history, but in her day, she was "influential." See Georgess McHargue, *Facts, Frauds, and Phantasms* (Garden City, NY: Doubleday, 1972).

38. McHargue, *Facts, Frauds, and Phantasms*, 66–84 is devoted to details about Andrew Jackson Davis, his life and his contributions to spiritualism.

Chapter 3: *Is That You, Mr. Splitfoot?*

1. This chapter looks closely at the birth of the Spiritualist Movement that began in the home of the Fox family in upstate New York. To piece the story together, many sources were used, including: interviews with the well-respected library historian at the Rochester (NY) Public Library; R. G. Pressing, *Rappings that Startled the World: Facts about the Fox Sisters* (Lily Dale, NY: Dale News) booklet; Robert Somerlott, *"Here, Mr. Splitfoot"—An Informal Exploration into Modern Occultism* (New York: Viking Press, 1971); McHargue, *Facts, Frauds, and Phantasms*; Martin and Birnes, *The Haunting of the Presidents: A Paranormal History of the U.S. Presidency*; Ruth Brandon, *The Spiritualists* (New York: Knopf, 1983); Ann Braude, *Radical Spirits* (Boston: Beacon Press, 1989); Slater Brown, *The Heyday of Spiritualism* (New York: Hawthorn Books, 1970); Rosemary Ellen Guiley, *The Encyclopedia of Ghosts and Spirits*; Herbert G. Jackson, *The Spirit Rappers* (Garden City, NY: Doubleday, 1972); R. Laurence Moore, *In Search of White Crows* (New York: Oxford University Press, 1977); Nancy Rubin Stuart, *The Reluctant Spiritualist: The Life of Maggie Fox* (Orlando, FL: Harcourt, 2005); Barbara Weisberg, *Talking to the Dead: Kate and Maggie Fox and the Rise of Spiritualism* (New York: HarperSanFrancisco, 2004); *ASPR Journal*, "Lily Dale" New York, 1908.

2. There has long been confusion about the ages of the Fox sisters. To the best of our ability, we have determined Margaretta was ten, and Catherine was seven years old at the time of their first spirit rappings on March 31, 1848. Some researchers have speculated that the girls might have been slightly older, and their mother reported their ages to make it seem the girls were younger, and so more publicly appealing. But there is no strong evidence to back up that theory. In any event, depending on the source used, you may find a contradiction in the ages of the two younger Fox sisters. However, it is not critical to their story.

3. Pressing, *Rappings*.

4. Ibid. With regard to Mrs. Margaret Fox, the girls' mother, she was asked to prepare a formal statement of the events of March 31, 1848, as the story gathered more public attention. The only local media at that time were newspapers that carried the story. The Lily Dale publications suggest that Mrs. Fox was willing to make her position publicly known. As a devout Christian, her first thought was that the rappings were something evil or demonic in nature. Mrs. Fox wanted it made clear that she knew nothing about the incident or the source of the noises other than what the girls had told family, friends, and neighbors. Therefore, she wrote about the rappings in her home only after they occurred, and it had become clear the events could not be kept from the public—believers and skeptics alike.

5. The Fox sisters were fortunate to have on their side the well-known editor of the *New York Tribune*, Horace Greeley. No doubt, the favorable publicity they received in his writing about them contributed to the attention they attracted from celebrities of the day, as well as average people.

6. Martin and Birnes, *The Haunting of the Presidents*.

7. Seybert Commission. Wikipedia. http://en.wikipedia.org/wiki/Seybert_Commission.

8. Spiritualism captured much of the nation's attention at a time when many new social and religious movements had taken place, including abolition, the first attempts at woman's rights, and even the birth of new belief systems including Mormonism, Shakers, and the Adventists. Added to that was the new invention: the telegraph (1844), which was the first instant communication, suggesting spirits might also communicate, especially in mesmeric trances. Spiritualism was spurred by the Civil War, which resulted in 600,000 casualties. The idea of talking to dead loved ones killed in the terrible conflagration was especially appealing to the bereaved, at a time when grief counseling as we know it did not exist. Bereaved parents were among the most ardent believers. Clergy could only advise prayers for the dead; mediums claimed to bring messages from them.

Chapter 4: *Spiritualism Spreading like Wildfire*

1. For this chapter, we used many of the same sources as in Chapter Three.

2. *ASPR Journal* (1913).

3. Hauck, *Haunted Places*.

4. Guiley, *Ghosts and Spirits*.

5. Notice that the major newspapers were skeptical or hostile to spiritualism, much as they remain today.

6. *Encyclopedia of Occultism and Parapsychology*.

7. Ibid.

8. Darwin knew his theory was so controversial that he waited many years before releasing it publicly in 1859.

9. The book was initially published in 1988.

10. McHargue, *Facts, Frauds, and Phantasms*, 59, 88.

11. Stuart, *The Reluctant Spiritualist*. Post's book in 1852 was titled *Voices from the Spirit World, Being Communications from Many Spirits*, by the hand of Isaac Post. Joel Martin also interviewed a friend of the Post family descendants who still resides in the Rochester, New York, area.

12. Table tipping became a popular social event throughout the country, as much as it was a spiritualist phenomenon. See McHargue, *Facts, Frauds, and Phantasms*.

13. *Encyclopedia of Occultism and Parapsychology*. (*See* Automatic Writing.)

14. McHargue, *Facts, Frauds, and Phantasms*; Lewis, *Afterlife Beliefs and Phenomena*.

15. Stuart, *The Reluctant Spiritualist*. See also, *Encyclopedia of Occultism and Parapsychology* (See Slate Writing).

16. McHargue, *Facts, Frauds*; Lewis, *Afterlife Beliefs and Phenomena*.

17. *Encyclopedia of Occultism and Parapsychology*; Lewis, *Afterlife Beliefs and Phenomena*; Guiley, *Encyclopedia of Ghosts and Spirits*.

18. Elizabeth Jenkins, *The Shadow and the Light: A Defence of Daniel Dunglas Home the Medium* (London: Hamish Hamilton, 1982), 235–237, 244–245.

19. There are literally thousands of books about Abraham Lincoln. To compile his biographical highlights here we used several: Carl Sandburg's famed books, *Abraham Lincoln: The Prairie Years* and *Abraham Lincoln: The War Years* (New York: Harcourt, 1939). Six volumes; John Alexander, *Ghosts: Washington's Most Famous Ghost Stories* (Washington, D.C.: Washington Books, 1987); Jim Bishop, *The Day Lincoln Was Shot* (New York: Harper & Row, 1964); Betty Boyd Caroli, *First Ladies* (New York: Oxford University Press, 1987); Richard N. Current, *The Lincoln Nobody Knows* (New York: Hill & Wang, 1958); David Herbert Donald, *Lincoln* (New York: Simon & Schuster, 1995); William A. DeGregorio, *The Complete Book of U.S. Presidents* (New York: Dember Books, 1989); Diana Dixon Healy, *America's First Ladies: Private Lives of Presidential Wives* (New York: Atheneum, 1988); Philip B. Kunhardt, Jr., Philip B. Kundhardt III, and Peter W. Kundhardt, *Lincoln: An Illustrated Biography* (New York: Portland House, 1992); Ward Hill Lamon, *The Life of Abraham Lincoln* (Boston: James R. Osgood and Company, 1872); Lloyd Lewis, *The Assassination of Lincoln: History and Myth* (Harcourt, Brace, 1929). Reprinted in 1994. New York: MJF Books; "Lincoln and the Supernatural." http://prairieghosts.com; Michael Lind, *What Lincoln Believed* (New York: Doubleday, 2004); Joel Martin and William J. Birnes, *The Haunting of the Presidents* (New York: Signet, 2003). Joel Martin also visited Springfield, Illinois, where Lincoln lived and practiced law prior to being elected president in 1860. Another visit was to Ford's Theatre in Washington, D.C., where Lincoln was assassinated on April 14, 1865; "Tragedy at Ford's Theatre," TV documentary, WNYC-TV, New York (1966); Nettie Colburn Maynard, *Was Abraham Lincoln a Spiritualist?* (Philadelphia: Rufus C. Hartranft, 1891); Sylvan Muldoon, *Psychic Experiences of Famous People* (The Aries Press, 1947); Barack Obama, "What I See in Lincoln's Eyes." *Time*, July 4, 2005; Ruth Painter Randall, *Mary Lincoln: Biography of a Marriage* (Little, Brown 1953).

20. This quote is attributed to the writings of Lincoln's Springfield law partner, William Herndon.

21. Martin and Birnes, *The Haunting of the Presidents*.

22. There are references to various spiritualist publications. We obtained them from sources, some quite obscure. Many of them contained the word "spiritualist" in their titles. One problem with these periodicals was that some published for only a brief period of time during the nineteenth century, and even changed titles with new ownerships.

22. Martin and Birnes, *The Haunting of the Presidents*; Martin Ebon, *Communicating with the Dead* (New York: New American Library, 1968).

23. All of the discussion about Nettie Colburn Maynard in this book is drawn from Mrs. Maynard's book, *Was Abraham Lincoln a Spiritualist?* (1891). Martin and Birnes worked from a privately owned original copy. Few traditional biographies of Lincoln mention Nettie Colburn, or if they do, it is with a brief or dismissive reference. Unfortunately, Martin and Birnes had written the chapters about the Lincolns before learning about a recent book, *The Psychic Life of Abraham Lincoln* by Susan Martinez (Franklin Lakes, NJ: New Page Books, 2007). However, we recommend the book for those interested in this subject.

24. Maynard, *Was Abraham Lincoln a Spiritualist?*

25. Ibid.

26. Ibid.

27. Ibid.

28. Ibid. The question of how much of an adherent President Lincoln was to spiritualism may never be fully answered. Very few so-called traditional or academically oriented historians and authors have long steered clear of the question as if it is beneath them. However, evidence suggests that Lincoln was, indeed, our most psychic president. To what extent spiritualism may have influenced his presidential and personal decisions is unclear. It is a worthy subject for open-minded historians to consider.

29. An account of Lincoln's dream premonitions and visions are told in *Ghosts and Haunts of the Civil War* by Christopher K. Coleman (New York: Barnes & Noble, 2003), 133–143. Also see Martin and Birnes, *The Haunting of the Presidents*; Martin Ebon, *Communicating with the Dead*; Sylvan Muldoon, *Psychic Experiences of Famous People*; Robert L. Van de Castle, *Our Dreaming Mind* (New York: Ballantine Books, 1994), 30.

30. Lincoln's dream premonition of his own assassination is generally considered the most famous of its kind to ever be experienced by a U.S. president. Typically, skeptics dismiss it, despite many witness accounts that Lincoln had a genuine prophetic dream. Lincoln, a fatalist, ignored the dream's warning and pleas from many close to him to exercise caution. See Muldoon, *Psychic Experiences of Famous People*, 155.

31. Coleman, *Ghosts and Haunts of the Civil War*; Martin and Birnes, *The Haunting of the Presidents*.

32. Bishop, *The Day Lincoln Was Shot*.

33. Ruth Painter Randall, *Mary Lincoln: Biography of a Marriage* (Boston: Little, Brown, 1953); Barbara Weisberg, *Talking to the Dead*, 206; Diana Dixon Healy, *America's First Ladies*.

34. *The Encyclopedia of Occultism and Parapsychology*, 891; Guiley, *The Encyclopedia of Ghosts and Spirits*, 314; *Into the Unknown*, 174, 227, 245; Lewis, *Encyclopedia of Afterlife Beliefs and Phenomena*, 334–335; Nandor Fodor, *Between Two Worlds*; Clement Cheroux, Andreas Fischer, and others, *The Perfect Medium: Photography and the Occult* (New Haven and London: Yale University Press, 2005). An exhibition with the same title, "The Perfect Medium: Photography and the Occult," Metropolitan Museum of Art, New York, September–December 2005.

Chapter 5: *Home and the Power of Levitation: A Remarkable Demonstration*

1. McHargue, *Facts, Frauds, Phantasms*, 92.
2. Gordon Stein, Ph.D., *The Sorcerer of Kings: The Case of Daniel Dunglas Home and William Crookes* (Buffalo, NY: Prometheus Books, 1993); Elizabeth Jenkins, *The Shadow and the Light: A Defence of Daniel Dunglas Home the Medium*; Harry Houdini, *A Magician Among the Spirits* (New York: Harper & Brothers, 1924), reprinted by Arno Press, 1972; Sylvan Muldoon, *Psychic Experiences of Famous People*, 54–57; Rogo, *Miracles* (see Levitation); *Encyclopedia of Occultism and Parapsychology* (Levitation, 749–758).
3. Stein, *The Sorcerer of Kings*, 72. Brewster was an obdurate skeptic of psychical events. When news that he'd been impressed by Home became public, Brewster wrote a letter to a London newspaper (1855) denying he'd been impressed with Home's demonstration. The publicity worked to Home's advantage. Home's book, *Incidents in My Life* (1863), chided Brewster's about-face.
4. *D. D. Home: His Life and Mission*, written by his wife was originally published in 1888.
5. The popular British poet Elizabeth Barrett Browning was impressed by D. D. Home's mediumship and believed in spiritualism. Her husband, the well-known poet Robert Browning, was hostile. There has long been speculation that Robert Browning actually despised Home because he believed the medium was a homosexual. He may also have been jealous of his wife Elizabeth's attention to Home's performances.
6. McHargue, *Facts, Frauds, and Phantasms*, 96.
7. Ibid, 97.
8. During the nineteenth century, media consisted entirely of newspapers, magazines, and other periodicals. Major publications were national magazines or large city newspapers. Home made good copy for reporters who often played fast and loose with the facts. Thus, outlandish tabloid claims could be made. Other publications, such as *The New York Times*, remained highly skeptical about anything involving spiritualism, understating even Home's inexplicable psychical demonstrations.

9. The respected scientist, Faraday, was a skeptic of spiritualism and psychical phenomena, branding it "superstition." Between 1860 and 1862, Faraday, then in his seventies, undertook his own investigation of the supernatural. It was within that period Faraday was invited to meet and observe D. D. Home. However, no séance took place because of Faraday's close-mindedness and unreasonable demands for conditions that no medium could meet. Elizabeth Jenkins, *The Shadow and the Light*, 177–178.

10. Elizabeth Jenkins, *The Shadow and the Light*; McHargue, *Facts, Frauds, and Phantasms*; Stein, *The Sorcerer of Kings*, 93–98, subtitled "D. D. Home and William Crookes." Some sources cite 1869 as the beginning of Crookes's tests of Home. However, several give a later date because Crookes's first attempt to present his findings about Home to the Royal Society was in 1871, the same year he published them in the *Quarterly Journal of Science*. Crookes, a believer in spiritualism, found a warmer reception in the 1880s when the Society for Psychical Research (SPR) was founded. For this chapter, we also used materials from SPR journals, as well as the books cited above.

11. *Encyclopedia of Occultism and Parapsychology*, 1071; Frank Podmore, *The Never Spiritualism*, reprinted by Arno Press, 1975; Podmore, *Mediums of the Nineteenth Century*, reprinted by University Books, 1963; McHargue, *Facts, Frauds, and Phantasms*, 100–103, 106–108; Stein, *The Sorcerer of Kings*, 17, 88, 97, 105.

Chapter 6: *Women at the Séance Table*

1. Several books compiled the text of this chapter, including Ann Braude, *Radical Spirits*; R. Laurence Moore, *In Search of White Crows*; Barbara Weisberg, *Talking to the Dead*; Mary Gabriel, *Notorious Victoria*; Nettie Colburn Maynard, *Was Abraham Lincoln a Spiritualist?*; Nancy Rubin Stuart, *The Reluctant Spiritualist: The Life of Maggie Fox*; Diana Dixon Healy, *America's First Ladies*; Barbara Goldsmith, *Other Powers: The Age of Suffrage, Spiritualism, and the Scandalous Victoria Woodhull* (New York: Knopf, 1998). This chapter should be read with an understanding of the era in which it took place: the nineteenth-century attitude toward women can barely be imagined from today's perspective. Mediumship offered one of the few opportunities for women to earn a living, albeit modest, with even a modicum of independence and control.

2. Significantly, at the time, the efforts for women's rights aligned with spiritualism. See Ann Braude, *Radical Spirits: Spiritualism and Women's Rights in Nineteenth Century America* (Boston: Beacon Press, 1989).

3. Ibid, 30, 37–38.

4. Maynard, *Was Abraham Lincoln a Spiritualist?*

5. Moore, *In Search of White Crows*.

6. Ibid.

7. The statement reads somewhat similar to present attitudes among some.

8. Both Emma Hardinge and Cora Richmond are discussed throughout Ann Braude's *Radical Spirits*.

9. Braude, *Radical Spirits*, 27. Tallmadge, an early convert to spiritualism during the 1850s, had been a U. S. senator (1833–34), then governor (1844–46). See also Stuart, *The Reluctant Spiritualist*.

10. Braude, *Radical Spirits*, 85. Braude's quote of medium Elizabeth Doten was taken from a graduate thesis written by Mary Farrell Bedarnowski in 1969. Bedarnowski went on to write articles about women and spiritualism.

11. Ibid.

12. Susan B. Anthony died in 1906. Her passing inspired the medium Elizabeth Watson to write the poem from which we quoted. It originally appeared in *The Life and Work of Susan B. Anthony* by Ida Harper, published in 1898.

13. Story of Achsa Sprague provided to authors (Martin and Birnes) by the Vermont Historical Society. Sprague, who lived in Vermont, was born around 1828. Sprague's poem "The Angel's Visit" was included with other materials about her.

14. A notable and controversial nineteenth-century suffrage activist and spiritualist, two excellent books about Woodhull are *Notorious Victoria* by Mary Gabriel, and *Other Powers* by Barbara Goldsmith. Both were used for this section about Woodhull who, in 1872, became the first woman to run for president of the United States.

15. Blavatsky was, arguably, the most fascinating woman of the spiritualist era—controversial, influential, and charismatic. She was the founder of the Theosophical movement. The sources for the portion of the book about her included a wealth of material. Her name and her contributions appear in a huge number of historical works about nineteenth-century spiritualism, as well as the accusations that her mediumship was fraudulent. Nonetheless, she has had lasting influence, especially bringing to America, teachings from Hindu philosophy.

We were able to locate many writings published by the Theosophical Society. One source was *Isis Unveiled*, a large, often unwieldy two volumes, written by Blavatsky and first published in 1877. She claimed "Masters of Wisdom" dictated the 1,200-page tome to her from the spirit world. Another work by her was *The Key to Theosophy*, reprinted in 1972. Other sources we used were the *Encyclopedia of Occultism and Parapsychology*; Peter Washington, *Madame Blavatsky's Baboon*; *Into the Unknown*; James R. Lewis, *Afterlife Beliefs*. Interviews conducted by Joel Martin with several self-described Theosophists.

16. *Encyclopedia of Occultism and Parapsychology*; Hauck, *The National Directory of Haunted Places*; Roger Somerlott, *Here, Mr. Splitfoot*.

17. Richard Hodgson, "Report on Phenomena Connected with Theosophy." Proceedings of the Society for Psychical Research (1885), Volume 3.

Chapter 7: *From Séance to Science*

1. The famed "White Crow" quote was made by William James in his address upon being named president of the newly formed American Society for Psychical Research (ASPR).

Proceedings of the ASPR 1 (July 1886). To this day, it is a well-known phrase within parapsychology. The title of the book *In Search of White Crows* by R. Laurence Moore (1977) is but one example.

2. R. G. Pressing, *Rappings That Startled the World: Facts About the Fox Sisters* (Lily Dale, New York) (Undated pamphlet).

3. Ibid.

4. *Encyclopedia of Occultism and Parapsychology*, 569–570.

5. Linda Simon, *Dark Light* (New York: Harcourt, 2004), 15.

6. Notable were Poe's short stories, "Mesmeric Revelation," and "A Tale of the Ragged Mountains." Poe wrote both in 1844.

7. McHargue, *Phantasms*, 53–57; *Encyclopedia of Occultism and Parapsychology*, 1215–1216.

8. Britten's book *Modern American Spiritualism* became an "important source for understanding the origin and spread of the movement worldwide," noted the *Encyclopedia of Occultism and Parapsychology*, 178.

9. Professor Henry Sidgwick's exact words are from his presidential address to the newly formed SPR, July 17, 1882.

10. *Phantasms of the Living* was published in 1886.

11. *SPR Journal* is officially known as the *Journal of the Society for Psychical Research*. It was initially known as *Proceedings of the Society for Psychical Research*.

12. It was published in 1950.

13. John G. Fuller wrote *The Airmen Who Would Not Die* in 1979. In it he refers to Sir Oliver Lodge's experiences.

14. Broughton made his comments in *Parapsychology: the Controversial Science* (1991).

15. Later, we will more fully discuss Dr. Rhine's work in parapsychology research. He was especially interested in extra-sensory perception (ESP), psychokinesis (PK), and deathbed visions. J. B. Rhine (1895–1980) holds a prominent place as an innovator in the research of parapsychology at Duke University in North Carolina, where he cofounded the famed Parapsychology Laboratory. With his wife, Louise, throughout the 1930s, he conducted extensive experiments of psychic phenomena by applying strict scientific principles. One important goal was to determine if extrasensory perception (ESP) could be statistically measured. ESP included telepathy and clairvoyance. The goal was to determine if simple shapes on cards could be transmitted from sender to receiver. Later, the Rhines tested psychokinesis (PK), the power of the human mind to cause objects to move. The Rhines brought psychic testing into a laboratory setting, a great achievement. One book the authors used for research was J. B. Rhine, *New Frontiers of the Mind* (New York: Farrar and Rinehart, 1939).

16. Simon, *Dark Light*.

17. Upton Sinclair, *Mental Radio*.

18. Laile Bartlett, *PSI Trek* (New York: McGraw-Hill Company, 1981).

Chapter 8: *A Magician Among the Spirits*

1. Sir Arthur Conan Doyle was a passionate defender of spiritualism. Any criticism from skeptics or debunkers was anathema to him.

2. The authors of *We Don't Die* are Joel Martin and Patricia Romanowski.

3. Arthur Ford's book referred to in this chapter is *Unknown But Known*.

4. This chapter was compiled from research drawn from several books, including Ronald Pearsall, *Conan Doyle: A Biographical Solution* (New York: St. Martin's Press, 1977); Andrew Lycett, *The Man Who Created Sherlock Holmes: The Life and Times of Sir Arthur Conan Doyle* (London: Wiedenfeld & Nicolson, 2007); Daniel Stashower, *Tellers of Tales: The Life of Arthur Conan Doyle* (New York: Henry Holt and Co., 1999); Russell Miller, *The Adventures of Arthur Conan Doyle: A Biography* (New York: Thomas Dunne Books, 2008); and Harry Houdini, *A Magician Among the Spirits* (Harper, 1924).

Books

Ahlstrom, Sydney E. *A Religious History of the American People*. New Haven, CT: Yale University Press, 1972.

Alexander, Dominic. *Spellbound: From Ancient Gods to Modern Merlins: A Time Tour of Myth and Magic*. Pleasantville, NY: Reader's Digest, 2002.

Alexander, John. *Ghosts: Washington Revisited*. Atglen, PA: Schiffer, 1998.

———. *Washington's Most Famous Ghost Stories*. Washington, DC: Washington Books, 1975.

Ambrosini, Maria Luisa, and Mary Willis. *The Secrets of the Vatican*. New York: Barnes & Noble Books, 1969.

Anderson, Jean. *The Haunting of America*. Boston: Houghton Mifflin, 1973.

Aronson, Marc. *Witch-hunt Mysteries of the Salem Witch Trials*. New York: Atheneum Books, 2003.

Baigent, Michael, and Richard Leigh. *The Temple and the Lodge*. New York: Arcade Publishing Company, 1989.

Bartlett, Laile. *PSI Trek*. New York: McGraw-Hill Company, 1981.

Baumer, Franklin L. *Religion and the Rise of Scepticism*. New York: Harcourt, Brace & Company, 1960.

Berlitz, Charles. *The Mystery of Atlantis*. New York: Grosset and Dunlap, 1969.

———. *Atlantis the Eighth Continent*. New York: G. P. Putnam's Sons, 1984.

Berry, Gerald L. *Religions of the World*. New York: Barnes & Noble, Inc., 1947.

Besterman, Theodore. *Collected Papers on the Paranormal*. New York: Garrett Publications, 1968.

Bishop, Jim. *The Day Lincoln Was Shot*. New York: Harper & Row, 1955.

———. *The Day Christ Died*. New York: Harper & Row, 1957.

Blavatsky, Helena Petrovna. *Isis Unveiled*. 2 vol. New York: J. W. Bouton, 1877.

Bliven, Bruce, Jr. *The American Revolution: 1760–1783*. New York: Random House, 1958.

Blumrich, Josef F. *The Spaceships of Ezekiel*. New York: Bantam Books, 1974.

Bond, Bryce. *A Touch of Alchemy: The Wisdom of Druid Chief Thomas Maughan*. New York: Parabond Productions, 1982.

Booth, Sally Smith. *The Witches of Early America*. New York: Hastings House, 1975.

Bosworth, F. F. *Christ, the Healer*. Old Tappan, NJ: F. H. Revell Company, 1974. (Originally printed in 1924.)

Bourne, Russell. *Gods of War, Gods of Peace: How the Meeting of Natives and Colonial Religions Shaped Early America*. New York: Harcourt, 2002.

Boyd, Gregory A., and Paul Rhodes Eddy. *Lord or Legend: Wrestling with the Jesus Dilemma*. Grand Rapids, MI: Baker Books, 2007.

Boyer, Paul, and Stephen Nissenbaum. *Salem Possessed*. Cambridge, MA: Harvard University Press, 1974.

Brandon, Ruth. *The Spiritualists: The Passion for the Occult in the Nineteenth and Twentieth Centuries*. New York: Alfred Knopf, 1983.

Brands, H. W. *The First American: The Life and Times of Benjamin Franklin*. New York: Doubleday, 2000.

Braude, Anne. *Radical Spirits: Spiritualism and Women's Rights in Nineteenth Century America*. Boston: Beacon Press, 1989.

Brodie, Fawn M. *Thomas Jefferson: An Intimate History*. New York: W. W. Norton, 1974.

Broughton, Richard S. *Parapsychology: The Controversial Science*. New York: Ballantine, 1991.

Brown, Slater. *The Heyday of Spiritualism*. New York: Hawthorn Books, 1970.

Buckland, Raymond. *Doors to Other Worlds*. St. Paul, MN: Llewellyn, 1993.

Burr, George Lincoln, ed. *Narratives of the Witchcraft Cases 1648–1706*. New York: Barnes & Noble, 1966.

Butler, Trent C. *Holman Bible Dictionary*. Tennessee: Holman Bible Publishers, 1991.

Carlson, Laurie Winn. *A Fever in Salem*. Chicago: Ivan Dee, 1999.

Carrington, Hereward and Nandor Fodor. *Haunted People: Story of the Poltergeist Down the Centuries*. New York: E. P. Dutton, 1951.

Carver, Mark C. *Secret Ritual and Manhood in Victorian America*. New Haven, CT: Yale University Press, 1989.

Cavendish, Marshall, ed. *Man, Myth and Magic*. North Bellmore, NY: Cavendish, 1995.

Chatelain, Maurice. *Our Ancestors Came from Outer Space*. New York: Dell Books, 1975.

Cheetham, Erika. *The Man Who Saw Tomorrow: The Prophecies of Nostradamus*. New York: Berkley Books, 1973.

Cheroux, Clement, Andreas Fisher, Pierre Apraxine, Denis Canguilhem, and Sophie Schmit. *The Perfect Medium: Photography and the Occult*. New Haven, CT: Yale University, 2005.

Christopher, Milbourne. *Houdini: A Pictorial Life*. New York: Thomas Y. Crowell, 1976.

Cohen, Daniel. *The Encyclopedia of the Strange*. New York: Avon Books, 1985.

———. *Civil War Ghosts*. New York: Scholastic Books, 1999.

Cohen, I. Bernard. *Benjamin Franklin: Scientist and Statesman*. New York: Charles Scribner's Sons, 1975.

Cohen, I. L. *The Secret of Stonehenge*. New York: New Research Publications, 1977.

Coleman, Christopher K. *Ghosts and Haunts of the Civil War*. New York: Barnes & Noble, 2003.

Collins, David R. *Shattered Dreams: The Story of Mary Todd Lincoln*. Greensboro, NC: Morgan Reynolds, 1994.

Cooper, Margaret. *Exploring the Ice Age*. New York: Atheneum Books, 2001.

Current, Richard N. *The Lincoln Nobody Knows*. New York: Hill and Wang, 1958.

Daraul, Arkon. *A History of Secret Societies*. New York: Citadel Press, 1962.

Deen, Edith. *All the Women of the Bible*. New York: HarperCollins, 1955.

Dickinson, Alice. *The Salem Witchcraft Delusion: 1692*. New York: Franklin Watts, 1974.

Donald, David Herbert. *Lincoln*. London: Johnathan Cape, 1995.

Donnelly, Ignatius. *Atlantis: The Antediluvian World*. New York: Gramercy, 1949. (Originally published by Harper's, 1882.)

Dreller, Larry. *Beginner's Guide to Mediumship*. York Beach, ME: Samuel Weiser, 1997.

Ebon, Martin. *Communicating with the Dead*. New York: New American Library, 1981.

———. *Miracles*. New York: Signet Books, 1981.

Edmonds, I. G. *D. D. Home: The Man Who Talked with Ghosts*. Nashville, TN: Thomas Nelson, Inc., 1978.

Eliot, Alexander. *Abraham Lincoln: An Illustrated Biography*. London: Bison Books, Ltd., 1985.

Ellis, Joseph J. *American Sphinx: The Character of Thomas Jefferson*. New York: Vintage Books, 1998.

———. *Passionate Sage: The Character and Legacy of John Adams*. New York: W. W. Norton, 1993.

———. *Founding Brothers: The Revolutionary Generation*. New York: Vintage Books, 2000.

———. *His Excellency George Washington*. New York: Alfred A. Knopf, 2004.

Elwood, Ann. *Weird and Mysterious*. New York: Globe Books, 1979.

Epstein, Perle. *The Way of Witches*. New York: Doubleday, 1972.

Estabrooks, G. H. *Hypnotism*. New York: E. P. Dutton, 1943, 1957.

Evans-Pritchard, E. E. *Theories of Primitive Religion*. London: Oxford University Press, 1965.

Finnegan, Jack. *The Archeology of World Religions*. Princeton, NJ: Princeton University Press, 1952.

Fisher, Paul A. *Behind the Lodge Door*. Illinois: Tan Books, 1988.

Fitzsimmons, Raymund. *Death and the Magician: The Mysteries of Houdini*. New York: Atheneum, 1981.

Flexner, James Thomas. *George Washington in the American Revolution*. Boston: Little, Brown and Company, 1967.

———. *Washington: The Indispensable Man*. Boston: Little, Brown and Company, 1969.

Fodor, Nandor. *Between Two Worlds*. New York: Parker Publishing Company, 1964.

Ford, Arthur. *Unknown But Known*. New York: Signet Books, 1968.

Freeman, Douglas Southall. *George Washington: A Biography, Leader of the Revolution*. Vol. 4. New York: Charles Scribner's Sons, 1951.

Fuller, Edmund, and David E. Green. *God in the White House: The Faiths of American Presidents*. New York: Crown, 1968.

Fuller, John G. *The Airmen Who Would Not Die*. New York: G. P. Putnam's Sons, 1979.

Fuller, Robert C. *Mesmerism and the American Cure of Souls*. Philadelphia: University of Pennsylvania Press, 1982.

Gabriel, Mary. *Notorious Victoria: The Life of Victoria: The Life of Victoria Woodhull, Uncensored*. Chapel Hill: NC: Algonquin Books, 1998.

————. *Religious Revolutionaries*. New York: Palgrave Macmillan, 2004.

Gauld, Alan. *The Founders of Psychical Research*. New York: Schocken Books, 1968.

Gaustad, Edwin, and Leigh Schmidt. *The Religious History of America*. New York: HarperSanFrancisco, 2002.

Gleick, James. *Isaac Newton*. New York: Pantheon Books, 2003.

Gleiser, Marcello. *The Prophet and the Astronomer*. New York: W. W. Norton, 2001.

Godbeer, Richard. *Escaping Salem: The Other Witch Hunt of 1692*. New York: Oxford University Press, 2005.

Goldsmith, Barbara. *Other Powers: The Age of Suffrage, Spiritualism, and the Scandalous Victoria Woodhull*. New York: Alfred A. Knopf, 1998.

Goldstein, Thomas. *Dawn of Modern Science*. Boston: Houghton Mifflin, 1980.

Goodman, Jeffrey. *Psychic Archaeology: Time Machine to the Past*. New York: Berkley Books, 1978.

Gordon, Mary. *Joan of Arc*. New York: Viking Books, 2000.

Grant, Neil. *How They Lived: The Egyptians*. New York: Mallard Press, 1990.

Green, Ruth. *The Born Again Skeptic's Guide to the Bible*. Wisconsin: Freedom From Religion Foundation, 1979.

Greenhouse, Herbert. *The Book of Psychic Knowledge*. New York: Taplinger Publishing Company, 1973.

Guiley, Rosemary Ellen. *Atlas of the Mysteries in North America*. New York: Facts on File, 1995.

————. *The Encyclopedia of Ghosts and Spirits*. New York: Facts on File, 1992.

Haberstein, Robert W., and William M. Lamers. *Funeral Customs the World Over*. Wisconsin: Bulfin Printers, 1963.

Hamilton, Margaret Lillian. *Is Survival a Fact?* London: Psychic Press, 1969.

Hampshire, Stuart. *The Age of Reason*. Boston: Houghton Mifflin, 1957.

Hansen, Chadwick. *Witchcraft at Salem*. New York: George Braziller, Inc., 1969.

Harpur, James. *The Miracles of Jesus*. Pleasantville, NY: Reader's Digest Association, 1997.

Harrison, Maureen, and Steve Gilbert, eds. *Abraham Lincoln: Word for Word*. San Diego, CA: Excellent Books, 1994.

Harvey, Andrew, ed. *Teachings of the Christian Mystics*. Boston: Shambhala, 1998.

Harwell, Richard, ed. *Washington*. New York: Charles Scribner's Sons, 1968.

Haskins, James, and Kathleen Benson. *Bound for America: The Forced Migration of Africans to the New World*. New York: Lothrop, Lee and Shepard Books, 1999.

Hauck, Dennis William. *Haunted Places: The National Directory*. New York: Penguin Books, 1996.

Heaney, John J. *The Sacred and the Psychic*. New York: Paulist Press, 1984.

Heckler-Feltz, Cheryl. *Heart and Soul of the Nation: How the First Ladies Changed America*. New York: Doubleday, 1997.

Herndon, William H., and Jesse W. Welk. *Herdon's Life of Lincoln*. Cleveland, OH: World Publishing Company, 1930. (Originally written in 1888.)

Hill, Brian. *Gates of Horn and Ivory*. New York: Taplinger Publishing, 1967.

Hill, Frances. *A Delusion of Satan: The Story of the Salem Witch Trials*. New York: Doubleday, 1995.

Hoare, Rodney. *The Turin Shroud Is Genuine*. New York: Barnes & Noble, 1995.

Holmes, A. Campbell. *The Facts of Psychic Science and Philosophy*. London: Kegan Paul, Trench, Trubner and Company, 1925.

Holzer, Hans. *Ghosts of New England*. Dublin, NH: Yankee Books, 1989.

———. *The Ghosts That Walk Washington*. Garden City, NY: Doubleday, 1971.

Houdini, Harry. *A Magician Among the Spirits*. New York: Arno Press, 1972. (Originally published in 1924.)

House, Brant. *Strange Powers of Unusual People*. New York: Ace Books, 1963.

Howard, Michael. *The Occult Conspiracy*. Vermont: Destiny Books, 1989.

Hudson, Winthrop S. *Religion in America*. New York: Macmillan Press, 1987.

Hutchison, William R. *Religious Pluralism in America*. New Haven, CT: Yale University Press, 2003.

Isaacson, Walter. *Benjamin Franklin: An American Life*. New York: Simon & Schuster, 2003.

Jackson, Herbert G. *The Spirit Rappers*. Garden City, NY: Doubleday, 1972.

James, E. O. *The Ancient Gods*. G. P. Putnam's Sons, 1960.

———. *Prehistoric Religion*. New York: Frederick A. Praeger, 1957.

Jenkins, Elizabeth. *The Shadow and the Light: A Defence of Daniel Dunglas Home the Medium*. London: Hamish Hamilton, Ltd., 1982.

Kaczmarek, Dale. *National Register of Haunted Locations*. Chicago: Ghost Research Society (booklet).

Kallen, Stuart A. *Pyramids*. San Diego, CA: Lucent Books, 2002.

———. *Witches*. San Diego, CA: Lucent Books, 2000.

Kaplan, Fred. *The Singular Mark Twain*. New York: Doubleday, 2003.

Karlesen, Carol F. *The Devil in the Shape of a Woman*. New York: W. W. Norton, 1987.

Kerr, Howard. *Mediums and Spirits*. Urbana, IL: University of Illinois Press, 1972.

Kerr, Howard, and Charles L. Crow. *The Occult in America*. Urbana, IL: University of Illinois Press, 1983.

Kaye, Marvin. *Haunted America*. New York: Barnes & Noble Books, 1990.

Kling, David W. *The Bible in History*. New York: Oxford University Press, 2004.

Koenig-Brickner. *365 Saints: Your Daily Guide to the Wisdom and Wonders of Their Lives*. New York: HarperSanFrancisco, 1995.

Kramer, Samuel Noah. *History Begins at Sumer*. Philadelphia: The University of Pennsylvania Press, 1981.

Kunhardt, Philip B., Jr., Philip B. Kunhardt III, and Peter W. Kunhardt. *Lincoln: An Illustrated Biography*. New York: Portland House, 1992.

Landis, Benson. *World Religions*. New York: E. P. Dutton and Company, 1965.

Landsburg, Alan, and Sally Landsburg. *In Search of Ancient Mysteries*. New York: Bantam, 1974.

Landua, Elaine. *The Sumerians*. Brookfield, CT: Milbrook Press, 1997.

Lassieur, Allison. *The Ancient Egyptians*. San Diego, CA: Lucent Books, 2001.

Lee, Tanja. *Benjamin Franklin*. San Diego, CA: Greenhaven Press, 2002.

Lellenberg, Jon, Daniel Stashower, and Charles Foley. *Arthur Conan Doyle: A Life in Letters*. New York: The Penguin Press, 2007.

Leone, Mark P. *Roots of Modern Mormonism*. Cambridge, MA: Harvard University Press, 1979.

Leoni, Edgar. *Nostradamus and His Prophecies*. New York: Bell Publishers, 1982.

Lewis, James R. *Encyclopedia of Afterlife Beliefs and Phenomena*. Detroit: Gale, 1994.

Lewis, Lloyd. *The Assassination of Lincoln: History and Myth*. New York: MJF Books, 1957. (Originally published in 1929 by Harcourt, Brace & Company.)

Liljencrants, Johan. *Spiritism and Religion: Can You Talk to the Dead?* New York: Devin-Adair Company, 1918.

Lodge, Sir Oliver. *Raymond; or, Life and Death*. London: Methuen, 1916.

Lycett, Andrew. *The Man Who Created Sherlock Holmes: The Life and Times of Sir Arthur Conan Doyle*. New York: Free Press, 2007.

MacNulty, W. Kirk. *Freemasonry: A Journey Through Ritual and Symbol*. New York and London: Thames and Hudson, 1991.

Magill, Frank, ed. *Great Events from History: American Series*. Englewood Cliffs, NJ: Salem Press, 1975.

Malbrough, Ray T. *The Magical Powers of the Saints*. St. Paul, MN: Llewellyn, 1998.

Marion, Jim. *The Death of the Mythic God*. Charlottesville, VA: Hampton Roads Publishing, 2004.

Markowitz, Harvey. *American Indian Biographies*. Pasadena, CA: Salem Press, 1999.

Marrs, Jim. *Rule by Secrecy: The Hidden History That Connects the Trilateral Commission, the Freemasons, and the Great Pyramids*. Perennial, 2000.

Martin, Joel, and William J. Birnes. *The Haunting of the Presidents: A Paranormal History of the U.S. Presidency*. New York: Signet Books, 2003.

Martinez, Susan B. *The Psychic Life of Abraham Lincoln*. Franklin Lakes, NJ: New Page Books, 2007.

Mather, Cotton. *Memorable Provinces, Relating to Witchcraft and Possessions*.

Maxwell-Stuart, P. G. *Witchcraft in Europe and the New World, 1400–1800*. New York: Palgrave, 2001.

Maynard, Nettie Colburn. *Was Abraham Lincoln A Spiritualist?* Philadelphia: Rufus C. Hartranft, 1891.

McCaffery, John. *Tales of Padre Pio: The Friar of San Giovanni*. New York: Image Books/Doubleday, 1981.

McCollister, John. *So Help Me God: The Faith of America's Presidents*. Louisville, Kentucky: John Knox Press, 1991.

McDannell, Colleen, and Bernhard Lang. *Heaven: A History*. New Haven, CT: Yale University Press, 1988.

McHargue, Georgess. *Facts, Frauds, and Phantasms: A Survey of the Spiritualist Movement*. Garden City, New York: Doubleday, 1972.

McNeill, W. H. *The Rise of the West: A History of the Human Community*. New York: New American Library, 1963.

Meyer, Marvin. *The Gnostic Discoveries*. New York: HarperSanFrancisco, 2005.

Miller, Karen, ed. *Paranormal Phenomena: Opposing Viewpoints*. Detroit: Greenhaven Press, 2008.

Monahan, Brent, ed. *The Bell Witch: An American Haunting*. New York: St. Martin's, 1977.

Montgomery, Ruth. *A Search for the Truth*. New York: Fawcett Crest, 1966.

———. *The World Before*. New York: Fawcett Crest, 1976.

Moore, R. Lawrence. *In Search of White Crows*. New York: Oxford University Press, 1977.

Muldoon, Sylvan. *Psychic Experiences of Famous People*. Chicago: Aries Press, 1947.

Murphy, Gardner. *Challenge of Psychical Research: A Primer of Parapsychology*. New York: Harper & Brothers, 1961.

Myers, F. W. H. *Human Personality and Its Survival of Bodily Death*. New Hyde Park, NY: University Books, 1961.

Nardo, Don. *Empires of Mesopotamia*. San Diego: Lucent Books, 2001.

———. *Living in Ancient Egypt*. Detroit: Greenhaven Press, 2004.

———. *Living in Ancient Greece*. Detroit: Greenhaven Press, 2004.

———. *Living in Ancient Rome*. San Diego: Lucent Books, 2001.

Neame, Alan. *The Happening at Lourdes*. New York: Simon & Schuster, 1967.

Nelson, Eric. *The Complete Idiot's Guide to the Roman Empire*. IN: Alpha Books, 2002.

Nesbitt, Mark. *Ghosts of Gettysburg*. Gettysburg, PA: Thomas Publications, 1991.

Nicolson, Adam. *God's Secretaries: The Making of the King James Bible*. New York: HarperCollins, 2003.

Norman, Michael and Beth Scott. *Haunted America*. New York: TOR, 1994.

————. *Historic Haunted America*. New York: TOR 1995.

Norton, Mary Beth. *In the Devil's Snare: The Salem Witchcraft Crisis of 1692*. New York: Alfred A. Knopf, 2002.

O'Neill, Terry, and Stacey L. Tripp. *Paranormal Phenomena: Opposing Viewpoints*. San Diego: Greenhaven Press, 1991.

Osofsky, Gilbert. *Harlem: The Making of a Ghetto: Negro New York, 1890–1930*. New York: Harper & Row, c. 1963.

Ostendorf, Lloyd, ed. *Lincoln's Unknown Private Life*. Mamaroneck, New York: Hastings House, 1993.

Padover, Saul K., ed. *A Jefferson Profile as Revealed in His Letters*. New York: John Day, 1956.

Parker, Derek, and Julia Parker. *Atlas of the Supernatural*. New York: Prentice-Hall, 1990.

Parker, Steve. *Benjamin Franklin and Electricity*. New York: Chelsea House, 1995.

Pauli, Hertha. *Bernadette and the Lady*. New York: Vision Books, 1956.

Pearsall, Ronald. *Conan Doyle: A Biographical Solution*. New York: St. Martin's, 1977.

Pellegrino, Charles. *Unearthing Atlantis: An Archaeological Odyssey*. New York: Random House, 1991.

Perret, Geoffrey. *Lincoln's War*. New York: Random House, 2004.

Perrin, Norman. *Rediscovering the Teaching of Jesus*. New York: Harper & Row, 1967.

Perry, Michael. *Psychic Studies: A Christian's View*. Wellingborough, Northamptonshire, UK: The Aquarian Press, 1984.

Picknett, Lynn, and Clive Prince. *Turin Shroud*. New York: HarperCollins, 1994.

Poe, Edgar Allan. *Tales of Horror and Suspense*. New York: Dover Publications, 2003.

Pollack, Susan. *Ancient Mesopotamia*. Cambridge: Cambridge University Press, 1999.

Press, Skip. *The Importance of Mark Twain*. San Diego: Lucent Books, 1994.

Pressing, R. G. *Rappings that Startled the World: Facts About the Fox Sisters*. Lily Dale, NY: Dale News (pamphlet).

Randall, Ruth Painter. *Mary Lincoln: Biography of a Mary Lincoln*. Boston: Little, Brown and Company, 1953.

Rawlings, Maurice. *Beyond Death's Door*. New York: Bantam Books, 1978.

Reader's Digest Association. *Into the Unknown*. Pleasantville, NY: Reader's Digest Association, 1981.

————. *Mysteries of the Unexplained*. Pleasantville, NY: Reader's Digest Association, 1982.

Redondi, Pietro. *Galileo Heretic*. Princeton, NJ: Princeton University Press, 1987.

Reichblum, Charles. *Strange and Fascinating Facts About the Presidents*. New York: Black Dog and Leventhal, 2004.

Richmond, Lewis. *Healing Lazarus*. New York: Simon & Schuster, 2002.

Ridley, Jasper. *The Freemasons: A History of the World's Most Powerful Secret Society*. New York: Arcade Publishing Company, 1999.

Rinn, Joseph F. *Sixty Years of Psychical Research*. New York: Truth Seeker Company, 1950.

Riva, Anna. *Devotions to the Saints*. Toluca Lake, CA: International Imports, 1982.

Roach, Marilynne K. *In the Days of the Salem Witchcraft Trials*. Boston: Houghton Mifflin, 1996.

Robb, Stewart. *Prophecies on World Events by Nostradamus*. New York: Ace Books, 1961.

Roberts, Henry C. *The Complete Prophecies of Nostradamus*. Oyster Bay, NY: Nostradamus Company, 1947. (Republished in 1982.)

Roberts, Nancy. *Civil War Ghosts and Legends*. Columbia, SC: University of South Carolina Press, 1992.

———. *Southern Ghosts*. New York: Doubleday & Company, 1979.

Robinson, John J. *Born in Blood: The Lost Secrets of Freemasonry*. New York: M. Evans and Company, 1989.

Robinson, Lynn A., and LaVonne Carlson-Finnerty. *The Complete Idiot's Guide to Being Psychic*. New York: Alpha Books, 1999.

Robinson, Lytle. *The Origin and Destiny of Man*. New York: Berkley Books, 1972.

Rogo, D. Scott. *Miracles: A Parascientific Inquiry into Wondrous Phenomena*. New York: Dial Press, 1982.

Ross, Nancy Wilson. *Joan of Arc*. New York: Random House, 1953.

Rossi, Renzo, and Andrea Due. *The First People*. New York: Macmillan Library Reference USA, 1996.

Ruffin, C. Bernard. *Padre Pio: The True Story*. Huntington, IN: Our Sunday Visitor, 1982.

Sanborn, Margaret. *Mark Twain: The Bachelor Years*. New York: Doubleday, 1990.

Sandburg, Carl. *Abraham Lincoln: The Prairie Years*. Volumes 1 and 2. New York: Charles Scribner's Sons, 1926.

———. *Abraham Lincoln: The War Years I–IV*. Volumes 3 through 6. New York: Charles Scribner's Sons, 1939.

Schraff, Anne. *Tecumseh: The Story of an American Indian*. MN: Dillon Press, 1979.

Seeger, Raymond John. *Benjamin Franklin: New World Physicist*. New York: Pergamon Press, 1973.

Segal, Alan F. *Life After Death: A History of the Afterlife in the Religions of the West*. New York: Doubleday, 2004.

Sellier, Charles E. *Miracles and Other Wonders*. New York: Dell Books, 1994.

Service, Pamela F. *Mesopotamia*. New York: Bench Mark Books, 1999.

Shindman, Ellen. *The African-American Answer Book*. PA: Chelsea House, 1999.

Simon, Linda. *Dark Light: Electricity and Anxiety from the Telegraph to the X-Ray*. New York: Harcourt, 2004.

Sitchin, Zecharia. *Divine Encounters: A Guide to Visions, Angels, and Other Emissaries*. New York: Avon Books, 1995.

———. *Genesis Revisited*. New York: Avon Books, 1990.

———. *The Stairway to Heaven*. New York: Avon Books, 1980.

———. *The 12th Planet*. Rochester, VT: Bear & Company, 1976.

———. *The Wars of Gods and Men*. New York: Avon Books, 1985.

Slemen, Thomas. *Strange But True: Mysterious and Bizarre People*. New York: Barnes & Noble Books, 1998.

Smith, Susy. *Prominent American Ghosts*. Cleveland: World Publishing Company, 1967.

Somerlott, Robert. *"Here, Mr. Splitfoot": An Informal Exploration into Modern Occultism*. New York: Viking Press, 1971.

Starkey, Marion L. *The Devil in Massachusetts*. New York: Anchor Books/Doubleday, 1949.

————. *The Visionary Girls: Witchcraft in Salem Village*. Boston: Little, Brown and Company, 1973.

Stashower, Daniel. *Teller of Tales: The Life of Arthur Conan Doyle*. New York: Henry Holt and Company, 1999.

Steiger, Brad. *Real Ghosts, Restless Spirits, and Haunted Places*. Canton, MI: Visible Ink Press, 2003.

Stein, Gordon. *The Sorcerer of Kings: The Case of Daniel Dunglas Home and William Crookes*. Buffalo, NY: Prometheus Books, 1993.

Stiebing, William H., Jr. *Ancient Astronauts, Cosmic Collisions and Other Popular Theories About Man's Past*. Buffalo, NY: Prometheus Books, 1984.

Stuart, Nancy Rubin. *The Reluctant Spiritualist*. Orlando, FL: Harcourt, 2005.

Sugden, John. *Tecumseh: A Life*. New York: Henry Holt and Company, 1997.

Sweet, William Warren. *Revivalism in America*. MA: Peter Smith, 1965.

Swisher, Clarice. *The Ancient Near East*. San Diego: Lucent, 1995.

Tatsch, J. Hugo. *Freemasonry: The Thirteen Colonies*. New York: Macoy Publishing and Masonic Supply Company, 1929.

————. *The Ghosts of Fredericksburg*. Williamsburg, VA: Progress Printing Company, 1991.

Taylor, L. B., Jr. *The Ghosts of Virginia*. Williamsburg, VA: Progress Printing Company, 1996.

————. *The Ghosts of Williamsburg*. Williamsburg, VA: Progress Printing Company, 1983.

Thurman, Robert A. F. *The Tibetan Book of the Dead*. New York: Bantam Books, 1994.

Thurston, Herbert. *Ghosts and Poltergeists*. Folcroft, PA: Folcroft Editions, 1976.

Time-Life Books, eds. *Hauntings*. New York: Barnes & Noble Books, 1989.

Tognetti, Arlene and Lisa Lenard. *The Complete Idiot's Guide to Tarot and Fortune-Telling*. New York: Alpha Books, 1999.

Tomlinson, R. G. *Witchcraft Trials of Connecticut*. Hartford, CT: Bond Press, 1978.

Toth, Max. *Pyramid Prophecies*. Rochester, VT: Destiny Books, 1979.

Toth, Max, and Greg Nielson. *Pyramid Power*. New York: Warner Books, 1974.

Trickey-Bapty, Carolyn. *Martyrs and Miracles: The Inspiring Lives of Saints and Martyrs*. MD: Halo Press, 1996.

Trouncer, Margaret. *Saint Bernadette*. New York: Sheed and Ward, 1958.

Truman, Margaret. *First Ladies*. New York: Random House, 1995.

Tuchman, Barbara W. *A Distant Mirror: The Calamitous 14th Century*. New York: Alfred A. Knopf, 1978.

Twain, Mark. *Mark Twain's Own Autobiography*. Madison, WI: University of Wisconsin Press, 1990.

Twigg, Ena. *The Woman Who Stunned the World*. New York: Manor Books, 1973.

Twohig, Dorothy, ed. *George Washington's Diaries: An Abridgement*. Charlottesville, VA: University Press of Virginia, 1999.

Underhill, Lois B. *The Woman Who Ran for President: The Many Lives of Victoria Woodhull*. Bridgehampton, NY: Bridge Works Publishing, 1995.

Van der Linde, Laurel. *The Devil in Salem Village: The Story of the Salem Witchcraft Trials*. Brookfield, CT: Milbrook Press, 1992.

Vickers, Brian, ed. *Occult and Scientific Mentalities in the Renaissance*. Cambridge: Cambridge University Press, 1984.

Vidal, Gore. *Lincoln*. New York: Ballantine Books, 1985.

Walsh, Michael. *Lives of the Saints*. New York: HarperCollins, 1956.

Ward, Geoffrey C., Ric Burns, and Ken Burns. *The Civil War: An Illustrated History*. New York: Alfred A. Knopf, 1990.

Washington, Peter. *Madame Blavatsky's Baboon: A History of the Mystics, Mediums, and Misfits Who Brought Spiritualism to America*. New York: Schocken Books, 1995.

Weisberg, Barbara. *Talking to the Dead*. New York: HarperSanFrancisco, 2004.

Weisman, Richard. *Witchcraft, Magic, and Religion in 17th Century Massachusetts*. Amherst, MA: University of Massachusetts Press, 1984.

Welch, William Addams. *Talks with the Dead*. New York: Pinnacle Books, 1975.

Westwood, Jennifer, ed. *The Atlas of Mysterious Places*. New York: Weidenfeld & Nicolson, 1987.

Wicker, Christine. *Lily Dale: The True Story of the Town that Talks to the Dead*. New York: HarperSanFrancisco, 2003.

Williams, Beryl, and Samuel Epstein. *The Great Houdini*. New York: Scholastic Books, 1951.

Williams, Mary E. *Opposing Viewpoints: Paranormal Phenomena*. Detroit: Greenhaven Press, 2003.

Williamson, Linda. *Contacting the Spirit World*. New York: Berkley Books, 1996.

Wilson, Ian. *Nostradamus: The Man Behind the Prophecies*. New York: St. Martin's Press, 2002.

Woods, Richard. *The Occult Revolution*. New York: Herder and Herder, 1971.

Woodward, Kenneth L. *Making Saints*. New York: Simon & Schuster, 1990.

Zall, Paul, ed. *Lincoln on Lincoln*. Lexington: University Press of Kentucky, 1999.

Reference Books

Amplified Bible, expanded edition: The Lockman Foundation. Grand Rapids, MI: Zondervan, 1987.

Asimov, Isaac. *Asimov's Biographical Encyclopedia of Science and Technology*. Second Revised Edition. Garden City, NY: Doubleday, 1964.

Doll, Eugene E. *The Ephrata Cloister: An Introduction*. Ephrata, PA: Ephrata Cloister Associates,1958. (Pamphlet) *www.ephratacloister.org*.

Great Events from History: Ancient and Medieval Series (three volumes) Frank N. Magill (ed.) Englewood Cliffs, NJ: Salem Press, Incorporated, 1972.

Great Events from History: American Series (three volumes) Frank N. Magill (ed.) Englewood Cliffs, NJ: Salem Press, Incorporated, 1975.

Grun, Bernard. *The Timetables of History: A Horizontal Linkage of People and Events*. New York: Simon & Schuster, 1975.

Lorie, Peter, and Manuela Dunn Mascetti. *The Quotable Spirit: A Treasury of Religious and Spiritual Quotations from Ancient Times to the Twentieth Century*. Edison, NJ: Castle Books, 1996.

Melton, J. Gordon. *Encyclopedia of Occultism & Parapsychology*. Fourth edition. Two volumes. Detroit: Gale Research, 1996.

Wigoder, Geoffrey, ed. *The New Encyclopedia of Judaism*. New York: New York University Press, 1989.

Oxford Desk Dictionary and Thesaurus, American Edition. New York: Berkley Books.

Time Almanac with Information Please. Boston: Time, Inc. (annual publication).

United States Bibliographic Directory of the American Congress, 1774–1996. Alexandria, Virginia: CQ Staff Directories, 1997.

World Almanac Book of the Strange. New York: Signet Books, 1977.

Periodicals
Magazines

AARPMagazine, America, American Heritage, Atlantic Monthly, Atlantis Rising, Fate, Guideposts, Harper's Bazaar, Ladies Home Journal, Life, MacLean's, National Geographic, New England Almanac and Farmer's Friend (1877), Illustrated Family Christian Almanac for the United States (1857), Newsmakers, Newsweek, Omni, People, Psychology Today, Reader's Digest, Saturday Evening Post, Scientific American, Skeptic, Skeptical Inquirer, Smithsonian, Spiritual Life, Time, UFO Magazine, U.S. News & World Report, Utne Reader, Vermont Life.

Newspapers

Akron Beacon-Journal, Baltimore Sun, Banner of Light, Boston Globe, Brooklyn Eagle, Chicago Tribune, Christian Science Monitor, Frank Leslie's Illustrated, Hartford Courant, New Orleans Picayune, Newark (NY) Herald, New York Daily News, New York Graphic, New York Herald, New York Post, New York Sun, New York Times, New York Tribune, New York

World, Newsday (NY), Rochester (NY) Democrat, USA Today, Virginia Gazette, Washington Post.

Journals

The A.R.E. Journal, The Christian Parapsychologist, Exceptional Human Experience, The Journal of the American Society for Psychical Research, The Journal of Parapsychology, Journal of Religion and Psychical Research, Journal of the Society for Psychical Research.

Articles

Accurso, Lina. "The Lady and the Peasant Girl: Saint Bernadette and the Miracle of Lourdes." *Psychic World*: Spring 1998.

Accurso, Lina. "The Miracle of Fatima: Will the Last Secret Be Revealed? *Psychic World*: Spring 1997.

Associated Press, "Three-century-old Virginia witch is exonerated," July 10, 2006.

Brown, David. "The Naming of America." *New York Post*, November 23, 2008.

CQ Researcher, "Protestants Today," December 2007.

Ellis, Joseph. "The Great Upheaval: America and the Birth of the Modern World, 1788–1800," book review. *New York Times*, September 30, 2007.

Jones, Dan. "Unearthing Stonehenge." *Smithsonian Magazine*, October 2008.

Lee, Hermione. "The Dysfunctional Jameses," book review. *New York Times*, July 6, 2008.

Journal of the American Society for Psychical Research, "Conscious Life in the Spirit World," by Professor William James. ASPR: 1914.

Journal of the American Society for Psychical Research, "Honesty and Dishonesty of Mediums." ASPR: 1914.

Journal of the American Society for Psychical Research, "Mark Twain's Premonition." ASPR: 1913.

Journal of the American Society for Psychical Research, "Mediumistic Investigations and Their Difficulties," by James H. Hyslop. ASPR: June 1913.

Journal of the American Society for Psychical Research, "Psychic Manifestations Among the Shakers." ASPR: 1938.

Journal of the American Society for Psychical Research, "The Margery Mediumship." April 1938.

Journal of the American Society for Psychical Research, "Visions of the Dying—Mrs. Piper." ASPR: 1907.

Journal of the American Society for Psychical Research, "Louisa May Alcott's Psychic Incident During 1850s." ASPR: 1913.

McFeatters, Dale. "Reconstructing most of the genetic code of the wooly mammoth." *New York Post*, November 25, 2008.

New York Daily News, "Prehistoric Science and Technology." March 13, 2008.

New York Times, "Awful Event—President Lincoln Shot by an Assassin." April 15, 1865.

New York Times, "Fort Sumter Fallen." April 15, 1861.

New York Times, "Military Rights of Colored Troops." July 4, 1863.

New York Times, "The Fall of Atlanta." September 3, 1864.

New York Times, "The Surrender." April 14, 1865.

New York Times, "Tremendous Artillery Duel" [Gettysburg]. July 6, 1863.

New York Times, Great battles: the "major events" of the Battle of Gettysburg. July 4, 1863.

Newsday, "Lost Cities Discovered: Fabled sites of ancient Egypt." June 4, 2000.

Newsweek, "Archaeology: From Iraq to Israel, the Race to Unearth the Bible." August 30, 2004.

Proceedings of the American Society for Psychical Research, "Lily Dale." ASPR: 1908.

Schwartz, Dr. Jacob. "Stone Ruins in America: the Mystery and the Myths." *Psychic World*: Spring 1998.

Sorensen, Ted. "Presence of Mind: Lincoln's Speeches." *Smithsonian*, October 2008.

Specter, Michael. "In Modern Russia, a Medieval Witch Hunt." *New York Times*, April 5, 1997.

Time (special issue), "Abraham Lincoln: An Illustrated History of His Life and Times." 2009.

U.S. News & World Report, "The American Revolution: Myths and Realities." July 7, 2008.

U.S. News & World Report, "Secrets of the Civil War." 2008 (special issue).

Wills, Garry. "Lincoln." *Life Magazine*, February 1991.

Libraries and Other Collections

American Society for Psychical Research, NY

Association for Research and Enlightenment: Edgar Cayce Foundation, Virginia Beach

Axinn Library of Hofstra University, Hempstead, NY

David Library, New Hope, PA

East Meadow (NY) Public Library

Metropolitan Museum of Art, NY

Morgan Library, NY

New Horizons Foundation, Toronto (Canada)

New York Public Library

Parapsychology Sources of Information Center, Dix Hills, NY

Rochester (NY) Public Library

Toronto Society for Psychical Research (Canada)

Vermont Historical Society

West Babylon (NY) Public Library

Web sites and On Line Sources

American Society for Psychical Research

www.aspr.com

Ancient Sumeria
   http://history-world.org/sumeria.htm
Sir David Brewster
   http//www.answers.com/topic/david-brewster
Death in Ancient Egypt—Resources and Sites
   http://oi.uchicago.edu
W. E. B. DuBois. *Encyclopedia of World Biography*. Biography Resource Center.
   http://galenet.galegroup.com/servlet/BioRC
Egyptian Mummies
   http://www.si.edu/Encyclopedia_Sinmnh/mummies.htm.
Fate Magazine
   www.fatemag.com
Ghost Research Society
   www.ghostresearch.org
Haunted Places in the District of Columbia
   www.theshadowlands.net
Deodat Lawson's A *Brief and True Narrative*
   http://www.piney.com/ColDeoLawSurp.html
The Salem Witch Trials of 1692. Salem Witch Museum.
   http://www.salemwitchmuseum.com/education/index/.shtml
Salem Witchcraft Project
   http://etext.virginia.edu/salem/witchcraft/archives
Seybert Commission
   http://en.wikipedia.org/wiki/Seybert-Commission
Society for Psychical Research, London, England
   www.spr.ac.uk/